The Physics of Duns Scotus

The Scientific Context of a Theological Vision

RICHARD CROSS

CLARENDON PRESS · OXFORD
1998

Oxford University Press, Great Clarendon Street, Oxford OX2 6DP

Oxford New York

Athens Auckland Bangkok Bogota Bombay Buenos Aires Calcutta
Cape Town Chennai Dar es Salaam Delhi Florence Hong Kong Istanbul
Karachi Kuala Lumpur Madras Madrid Melbourne Mexico City Mumbai
Nairobi Paris Singapore São Paulo Taipei Tokyo Toronto Warsaw

and associated companies in
Berlin Ibadan

Oxford is a registered trade mark of Oxford University Press

Published in the United States
by Oxford University Press Inc., New York

British Library Cataloguing in Publication Data
Data available

Library of Congress Cataloging in Publication Data
The physics of Dun Scotus: the scientific context of a
theological vision/Richard Cross
Includes bibliographical references and indexes.
1. Duns Scotus, John, ca. 1266–1308. 2. Philosophy of nature–History.
3. Physics–Philosophy–History. I. Title.
B765.D74C76   1998   113'.092–dc21   98-4472
ISBN 0-19-826974-9

1 3 5 7 9 10 8 6 4 2

Typeset by J&L Composition Ltd, Filey, North Yorkshire
Printed in Great Britain on acid-free paper by
Bookcraft (Bath) Ltd., Midsomer Norton

In memory of my mother
Jill Margaret Pride
1933–1997

PREFACE

My original purpose in setting about the research for this book was to provide some sort of metaphysical background to Scotus's account of a central theological doctrine—one which I explored a few years ago in my doctoral thesis—the doctrine of the hypostatic union (i.e. the doctrine that the person of Jesus Christ has both divine and human natures). As I worked, however, the book took on a rather different shape. This was in part the consequence of a request from Richard Sorabji and Charles Burnett to deliver a paper on part and whole in Scotus at the Warburg Institute in 1991. The result—on Scotus's natural philosophy—has turned out to have direct relevance to a rather larger number of theological doctrines than just Christology. I hope in future studies to exploit some of the material here in more obviously theological ways. Since my aim is to explain an aspect of Scotus's philosophy, I eschew theological discussions here. I believe that the results are of sufficient interest in themselves to justify this approach.

Much of the research for the book was done in 1991–3 while I was Bampton Junior Research Fellow at St Peter's College, Oxford, and my first thanks must go to the trustees of the Bampton Fund, who financed the post, and the Master and Fellows of St Peter's, for providing a stimulating academic environment and incomparable hospitality. Some of the material in Chapters 1, 5, and 6 first appeared in *Vivarium*, 33 (1995), 137–70, and is reproduced here by kind permission of Brill, Leiden.

Various people have helped me in diverse ways in the writing of the book. John Marenbon and an anonymous reader for OUP provided detailed comments on two earlier drafts of Chapters 2–5. Rory Fox kindly read drafts of Chapters 7, 8, 12, and 13, and provided many useful criticisms and corrections. My colleague at Oriel, Richard Swinburne, read a very early version of what was to become Chapter 5. Both it and parts of Chapter 6 would look very different from the way they do now without his penetrating advice. Tim Jones, John

Roche, and Rowland Stout helped in different ways with problems I encountered. Jeremy Catto kept me ever mindful of the tremendous dynamism and vitality of Scotus's thought. Mistakes, of course, are mine; I hope at least that I have not made any by ignoring the sensible advice of others. As with everything I do, I would like to thank Essaka Joshua—especially here for the theological subtitle.

Oriel College,
Oxford.

CONTENTS

Contents   xi

ABBREVIATIONS

Albert of Saxony
  In Ph.   *Quaestiones in Octo Libros Physicorum*

Albert the Great
  In Sent.   *Commentarii in Libros Sententiarum*

Aquinas, Thomas
  In Gen. corr.   *In Aristotelis Librum De Generatione et Corruptione*

  In Ph.   *In Octo Libros Physicorum Aristotelis Expositio*
  Quod.   *Quaestiones Quodlibetales*
  ST   *Summa Theologiae*

Aristotle
  An. post.   *Analytica posteriora*
  Cael.   *De caelo*
  Cat.   *Categoriae*
  De an.   *De anima*
  De iuv.   *De iuventute*
  Eth. Nic.   *Ethica Nicomachea*
  Gen. corr.   *De generatione et corruptione*
  Metaph.   *Metaphysica*
  Ph.   *Physica*
  Top.   *Topicia*

Augustine
  Conf.   *Confessions*

Averroës
  In Cael.   *In libros de Caelo*
  In Gen. corr.   *In libros de Generatione et Corruptione*
  In Metaph.   *In libros Metaphysicorum*
  In Ph.   *In libros Physicorum Aristotelis*

Avicenna
  Metaph.   *Metaphysica (Liber de Philosophia Prima sive Scientia Divina)*

Bacon, Roger
  Op. Maius   *Opus Maius*

Boethius
  De Trin.   *De Trinitate*
  Comm. in Isag. ed. secunda   *In Isagogen Porphyrii Commenta. Editio Secunda*

Bonaventure
  In Sent.   *Commentaria in Quatuor Libros Sententiarum*

Buridan, John
  In Ph.   *Quaestiones super Octo Physicorum Libros Aristotelis*

Burley, Walter
  De Inst.   *De Primo et Ultimo Instanti*
  De Int.   *De Intensione et Remissione Formarum*
  In Ph.   *In Physica Aristotelis Expositio et Quaestiones*

Duns Scotus, John
  Add. Mag.   *Additiones Magnae*
  De Primo Princ.   *De Primo Principio*
  In De an.   *Quaestiones super libros De Anima*
  In Metaph.   *Quaestiones super libros Metaphysicorum*
  In Periherm.   *Quaestiones super librum Perihermeneias*
  Lect.   *Lectura*
  Ord.   *Ordinatio*
  Quod.   *Quodlibetum*
  Rep.   *Reportatio Parisiensis*

Francis of Marchia
  In Sent.   *In Sententias*

Giles of Rome
  Quod.   *Quodlibeta*
  Th. de Corp. Christi   *Theoremata de Corpore Christi*
  In Ph.   *In Libros de Physica auditu Aristotelis*

Godfrey of Fontaines
  Quod.   *Quodlibeta*

Henry of Ghent
  Quod.   *Quodlibeta*

Hugh of St Victor
  De Sac.   *De Sacramentis Christianae Fidei*

Marston, Roger
   Quod.   *Quodlibeta*
Olivi, Peter John
   In Sent.   *Quaestiones in Libros Sententiarum*
Peter of Spain
   Syncat.   *Syncategoreumata*
Richard of Middleton
   Qu. Disp.   *Quaestiones Disputatae*
Siger of Brabant
   In. Ph.   *Quaestiones super Physica Aristotelis*
Simplicius
   In Cat.   *Scolia in Praedicamenta Aristotelis*
Sutton, Thomas
   Qu. Ord.   *Quaestiones Ordinariae*
William of Auxerre
   Sum. Aur.   *Summa Aurea*
William of Ockham
   De Quant.   *De Quantitate*
   Op. Theol.   *Opera Theologica*
   Quod.   *Quodlibeta Septem*
   Rep.   *Reportatio*
William of Ware
   In Sent.   *In Sententias*

ENGLISH TRANSLATIONS

Alluntis and Wolter   John Duns Scotus, *God and Creatures: The Quodlibetal Questions*, ed. Felix Alluntis and Allan B. Wolter (Princeton and London: Princeton University Press, 1975)

Freddoso and Kelley   William of Ockham, *Quodlibetal Questions*, trans. Alfred J. Freddoso and Francis E. Kelley, Yale Library of Medieval Philosophy (2 vols., New Haven and London: Yale University Press, 1991)

Spade   Paul Vincent Spade (trans. and ed.), *Five Texts on the Medieval Problem of Universals: Porphyry, Boethius, Abelard, Duns Soctus, Ockham* (Indianapolis and Cambridge: Hackett, 1994)

MANUSCRIPT SIGLA

A   Assisi, Biblioteca Communale, MS 137
F   Florence, Biblioteca Laurenziana, MS Lat. Plut. 33, Dext. 1
G   Cambridge, Gonville and Caius College, MS 448/409
M   Oxford, Merton College, MS 59

1

Introduction: Physics and Duns Scotus

1. DUNS SCOTUS AND PHYSICS

Imagine a radical movement which had suffered an emphatic defeat. So emphatic, in fact, that it seemed unlikely to resurface for the length of a lifetime, if even then . . . . It would now be less a matter of hotly contesting [this movement's] notions than of contemplating them with something of the mild antiquarian interest with which one might regard Ptolemaic cosmology or the scholasticism of Duns Scotus.[1]

Terry Eagleton may be right in so describing postmodernism. But is he right about Duns Scotus? Is Scotus a figure of interest (and of eccentric interest at that) merely to the historian of ideas? There are (of course) some well-known Scotist *loci* which still directly inform modern philosophical discussion, at least in the analytic tradition. Perhaps the most obvious is Scotus's famous theory of individuation. According to this theory, individuation is explained by each individual having its own non-repeatable property, labelled 'haecceity' ('thisness'). Almost as famous is Scotus's defence of what philosophers call 'contra-causal' freedom: freedom to bring about not-*a* even if all the conditions necessary for bringing about *a* obtain. Tied in with this is Scotus's careful formulation of the concept of logical possibility, which has recently been so ably described by Simo Knuuttila.[2] All three of these central philosophical concepts can reasonably be held to have received their first theoretical treatment at the hands of Scotus. In philosophical theology, Scotus's devastating critique of Aquinas's theory of religious language is central to much modern discussion of the issue.

Having said all this, there is a lot of Scotus's work that still awaits

---

[1] Terry Eagleton, *The Illusions of Postmodernism* (Oxford and Cambridge, Mass.: Blackwell, 1996), 1.

[2] See Simo Knuuttila, *Modalities in Medieval Philosophy*, Topics in Medieval Philosophy (London and New York: Routledge, 1993), ch. 4.

exploration. Here, I want to look at some of this uncharted territory: the central concepts in Scotus's natural philosophy, or physics. I do not claim that there are no parts of Scotus's physics which are interesting chiefly because of the place they have in the history of ideas; which, less sympathetically, are of merely antiquarian interest. It would indeed be strange if this were not the case. But it is rare to find an issue on which Scotus did not have something interesting to say. As we shall see, some of his ideas had a role in the development of some central concepts in physics. Perhaps the most suggestive and fruitful aspect of Scotus's thought which we shall encounter here, however, is one which should properly be classified as a part of metaphysics: Scotus's nuanced account of the different sorts of *unity* which can be exhibited by different sorts of composite object. Scotus also provides a reasonably explicit account of the unity of perduring items such as processes. Equally, as we shall see, he argues that principled reasons can be found for distinguishing essential properties from accidental properties: a manœuvre sufficient for a defence of essentialism.[3]

In the philosophy of physics, too, Scotus's discussions are of more than merely historical interest. He provides an engrossing argument to show that the Thomist (and possibly Aristotelian) concept of prime matter is incoherent. I examine this in Chapter 2. He attempts to show that there are some good physical reasons for accepting what we would call mind–body dualism. We shall look at this material in Chapter 4. He formulates reasonably clear accounts of space and time, and provides useful arguments against theories that space and time are what we would label 'granular'. He also suggests a way to give an account of the flow of time.

This does not mean that Scotus never made mistakes, and I shall draw attention to places where I think Scotus might have gone wrong as I discuss his different views. I have decided to adopt a methodology which perhaps requires justification. In particular, I have tended to allow Scotus certain presuppositions which would have been generally accepted by his contemporaries. I have then tried to scrutinize Scotus's arguments for their validity and consistency. So I take Scotus to task on grounds which he and his contemporaries would have accepted, but not always on grounds which we would accept. (It should, I hope, be reasonably obvious which of Scotus's presuppositions we should

---

[3] Curiously, Eagleton—like Duns Scotus—seems to think that essentialism is something worth defending: see his *Illusions of Postmodernism*, 103–4.

accept, and which we should not.) There is, I believe, a good reason for this methodology. It is clear from Scotus's practice that he regarded validity, consistency, and clarity as necessary features of good arguments. If we did not subject his arguments to the same rigorous criticism as he applied to the arguments of others, we should be doing him an injustice, failing to take him seriously as a philosopher. And Scotus is a philosopher of the first rank, one who deserves to be taken extremely seriously.[4]

The springboard for medieval discussions of physics was Aristotle's work of the same name. In the *Physics*, Aristotle's major concern is with natural bodies, specifically as objects which *change* and *move*.[5] When discussing Aristotle's division of the theoretical sciences into mathematics, physics, and first philosophy (i.e. what we and Scotus would call metaphysics), Scotus puts it as follows:

Bodily substance . . . considered . . . in so far as it has form, which is the principle of determinate operation, motion, and rest, has many passions inhering in it, which can be known by the way of sense. Therefore there will be . . . a theoretical [science] regarding these things, which is called 'physics' or 'natural [science]'.[6]

The medievals were far more sensitive than Aristotle was to the idea that physical reality should ultimately admit of *mathematical* description. So I shall also be interested here in some features of material substance which Scotus would probably want to classify as part of mathematics:

There remains . . . bodily substance, in which considered absolutely continuous quantity primarily inheres, and through the medium of quantity all those things which follow quantity . . . And these passions are known of it from

---

[4] Whether or not we agree with Alexander Broadie's recent provocative claim that he is 'Scotland's greatest philosopher' is perhaps an open question (see his *The Shadow of Scotus: Philosophy and Faith in Pre-Reformation Scotland* (Edinburgh: T. and T. Clark, 1995), 11). But this is no mean praise.   [5] See Arist. *Ph.* 3. 1 (200^b12–14).
[6] Scotus, *In Metaph.* 6. 1, n. 11 (*Opera omnia*, ed. Luke Wadding (12 vols., Lyons: Durand, 1639), iv. 653^b), with reference to Arist. *Metaph.* 6. 1 (1025^b3–1026^a32). See also Boethius, *De Trin.* 2 (*The Theological Tractates: The Consolation of Philosoply*, ed. H. F. Stewart, E. K. Rand, and S. J. Tester, Loeb Classical Library (Cambridge, Mass.: Harvard University Press; London: Heinemann, 1978), 8): 'Theoretical science may be divided into three: physics, mathematics and theology. Physics deals with motion and . . . is concerned with the forms of bodies together with their constituent matter.' On Scotus here, see Ignacio Miralbell, 'La distinción entre metafísica, matemática y física según Duns Escoto', in Leonardo Sileo (ed.), *Via Scoti: Methodologica ad mentem Joannis Duns Scoti. Atti del Congresso Scotistico Internazionale. Roma* 9–11 Marzo 1993, (2 vols., Rome: Antonianum, 1995), i. 348–58. On the aims and scope of medieval physics, see Marshall Clagett, 'Some General Aspects of Medieval Physics', *Isis*, 39 (1948), 29–44.

principles known by way of sense. Therefore there can be, and is, a subject of a theoretical science open to our capacity other than metaphysics. And this is called mathematics. Although it concerns the quantum or quantity, since the mathematician does not often relate quantity to bodily substance, nevertheless bodily substance is the first subject, containing everything [mathematical] in potentiality [*virtute*].[7]

Aristotle too treats of these issues—quantity, extension, and (anti-) atomism—in his *Physics*; and we need an understanding of some of these 'mathematical' issues to get a clear grasp of Scotus's accounts of the nature of body, space, motion, and time.

This does not mean that I shall discuss everything which Aristotle discusses in his *Physics*. There are some aspects of Aristotelian physics which Scotus simply was not interested in. Perhaps the most obvious is *dynamics*, about which Aristotle has quite a lot to say. (I shall try to show in Chapter 9 that Scotus had an intuitive grasp of the concept of *mass*, though it is a concept so basic that it is articulated without the concepts from dynamics which are required for a sophisticated account. Equally, Scotus, as we shall see in Chapter 10, began to develop some philosophical ideas which turned out to be important in the growth of *kinematics*: the study of the temporal and spatial features of motion.) More important, there are some topics which Scotus deals with which I do not want to discuss here. The largest omissions I shall make are discussions of efficient and final causality in Scotus. Part of my reason for this is that I agree with Scotus's claim that these are really matters for *metaphysics*.[8] But a good discussion of, say, efficient causality in Scotus would in any case easily require a book-length study in itself.[9] I do not discuss Scotus's cosmology—not because it is not interesting in itself, but because my interests here are

[7] Scotus, *In Metaph.* 6. 1, n. 11 (Wadding edn., iv. 653[b]).

[8] For causality as one of the transcendentals, see Allan B. Wolter, *The Transcendentals and their Function in the Metaphysics of Duns Scotus*, Franciscan Institute Publications, Philosophy Series, 3 (St Bonaventure, NY: The Franciscan Institute, 1946), 138, 141–5; for the transcendentals as the object of metaphysics, see Scotus, *In Metaph.*, prol., n. 10 (Wadding edn., iv. 507[b]–8[a]).

[9] See e.g. R. Effler, *John Duns Scotus and the Principle 'Omne quod movetur ab alio movetur'*, Franciscan Institute Publications, Philosophy Series, 15 (St Bonaventure, NY: The Franciscan Institute, 1962), Peter King, 'Duns Scotus on the Reality of Self-Change', in Mary Louise Gill and James G. Lennox (eds.), *Self-Motion from Aristotle to Newton* (Princeton: Princeton University Press, 1994), 229–90, and recently Michael Sylwanowicz, *Contingent Causality and the Foundations of Duns Scotus' Metaphysics*, Studien und Texte zur Geistesgeschichte des Mittelalters, 51 (Leiden, New York, and Cologne: Brill, 1996).

in the medium-sized bodies which we encounter on a day-to-day basis: what the medievals would have called 'sublunar' bodies.[10] One very medieval interest is the nature of light, again a topic which will have to be dealt with elsewhere.[11] Neither am I interested in Scotus's views on scientific method. Hence I do not discuss his account of deductive reasoning.[12] And his famous formulation of the principles of inductive reasoning has already been treated briefly by another author.[13] Equally, there are some features of Scotus's physics which do not find a place in Aristotle. Not all of his nuanced discussion of motion, which I deal with in Chapters 9, 10, and 12, has parallels in Aristotle. In particular, Scotus's account of changes in the degree of a quality addresses questions which arose through readings of Averroës and Avicenna.

Scotus's account, like Aristotle's, is not empirical. He is more interested in theory: specifically, which sorts of theory should be true, and which sorts false. Scotus is in fact an acute (if somewhat eccentric) commentator on Aristotle. His discussions sometimes anticipate the kinds of problems which engage contemporary critics of Aristotle's thought. I shall, without going into too much detail, try to highlight some of these as I proceed.

2. PHYSICS AND THEOLOGY

There seem to me to be good historical and philosophical reasons for taking a look at Scotus's physics. But there is another reason too. The importance of Scotus in the history of *theology* goes without saying. And a number of his theological theories—divine timelessness, angels and the human soul, grace, the Incarnation, the Immaculate Conception,

---

[10] On astronomy, see Scotus, *Ord.* 2. 14. 1–3 (Wadding edn., vi. 721–45); *idem, Lect.* 2. 14. 1–4 (*Opera omnia*, ed. C. Balić *et al.* (Vatican City: Vatican Polyglot Press, 1950–), xix. 111–35). For a useful delineation of the distinction between physics and what we would call cosmology, see Edward Grant, *Planets, Stars, and Orbs: The Medieval Cosmos, 1200–1687* (Cambridge, New York, and Melbourne: Cambridge University Press, 1994), 5–9.

[11] For Scotus's treatment of it, see *Ord.* 2. 13. un. (Wadding edn., vi. 703–12); *Lect.* 2. 13. un. (Vatican edn., xix. 103–10).

[12] On Scotus's logic, see recently Roman M. Olejnik, 'Attualità delle leggi logiche in Giovanni Duns Scoto', in Sileo (ed.), *Via Scoti*, ii. 1073–90.

[13] See the rather cursory discussion of *Ord.* 1. 3. 1. 4, nn. 235–7 (Vatican edn., iii. 141–4), in A. C. Crombie, *Robert Grosseteste and the Origins of Experimental Science 1100–1700* (Oxford: Clarendon Press, 1953), 169.

transubstantiation—cannot be properly understood without a grasp of Scotus's physics. I shall not discuss any of these issues in detail in what follows. But the choice of the word 'context' in the subtitle of the book is deliberate. I hope that, by the end of my study of Scotus's physics, the dynamic of Scotus's view of the connectedness of physics and theology will be clear. Scotus never allows his theology to drive or determine his physics. He provides *philosophical* arguments—sound or unsound irrespective of any information derived from divine revelation—for all of the positions discussed here. It is true that he also provides theological arguments in favour of some of his physical theories. But he never defends any theory merely by invoking theological arguments, and there are several theories he defends by invoking only non-theological arguments. This is not to say that the *motivation* behind Scotus's discussion of these scientific matters may not have been theological. There is no obvious way of telling about this. But the structure and basic thrust of his arguments, as he presents them, are clear: physics, as discovered independently of theology, is wholly consistent with theology. So Scotus can allow his views on physics to determine at least in part the way in which he spells out his account of Christian orthodoxy. This does not mean that Scotus's physics leads him to adopt any heterodox theological views; rather like Aquinas, Scotus does not seem to perceive any real conflict. Of course, between Aquinas and Scotus were the monumental condemnations of 1270 and especially of 1277.[14] As we shall see in Chapter 11 below, Scotus attempts to provide good philosophical reasons for rejecting the relevant articles condemned at Paris, and he generally (though oddly, not always) defends the Oxford condemnation too, as we shall see in Chapters 3 and 4.

---

[14] For the condemnation of 219 articles by Stephen Tempier at Paris in 1277, see *Cartularium Universitatis Parisiensis*, ed. H. Denifle and E. Chatelain (4 vols. Paris: Delalain, 1889–97), i. 543–55; English translation in Ralph Lerner and Muhsin Mahdi (eds.), *Medieval Political Philosophy: A Sourcebook* (New York: The Free Press of Glencoe, 1963), 338–54. For a commentary see R. Hissette, *Enquête sur les 219 articles condamnés à Paris le 7 Mars 1277*, Philosophes médiévaux, 22 (Louvain: Publications Universitaires de Louvain; Paris: Vander Oyez, 1977). On their significance for natural philosophy, see Edward Grant, 'The Effect of the Condemnation of 1277', in Norman Kretzmann, Anthony Kenny, and Jan Pinborg (eds.), *The Cambridge History of Later Medieval Philosophy* (Cambridge: Cambridge University Press, 1982), 537–40. For the Oxford articles, see *Cartularium Universitatis Parisiensis*, i. 558–9. They are usefully discussed in Frederick J. Roensch, *Early Thomistic School* (Dubuque, Ia.: Priory Press, 1964), 13–19.

3. METAPHYSICS

I have already mentioned the central metaphysical question which we will come across when discussing Scotus's physics: that of *unity*. In one important passage, Scotus distinguishes six different senses of 'unity':

(i)   The unity of aggregation;
(ii) The unity of order;
(iii) Accidental unity;
(iv) Substantial unity (viz. the unity of a substance composed of really distinct parts);
(v)   The unity of simplicity (viz. the unity of a substance composed of merely formally distinct parts);
(vi) Formal identity (viz. unity which has no parts at all, either really distinct or formally distinct).[15]

I shall label these different types of unity respectively 'unity$_1$' to 'unity$_6$'. Scotus, as we shall see in Chapter 8, allows another sense of 'unity' as well:

(vii) The unity of homogeneity.

I shall label this type of unity 'H-unity'.

An example of unity$_1$ is a heap or bundle of anything; of unity$_2$ a series of efficient causes;[16] of unity$_3$, a white man; of unity$_4$, a human being; of unity$_5$, the human soul. (The case of unity$_6$ is rather complex, and I do not need it for what follows.) Scotus's favourite example of H-unity is a puddle of water. I shall deal with unity$_1$ in Chapters 5 and 6, with unity$_3$ in Chapter 6, with unity$_4$ in Chapter 5, with unity$_5$ (briefly) in Chapters 3 and 4, and with H-unity in Chapters 8–10, and (briefly) 12. What will emerge, I believe, is that Scotus has a profound and brilliant account of the different senses of 'unity'. I shall argue that, in particular, his account of unity$_4$ has much to offer to contemporary discussions.

In the above list, both unity$_5$ and unity$_6$ involve Scotus's well-known 'formal distinction', a Scotist theory of which we shall need some knowledge in what follows. Roughly, two realities[17]—two aspects of

[15] Scotus, *Ord.* 1. 2. 2. 1–4, n. 403 (Vatican edn., ii. 356–7).
[16] Scotus, *De Primo Princ.* 3. 49 (ed. Allan B. Wolter, 2nd edn. (Chicago: Franciscan Herald Press, [1982]), 64/5–66/7).
[17] 'Reality' is one of a series of terms which Scotus uses to refer to the merely formally distinct parts of some whole. Other terms include 'formality', 'aspects' (*rationes*), 'formal aspects', 'intentions', and 'real aspects': see Marilyn McCord Adams, 'Universals in the Early Fourteenth Century', in Kretzmann *et al.* (eds.), *Cambridge History of Later Medieval Philosophy*, 411–29, p. 415.

one thing—are formally distinct if and only if they are both (a) really identical and (b) susceptible of definition independently of each other.[18] Scotus's criterion for real identity is real inseparability. In fact, real inseparability (such that the real separation of two or more realities is *logically impossible*) is *necessary and sufficient* for real identity.[19] Conversely, real separability is necessary and sufficient for real distinction. More precisely, two objects *x* and *y* are inseparable if and only if, both, it is not possible for *x* to exist without *y*, and it is not possible for *y* to exist without *x*; conversely, two objects *x* and *y* are separable if and only if at least one of *x* and *y* can exist without the other. (I shall label this the 'separability criterion'.) On this showing, two really identical but formally distinct realities will be something like essential (i.e. inseparable) properties of a thing. I suspect that most of them will count as *abstract* items.[20] But I do not want to become involved here in a detailed discussion of Scotus's formal distinction.

Scotus makes use of his formal distinction in his account of individuation. He argues that any individual created item (including a composite substance) can be analysed into two really identical but formally distinct aspects: essence and individuating feature or haecceity.[21] What this amounts to, roughly, is that any individual created item

---

[18] For Scotus's formal distinction, see usefully his *Ord.* 1. 8. 1. 4, n. 193 (Vatican edn., iv. 261–2). For a thorough discussion, see Maurice J. Grajewski, *The Formal Distinction of Duns Scotus: A Study in Metaphysics*, The Catholic University of America Philosophical Series, 90 (Washington: Catholic University of America Press, 1944). For a more rigorous presentation, see the account by Adams, 'Universals in the Early Fourteenth Century', 412–17; also Allan B. Wolter, 'The Formal Distinction', in John K. Ryan and Bernardine M. Bonansea (eds.), *John Duns Scotus, 1265–1965*, Studies in Philosophy and the History of Philosophy, 3 (Washington: Catholic University of America Press, 1965), 45–60, repr. in Allan B. Wolter, *The Philosophical Theology of John Duns Scotus*, ed. Marilyn McCord Adams (Ithaca, NY, and London: Cornell University Press, 1990), 27–41.

[19] See esp. Scotus, *Quod.* 3, n. 15 (Wadding edn., xii. 81; Alluntis and Wolter, 73–4 n. 3. 46) for the *sufficiency* of inseparability for real identity; and *idem, Ord.* 2. 1. 4–5, n. 200 (Vatican edn., vii. 101) for the *necessity* of inseparability for real identity. We shall encounter this principle on many different occasions below.

[20] Not all of them will. An individual haecceity is non-repeatable, and *a fortiori* not an abstract object. On this see Rega Wood, 'Individual Forms. Richard Rufus and John Duns Scotus', in Ludger Honnefelder, Rega Wood, and Mechthild Dreyer (eds.), *John Duns Scotus: Metaphysics and Ethics*, Studien und Texte zur Geistesgeschichte des Mittelalters, 53 (Leiden, New York, and Cologne: Brill, 1996), 251–72.

[21] For the relevance of Scotus's formal distinction to his account of individuation, see Scotus, *Ord.* 2. 3. 1. 1, n. 32 (Vatican edn., vii. 403; Spade, 63–4); 2. 3. 1. 5–6, nn. 179–80, 192 (Vatican edn., vii. 479, 486; Spade, 104, 108). On Scotus's account of individuation in general, see ibid. 2. 3. 1 *passim* (Vatican edn., vii. 391–516; Spade, 57–113); also Adams, 'Universals in the Early Fourteenth Century', 412–17; Tamar M. Rudavsky, 'The Doctrine of Individuation in Duns Scotus', *Franziskanische Studien*, 59 (1977), 320–77, and 62

has two different essential properties: its nature or kind and its individuating, non-repeatable haecceity.

4. HISTORY

Most of the issues I look at in this book have a certain historical background, often (though not always) stemming from Aristotle, sometimes read through the spectacles of the great Islamic philosophers Avicenna and Averroës. Wherever possible, I try to give some sort of account of this. Scotus's own discussions were also often directed against specific contemporary opponents of his from Paris and (in the case of Roger Bacon, Roger Marston, William of Ware, and Walter Burley) Oxford: Bonaventure (*c*.1217–74), Aquinas (*c*.1225–74), Roger Bacon (*c*.1214–92/4), Henry of Ghent (*c*.1217–93), Giles of Rome (*c*.1243/7–1316), Roger Marston (studying at Paris *c*.1270; d. (?)1303), Richard of Middleton (*c*.1249–1302), Godfrey of Fontaines (1250–1306/9), William of Ware (fl. 1290), and Walter Burley (*c*.1275–1344/5).[22] When Scotus is clearly

---

(1980), 62–83; Allan B. Wolter, 'Scotus's Individuation Theory', in *Philosophical Theology of John Duns Scotus*, 68–97; *idem*, 'John Duns Scotus', in Jorge J. E. Gracia (ed.), *Individuation in Scholasticism: The Later Middle Ages and the Counter-Reformation 1150–1650*, (Albany, NY: State University of New York Press, 1994), 271–98; Woosuk Park, 'The Problem of Individuation for Scotus: A Principle of Indivisibility or a Principle of Distinction?', *Franciscan Studies*, 48 (1988), 105–23; also *idem*, 'Understanding the Problem of Individuation: Gracia vs. Scotus', in Honnefelder *et al.* (eds.), *John Duns Scotus*, 273–89, commenting on Jorge J. E. Gracia, 'Individuality and the Individuating Entity in Scotus's *Ordinatio*: An Ontological Characterization', in Honnefelder, *et al.* (eds.), *John Duns Scotus*, 229–49. Scotus's basic account of individuation makes it clear that what is at issue is the indivisibility of a concrete entity into what he labels 'subjective parts' (*Ord.* 2. 3. 1. 2, n. 48 (Vatican edn., vii. 412–13; Spade, 69); 2. 3. 1. 4, n. 76 (Vatican edn., vii. 426–7; Spade, 76)). What he is getting at is that, unlike an essence, an individual is a non-repeatable item: and it is this non-repeatability which, for Scotus, requires explaining.

[22] Potted biographies, with short bibliographies, for most of these thinkers can be found in Kretzmann *et al.* (eds.), *Cambridge History of Later Medieval Philosophy*. For Roger Marston see A. B. Emden, *A Biographical Register of the University of Oxford to A. D. 1500* (3 vols., Oxford: Clarendon Press, 1957–9), ii. 1230^{b}–1^{b}. For Richard of Middleton, see Edgar Hocedez, *Richard de Middleton: sa vie, ses oeuvres, sa doctrine*, Spicilegium Sacrum Lovaniense. Études et documents, 7 (Louvain: 'Spicilegium Sacrum Lovaniense' Bureaux; Paris: Honoré Champion, 1925). For William of Ware, see A. Daniels, 'Zu den Beziehungen zwischen Wilhelm von Ware und Johannes Duns Scotus', *Franziskanische Studien*, 4 (1917), 221–38; Joseph Lechner, 'Die mehrfachen Fassungen des Sentenzkom mentars des Wilhelm von Ware, O.F.M.', *Franziskanische Studien*, 31 (1949), 99–127; Gedeon Gál, 'Gulielmi de Ware, O.F.M. Doctrina Philosophica per Summa Capitula Proposita', *Franciscan Studies*, 14 (1954), 155–80, 265–92; Ludwig Hödl, 'Untersuchungen zum scholastischen Begriff des Schöpferischen in der Theologie des Wilhelm von Ware

opposing one or more of these writers, I try to give an account of his opponents' views. (Scotus, perhaps more elaborately than any other scholastic, formulates his own opinion dialectically, by eliminating the views of his opponents.) I would like to have shown the extent to which Scotus draws positively on these writers as well. But to do this adequately would require a book in itself; and in any case, whether the positions Scotus defends are original or not, his *arguments* for these positions usually are. So I have decided to concentrate on Scotus here, perhaps leaving detailed discussion of the writers immediately preceding Scotus to another time.

5. TEXTS

Scotus's discussions of issues in physics are scattered throughout his works, and, as we shall see, Scotus sometimes changed his mind. Almost all of his works, unfortunately, remained incomplete at his untimely death in 1308.[23] I shall make use of his three commentaries on the four books of the *Sentences* of Peter Lombard: the early Oxford *Lectura* (books 1 and 2 pre-1300), the magisterial *Ordinatio* (Scotus's 'edited' version of his lectures, started *c.*1300 and incomplete in 1308), and the short, late *Reportatio Parisiensis* (student notes of his Paris lectures, perhaps checked by Scotus around 1305).[24] Scotus's *De Primo Principio*, a treatise on the existence and nature of God, is also generally held to be a late work, compiled from the *Ordinatio*, possibly with the help of an assistant.[25] I also use Scotus's early questions on Aristotle's *De interpretatione* and *De anima* as well as his questions on the *Metaphysics* (a mainly early work probably started in Oxford, though we know that parts of it—at least book 9, and possibly the

OM', in Burkhard Mojsisch and Olaf Pluta (eds.) *Historia Philosophiae Medii Aevi: Studien zur Geschichte der Philosophie des Mittelalters*, (2 vols., Amsterdam: Grüner, 1992), i. 387–408. On Scotus's life, see most recently Allan B. Wolter, 'Reflections on the Life and Works of Scotus', *American Catholic Philosophical Quarterly*, 67 (1993), 1–36; *idem*, 'Duns Scotus at Oxford', in Sileo (ed.), *Via Scoti*, i. 183–91; William J. Courtenay, 'Scotus at Paris', in Sileo (ed.), *Via Scoti*, i. 149–64.

[23] For Scotus's works, see Vatican edn., i. 140*–75*; xix. 41*–6*.

[24] See C. Balić, *Les Commentaires de Jean Duns Scot sur les quatre livres des Sentences*, Bibliothèque de la Revue d'Histoire Ecclésiastique, 1 (Louvain: Bureaux de la Revue d'Histoire Ecclésiastique, 1927), 25–33.

[25] See John Duns Scotus, *A Treatise on God as First Principle*, ed. Allan B. Wolter, pp. ix–xiii.

last four books (i.e. 6–9)—should be dated late in Scotus's career).[26] Finally, I use Scotus's *Quodlibet*, a late work dating from his regency at Paris (i.e. between 1305 and (probably) 1307).[27] Difficulties in dating Scotus's works sometimes make it difficult to trace the changes in his thought. I am assuming that books 1 and 2 of the *Ordinatio* represent fairly early work, probably pre-dating Scotus's Parisian sojourn,[28] and that books 3 and 4 can reasonably be given a rather later date. Scotus's most mature thought is represented in the *Reportatio Parisiensis* and the *Quodlibet*.[29]

[26] See Stephen D. Dumont, 'The Question on Individuation in Scotus' "Quaestiones super Metaphysicam" ', in Sileo (ed.), *Via Scoti*, i. 193–227; also Timothy B. Noone, 'Scotus' Critique of the Thomistic Theory of Individuation and the Dating of the "Quaestiones in Libros Metaphysicorum", VII q. 13', in Sileo (ed.), *Via Scoti*, i. 391–406, pp. 394–6. Allan B. Wolter notes, on the basis of the work done by Dumont and Noone, that book 7 of the *Metaphysics* questions dates from between book 2 of the *Ordinatio* and book 2 of the *Reportatio*: see his 'Reflections about Scotus's Early Works', in Honnefelder *et al.* (eds.), *John Duns Scotus*, 37–57, p. 52. In Ch. 13 below I shall try to give some reasons to confirm that book 5 of the *Metaphysics* questions should be dated before the *Lectura*, and thus that at least books 1–5 should be given an early date.

[27] For the date, see Courtenay, 'Scotus at Paris', 162.

[28] On this, see Wolter, 'Reflections about Scotus's Early Works', 49.

[29] Not all of these works yet exist in critical editions. I have used the Vatican edition where possible for the *Lectura* and the *Ordinatio*. For parts of the *Ordinatio* which do not yet exist in the Vatican edition, I have used the Wadding edition, checked against MS A for books 3 and 4. I do not signal the folio references to MS A unless there is a significant difference (i.e. one affecting the sense of Scotus's argument) from the text of the Wadding edition. Where there is such a difference, I give the Latin text from MS A in a footnote, along with the exact folio reference to it. The parts of book 2 of the *Ordinatio* which do not appear in the Vatican edition are more problematic. According to the Vatican editors, none of book 2 in MS A, with the exception of distinction 1 and nn. 1–485 of distinction 2, represents a reliable text of the *Ordinatio* (see Vatican edn., iii. 3*). And it is not yet clear what editorial strategy the Vatican editors will use for the rest of book 2. In the light of this, I have decided to make do with the text in the Wadding edition for the rest of book 2. The most important topics, however, are clearly covered in the *Lectura*, and the Wadding text of the *Ordinatio* adds nothing of substance to the *Lectura* account in the distinctions relevant to my purposes. So I base my account on this early version of book 2, making use of the *Ordinatio* and *Reportatio Parisiensis* (both in the Wadding edition) where they add to the *Lectura* version. I have likewise used the Wadding edition for the *Quodlibetum*, making use of an English translation published as *God and Creatures: The Quodlibetal Questions*, ed. Felix Alluntis and Allan B. Wolter (Princeton and London: Princeton University Press, 1975), a version checked against the best Latin manuscripts. For books 2–4 of the *Reportatio Parisiensis*, I have used the Wadding edition. For book 1 I have used MS M. Book 1 in Wadding is a version of *Additiones Magnae*, a set of additions compiled by William of Alnwick from the oral teaching of Scotus. I occasionally refer to these, using the text (printed as book 1 of the *Reportatio*) found in vol. 11 of the Wadding edition. (I have checked this against Oxford, Merton College, MS 87, fos. 1–86, and only use passages which can be found in this manuscript.) I have likewise used the Wadding edition for the various questions on works of Aristotle.

I hope the structure that I have decided to follow is reasonably self-explanatory. Chapters 2–5 are an account of material substance and its essential components. Chapter 6 provides a general account of the accidental properties of a material substance. Chapter 7 provides an account of quantity and Scotus's basic rejection of atomism. Chapter 8 gives a general theory of homogeneity, including an account of homoeomeric substances. (Scotus's account of such substances cannot be understood without a clear understanding of his anti-atomistic physics.) Chapters 9 and 10 consider Scotus's account of changes in quantity and quality. Chapter 11 gives Scotus's account of space, and Chapters 12 and 13 his general account of motion and the nature of time.

2

Prime Matter

Aristotle analysed material substances into two components: matter and form.[1] One of his motivations for so doing was to provide an explanation of the physical phenomena of generation and corruption.[2] When something—say the dog Fido—ceases to exist, we can generally talk of something (not the dog Fido) being *changed*. There is something that was Fido that has changed into something else—a rotting carcass. On at least some readings of Aristotle, this account can be generalized to mean that there is some one thing, labelled *prime matter*, which remains constant in every change. Someone who accepted the existence of prime matter as a component part of a substance might well want to talk of change in terms of prime matter's losing some properties and gaining others. When Fido dies, for example, we might want to claim that some prime matter has lost some or all of its dog-like properties, and gained in their stead carcass-like properties. Someone could, of course, accept the claim that prime matter exists without thereby being committed to the view that prime matter was the *only* thing which remained constant in any change. As we shall see, Scotus accepts that there are some substantial changes in which only *some* of a thing's properties are lost. Where we might talk of properties here, Aristotle and the medievals talked of *form*, or, more precisely, *substantial form*. A substantial form, roughly speaking, is that property or set of properties in virtue of which a material substance is a substance of such-and-such a kind.

In this chapter, I shall examine Scotus's account of prime matter. In Chapter 3, I shall examine his account of substantial form. In Chapter 4, I shall examine those non-standard cases in which a composite substance essentially contains more than one substantial form. In Chapter 5, I will discuss Scotus's claim that a composite of prime

---

[1] See e.g. Arist. *Metaph.* 7. 3 (1028^{b}36–1029^{a}27); *idem, Ph.* 1. 7 (190^{b}12–191^{a}13).
[2] See Arist. *Ph.* 1. 7 (189^{b}30–2); *idem, Gen. corr.* 1. 3 (319^{a}29–^{b}4); 2. 1 (329^{a}24–32).

matter and substantial form is more than just the aggregate of these two parts.[3]

Scotus's account of matter is rather distinctive, and can usefully be looked at under four headings: (i) Scotus's claim that matter exists; (ii) that, as such, matter has an essence, or some properties, all its own; (iii) that it is logically possible for individual matter to exist independently of any form; (iv) that matter is an essential part of a material substance.[4] Of the four sections under these headings, the first three provide the basic account of Scotus on matter. The last offers more complex refinements to the account.

1. THE EXISTENCE OF MATTER

Scotus offers a series of arguments to demonstrate:

  (1) Matter exists.[5]

---

[3] In what follows, I shall use 'matter' to mean 'prime matter', and 'form' to mean 'substantial form', unless I expressly note otherwise. As we shall see, Scotus holds that each of matter, form, and composite substance has an essence. When I want to refer to the essences of these items, I shall talk about 'matter as such', 'form as such', and '(composite) essence'. When I want to refer to one or more individual instance of these items, I shall talk about 'individual matter', 'individual form', and '(composite) substance'.

[4] Scotus also holds that the existence of matter is a logically necessary feature of any world which contains finite agents capable of producing substances, and that this claim can be shown to be true (such that it is not, for example, merely an article of faith). I examine these claims in the Appendix.

[5] Scotus *Lect.* 2. 12. un., nn. 11–21 (Vatican edn., xix. 72–7). For accounts of Scotus's position on prime matter, see Etienne Gilson, *Jean Duns Scot: Introduction à ses positions fondamentales*, Études de philosophie médiévale, 42 (Paris: Vrin, 1952), ch. 6; Marilyn McCord Adams, *William Ockham*, Publications in Medieval Studies, 26 (2 vols., Notre Dame, Ind.: University of Notre Dame Press, 1987), ii. 642–7; and Simona Massobrio, 'Aristotelian Matter as Understood by St Thomas Aquinas and John Duns Scotus' (unpublished doctoral dissertation, McGill University, 1991), 194–244; for an account of Scotus's hylomorphism, see Allan B. Wolter's commentary on Scotus's *A Treatise on God as First Principle*, 2nd edn. (Chicago: Franciscan Herald Press, [1982]), 197–207. Some of the issues which I discuss throughout Chs. 2–4 are dealt with briefly in Celina A. Létora Mendoza, 'Escoto y el hilemorfismo aristotélico: Cuestiones metodológicas', in Leonardo Sileo (ed.), *Via Scoti: Methodologica ad mentem Joannis Duns Scoti. Atti del Congresso Scotistico Internazionale. Roma 9–11 Marzo 1993* (2 vols., Rome: Antonianum, 1995), ii. 765–81. On matter in general, see Ernan McMullin (ed.), *The Concept of Matter* (Notre Dame, Ind.: University of Notre Dame Press, 1963); on Scotus, see ibid. 151–2. Prospero Stella's account of Scotus on matter, in his generally useful *L'Ilemorfismo di G. Duns Scoto*, Pubblicazione del Pontificio Ateneo Salesiano. II. Testi e studi sul pensiero medioevale, 2 (Turin: Società Editrice Internazionale, 1955), part 1, uses the version of *Ord.* 2. 12 found in MS A. As I noted in Ch.1 n. 29, the Vatican editors do not regard this

Scotus's arguments draw on the intuition that the existence of changes from one substance to another—that is, of generation and corruption— entails the existence of prime matter. He argues that

(A) Generation exists,[6]

on the standard Aristotelian understanding of generation, entails

(2) There exists a subject remaining constant over the process of generation,

(3) There exists something having a natural inclination to the end term of generation (i.e. something for which the inherence of any sub- stantial form is a natural state), and

(4) There exists the privation of the form of a yet-to-be-generated substance.

Scotus argues further that

(A*) Corruption exists

entails

(5) There exists something intrinsic to a substance in virtue of which that substance is corruptible.

((A) and (A*) are equivalent, since it is possible for the process of generation to take place if and only if some substance is corrupted.) Scotus's argument is that each of (2)–(5) entails (1), on the grounds that only matter (and not form) can satisfy the descriptions in (2)–(5).

The presuppositions in the argument from (2) to (1)[7] are straight- forwardly Aristotelian: only matter (and not form) remains over every

---

part of MS A as a reliable source for Scotus's commentary. (On this, see also Wolter, in Scotus, *Treatise on God as First Principle*, 200.) Given the problems surrounding the text of the *Ordinatio* here, I base my account primarily on the *Lectura*, using the *Reportatio Parisiensis* for material not found in the *Lectura*, and occasionally referring to the *Ordinatio* discussion, both in the Wadding edition and MS A. In what follows, I use capital roman letters to indicate *axioms* in Scotus's arguments, and arabic numbers to indicate claims inferred from the axioms.

[6] Scotus offers a complex argument to show that (A) is true in all worlds which contain created substances capable of producing other such substances. I discuss it in the Appen- dix. For detailed discussion of Scotus's analysis of change, see Peter King, 'Duns Scotus on the Reality of Self-Change', in Mary Louise Gill and James G. Lennox (eds.), *Self-Motion from Aristotle to Newton* (Princeton: Princeton University Press, 1994), 229–90, pp. 229–31.

[7] Scotus, *Lect.* 2. 12. un., n. 11 (Vatican edn., xix. 72–3).

substantial change.[8] Likewise for the argument from (3) to (1). The idea behind (3) is that, for generation to be a natural process, there must exist something for which the inherence of *any* substantial form is a natural state.[9] But, as Scotus understands form, it will fail to match this description.[10] Furthermore, form cannot possibly be the subject of a property satisfying the condition set out in (4).[11] So each of (3) and (4) entails (1). Equally, form cannot satisfy the description in (5), since, if it could, it would follow that immaterial substances (i.e. subsistent forms) were corruptible, which, on standard medieval accounts, is false. But it is possible for matter to satisfy the description in (5); and thus, since *only* matter can satisfy it, (5) entails (1).[12]

How successful are Scotus's arguments in favour of the existence of prime matter? In terms of empirical fact, it seems clear that a change from one substance to another requires some features to remain constant. It might even be an empirical fact that there is some most basic kind of stuff, or some most basic physical constituents of things, which remain constant over all sorts of substantial change. But I do not see that Scotus's arguments, as they stand, successfully demonstrate this second claim. What they do show is that *some* features remain in common over substantial changes if these changes take place by generation—rather than by, say, creation or transubstantiation.[13]

[8] For (2), Scotus refers to Arist. *Ph.* 1. 7 (190ᵃ14–21); *idem, Gen. Corr.* 1. 1 (319ᵇ6–320ᵃ3); *idem, Metaph.* 12. 2 (1069ᵇ3–9) and 12. 2–3 (1069ᵇ32–1070ᵃ2), 'et alibi pluries': the Vatican editors suggest *Metaph.* 7. 8 (1033ᵃ24–6), 7. 9 (1034ᵇ7–19), 8. 5 (1044ᵇ21–1045ᵃ5): see Vatican edn., xix. 72–3. For a similar argument drawing on Aristotle's remarks in *Ph.* 5. 2 (226ᵃ10–11), see Scotus, *Ord.* 2. 1. 4–5, n. 204 (Vatican edn., vii. 103).
[9] The insight is Aristotle's: see *Ph.* 1. 9 (192ᵃ22–5).
[10] Scotus, *Lect.* 2. 12. un., n. 17 (Vatican edn., xix. 74).
[11] Ibid. n. 18 (Vatican edn., xix. 74–5). For the entailment from (A) to (4), see Arist., *Ph.* 5. 1 (225ᵃ12–20). Scotus elsewhere makes it clear that matter is correctly described as having 'privative privation', as opposed to 'positive privation'. The distinction to which Scotus is drawing our attention is between the kind of privation which results from the *non-activity* of some agent and the kind of privation which results from the *activity* of some agent. In the first case, an item fails to have some form since the agent required to produce the form fails to produce it. In the second case, an item fails to have some form because some agent prevents the existence of a form which would otherwise—but for the activity of the agent—exist. In order for matter to have a form, the activity of some agent is required over and above the activity which produced the matter in the first place. Matter therefore has privative privation: see Scotus, *Ord.* 2. 1. 3, n. 167 (Vatican edn., vii. 85); also 2. 1. 2, n. 61 (Vatican edn., vii. 35).
[12] Scotus, *Lect.* 2. 12. un., n. 19 (Vatican edn., xix. 75–6). In his *Metaphysics* questions, Scotus gives a further rather interesting argument for the existence of prime matter. I discuss it briefly in the Appendix, n. 6.
[13] For creation and transubstantiation, see Appendix.

2. THE NATURE OF MATTER

Suppose, however, that Scotus is in fact correct that there is some most basic stuff which remains constant over all substantial changes. One question which we could sensibly ask about this stuff is whether or not it has any essential properties all its own. For example, I take it that quarks, leptons, and bosons *might* be basic, irreducible physical constituents of things, and that in principle they would admit of some kind of general description.[14] According to Scotus, any most basic stuff remaining constant over all substantial changes must in principle have some properties all its own; it must have a *nature*. His opponent here is Aquinas. Aquinas argues that, although it is true that matter exists, matter is merely pure potentiality: the thinnest possible existent, in itself lacking any genuine attribute whatsoever. On this account, matter really does exist, but only when united to some form.[15] Aquinas thus subscribes to the view that matter in itself has no properties other than being pure potentiality. Scotus argues against this conception of matter in two ways. First, no actual existent could in fact be pure potentiality. Pure potentiality, as Scotus construes it, is the kind of property which could be had only by non-existent items. Secondly, if matter were pure potentiality, it would not be possible for it to perform the functions assigned to it by Aristotle.

Scotus argues for the first of these by means of a distinction between two relevant senses of 'potentiality'. (i) An item is in *objective* potentiality if it can (but does not) exist. As Scotus puts it, it is the *object* or *end term* of some active power. Scotus's example is the Antichrist: a creature who, according to Scotus, does not now exist, but will exist in the future. (Whether or not possible objects which are never actualized—the Antichrist's twin brother, for example—are in objective potentiality remains unclear.[16]) (ii) An item is in *subjective* potentiality

---

[14] Scotus, as we shall see in Ch. 7, would deny that things like quarks could be the most basic constituents of material substances, since he holds that any physical substance is in principle infinitely divisible: there are no smallest indivisible particles out of which it is made.

[15] See e.g. Aquinas, *Quod.* 3. 1. 1 (ed. R. M. Spiazzi (Turin and Rome: Marietti, 1949), 39[a-b]).

[16] On this problem, see Ansgar Santogrossi, 'Duns Scotus on the Potency Opposed to Act in *Questions on the Metaphysics*', *American Catholic Philosophical Quarterly*, 67 (1993), 55–76, pp. 62–3; also John F. Boler, 'The Ontological Commitment of Scotus's Account of Potency in his *Questions on the Metaphysics*, Book IX', in Ludger Honnefelder, Rega Wood, and Mechthild Dreyer (eds.), *John Duns Scotus: Metaphysics and Ethics*, Texte und Studien zur Geistesgeschichte des Mittelalters, 53 (Leiden, New York, and Cologne: Brill, 1996), 145–60.

if it is an existent which can be (but is not) φ.[17] On these definitions, it is clear that objective potentiality is a property which can be had only by *non-existent* items; likewise, subjective potentiality is a property which can be had only by *existent* items. As Scotus construes Aquinas's account of matter, it amounts to the claim that matter has objective potentiality; and therefore (since objective potentiality is a property only of non-existent items) that matter does not exist.[18] Underlying this seems to be the intuition that anything which exists has some kind of actuality, and hence that it cannot be pure potentiality. There is a sense in which Aquinas would agree with this. Matter exists only when united to form. Scotus's worry is that Aquinas's account simply *reduces* matter to form: that is, that Aquinas's talk of matter ultimately says nothing which cannot be captured equivalently by some of the ways we talk about form.

Secondly, if matter is pure potentiality—or if it is in objective potentiality—then, Scotus reasons, it cannot satisfy any of the basic Aristotelian descriptions of matter. Scotus lists these descriptions as follows:[19]

(i)   Matter is a principle.[20]
(ii)   Matter is a cause.[21]
(iii) Matter is a part of a generated substance.[22]
(iv)   Matter is the subject of substantial change.[23]
(v)   Matter remains the same under each term of a substantial change.[24]

To this list, Scotus adds a sixth, theological claim:

---

[17] Scotus, *Lect.* 2. 12. un., n. 30 (Vatican edn., xix. 80); see also ibid. nn. 61–4 (Vatican edn., xix. 92–4); *idem, In Metaph.* 7. 5, n. 2 (Wadding edn., iv. 680[b]); 9. 2, nn. 8–12 (Wadding edn., iv. 763[a]-4[b]). For discussions in the literature, see, in addition to Santo-grossi, Adams, *William Ockham*, ii. 640–1; Allan B. Wolter, *The Philosophical Theology of John Duns Scotus*, ed. Marilyn McCord Adams (Ithaca, NY, and London: Cornell University Press, 1990), 16; and, definitively, King, 'Duns Scotus on the Reality of Self-Change', 246–50. Note that subjective potentiality and objective potentiality are contraries: nothing can exhibit both of them in the same respect. There is no evidence that Scotus would want to claim that matter exhibits objective potentiality as well as subjective potentiality. (For the opposite claim, see Massobrio, 'Aristotelian Matter', 205.)
[18] Scotus, *Lect.* 2. 12. un., n. 31 (Vatican edn., xix. 80); *idem, In Metaph.* 7. 5, n. 2 (Wadding edn., iv. 180[b]).
[19] Scotus, *Lect.* 2. 12. un., n. 29 (Vatican edn., xix. 79–80).
[20] Arist. *Ph.* 1. 7 (190[b]17–20).   [21] Ibid. 2. 3 (194[b]23–6).
[22] Arist. *Metaph.* 5. 2 (1013[a]24–5), 7. 7 (1032[b]31–1033[a]1), 7. 10 (1035[a]1–3, 1035[b]31–3).
[23] Arist. *Ph.* 5. 2. (226[a]11–12).
[24] Arist. *Cael.* 2. 3 (286[a]25); *idem, Metaph.* 10. 4 (1055[a]30).

(vi) Matter is something created.[25]

Scotus argues that if matter has objective potentiality, then it does not exist at all; and something which does not exist clearly cannot satisfy any of these conditions.[26] Most interesting is Scotus's (brief) discussion of condition (v). He reasons that items in objective potentiality are individuated by their actualization: some objectively potential item is different from some other objectively potential item just in virtue of the fact that, when the items actually exist, they are different from each other. Thus, if matter merely had objective potentiality, we could not speak of it retaining numerical identity over a substantial change. Matter would in effect be individuated by form. Thus, if the form is *completely* different, so matter is too.[27] Again, the basic intuition here is that nothing which actually exists could be pure potentiality. There is a sense, of course, in which Aquinas agrees with this. Matter on his account is just the potentiality that a substance has for becoming something else. Being pure potentiality, on this account, is not some genuine sort of property; it is more a *lack* of properties. But Scotus holds that this basic Thomist intuition, that nothing can (actually) be pure potentiality, is inconsistent with the claim that matter could retain numerical identity over a substantial change.[28]

Matter according to Scotus does not exhibit objective potentiality; so he argues that it must instead exhibit subjective potentiality:

[Matter] is therefore a being in potentiality in the second way, as some positive being which naturally receives act, and which is a being in potentiality to all the acts which it can receive.[29]

This amounts to the claim that matter has some actuality of its own: there is something (beyond pure potentiality) 'which [matter] is all the time'.[30] Scotus thus modifies Aristotle's straightforward identification

---

[25] See e.g. Augustine, *Conf.* 12. 8, n. 8 (ed. James J. O'Donnell (3 vols., Oxford: Clarendon Press, 1992), i. 166).

[26] Scotus, *Lect.* 2. 12. un., nn. 32–6 (Vatican edn., xix. 80–2).

[27] Ibid. n. 35 (Vatican edn., xix. 81–2).

[28] For a discussion of some related difficulties in Aristotle's account of prime matter, see Daniel W. Graham, *Aristotle's Two Systems* (Oxford: Clarendon Press, 1987), 226–8, and the literature cited there.

[29] Scotus, *Lect.* 2. 12. un., n. 37 (Vatican edn., xix. 82).

[30] See Christopher Martin, *The Philosophy of Thomas Aquinas: Introductory Readings* (London and New York: Routledge, 1988), 65, where Martin notes that, on Aquinas's account of matter, 'there is not anything . . . which it is all the time'; and Scotus's opposite claim well brings out the difference between the two thinkers.

of matter with potentiality, and form with actuality. There is, of course, a sense in which matter cannot be actual. It cannot be actual in just the way that a form is actual. Matter can never *inform* some other entity; it can never be the form of something. Thus, nothing is subjectively potential to matter.[31] On the other hand, both matter and form are actual in the sense of being items that exist in reality, outside their causes. Thus, they both have the actuality which is the correlative of objective potentiality.[32] It would be tempting to make the further claim that form is never subjectively potential to anything else. But, as we shall see in Chapter 4, Scotus believes that for some types of substances we can properly talk of a series of forms arranged hierarchically, such that lower forms—or at least the lower-order composites of matter and a lower form—are subjectively potential to higher forms.

As we might expect in the light of this discussion, Scotus claims unequivocally that prime matter has an essence or quiddity:

Every quidditative entity (whether partial or total) in some genus is of itself indifferent as a quidditative entity to this [individual] entity and that, such that, as a quidditative entity, it is naturally prior to this [individual] entity in so far as it is *this*. As naturally prior, just as it does not belong to it to be a *this*, so the opposite of being a *this* is not incompatible with it from its notion. And just as a composite, in so far as it is a nature, does not include its individual entity in virtue of which it is formally *this*, so neither does matter, in so far as it is a nature, include its individual entity in virtue of which it is *this matter*, nor does form, in so far as it is a nature, include its [individual entity in virtue of which it is *this form*].[33]

This passage makes clear that matter has an essence (albeit one which is *naturally* (though not logically necessarily) a component part of

---

[31] In his early (incomplete) questions on Aristotle's *De Anima*, Scotus seems to suggest the opposite thesis. He argues that a human soul includes the same sort of matter as a body has, and that the soul (including its matter) inheres in a human body (which itself includes matter): see Scotus, *In De an.* 15, nn. 6 and 11 (Wadding edn., ii. 532[a] and 533[b]). But the *De anima* questions are possibly not all by Scotus (see C. Balić, 'The Life and Works of John Duns Scotus', in John K. Ryan and Bernardine M. Bonansea (eds.), *John Duns Scotus, 1265–1965*, Studies in Philosophy and the History of Philosophy, 3 (Washington: Catholic University of America Press, 1965), 1–27, p. 22), and Scotus's other early works do not subscribe to the doctrine of the hylomorphic composition of spiritual substances.

[32] Scotus, *Lect.* 2. 12. un., nn. 38 and 42 (Vatican edn., xix. 82 and 84–5).

[33] Scotus, *Ord.* 2. 3. 1. 5–6, n. 187 (Vatican edn., vii. 483; Spade, 106–7), my italics; see also ibid. 2. 3. 1. 4, n. 114 (Vatican edn., vii. 447; Spade, 87); 2. 3. 1. 5–6, nn. 138–40, 211 (Vatican edn., vii. 462–3, 494; Spade, 95, 113); 3. 22. un., n. 7 (Wadding edn., vii. 443); *idem, In Metaph.* 7. 16, nn. 3, 5–6 (Wadding edn., iv. 717[b], 718[a-b]).

some composite essence). Since matter has an essence, it has essential properties. Quantity is not numbered amongst the essential properties of matter. Thus, matter has its properties *prior* to the inherence of quantity.[34] (I discuss this point in further detail in Chapters 8 and 9.)

As the quoted passage makes clear, Scotus also holds that matter itself requires individuation, which must be brought about *independently* of the composite substance of which individual matter is a part, and independently of the substantial form to which individual matter is united. This claim is in any case entailed by Scotus's claim that matter retains numerical identity over a substantial change.

Clearly, if matter is to have an essence, then it should be possible to know this essence. God can know the essence of matter, since there is an idea of matter in the divine mind. According to Scotus, God can only create what he can know. But God can create matter. So God can know matter.[35] Furthermore, Scotus argues that it is possible to abstract a common concept of matter from the various instances of matter.[36] Nevertheless, there is a restriction on how well a created intellect can know matter. Scotus argues that, just as form has more actuality than matter, so too it is more cognizable. Furthermore, just as form in some sense gives existence to matter, so too it gives a certain kind of cognizability to matter. Something can be known (if at all) in so far as it is actual.[37] But we cannot know the essence of matter without deliberately adverting to its role in a matter–form composite;

---

[34] Scotus, *Ord.* 2. 3. 1. 4, n. 114 (Vatican edn., vii. 447; Spade, 87–8); *idem, Rep.* 2. 12. 2, n. 7 (Wadding edn., xi. 322ᵇ). Matter does not, however, have any sort of *extension* prior to the inherence of quantity, as Massobrio interestingly suggests: see her 'Aristotelian Matter', 208–17. I give my reasons for disagreeing with her interpretation in Ch. 8 n. 40.
[35] Scotus, *Rep.* 2. 12. 2, n. 10 (Wadding edn., xi.323ᵃ); *idem, Ord.* 2. 12. 1, n. 20 (Wadding edn., vi. 676).   [36] Scotus, *Ord.* 3. 22. un., n. 7 (Wadding edn., vii. 443).
[37] Ibid. n. 16 (Wadding edn., vii. 448); the version in MS A, fo. 164ᵛᵃ, differs somewhat from that in Wadding: 'Ad secundum, cum dicitur quod quid est est principium cognoscendi et materia eius est ignota, dico quod habens materiam partem sui non cognoscitur nisi cognita materia sui. Nunquam enim homo haberet scientiam de substantia composita nisi cognosceret eius materiam: aliter omnis cognitio scientifica esset simplicium et immaterialium, secundum quod scientia est de rebus. Tamen quamvis requiritur cognitio materiae ad hoc quod cognoscatur substantia rei materialis, aliter tamen est materia causa cognoscendi, et aliter forma: sicut enim causae differunt in entitate et perfectione et causalitate in causando, ita et in causando cognoscibilitatem illius cuius sunt causae differunt: sicut enim forma est magis ens quam materia, ita magis causat entitatem cuius est forma quam materia et per consequens magis causat cognoscibilitatem ipsius: et quia materia non habet esse perfectum nisi per formam dantem esse tale ultimate in effectu, ideo forma et facit cognoscere materiam, et ultra est ratio cognoscendi compositum. Est ergo materia ignota quia non perfecta ratio cognoscendi'; see also Scotus, *In Metaph.* 7. 16, n. 4 (Wadding edn., iv. 717ᵇ).

as Scotus puts it, we can know matter only by analogy with form. This is not true of all intelligent beings. God and angels can know matter in itself. But the limited nature of the human mind means that it cannot achieve this kind of knowledge.[38] In claiming that we can get some idea of the essence of matter by analogy with form, Scotus means that we can know that something remains constant over a substantial change, and that the essence of matter must be such that it can explain this constancy.[39] Furthermore, we can know that it is in virtue of matter that something is mutable, or generable and corruptible.[40] These, of course, are minimal sorts of description; but they are, according to Scotus, the best that the human mind can offer.

There is a lot to be said in favour of Scotus's claim that matter has some properties of its own. Aristotle reasons, correctly, that to lack any attribute whatsoever is to be nothing;[41] and Aquinas's account of prime matter amounts to the claim that matter is *in itself* completely lacking in (genuine) attributes. It seems difficult to square Aquinas's account of matter with the claim that something must remain *unchanged* over a substantial change. If matter is just the potentiality that some substance has for becoming some completely different substance, then it is difficult to see how that potentiality could remain over the change. Thus, Aquinas's account—unlike Scotus's—cannot allow for the relevant continuity claim which would distinguish generation and corruption from transubstantiation, creation, and annihilation.[42] Matter, according to Scotus, has some properties all of its own. Furthermore, not only are these properties essential to matter, but being properties of matter is essential to them. There is no even more basic stuff underlying prime matter. Scotus's main problem is that *we* cannot know what these features are. But he has at least taken a step in the right direction by claiming that there must be some such features. Any kind of empirical enquiry into the nature of matter must presuppose that matter has some properties. Aquinas's prime matter—the most basic stuff in the universe—is completely inaccessible to scientific

---

[38] Scotus, *Lect.* 2. 12. un., n. 79 (Vatican edn., xix. 101); *idem, Ord.* 2. 12. 1, n. 20 (Wadding edn., vi. 676).   [39] Scotus, *Lect.* 2. 12. un., n. 78 (Vatican edn., xix. 100–1).

[40] Scotus, *Ord.* 3. 22. un., n. 16 (Wadding edn., vii. 448); for the text in MS A, see n. 37 above; see also idem, *Lect.* 2. 12. un., nn. 78–9 (Vatican edn., xix. 100–1).

[41] Arist. *Gen. corr.* 1. 3 (317^b11–13).

[42] In MS A, the point is made beautifully: 'Si materia non maneret, generatio esset vera transubstantiatio': *Ord.* 2. 12. un. (MS A, fo. 130ra, printed in Stella, *L'Ilemorfismo*, 311). I discuss creation and transubstantiation in the Appendix.

investigation. We should not, then, underestimate the importance of Scotus's arguments against Aquinas here.

3. MATTER WITHOUT FORM

More controversial is Scotus's conclusion:

(6) It is possible that matter exists without form.[43]

The claim, of course, admits of two interpretations:

(6*) For every individual matter *m* and every individual form *f*, it is possible that *m* exists without *f*.

(6**) For every individual matter *m*, it is possible that, for every individual form *f*, *m* exists without *f*

(i.e. it is possible for matter to exist without any individual form whatever).[44] (6*) is wholly uncontroversial. All it implies is that different forms could (at different times) belong to one lump of matter. One way in which individual matter can exist without *this* individual form is if it exists with *that* individual form. But (6**)—the conclusion Scotus really wants to defend—is highly questionable.

Scotus gives four arguments for (6). At the end of the final one he provides an argument, which I shall label '(M)', to allow us to infer (6**) from (6*). Since he really needs this argument for three of his four arguments in favour of (6), I discuss (M) first, and then look at two of his arguments in favour of (6).

(M) (p1) If an individual item *x* is necessarily related to a genus φ, then *x* is necessarily related to a species χ of φ.

(p2) If *x* is necessarily related to a species χ, then *x* is necessarily related to an individual instance *y* of χ.

(p3) It is not the case that an individual lump of matter *m* is necessarily related to an individual form.[45]

---

[43] Although he is aware of the distinction, Scotus does not always distinguish carefully between *de re* and *de dicto* modalities—i.e. between modalities attaching to objects and modalities attaching to propositions. I generally take his modalities as *de dicto*, which I translate as 'It is possible that p'. When Scotus seems to have a *de re* modality in mind, or require it for his argument, I translate it as 'It is possible for *x* to *F*'.

[44] By 'individual form', I mean an individual instance of a specific kind: see n. 3 above and Ch. 4.

[45] Where 'individual form' satisfies the description 'individual instance of a species'.

(c1) It is not the case that *m* is necessarily related to a species of form ((p2) and (p3)).

(c2) It is not the case that *m* is necessarily related to the genus of form as such ((p1) and (c1)).[46]

(p3) follows from the claim that matter retains numerical identity over a substantial change. It is in fact equivalent to (6*). According to (p3), there is no one individual form which is essential to any lump of matter; and this is just what (6*) claims. (c2) is equivalent to (6**). According to (c2), there is no lump of matter which has form essentially; and this is just what (6**) claims. So (M) will provide a route from the relatively uncontroversial (6*) to the questionable claim (6**).

But (M) looks faulty, because (p1) and (p2) are false. Scotus justifies (p1) by the following principle:

(B) If an individual item *x* is contingently related to a species of a genus φ, then *x* is contingently related to φ.[47]

(B) and (p1) are equivalent: if a property is contingent (as in (B)), then it is non-necessary (as in (p1)); and vice versa. But both (B) and (p1) are false. The error is one of scope, and can be clearly seen if we express (B) formally:

(B*) $\vdash \forall x (\forall y \Diamond \neg Rxy \rightarrow \Diamond \forall y \neg Rxy)$

(i.e. for every *x* and every *y*, if it is possible that *x* is not related to *y*, then, for every *x*, it is possible that, for every *y*, *x* is not related to *y*). It does not follow, for example, that, if I am contingently 68 inches tall, then I could in principle have *no* height at all.[48] ((p2) is false for analogous reasons.) (B*) is, of course, just the inference from (6*) to (6**) expressed formally. So it is difficult to see how (M) is really any help in Scotus's argument.

The failure of (M) creates difficulties for Scotus's attempt to show that it is possible for matter to exist without any form at all. Scotus uses (M) to justify one of his arguments to (6) construed as (6**).[49] (M) is in fact required—as I just noted—for three of them. I discuss one of these here. The argument derives (6) from

[46] Scotus, *Rep.* 2. 12. 2, n. 6 (Wadding edn., xi. 322ᵃ); *idem, Ord.* 2. 12. 2, n. 4 (Wadding edn., vi. 665).   [47] Scotus, *Rep.* 2. 12. 2, n. 6 (Wadding edn., xi. 322ᵃ).

[48] See Ch. 7 below for a rejection of this principle by Scotus in a different context; also Scotus, *Rep.* 2. 15. un., n. 4 (Wadding edn., xi. 343ᵇ).

[49] Scotus, *Rep.* 2. 12. 2, n. 6 (Wadding edn., xi. 322ᵃ); *idem, Ord.* 2. 12. 2, n. 4 (Wadding edn., vi. 682).

(1*) Matter is really distinct from form,

(7) Matter is naturally prior to substantial form,

and part of the separability criterion for real distinction discussed in Chapter 1:

(C) If *x* is really distinct from, and naturally prior to, *y*, then it is possible for *x* to exist without *y*.

(7) is justified by the claim, already noted, that matter receives form, and

(D) A recipient is naturally prior to what it receives.[50]

But this argument is highly ambiguous, depending upon whether it is read to be about *individual* matter and *individual* form, or about matter *as such* and form *as such*.[51] If we read the arguments in the first way, as about individual matter and individual form, then (6) will amount to (6*). Read thus, the argument is sound. The conclusion, however, is not as strong as that which Scotus requires. If we read the argument in the second way, as about matter as such and form as such, then (C) looks inapplicable: matter as such does not *exist* at all, and *a fortiori* cannot exist without form as such. Scotus's argument (M), would, of course, allow him to infer (6**) from (6*). But, as we have seen, (M) is not successful.

Scotus's other argument is rather different. He reasons that

(E) God creates individual matter directly

entails

(8) God can conserve individual matter directly.

Scotus argues that (8) entails (6**).[52] 'Directly' here translates the Latin *immediate*, and means 'without any other cause'. The argument is deceptively appealing. It is clearly the case that individual matter cannot be produced by any created agent at all; this is why the claim

---

[50] Scotus, *Rep.* 2. 12. 2, n. 4 (Wadding edn., xi. 321^b). Scotus's notion of natural priority is in essence reasonably simple to grasp. If two items *x* and *y* are really distinct, then *x* is naturally prior to *y* if and only if it is possible that *x* exists without *y*, and not possible that *y* exists without *x*. If two formalities *x* and *y* are formally distinct, then *x* is naturally prior to *y* if and only if it is possible that *x* is defined without reference to *y*, and not possible that *y* is defined without reference to *x*. Note that natural priority, as understood by Scotus, does not entail actual temporal priority.

[51] For my terminology here, see n. 3 above.

[52] Scotus, *Rep.* 2. 12. 2, n. 6 (Wadding edn., xi. 322^a).

that God creates individual matter directly looks convincing. But it overlooks the possibility that the existence of form might be (as Aquinas would reason) a *necessary condition* for the existence of individual matter,[53] even if form does not itself have any efficiently causal role in the production of individual matter. In this case, it would be false to claim that God creates individual matter 'directly'.

Since Scotus's arguments for (6**) fail to demonstrate the required conclusion, I conclude that Scotus in fact fails to show that it is possible for matter to exist without form. This does not of course entail that individual matter fails to be really distinct from every individual form. Neither does it entail that it is *impossible* for matter to exist without any form at all. So its failure will not, I think, be fatal for Scotus's metaphysics of matter.

4. MATTER ESSENTIAL TO MATERIAL SUBSTANCE

Scotus claims that (individual) matter and (individual) form are both essential components of a material substance. Scotus's technical term for matter and form is 'essential parts'.[54] While this is suggestive of the thesis I wish to demonstrate, it hardly counts as conclusive evidence: *prima facie*, 'essential parts' is a phrase which could describe all sorts of parts, not just matter and form. It is thus difficult to see what *descriptive* value its use as a technical term actually has. Scotus offers a comprehensive study of the essentiality of matter in *Ordinatio* 3. 22. un., in which he clearly makes the point that matter is essential to any material substance.[55] The claim that substance is just form—which Scotus opposes in *Ordinatio* 3. 22. un.—is one out of a total of four reductionistic accounts of material substance considered by Scotus. I shall label them 'R1'–'R4'.

R1: substance is just form.
R2: substance is just matter.
R3: substance is just the aggregate of matter and form.
R4: substance is just the aggregate of matter, form, and the relation between matter and form.

---

[53] By claiming that the existence of form might be a necessary condition for the existence of matter, I do not mean that the form must *pre-exist* the matter; just that, necessarily, if matter exists, then form does too.

[54] Scotus, *Ord.* 1. 8. 1. 1, n. 7 (Vatican edn., iv. 154–5).

[55] Scotus also discusses the issue more briefly at *In Metaph.* 7. 16 (Wadding edn., iv. 716[a]–19[a]).

I consider R1 in this chapter, R2 in the next chapter, and R3 and R4 in Chapter 5.

R1 is a generalization of a Platonist account of what it is to be a human being. On this account, a human being is just a soul. This soul makes use of a human body.[56] In R1, this claim is generalized to mean that a substance—or, more precisely, the essence or quiddity of a substance—is just form.[57] As Scotus discusses this theory, it becomes apparent that there are two issues at stake: (i) that individual substance must include individual matter and individual form as essential parts; (ii) that essence must include matter as such and form as such.[58] In his attempt to refute R1, Scotus argues from (i) to (ii). If individual matter is *essential* to individual substance, then matter as such must be part of the essence of material substance. As some of the arguments below make clear, Scotus claims that (ii) is properly explanatory of (i). The claim that material substance as such is just form as such amounts to the following claim:

(9) An essence does not include matter as such.

(9), I take it, is the basic metaphysical claim of R1. Setting aside arguments from authority, Scotus gives three arguments in favour of something like (9), of which I will give the most interesting one here, along with Scotus's reply.

Scotus's opponent derives (9) from

(F) If a feature φ prevents an essence *E* from being the same as an individual substance, then it is not possible that φ is a part of *E*,

together with the Aristotelian claim

[56] Scotus (rightly) attributes this account of what it is to be a human being to Hugh of St Victor (Scotus, *Ord.* 3. 22. un., n. 2 (Wadding edn., vii. 441)): see Hugh of St Victor, *De Sac.* 2. 1. 11 (Migne, clxxvi, cols. 401B–411D, esp. 410D–411B; trans. Roy J. Deferrari, (Cambridge, Mass.: The Medieval Academy of America, 1951), 247–9).

[57] See Scotus, *Ord.* 3. 22. un., n. 3 (Wadding edn., vii. 441). According to the marginal annotation in the Wadding edition, this position is to be attributed to Albert the Great. The annotators do not cite a passage, however, and in his commentary on the *Sentences*, 3. 22. 1 ad 1, Albert clearly rejects an identification of substantial form with essence (*Opera Omaia*, ed. S.C.A. Borgnet (38 vols, Paris: Vivès, 1890–9), xxviii. 385ᵇ–6ª). For some of the ambiguities and difficulties in Albert's use of the terms 'form' and 'essence', see Georg Wieland, *Untersuchungen zum Seinsbegriff im Metaphysikkommentar Alberts des Großen*, Beiträge zur Geschichte der Philosophie und Theologie des Mittelalters, N. F., 7 (Münster: Aschendorff, 1971), 18–40.

[58] For the distinction, see Scotus, *Ord.* 3. 22. un., n. 8 (Wadding edn., vii. 443–4); *idem*, *In Metaph.* 7. 16, nn. 3 and 6 (Wadding edn., iv. 717ᵇ and 718ª).

(G) Matter is a feature which prevents an essence from being the same as an individual substance.[59]

A feature which prevents an essence from being the same as an individual substance will be an individuating feature *over and above* the essence which it individuates. (An essence as such which was the same as an individual substance would have to be a self-individuating essence admitting necessarily of no more than one instantiation.) Thus construed, (F) looks analytic. Material substances, according to Scotus, fail to satisfy the criterion in (F). Presumably, the argument is that the essence of a material substance does not contain within itself a principle of numerical distinction: it must be individuated by something other than itself.[60]

Scotus's reply to this argument draws on his view that matter cannot be responsible for individuating material substances. He thus holds that (G) is false: there is no sense in which matter prevents a substance from being really the same as its essence.[61] (Someone who thought that matter individuated would probably want to identify essence with *form*, and thus be an adherent of R1.[62]) Scotus claims as Aristotelian the position that matter as such is a part of the essence as such, and that individual matter is a part of individual substance.[63] In fact, Scotus holds that all substances are really (though not formally) identical with their quiddities.[64] What Scotus means is that an individual substance can be seen, metaphysically, as a composite of two parts which are really identical with each other (and therefore with the substance itself), one of which is quiddity or essence as such (what Scotus labels 'common nature'), the other of which is individuating principle. These parts are formally distinct from each other, and each is therefore formally distinct from the whole individual composite. Thus, a composite is not formally identical with its quiddity.[65]

---

[59] Arist. *Metaph.* 7. 11 (1037^{b}3–7).

[60] Scotus, *Ord.* 3. 22. un., n. 4 (Wadding edn., vii. 442); see also *idem, In Metaph.* 7. 16, n. 2 (Wadding edn., iv. 716^b).

[61] On this, see also Scotus, *Ord.* 2. 3. 1. 5–6, n. 206 (Vatican edn., vii. 492; Spade, 112).

[62] Aristotle himself sometimes seems apt to take this view: see e.g. *Metaph.* 7. 3 (1029^{a}26–33), though see also below, Ch. 3 n. 3.

[63] See Scotus, *Lect.* 2. 12. un., nn. 29, 33 (Vatican edn., xix. 79–81).

[64] See Scotus, *Ord.* 2. 3. 1. 1, n. 32 (Vatican edn., vii. 403; Spade, 63–4); 2. 3. 1. 5–6, nn. 172, 204–5 (Vatican edn., vii. 476, 491–2; Spade, 102, 111–12).

[65] Scotus, *Ord.* 3. 22. un., n. 11 (Wadding edn., vii. 445); MS A, fo. 164ra has: 'Quod quid est in materialibus est idem cum eo cuius est, ut quod quid est hominis est cum homine per se et primo, et est idem cum hoc homine per se et non primo (sicut hic homo habet definitionem sive quod quid est, sic est idem sibi cuius est, vel non idem)'; see also *idem, In Metaph.* 7. 16, nn. 3–4 (Wadding edn., iv. 717^b).

Scotus here does not take issue with his opponent's inference from (G) (the claim that matter individuates) to R1. His reply will thus show that anyone rejecting R1 will have to reject the claim that matter individuates. Scotus thinks, however, that there are good reasons for rejecting R1. His arguments against R1, if successful, would thus have the further result of showing that matter cannot be responsible for individuating material substances. The arguments all turn on Aristotelian sorts of claims which the determined defender of R1 could deny; though not all of the claims could, I think, be *plausibly* denied:

(i)   Matter is the material cause of a composite substance,
(ii) Matter is essentially part of a composite substance,
(iii) It is possible for form to make a *per se* unity with some other entity,
(iv) There exists a body essentially including something that is in potentiality to different substantial forms.

Only the last of Scotus's arguments—that from (iv)—is successful, as far as I can tell. I shall discuss some of his other arguments first, and then give an account of the successful argument.

The first of the four claims which Scotus uses to try to reject R1 is straightforwardly Aristotelian.[66] Scotus argues that if (i) is false, it will follow that matter does not exist at all, presumably on the grounds that a material cause is necessarily an *essential* part of the composite substance of which it is a cause.[67] But, of course, the adherent of R1 would deny the claim that every material cause is an essential part of the composite substance which it causes, and Scotus's argument will thus fail to convince the determined defender that R1 is false.

The argument from Scotus's second claim fares little better. Scotus argues that (ii), coupled with

(1)   Matter exists,

---

[66] See Arist. *Ph.* 2. 3 (194^{b}23–6).

[67] Scotus, *Ord.* 3. 22. un., n. 6 (Wadding edn., vii. 443); MS A, fo. 164ra reads: 'Item cuius essentia est secundum se incausata, illud cuius est essentia est incausatum: quia quod aliquid causetur et essentia eius quae est eadem sibi per realem identitatem non causetur nihil est dictum. Patet igitur maior; ergo eodem addito utrobique, illud <est incausatum> cuius essentia est incausata causis intrinsecis, quia non habet materiam causam sui et per consequens est incausata materialiter; igitur quaelibet substantia materialis est incausata materialiter. Sed frustra ponitur materia in substantia materiali, nisi esset causa sui. Ergo sequitur (si verum est concessum) quod materia nihil est.' (My additions here are given in angle brackets.)

entails the falsity of R1. The central claim of R1 is

(9) An essence does not include matter as such.

But (ii) entails

(10) Matter as such is not a complete essence,

and Scotus accepts as a general principle

(H) Everything in a genus is either a complete essence or is included in an essence.

(H), (9), and (10) entail

(11) Matter as such fails to be in a genus,

which, along with

(I) Everything which fails to be in a genus is either God or nothing,

entails

(12) Matter as such is either God or nothing.

Unsurprisingly, Scotus holds that it is not the case that matter as such is God. So he reasons that R1 entails

(13) Matter as such is nothing.

(13) contradicts (1), which Scotus accepts.[68] Scotus's argument, however, depends on his opponent accepting (I), along with (ii) and the principle it entails, (10). (I) looks fairly questionable. Aquinas, for example, would deny that 'being' is a genus;[69] and, oddly, Scotus's official account of the transcendental attributes—of which 'being' is one—entails that such attributes fail to be in a genus.[70] Equally, the adherent of R1 might want to claim that

(10′) Matter as such is a complete essence.

Scotus's argument will not dislodge this person's commitment to R1.

Whatever his view on (10′), the adherent of (R1) will certainly want to hold

[68] Scotus, *Ord.* 3. 22. un., n. 6 (Wadding edn., vii. 443).

[69] *ST* 1. 3. 5 (ed. Petrus Caramello (3 vols., Turin and Rome: Marietti, 1952–6), i. 18ᵃ).

[70] Scotus, *Ord.* 1. 8. 1. 3, n. 136 (Vatican edn., iv. 221). On the transcendentals in Scotus, see Allan B. Wolter, *The Transcendentals and their Function in the Metaphysics of Duns Scotus*, Franciscan Institute Publications, Philosophy Series, 3 (St Bonaventure, NY: The Franciscan Institute, 1946).

(14) Every form as such is a complete essence,

which is entailed by the basic R1 principle (11). Scotus's argument against R1 from (iii) attacks (14). Briefly, Scotus argues that someone accepting that (14) is true of the forms of material substances will be committed to the view that a composite substance is just a bundle (*acervus*) of parts (where the relevant parts are matter and form): a claim which, according to Scotus, is contradicted by Aristotle.[71]

In principle, Scotus's attack on R1's (14) seems on the right lines. No one committed to (14) could accept that matter could be *essential* to a material substance. Such an R1 adherent could argue that (14) will allow matter to be an accidental part of a material substance. Scotus's attack would amount to the rather stronger claim that such a substance would fail to be a *composite* of matter and form at all: it could be no more than an *aggregate* of matter and form.[72] Scotus's final attack on R1, however, shows that neither of these two possible R1 claims (viz. that matter is an accidental part of a composite, or that a material substance is no more than an aggregate of matter and form) can square with the empirical claims

(A) Generation exists

and

(A*) Corruption exists.

There is a crucial principle (which Scotus does not spell out):

(J) Every body for which being corrupted is possible will include essentially something which is in potentiality to different substantial forms,

which with (A*) clearly entails

(iv) There exists a body essentially including something that is in potentiality to different substantial forms.

Scotus takes 'something that is in potentiality to different substantial forms' as a description referring properly only to prime matter. The adherent of R1 will clearly deny (iv), which amounts to the claim that matter is essential to a material substance. The R1 adherent will thus

---

[71] Arist. *Metaph.* 8.6 (1045ᵃ8–10); Scotus also refers to *Metaph.* 8. 1 (1042ᵃ29–31): see Scotus, *Ord.* 3. 22. un., n. 6 (Wadding edn., vii. 443). For two related arguments, see ibid. n. 5 (Wadding edn., vii. 443), and nn. 7–8 (Wadding edn., vii. 443–4).

[72] I deal with these distinctions in detail in Ch. 5.

have to deny either (A*) or (J). Denying (A*) would not look to me to be very desirable, since it seems to involve a commitment to the view that substances are changed into other substances, if at all, by *transubstantiation*.[73] If (A*) is true, then there will have to be a sense in which material bodies are composites of matter and form. The R1 version of this claim is that matter is an accidental part of a composite substance: that is, that (J) is false. But an accidental part of a body *b* is a part which *b* can exist without. And if *b* were to exist without its matter for a period of time *t*, it would presumably be incorruptible for the duration of *t*. Since on R1 any body can exist without matter, R1 entails that every body is in principle incorruptible. And this looks false.[74]

Scotus's discussion of R1 makes it clear that he holds that essence as such is a composite of matter as such and form as such, and that this individual substance is essentially a composite of individual matter and individual form. Of his arguments against R1, the last looks as though it might present difficulties even for a determined non-Aristotelian defender of R1, since it highlights some empirically implausible claims which result from accepting R1. Equally, Scotus's argument against his opponent's attempt to prove R1 shows that R1 could only be accepted by someone who claimed that material substances are individuated by their matter—a claim which Scotus certainly rejects.

In this chapter, I have tried to show how Scotus defends four claims: (i) that matter exists; (ii) that it has some properties all its own; (iii) that it is logically possible for individual matter to exist independently of any form; (iv) that matter is essential to a material substance. I have argued that Scotus's attempts to defend (ii) should be judged successful by anyone accepting Scotus's intuition that pure potentiality has insufficient ontological thickness to allow spatio-temporal continuity. I suspect that the truth of (ii) is important for the physical sciences in general. Furthermore, Scotus's defence of (iv) seems unequivocally successful.

---

[73] In the Appendix I shall give some reasons why Scotus would want to deny that, in any natural process of substantial change, substances are transubstantiated into each other.

[74] Scotus, *Ord.* 3. 22. un., n. 9 (MS A, fo. 164ra; Wadding edn., vii. 445). In *idem, Lect.* 2. 12. un., nn. 11–16 (Vatican edn., xix. 72–4), Scotus argues similarly, and at n. 16 (Vatican edn., xix. 74) notes that the opposing position would amount to the claim that a natural agent was capable of creation.

On the other hand, although (i) may be true, I have argued that Scotus does not successfully show that there could not be more than one sort of prime matter. Equally, his defence of (iii) is unsuccessful. But I do not think he needs (iii) for his crucial claim (ii), so I do not think that we need to regard his failure to defend (iii) successfully as critical for the success of his basically anti-Thomist account of matter.

3
Substantial Form

As we saw in the previous chapter, talk of substantial form is one way of talking about some of the essential properties of a substance. Scotus claims that instantiated substantial forms are individuals that are themselves essential parts of individual composite substances. I discuss this claim in the first section of this chapter. Since Scotus holds that substantial forms are individuals, he needs to give some kind of account of how such forms are naturally produced. In doing this, he rejects a vitalistic account of matter, according to which all forms exist inchoately in matter—what the medievals called *rationes seminales*. I discuss this in the second section.

1. INDIVIDUAL FORMS

Scotus holds that an instantiated substantial form, just like prime matter, is an individual item or object.[1] In making this claim, Scotus is not alone. Aquinas holds that an instantiated substantial form is an individual (rather than a universal).[2] Aquinas's claim is that a sub-

---

[1] On Scotus's account of substantial form, see Prospero Stella, *L'Ilemorfismo di G. Duns Scoto*, Pubblicazione del Pontificio Ateneo Salesiano. II. Testi e studi sul pensiero medioevale, 2 (Turin: Società Editrice Internazionale, 1955), part 2.

[2] See e.g. *ST.* 1. 50. 2 c. (ed. Petrus Caramello (3 vols., Turin and Rome: Marietti, 1952–6), 253^b); see also Peter Geach, 'Form and Existence', in Anthony Kenny (ed.), *Aquinas: A Collection of Critical Essays*, Modern Studies in Philosophy (London and Melbourne: Macmillan, 1969), 29–53, pp. 35–41, and the comments in Christopher Hughes, *On a Complex Theory of a Simple God: An Investigation in Aquinas' Philosophical Theology*, Cornell Studies in the Philosophy of Religion (Ithaca, NY, and London: Cornell University Press, 1989), 10–20; Gyula Klima, 'On Being and Essence in St Thomas Aquinas's Metaphysics and Philosophy of Science', in Simo Knuuttila *et al.* (eds.), *Knowledge and the Sciences in Medieval Philosophy: Proceedings of the Eighth International Congress of Medieval Philosophy*, Publications of the Luther–Agricola Society (3 vols., Helsinki: Yliopistopaino, 1990), ii. 210–22, pp. 210–11. On individuation generally in Aquinas, see Joseph Owens, 'Thomas Aquinas', in Jorge J.E. Gracia (ed.), *Individuation in Scholasticism: The Later Middle Ages and the Counter-Reformation, 1150–1650*, SUNY Series in

stantial form is individuated in virtue of its inhering in this lump of matter, and being a part of this individual substance. A form is not an item *in its own right*. But Scotus claims that it is individuated independently of the individuation of the prime matter to which it is united, and independently of the composite substance of which it is a part.[3]

The claim, made by both Aquinas and Scotus, that forms are individuals, is *prima facie* surprising. On one plausible hylomorphic account of material substances, matter is an individual concrete object, and form is an *abstract* object: perhaps a way in which matter is structured to be this or that sort of substance. Scotus considers this account of matter and substantial form when discussing a reductionistic account of material substance which I have labelled 'R2'. As Scotus understands R2—substance is just matter—it entails that there is only one concrete or individual part of a material substance. This part is *matter*. Form is just the way in which matter is structured. R2 is held by Richard of Middleton.[4] The version of the discussion found in MS A puts the point most succinctly:

A generable thing is simple, and some claim that it is only matter, and some that it is only form. But they mean the same thing. Those who claim that it is just matter claim that matter progresses in its grades (which are not other than the essence of matter), just as an unterminated dimension progresses up to its

Philosophy (Albany, NY: State University of New York Press, 1994), 173–94, and the works cited there; also, usefully, Christopher Hughes, 'Matter and Individuation in Aquinas', *History of Philosophy Quarterly*, 13 (1996), 1–16.

[3] Scotus, *Ord.* 2. 3. 1. 5–6, n. 187 (Vatican edn., vii. 483; Spade, 106–7), quoted in Ch. 2. Scotus's argument in this passage seems to be that matter and form are separate quiddities, and that any quiddity requires its *own* individuation. In arguing that a form is an individual which is individuated independently of the composite of which it is a part, Scotus looks a bit like a modern reading of Aristotle, according to which Aristotle holds that a form is an individual: see e.g. Michael Frede, *Essays in Ancient Philosophy* (Oxford: Clarendon Press, 1987), 65–71. But there are differences between Frede's account and that of Scotus. Frede argues that Aristotle holds a form to be an individual on the grounds that Aristotle, in *Metaph.* 7, identifies form with substance. Scotus, however, holds that substance is to be identified as the composite of matter and form. Equally, Frede argues that a form is individuated by its *history* (*Essays*, 69). But Scotus would argue that the history of an item is a contingent matter, and hence that Frede's account of the individuation of a form violates the thesis, which I note in Ch. 6, that no item is individuated by one or more of its accidental properties. In the passage just referred to, Scotus argues that a form is individuated by its haecceity.

[4] Richard of Middleton, *De Gradu Formarum* 3 (in Roberto Zavalloni, *Richard de Mediavilla et la controverse sur la pluralité des formes*, Philosophe médiévaux, 2 (Louvain: L'Institut Supérieur de Philosophie, 1951), 121–2); also *idem, Qu. Disp.* 17 (Vatican Library, MS Lat. 868, fo. 46va), quoted in Vatican edn. of Scotus, xix. 77–8.

end term. (A finite quantity is not something other than an infinite one, but is an intrinsic end term; and in some way a quantity is said to be composed of an infinite one and an end term.) In this way, substantial form is said to be the intrinsic end term of matter, and thus is said to be composed from that unterminated thing and [its] end term. Others call this form.[5]

The basic claim here is that a composite of matter and form is just one item, and does not have different individuals as *parts*. Rather, the composition consists in individual matter being actualized up to a particular point (a grade or degree of matter). This is a particular way of talking about the basic claim that a substance is not bare matter, but matter existing in a particular way or mode. We might want to characterize R2 by claiming that form is no more than a structuring of individual matter.

There is much to be said for R2. We would not usually think of forms or properties as individuals. We usually think of properties as *repeatable*, and that non-repeatability (as Scotus frequently points out) is sufficient for individuality.[6] Scotus, however, holds that there is good reason for thinking that R2 is false. In the *Ordinatio*, Scotus uses the arguments in favour of the reality of matter, given in section 1 of Chapter 2, against this view. I do not think that he should do this. We could easily hold that matter is an individual without being committed to the further claim that form is. Scotus gives two further arguments, however, to show that R2 is false. The arguments, of which I give one here, are more fully developed in the early *Lectura*.

According to Scotus, Richard of Middleton's view, R2, entails that all forms are of just one species, since it entails

(1) The only essence in a substance composed of matter and form is the essence of matter.

And, according to Scotus, (1) entails

(2) Form is the same kind of thing as matter.

[5] Scotus *Ord.* 2. 12. un. (MS A, fo. 129[vb]; printed in Stella, *L'Ilemorfismo di G. Duns Scoto*, 309–10); see ibid. 2. 12. 1, n. 3 (Wadding edn., vi. 665); *idem, Lect.* 2. 12. un., n. 23 (Vatican edn., xix. 77–8).

[6] See e.g. Scotus, *Ord.* 2. 3. 1. 2, nn. 48, 57 (Vatican edn., vii. 412–13, 416–17; Spade, 69, 71); 2. 3. 1. 4, nn. 76, 111 (Vatican edn., vii. 426–7, 446; Spade, 76, 87). For a discussion of the issue in the *Lectura*, see Woosuk Park, 'The Problem of Individuation for Scotus: A Principle of Indivisibility or a Principle of Distinction?', *Franciscan Studies*, 48 (1988), 105–23.

This, Scotus claims, is problematic, since, given that matter is just of one species, (2) entails

    (3) All forms are of the same species.[7]

(3) is false; hence (1) is. As Scotus understands (1), it is clear that its falsity will entail that both form and matter are individuals instantiating (different) essences.

(2) is one of the articles condemned at Oxford in 1277 by Robert Kilwardby.[8] So Scotus's argument represents an attempt to show that there are good philosophical reasons for accepting Kilwardby's teaching here. Richard of Middleton, of course, would not accept the inference from (1) to (2). He spells out the specific or sortal differences between substances in terms of *modal distinctions*: a species of substance is just matter existing in a particular mode, such that a different mode of existing is a sufficient condition for sortal difference. To get a substance of kind *F*, on this view, all we need is matter organized in an *F*-like mode or manner; to get a substance of kind *G*, all we need is matter organized in a *G*-like mode or manner. It is easy to see how on this sort of view a substance will contain just one essence. (The point is, presumably, that if one allows that there is just *one* essence in a composite substance, then one will have little difficulty giving a principled account of the *unity* of that substance.) We might want to make much the same point by claiming that different structures of matter are sufficient for sortal difference. But Scotus's inference from (1) to (2) is perhaps a bit more subtle than this reading suggests. His point is that structure is not in itself sufficient to explain sortal difference. What we need, according to Scotus, is an explanation of how different structures of matter could yield different sorts of substance.

By rejecting R2 in just this way, Scotus presumably wants us to accept that the sortal differences between substances can be explained only if we posit that the substantial forms of these substances are themselves specifically different items, such that the sortal differences between *substantial forms* are explanatory of the sortal differences between *substances*. If this is what Scotus means, it seems difficult to see how his theory could really be an improvement on Richard's. It is

---

[7] Scotus, *Lect.* 2. 12. un., n. 56 (Vatican edn., xix. 90). For the second argument, see ibid. n. 57 (Vatican edn., xix. 91).

[8] The condemned article (14 'in naturalibus') reads: 'That matter and form are not distinguished by essence': see *Cartularium Universitatis Parisiensis*, ed. H. Denifle and E. Chatelain (4 vols., Paris: Delalain, 1889–97), i. 559.

just as difficult to see how individual substantial forms can be used to explain sortal differences as it is to see how different arrangements of matter can be used to explain sortal differences.

Scotus holds, as I have pointed out, that form is individuated independently of matter.[9] He does not argue for this claim. But presumably he would appeal to his theory that the form and matter of a material substance are two different essences to support his claim that matter cannot account for the individuation of form. Given his claim that matter and form are individuated independently of each other, it is no surprise that Scotus holds that it is possible (logically possible, not naturally possible) for any individual substantial form to exist in separation from the matter to which it is naturally united—indeed, separately from any matter whatsoever. In the *Reportatio Parisiensis*, Scotus offers arguments on both sides of the question. One of the arguments cited in the previous chapter in favour of the possibility of the independent existence of matter is that matter is both really distinct from, and naturally prior to, form. On Scotus's standard account of real distinction and natural priority, this would mean that matter could exist without form, but that form could not likewise exist without matter. Hence Scotus is able to raise the following objection and reply:

Bodily matter is more dependent on bodily form than the other way round. But bodily form cannot exist without matter (since it would then be immaterial and consequently intellectual), as Avicenna claims 1 Met. c. 4.[10] [Reply] I say that matter is less dependent on bodily form than material form is on matter, since it is prior by origin—even though form is more perfect. And hence there is no likeness.[11]

But Scotus is not entirely satisfied with this account, and offers an alternative. On standard Aristotelian accounts of what it is to be a substantial form, a substantial form can be said to be the *formal cause* of the composite of which it is a part. Accepting the general principle

---

[9] See Scotus, *Ord.* 2. 3. 1. 5–6, n. 187 (Vatican edn., vii. 483; Spade, 106–7).

[10] This is a rogue reference. In *Metaph.* 2.2 (ed. S. van Riet, Avicenna Latinus (3 vols., Louvain: Peeters; Leiden: Brill, 1977–83), i. 82), Avicenna argues that bodily form cannot exist without matter; but he does not do so on the grounds that 'it would then be immaterial and consequently intellectual'; see also ibid. 2. 4 (i. 92).

[11] Scotus, *Rep.* 2. 12. 2, n. 12 (Wadding edn., xi. 323[b]).

(A) If form is not the formal cause of matter, and if form is an absolute entity, then it is possible that form exists without matter

(where the domain of (A) is material forms, those which naturally inhere in matter), and accepting that form satisfies the conditions set out in the antecedent of (A), Scotus infers

(4) It is possible that form exists without matter.[12]

(Form is, of course, the formal cause not of matter but of the composite.) (A), however, looks false here. The point of (A), presumably, is that matter is not a necessary condition for the existence of form. But it is difficult to see how (A) successfully makes this point. We might think that something could both be an absolute entity and fail to be the formal cause of matter, and yet still be such that it cannot exist without matter. For example, if we believe (i) that the existence of matter is a necessary condition for the existence of a composite, and (ii) that the existence of the composite is a necessary condition for the existence of form, then we will believe (A) to be false.

Scotus, however, would argue that the crucial claim made in (A) is that form is an absolute entity. An absolute entity is an entity which does not have as an essential property a relation to any other created entity. Thus, if form is an absolute entity, then it cannot have as an essential property a relation to matter.[13] Scotus presents a highly compressed argument against the claim, made by Avicenna,[14] that a relation to matter is an essential property of form. Accepting the general principle

(B) If an individual substantial form is essentially a relational item, then a substantial change is less perfect than an accidental change in the categories of quality or quantity,

Scotus reasons that

(C) It is not the case that a substantial change is less perfect than an accidental change in the categories of quality or quantity,

entails

(5) It is not the case that an individual substantial form is essentially a relational item.[15]

[12] Ibid.; see also Scotus, *In Metaph.* 7. 16, n. 8 (Wadding edn., iv. 719ᵃ).
[13] Scotus, *Lect.* 2. 12. un., nn. 54–6 (Vatican edn., xix. 90).
[14] Avicenna, *Metaph*, 2. 4 (i. 92).
[15] Scotus, *Lect.* 2. 12. un., n. 55 (Vatican edn., xix. 90).

Scotus does not in the text offer any argument for either of the premises. (C) might be taken as obvious to anyone who naturally views the world as arranged hierarchically in terms of perfection—something the medievals were wont to do. (B) presupposes that an accidental change in the category of quality or quantity will involve the acquisition of a new absolute or non-relational item (i.e. one which fails to be essentially related to any created thing). So (B) presupposes that quality and quantity count as non-relational items. Scotus does have some argument for the fairly controversial last claim here. (I discuss the argument in Chapter 6.) Nevertheless, someone who accepted Scotus's argument about the non-relational character of quantity and quality, and who was happy to make just the hierarchical classification which Scotus makes of degrees of perfection in changes issuing in relational and non-relational items, would be happy to accept this argument.

As we have seen, Scotus holds that a substantial form has an essence.[16] This presumably means that it has certain essential properties. Scotus discusses in any detail only one case of the sorts of properties had by a substantial form. The case is the human soul. He argues that the essential properties of a human soul are formally distinct parts of the soul.[17] Presumably Scotus would make the same claim for the properties of any substantial form. Scotus is clear that there is one property which is essential to every substantial form. Every form is *naturally* (though not logically necessarily) a component part of some further composite item.[18] Furthermore, as (M) in Chapter 2 makes clear, Scotus is happy to accept that substantial forms can be classified according to different species. Presumably, though Scotus does not make this point explicitly, he would regard specific differences between various substantial forms as corresponding on a one-to-one basis with specific differences between various composite essences. This certainly seems presupposed by Scotus's argument against R2.

In this section, I have given Scotus's basic account of substantial form. (I deal with Scotus's (fairly agnostic) account of form as actuality in Chapter 5.) Scotus holds that a substantial form is an individual with

---

[16] See also Scotus, *Ord.* 2. 3. 1 .5–6, n. 187 (Vatican edn., vii. 483; Spade, 106–7).

[17] I discuss this in Ch. 4 below.

[18] Scotus, *Ord.* 2. 3. 1. 5–6, n. 187 (Vatican edn., vii. 483; Spade, 106–7). For the human soul's tendency to be a part of a composite, see ibid. 3. 1. 1, n. 11 (Wadding edn., vii. 16). Scotus would want, I suppose, to make the same claim for any substantial form.

an essence separate from its matter. This individual is individuated independently of its matter, and can exist apart from any matter whatsoever. Whether or not the view that the forms of material substance are individuals can be successfully defended is not clear to me. I have suggested that an account of substantial form as *structure* will probably be sufficient to do all the metaphysical work Scotus needs. On the other hand, Scotus is right to hold that an argument needs to be given for the existence of individual forms. So his view represents an improvement on that of Aquinas. Aquinas holds that the forms of material substances are individual; but, as Hughes notes, 'One gets the impression that Aquinas thought it obvious enough that properties in distinct subjects must be distinct, that no argument to that effect was needed.'[19] Whatever we think of Scotus's argument, it is to his credit that he sees the need to give one.

2. RATIONES SEMINALES

Conceiving instantiated form as an individual item leaves Scotus with some difficult problems with regard to the generation and corruption of composite substances. On standard Aristotelian accounts of generation, for example, a new substance is produced in virtue of the fact that matter begins to have some properties which it did not previously have. But the properties, or form, are not *items*, and thus do not begin to exist.[20] On Scotus's account, however, an instantiated form counts as an individual item in itself. Thus, while he would agree with the Aristotelian account—that in generation a new substance begins to exist in virtue of the union of form and matter—he would add that a new form itself begins to exist.

The problem which arises if generation is thus described is that it looks as if the new form is produced out of nothing: that is, that it is created. Henry of Ghent, a few years previously, had considered just this problem. One answer he considered consists in adapting the Augustinian claim, mediated via Bonaventure, that matter contains

---

[19] Hughes, *On a Complex Theory of a Simple God*, 12.
[20] For a defence of this sort of view, see e.g. Aquinas, *ST* 1. 110. 2 (i. 520[b]); also 1. 45. 8 (i. 234[a]); 1. 65. 4 (i. 321[a]). How Aquinas reconciles his adherence to this account of generation with his adherence to the claim that forms are individuals remains unclear to me.

all forms in embryo: the so-called *rationes seminales*.[21] This kind of theory exists in several versions, and is made use of in a number of different contexts.[22] Here, I shall be interested just in the following version:

> (6) Prime matter has as a property a set of active causal powers (in virtue of the inherence of a lesser degree of a form) as a result of which it has the capacity to receive different substantial forms, such that for each kind of substantial form which prime matter can receive, it has an active causal power corresponding to that kind,

which forms the central claim of Henry's proposal.[23] As Henry understands the position, it entails that the set of active powers is to be identified as the inherence of a set of inchoate universal forms, with one such form corresponding to each species of substance and accident.[24] In fact, Henry rejects this theory in favour of a more recognizably Aristotelian position.[25] One of his objections is that (6) entails that substantial forms can admit of degrees. The idea is that the inchoate universal form is a lesser degree of a fully instantiated form. Scotus accepts this objection, since he denies that substantial forms can admit of degrees.[26]

[21] On Augustine's theory, see Etienne Gilson, *The Christian Philosophy of Saint Augustine*, trans. L. E. M. Lynch (London: Gollancz, 1961), 206–8; on Bonaventure, see *idem*, *The Philosophy of St Bonaventure*, trans. Illtyd Trethowan and F. J. Sheed (London: Sheed and Ward, 1938), ch. 10; Conrad John O'Leary, *The Substantial Composition of Man According to Saint Bonaventure* (Washington: Catholic University of America Press, 1931), 49–60; E. Bettoni, *Saint Bonaventure*, trans. Angelus Gambatese (Notre Dame, Ind.: University of Notre Dame Press, 1964), 76–82; and John Francis Quinn, *The Historical Constitution of St Bonaventure's Philosophy* (Toronto: Pontifical Institute of Mediaeval Studies, 1973), 110–12, 310–13.

[22] For example, *ratio seminalis* can refer to an active power possessed by semen. This power was held to alter the qualities of the pre-existing substance, such that a new substance could be generated from the old: see Scotus, *Lect.* 2. 18. 1–2, nn. 15–58 (Vatican edn., xix. 158–69). (The actual agent held to be responsible for generation was the sun: ibid. n. 37 (Vatican edn., xix. 163).) Scotus deals with the generative process in compounds and elements in ibid. nn. 43 and 46–7 (Vatican edn., xix. 165), respectively.

[23] For other versions of the *rationes seminales* theory, see Scotus, *In Metaph.* 7. 12, n. 2 (Wadding edn., iv. 694^{a-b}).

[24] Henry, *Quod.* 4. 14 ((2 vols., Venice, 1613), i. 174vb–5rb).

[25] Ibid. (Venice edn., i. 175rb–7rb, 180rb–1vb). A few years later, something like the position which Henry rejects was taken by Roger Marston: see his *Quod.* 2. 22 (Zavalloni, *Richard de Mediavilla*, 184–5). Henry's *Quod.* 4 is dated to 1279, Marston's *Quod.* 2 probably to 1282–4: see Zavalloni, *Richard de Mediavilla*, 506–7.

[26] For the objection, see Scotus, *In Metaph.* 7. 12, n. 3 (Wadding edn., iv. 694^b). For the claim that substantial forms do not admit of degrees, see *idem*, *Ord.* 4. 11. 3, n. 44 (Wadding edn., viii. 648).

For Henry, the reason why (6) might appear attractive is that it avoids the creation difficulty outlined above. Accepting the following Aristotelian principle

> (D) If, in the production of a substance, matter contributes nothing to the form of the new substance, then the production of the substance will be either creation or some process doing violence to the matter,[27]

Henry infers that, since the consequent of (D) is false,

> (7) In the production of a substance, matter contributes to the form of the new substance

is true. But, Henry reasons, (7) entails (6). Hence, accepting (6) is necessary to avoid the creation difficulty.[28] Presumably, Henry understands (7) to mean that matter must have an active role in the generation of substance (we might say that matter must make an *active* contribution to the process); and he sees (6) as the only way of securing this.

Scotus does not believe that (6) succeeds in avoiding the creation difficulty. He reasons that (6) alone cannot explain how at least some of the new form fails to be created:

Suppose that there are certain pre-existing things [in matter]. Either something new (none of which pre-existed) exists by generation, or not. If it does, then whatever pre-exists is needlessly posited to avoid the creation difficulty, because something—howsoever little—is new, and does not [come to] exist from any of its [parts]. If [nothing new exists by generation], then there will be no generation.[29]

Coupled with the principle of parsimony ('plurality should not be posited unnecessarily'),[30] Scotus reasons that, since it is not necessary to posit *rationes seminales* to avoid the creation difficulty, we should not posit such *rationes seminales.*[31]

---

[27] See Arist. *Eth. Nic.* 3. 1 (1110^b15–18). Aristotle's concern here is with compulsory action as opposed to voluntary action, but it is easy to see how Henry adapts the text for a different purpose.

[28] Henry, *Quod.* 4. 14 (Venice edn., i. 174vb). Henry later responds to this argument by noting that its truth entails the false claim that substantial forms admit of degrees: ibid. (Venice edn., i. 179rb).

[29] Scotus, *Lect.* 2. 18. 1–2, n. 62 (Vatican edn., xix. 170); see *idem, In Metaph.* 7. 12, n. 4 (Wadding edn., iv. 695^a).

[30] Scotus attributes the principle of parsimony to Aristotle, *Ph.* 1: see Scotus, *Ord.* 4. 11. 3, n. 27 (Wadding edn., viii. 630). Perhaps he is thinking of Arist. *Ph.* 1. 6 (189^a15–16).

[31] Scotus, *Lect.* 2. 18. 1–2, n. 64 (Vatican edn., xix. 171). Among the articles condemned at Oxford in 1277 was the following (3 'in naturalibus'): 'That there is no active power in matter': see *Cartularium Universitatis Parisiensis*, i. 559. (E) entails that the condemned proposition is false, and represents one way of spelling out what an orthodox position

Underlying Scotus's argument here is a principle which we shall come across again in subsequent chapters:

> (E) It is not possible that change occurs without the production and/or destruction of an individual thing.[32]

(E) explains Scotus's crucial claim, made in the last sentence of his argument against (6), that if the *whole* form pre-exists in any sense in the matter, then it is not possible for any real change to occur. Scotus's opponent, however, could deny the inference from (E) to the claim that it is not possible for the whole form to exist *in any sense* in the matter. The adherent of (6) would want to claim that the whole form exists first potentially in the matter, and later actually in the composite. Thus the fundamental metaphysical disagreement between Scotus and an adherent of (6) lies deeper than Scotus's acceptance of (E); specifically, it lies in the fact that Scotus has basically only two models for the actualizing of a passive potentiality: (i) the actualization of a subjective potentiality; (ii) the actualization of an objective potentiality. The first of these entails the addition of some new form to some already existing subject. It thus involves in some sense the existence of both the form and the subject as *parts* of some new whole. The second entails that some non-existing item become an existing item. On this scheme, it would make no sense to talk of a whole item existing potentially. A whole item x is in (objective) potentiality at t, if and only if x does not exist at t and will exist at t_n. But the metaphysic of some of Scotus's opponents allows for some one whole item to *exist* first potentially and then actually: thus, x exists potentially at t and actually at t_n. In this case, the *whole* form somehow exists potentially in the matter prior to its actualization. (We shall come across this problem again (along with Scotus's adherence to (E)) in Chapter 10, when looking at the problem of the intensification and remission of qualities.)

---

should look like. Scotus, of course, rejects (E), and I have furthermore found no evidence that he would want to reject the condemned proposition. Perhaps the force of the Oxonian condemnations was not felt in the same way as that of the Parisian ones. But Scotus sometimes refers to matter as a 'concause' in generation, so perhaps he would want to classify material causality as some sort of active causal power: see *Ord.* 4. 12. 4, n. 23 (Wadding edn., viii. 768), discussed below in the Appendix.

[32] For (E), see *Ord.* 1. 30. 1–2, n. 41 (Vatican edn., vi. 186); *Lect.* 1. 39. 1–5, n. 73 (Vatican edn., xvii. 504); and especially the texts cited below, Ch. 6 n. 39, and Ch. 10 n. 27.

Since Scotus denies the usefulness of (6) in avoiding the creation difficulty, he has to provide a different account of generation which will do this. He does this by offering the following definition of 'creation':

> Creation $=_{df}$ The production p of some item or items by an agent a, such that no item other than a is a necessary condition for p.[33]

The natural generation of a composite (and the consequent production of a form) does not satisfy this definition, since it is impossible for generation to take place—and thus for the consequent production of a form to take place—unless there exists some matter in subjective potentiality to the form.[34] The definition of creation proposed here seems fairly uncontroversial, and it clearly entails that generation, even if it involves the production of a new form, is not creation.

Given an account of forms as individuals, there seems to be a good reason for wanting to accept Scotus's rather counter-intuitive claim that form is individuated independently of the matter to which it is united. Form seems able to persist even when the matter to which it is united is replaced (gradually) by different matter. We generally suppose that a thing's properties can remain constant over time even if its basic constituent stuff has gradually been replaced by other constituent stuff. I have the same DNA configuration, for example, as I had when a child, even if I no longer have any of the same matter as I had when a child. On the other hand, I do not think we should accept Scotus's claim that the form of a material substance could exist without any matter at all.

Granted that form is an individual item, Scotus is surely right to reject the *rationes seminales* theory. For the reason pointed out by Scotus, such a theory cannot do the explanatory work required of it. On the view which Scotus rejects, the properties of higher-order composites somehow pre-exist potentially in matter. Scotus objects that it is not possible for these inchoate properties to be *sufficient* for the existence of higher-order properties, and hence that these inchoate properties cannot do the relevant explanatory work. It seems to

---

[33] Scotus, *Ord.* 4. 11. 1, n. 10 (Wadding edn., viii. 590).
[34] Scotus, *Lect.* 2. 18. 1–2, n. 70 (Vatican edn., xix. 174); see also ibid. 2. 12. un., nn. 63–5 (Vatican edn., xix. 93–5).

me to be quite right to reject a vitalistic account of this sort, and Scotus's argument highlights a way in which accepting such an account of matter fails to achieve the kind of result it sets out to achieve.[35]

[35] We might note in passing that Scotus's argument should make us wary of attributing the rejection of such vitalistic accounts of matter merely to 'the philosophers of the seventeenth century': for the attribution, see David Charles, 'Matter and Form: Unity, Persistence, and Identity', in T. Scaltsas, D. Charles, and M. L. Gill (eds.), *Unity, Identity, and Explanation in Aristotle's Metaphysics*, (Oxford: Clarendon Press, 1994), 75–105, p. 79.

4
The Plurality of Forms

According to Aquinas, it is not possible for a composite substance to have more than one substantial form. We shall see some of his reasons for this below. Scotus, on the other hand, argues that some composite substances have more that one substantial (i.e. essential) form. As Scotus makes clear, we should not posit more than one substantial form if just one will do; we should only posit more than one form if we need other forms to do some *explanatory* work which cannot be done if we posit just one form in a composite. Scotus believes, in fact, that just one form is all we need to posit in the case of non-living composites; but he also believes that, in the case of living beings, we do indeed need to posit more than one form. The forms which Scotus posits are (i) the form of the body, (ii) the animating form or soul, and (iii) (probably) the forms of the body's organs. Scotus also claims that it is not necessary to posit the forms of the elements in a mixed (compound) substance. I begin by considering the theories of Scotus's opponents here, Aquinas and Henry of Ghent, and Scotus's objections to these theories. I then outline Scotus's own theories.

1. THOMAS AQUINAS

Scotus gives three Thomist arguments in favour of a unitarian theory, and adds a further argument of his own. I give two of these, and label them '(A.1)' and '(A.2)'. Scotus also gives three arguments from Henry of Ghent in favour of a unitarian theory. One of these is much the same as (A.2), and I will discuss it with (A.2). I discuss two other of Henry's arguments in the next section.

(A.1) Thomas holds that

(A) A substance has only one substantial existence.

He reasons that (A) entails

(1) A substance has only one substantial form,

on the grounds that the presence of exactly one form is a necessary condition for the presence of exactly one existence.[1]

(**A.2**) According to Aquinas, accepting the plurality theory would prevent any principled distinction between an accidental form and a substantial form. He reasons that there are three differences between accidental forms and substantial forms. (i) A substance exists *simpliciter* in virtue of its substantial form, whereas it exists in a particular way (*secundum quid*) in virtue of its accidental forms. (ii) The recipient of a substantial form is something which is pure potentiality, whereas the recipient of an accidental form is something which is itself an actual existent. (iii) A substance is generated *simpliciter*, since it is produced from pure potentiality to existence *simpliciter*; whereas an accident is generated only in a derivative sense (*secundum quid*), since it is produced in existence such that it exists in a particular way (*secundum quid*)—that is, as a property of a substance. Aquinas reasons that, if there is more than one substantial form in a composite substance, these three distinctions will break down. The lowest form in any pluriformed composite will satisfy the conditions set out for a substantial form. But any higher form will satisfy the conditions set out for an accidental form, since (i) it will supervene on an already existent substance, and therefore merely be that in virtue of which a substance exists in a particular way; (ii) its recipient will be an actual existent; and (iii) it will be produced in existence such that it exists in a particular way.[2]

[1] Scotus, *Ord.* 4. 11. 3, n. 25 (Wadding edn., viii. 629); see Aquinas, *ST* 1. 76. 3 (ed. Petrus Caramello (3 vols., Turin and Rome: Marietti, 1952–6), i. 362ᵇ). The literature on Aquinas's account of existence is extensive. John F. Wippel, 'Aquinas's Route to the Real Distinction: A Note on *De Ente et Essentia*, c. 4', *Thomist*, 43 (1979), 279–95, reprinted, together with a reply to criticisms by Joseph Owens, as 'Essence and Existence in the *De Ente*, ch. 4', in John F. Wippel, *Metaphysical Themes in Thomas Aquinas*, Studies in Philosophy and the History of Philosophy, 10 (Washington: Catholic University of America Press, 1984), 107–32, and *idem*, 'Essence and Existence in Other Writings', in *Metaphysical Themes*, 133–61, both provide full bibliographies, to which we might add Stephen Theron, 'Esse', *New Scholasticism*, 53 (1979), 206–20; Scott MacDonald, 'The *Esse/Essentia* Argument in Aquinas's *De ente et essentia*', *Journal of the History of Philosophy*, 22 (1984), 157–72; Gyula Klima, 'On Being and Essence in St Thomas Aquinas's Metaphysics and Philosophy of Science', in Simo Knuuttila *et al.* (eds.), *Knowledge and the Sciences in Medieval Philosophy: Proceedings of the Eighth International Conference of Medieval Philosophy*, Publications of the Luther–Agricola Society (3 vols., Helsinki: Yliopistopaino, 1990), ii. 210–22, and *idem*, 'The Semantic Principles Underlying St Thomas Aquinas's Metaphysics of Being', *Medieval Philosophy and Theology*, 5 (1996), 87–141.

[2] Aquinas, *ST* 1. 76. 4 (i. 364ᵃ); Scotus, *Ord.* 4. 11. 3, n. 26 (Wadding edn., viii. 630).

Scotus cites many of the same points when discussing Henry's unitarian theory, but adds a useful clarification. A pluralist objector suggests that substantial forms could be distinguished from accidental forms on the grounds that, necessarily, a substantial form is added to an object which is essentially incomplete, whereas an accidental form is added to an object which is essentially complete. Henry replies, however, that a pluralist can have no non-question-begging way of distinguishing complete objects from incomplete objects. Hence, such a distinction will not provide the means for a principled distinction between substantial and accidental forms.[3]

2. HENRY OF GHENT

Henry of Ghent believes that in all composites *except human beings* we should posit just one substantial form. Scotus agrees that more than one form should be posited in a human composite. But he holds that there are some other substances as well—plants and animals, for example—which have more than one substantial form. Henry has two arguments to show that we should posit more than just one substantial form in the case of human beings. I will look first at Henry's main unitarian arguments, labelled '(B.1)' and '(B.2)': that is, his arguments for there being just one substantial form in all composites except for human beings. I shall then consider his arguments in favour of positing more than one form in the case of human beings.

Henry does not accept (1) as it stands, and argues instead for the related

(1*) A substance has only one naturally produced substantial form,

where 'naturally produced' means 'produced in virtue of the causal powers of some created agent'. Henry's reason is that (1*), unlike (1), is consistent with his claim

(2) A human being has two numerically distinct substantial forms,

which I discuss below. (B.1) Henry argues that if (1*) is false, then exactly one of

---

[3] Henry, *Quod.* 4. 13 ((2 vols., Venice, 1613), 164^{va-b}, 165vb–6ra); Scotus, *Ord.* 4. 11. 3, n. 34 (Wadding edn., viii. 639).

(3) The many forms in a pluriformed composite are produced from one potentiality in matter

and

(4) The many forms in a pluriformed composite are produced from many potentialities in matter

is true. Henry offers two different attempts to reduce (3) to absurdity. I label them '(i)' and '(ii)'. He also offers an argument to reduce (4) to absurdity, which I label '(iii)'. Scotus adds another, which I label '(iv)'.

(i) The many forms in any putative pluriformed composite belong to the same species. Accepting the Averroistic principle

(B) Specific distinction of the forms which actualize potentialities in matter is a necessary and sufficient condition for the numerical distinction of potentialities in matter,[4]

(3) therefore entails

(5) Two forms of the same species actualize one potentiality in matter.

But (5), on standard medieval accounts, is false. Hence (3) is too.[5]

(ii) (3) entails

(6) Many acts inhere in one potentiality,

which entails the falsity of the Aristotelian position

(C) Distinction of acts is a necessary and sufficient condition for the distinction of potentialities.[6]

But Henry accepts (C). Hence he reasons that (3) is false.[7]

(iii) Taking the other horn of the dilemma, Henry reasons that (4), together with the general principle

(D) It is not possible that potentialities are ordered to each other

entails

---

[4] See Averroës, *In Metaph.* 12. 11 (*Aristotelis Opera cum Averrois Commentaria* (11 vols., Venice, 1550) viii. 140ra).

[5] Henry, *Quod.* 4. 13 (Venice edn., i. 165ra); Scotus, *Ord.* 4. 11. 3, n. 33 (Wadding edn., viii. 639).   [6] Arist. *Ph.* 3. 1 (201[a]35–[b]1).

[7] Henry, *Quod.* 4. 13 (Venice edn., i. 165[ra]); Scotus, *Ord.* 4. 11. 3, n. 33 (Wadding edn., viii. 639). My formulations of (B) and (C) are stronger than those suggested by Henry. They are, however, necessary for the success of Henry's argument. Scotus discerns two arguments in Henry's one.

(7) It is not possible that the forms in a pluriformed composite are ordered to each other.

Supposing for the sake of argument that a plurality theory is true, however, (7) will then be false, since if the various substantial forms fail to be ordered to each other in terms of potentiality and actuality, it is impossible for them all to be united as parts of just *one* composite substance. The point of (D), presumably, is that one potentiality cannot be potential to another potentiality: by definition, potentialities are potential to *actualities*. Granted the truth of (D), Henry's claim is thus that the plurality theory is inconsistent, entailing both that (7) is true and that (7) is false.[8]

(iv) Scotus offers a further argument against (4). He reasons that

(E) Anything which includes a number of different potentialities has merely accidental unity.

But on (4), matter includes a number of different potentialities. Hence, (4) and (E) entail

(8) Matter has merely accidental unity.

But (8) is false. Therefore, granted (E), (4) is false.[9] As Scotus's reply to this argument makes clear, the grounds for supposing (E) to be true are that the different potentialities included in a substance are necessarily accidental *to each other*.[10] Scotus, as we shall see, argues that (E) is false. Since, according to Henry, both (3) and (4) are false, it follows that (1*) is true.

Henry has a further argument for (1*).

(B.2) Henry accepts

(9) There is one natural mutation in the generation of one substance,

where 'natural mutation' refers to a mutation brought about in virtue

---

[8] Henry, *Quod.* 4. 13 (Venice edn., i. 165rb); Scotus, *Ord.* 4. 11. 3, n. 34 (Wadding edn., viii. 639).

[9] Scotus, *Ord.* 4. 11. 3, n. 34 (Wadding edn., viii. 639). The argument is not found in just this form in Henry; perhaps it is based on *Quod.* 4. 13 (Venice edn., i. 165va): 'Et ideo (ut determinat ibidem) quod materia est una secundum substantiam, et plures secundum potentias et habilitates ad formas, hoc est causa in multitudine entium ex eadem materia. Si vero diversae formae per diversos motus aut mutationes simul existentes per naturam producantur in esse, hoc non contingit nisi quia illud quod movetur est unum, non per se, sed secundum accidens, secundum quod dicit Philosophus in quinto Physicorum.' [10] Scotus, *Ord.* 4. 11. 3, n. 42 (Wadding edn., viii. 646).

of the causal powers of some created agent. He reasons that (9), together with an Aristotelian claim

> (F) Numerical distinction of naturally produced forms is a necessary and sufficient condition for the numerical distinction of natural mutations,[11]

entails (1*).[12] On the basis of a passage from Boethius,[13] Henry argues that satisfying (9), and therefore (1*), is a necessary condition for an object to exhibit substantial unity. (As we shall see, Henry allows that there can be more than one substantial form in a composite substance just if one of the forms is created by God.)

(9)—and therefore (B.2)—seems open to an obvious objection, however: it ignores the empirical fact of the way in which substances are actually generated. As an objector asks, is it not the case that the *parts* of a substance are frequently generated *before* the whole substance is?[14] Henry clearly believes that (1*) is true despite this objection. (Perhaps he is strongly persuaded by (B.1).) So he replies to this

---

[11] The claim is very loosely derived from Arist. *Ph.* 5. 1 (224^{b}7–8).

[12] Scotus, *Ord.* 4. 11. 3, n. 33 (Wadding edn., viii. 638). MS A, fo. 214vb, has: 'Omne quod est, ideo est, quia unum numero est, secundum Boethium, libro de Unitate et Uno. Igitur ad quamlibet rem naturalem unam est una mutatio numero. Sed una mutatio distinguitur genere, specie et numero per formam terminantem (5 Physicorum). Ergo unius mutationis, qua producitur una res naturalis sunt multae generationes partiales, et illae sunt ad diversas formas tanquam ad proprios terminos. Contra: aut istae plures formae educuntur de una potentia materiae, aut de diversis. Non de una, quia secundum Commentatorem 22 commento 12 Metaphysicae, numerus potentiarum in materia est secundum numerum specierum, et ita istae duae formae, quibus una esset potentia, essent eiusdem speciei. Sed tales duas impossibile est esse simul in eodem'; I take it that the reading in the Wadding edition is better, spelling out the steps necessary to Scotus's argument far more explicitly. See also Henry, *Quod.* 4. 13 (Venice edn., i. 164vb–5va). For a detailed discussion of Henry's *Quodlibet* 4. 13, see Roberto Zavalloni, *Richard de Mediavilla et la controverse sur le pluralité des formes*, Philosophes médiévaux, 2 (Louvain: L'Institut Supérieur de Philosophie, 1951), 288–92. Henry actually claims only

> (F*) Numerical distinction of forms is a sufficient condition for the numerical distinction of natural mutations.

But his argument requires my stronger formulation—viz. (F)—and Henry doubtless supposes that the *only* way in which a natural mutation is individuated is in virtue of the numerical distinction of forms.

[13] Boethius, *Comm. in Isag. ed. secunda*, 1. 10 (ed. Samuel Brandt, Corpus Scriptorum Ecclesiasticorum Latinorum, 48 (Vienna: Tempsky; Leipzig: Freytag, 1906), 162): 'Omne quod est, idcirco est, quia unum est.' The precise role of this claim (which Henry quotes) as a premiss in his argument is unclear.

[14] Scotus, *Ord.* 4. 11. 3, n. 33 (Wadding edn., viii. 638–9; for the (unsatisfactory) version of the text in MS A, see n. 12 above); see Henry, *Quod.* 4. 13 (Venice edn., i. 165ra).

simply by arguing that, despite *prima facie* empirical evidence to the contrary,

(9′) For some substance *s*, there is more than one natural mutation in the generation of *s*,

is false. By (F), (9′) entails the contradictory of (1*); but Henry is convinced that (1*) is true. On this position, Henry could give an account of the empirical data of generation by claiming that the forms of the parts do not retain numerical identity on becoming parts of a whole.

Henry holds the unitarian thesis just outlined for all non-rational material substances. But he believes that it does not obtain in the case of rational material substances: that is, in the case of human beings.[15] Thus, inanimate objects, plants, and non-human animals all satisfy the unitarian thesis. Henry's acceptance of (1*) allows him room to accept a plurality theory with regard to those substances which are not produced merely in virtue of the causal powers of created agents. Henry has a number of arguments for his position. I give two of them, labelled '(C.1)' and '(C.2)'.

(C.1) Henry's most important argument attempts to show that

(10) For any two agents simultaneously and directly producing some one substance, exactly one of them is God.[16]

The argument presupposes the following principle (which Henry does not spell out):

(G) A created agent produces a substantial form just if it produces that form from a potentiality in matter.

On (G), if two created agents can simultaneously and directly cause some substance, each will have to produce a substantial form from a potentiality in matter. According to Henry, the consequent here entails that

(4) The many forms in a pluriformed composite are produced from many potentialities in matter

is true. But Henry's argument (B.1) demonstrates that (4) is false. Hence,

---

[15] On Henry's plurality theory, and developments thereof, see Zavalloni, *Richard de Mediavilla*, 491–2.

[16] In (10), I use 'simultaneously and directly' to exclude (i) the two causes acting *sequentially*; (ii) the two causes being ordered as primary and secondary causes, such as obtains, according to the schoolmen, in the case of divine and creaturely co-causality in the natural production of any effect.

> (11) It is not possible that two created agents simultaneously and directly produce one substance,

which is equivalent to (10). Since, according to Christian orthodoxy, it is necessarily the case that a human soul cannot be produced in virtue of the causal powers of any created agent, and is contingently the case that every other embodied form is produced in virtue of the causal powers of some created agent, we can conclude

> (2*) Only a human being has two numerically distinct substantial forms.[17]

(It is not clear to me why Henry thinks that (G) entails (4). It seems to me that it clearly entails that just one of (3) and (4) be true, without giving any reason for preferring one over the other. The truth of either (3) or (4) (though not both) is *presupposed* by the plurality theory.)

(C.2) The axiom for Henry's second argument is:

> (H) Generic diversity between any two agents *a* and *b*, together with generic diversity between the two mutations *m* and *n*, where *m* is caused by *a* and *n* is caused by *b*, are jointly sufficient for the numerical distinction of the two forms *p* and *q*, where *p* is the end term of *m*, and *q* the end term of *n*.[18]

He reasons that, according to Christian orthodoxy, God is directly responsible for creating the human soul. Because of this, human beings are quite unlike any other material object. But a human body is produced in virtue of the causal powers of created agents. Furthermore, God's activity in creating the human soul is generically diverse from the relevant activity of the created agents generating the human body, since the action of the created agents, unlike God's action, requires matter. Hence, from (H),

> (2) A human being has two numerically distinct substantial forms.

(2), of course, amounts to the claim that the plurality theory is true of human beings.[19]

Henry's theory is, I would judge, preferable to Aquinas's. On

---

[17] Henry, *Quod.* 4. 13 (Venice edn., i. 172va); Scotus, *Ord.* 4 .11. 3, n. 35 (Wadding edn., viii. 640). [18] Henry derives these loosely from Arist. *Ph.* 5. 4 (228^{a}10–19).
[19] Scotus, *Ord.* 4. 11. 3, n. 35 (Wadding edn., viii. 639–40); the passage in MS A, fo. 215ra, ends as follows: 'Et confirmatur ratio, quia si idem sit per se terminus utriusque agentis, aut idem compositum, aut eadem forma. Si primum detur, ergo homo creatus, quia est per se terminus creationis. Si forma, ergo per se est forma a propagante, quia per se terminus actionis eius. Et utrumque est inconveniens.' See Henry, *Quod.* 4. 13 (Venice edn., i. 167ra).

Aquinas's account of the human soul, the soul is both created directly and the form of the body. This entails that a human body is a very different sort of thing from any non-human animal body: its form is something created directly by God, not something produced naturally, which is an extremely counter-intuitive thesis (although not one which, it seems, troubled Aquinas).[20] Henry's theory also allows him to explain the apparent persistence of a human body through death. But Henry's theory will not allow him to explain the apparent persistence of a non-human animal body through death, and, as we shall see, Scotus finds some other problems with Henry's theory too.

3. AGAINST THOMAS AQUINAS AND HENRY OF GHENT

Adherents of the plurality thesis have a number of standard theological arguments against (1).[21] Scotus gives one of these in the context of a general refutation of the unitarian view, and he gives two more as a general refutation of Aquinas's unitarian thesis. These three arguments (of which I shall give the two simplest) are based on theological premisses. Scotus later gives detailed replies to the arguments of Aquinas and Henry. It is in these that the real philosophical work is done.

I give the theological arguments first. (i) When Christ died, his soul was separated from his body. According to Church doctrine, the body of Christ retained its identity when he died. But if there is no other substantial form in Christ apart from the intellectual soul, then the body will not be able to retain its identity when it dies. It will have to have a new substantial form.[22]

(ii) The second is a rather more complicated version of the first. According to the medieval doctrine of transubstantiation, the bread in the Eucharist is turned into Christ's body, such that only the appearance (*species*) of bread remains. Suppose that some of the bread consecrated at the Last Supper was kept until after Christ's death. When Christ died, his soul was separated from his body. What happened to the body which existed in the species of the bread? It clearly cannot be animate, since the body is one and the same as

---

[20] I discuss this matter briefly in my 'Aquinas and the Mind–Body Problem', in John Haldane (ed.), *Thomistic Papers* (forthcoming).

[21] For some of these arguments, and some of the people using them, see Zavalloni, *Richard de Mediavilla*, 317–19.

[22] Scotus, *Ord.* 4. 11. 3, n. 31 (Wadding edn., viii. 632).

Christ's (now dead) body. So it must be inanimate. Hence, the body
(in the Eucharistic species) must be able to retain identity independent
of its having a soul. But it cannot do this unless it has some substantial
form, independent of the soul.[23]

Scotus provides two non-theological arguments to show that both
(1) and (1*) are false.

(D.1) The first argument is based on the principle of non-
contradiction coupled with a fairly safe empirical observation. Scotus
reasons that

(I) A body remains the same through death

entails

(12) Some substantial form of the body remains the same through death.

His reason is that he accepts the general principle

(J) The persistence of a body is a sufficient condition for the persistence
of some substantial form.[24]

Presumably both Aquinas and Henry accept (J), but would not feel
compelled to accept (I).[25] But (I) seems intuitively plausible, and is
certainly more in accord with the empirical data. While the dead object
in the vase on my desk might not be a rose, and thus might not be the
same rose as the one that was in my garden a few days ago, it looks as
though it will still be the same *body* as the rose-body that was in my
garden a few days ago.[26]

---

[23] Ibid. n. 28 (Wadding edn., viii. 630).   [24] Ibid. n. 54 (Wadding edn., viii. 653).

[25] Adams points out that, 'A unitarian would see the issue as already begged in Scotus's
first premiss: the body *remains*': Marilyn McCord Adams, *William Ockham*, Publications
in Medieval Studies, 26 (2 vols., Notre Dame, Ind.: University of Notre Dame Press,
1987), ii. 648.

[26] (I) constitutes a rejection of proposition 13 'in naturalibus' condemned by
Kilwardby at Oxford in 1277: 'That a body living and dead is equivocally a body, and
that a dead body [considered] as a dead body is a body in a derivative sense [*secundum
quid*]': see *Cartularium Universitatis Parisiensis*, ed. H. Denifle and E. Chatelain (4 vols.,
Paris: Delalain, 1889–97), i. 559. So Scotus's (D.1), if successful, is a defence of the
philosophical good sense of Kilwardby's theologically motivated condemnation. In
fact, I do not know a way to show that, for example, the rose-body in the vase is the
same body as the rose that was in my garden. The dead rose-body, after all, behaves in a
very different way from a living rose. On the other hand, *qua* body the living rose and the
dead one have obvious properties in common, right down to the molecular level. The
differences between the two seem all to be reducible to the presence or absence of *vital*
activity. Scotus's plurality position seems to me to account for both the perceived
similarities and the obvious differences between the dead rose and the living rose.

(D.2) Scotus accepts the following principle:

> (K) It is not possible that specifically the same form is invariably pro-
> duced by specifically different agents.

From the empirical generalization

> (L) The corruption of an animate body, whatsoever the species of the
> agent, invariably results in a corpse,

he infers

> (13) The corruption of an animate body, whatsoever the species of the
> agent, invariably results in specifically the same form,

on the grounds that a corpse of such-and-such a kind has the form of
such-and-such a species. Supposing that it is possible for an animate
body to be corrupted by specifically different agents, (K) and (13) entail

> (14) It is not possible that the corruption of an animate body is the result
> of the production of any form,

and, equivalently,

> (14*) It is not possible that the generation of a corpse is the result of the
> production of any form.

Given that a corpse has a substantial form, and that this form is not
created directly by God, (14*) entails

> (12) Some substantial form of the body remains the same through death.

A corpse is not, of course, identical with the animate substance out of
which it is generated. Therefore, it cannot have all the substantial
forms once had by the animate substance. The generation of a corpse
must consist merely in the loss of one or more substantial forms which
were once had by the animate substance. Hence, (12) entails

> (15) An animate substance has at least two substantial forms.

In fact, the corpse has the same shape and form as the body, but none
of the body's living functions. So the bodily form must survive, and the
form which is lost must be the animating soul.[27]

---

[27] Scotus, *Ord.* 4. 11. 3, n. 38 (Wadding edn., viii. 641). In MS A, fo. 215[ra], (K) is
formulated as 'Non potest irregulariter esse idem effectus a quibuscumque et quantumcumque diversis agentibus'. '[I]rregulariter' is probably a mistake, unless it is intended to
imply that the production of the various different effects does not conform to any
obvious law (*regula*).

A unitarian could, of course, either deny (implausibly) that the bodies are of the same type, or deny (rather more plausibly) that (K) is true. But it would be intuitively odd to claim that, to use some of Scotus's examples, a knife, or even water, could produce the form of an ox corpse.[28] I think we must accept that Scotus's arguments against the pluralist position rely on our *intuitions* about things. How we assess his arguments will depend on how willing we are to abandon our plausible intuitions in favour of *prima facie* less plausible, non-intuitive accounts. And how willing we might be to do this will depend on our view of the strengths of the *other* unitarian arguments given above. By attempting to show that these other arguments are not effective, Scotus reduces—or eliminates—the need for us to abandon some of our intuitions about the identity of a corpse.

Scotus provides replies to the arguments marshalled in favour of their positions by Aquinas and Henry.

(A.1′) Scotus accepts

(A) A substance has only one substantial existence.

But he does not accept the inference to (1). He reasons that the one substantial existence of a whole composite can be composed of many partial existences, such that each partial existence could correspond to some substantial form. On this account, the unity of the one substantial existence would be contingent upon the capacity of the various forms to constitute some whole. So each partial existence would correspond to some partial form. The substantial existence referred to in (A) would refer to the existence which would correspond to the whole composite quiddity or essence.[29]

Scotus's account of existence here, and the sense he gives to (A), trades on an account of existence which is vastly different from that of Aquinas. As Scotus understands him, Aquinas argues for a distinction between existence and essence, such that it is possible for existence to be simple even if essence is complex.[30] But Scotus reasons that the

[28] Scotus, *Ord.* 4. 11. 3, n. 38 (Wadding edn., viii. 641).
[29] On the unity of a whole quiddity composed of matter as such and form as such, see Ch. 5.
[30] I examine Aquinas's account of the simplicity of existence in another context: see my 'Aquinas on Nature, Hypostasis, and the Metaphysics of the Incarnation', *Thomist*, 60 (1996), 171–202, pp. 186–98.The idea is that all the various concrete essential parts of a substance somehow share in the one existence of the substance.

complexity of existence corresponds exactly to the complexity of essence:

I do not know that fiction according to which existence is something that supervenes on an essence, [and which is] non-composite even if the essence is composite. In this way, the existence of the whole composite includes the existence of all the parts, and it includes the many partial existences of the many parts or forms [of the whole composite], just as the whole being [made up] of many forms includes those partial actualities.[31]

Scotus follows this with an account of in what way the partial forms and partial existences can be united to make just one being. I will discuss this in Chapter 5.

(A.2') Scotus answers Aquinas's second point by proposing a slightly different distinction between existence *simpliciter* and existence *secundum quid*. On Scotus's distinction, existence *simpliciter* is necessarily naturally prior to existence *secundum quid*, and the two existences are thus correctly distinguished in terms of relations of natural priority/posteriority. But Scotus has no explanation for the fact that some forms are of the kind which give existence *simpliciter*, and other forms are of the kind which give existence *secundum quid*: 'Whatever kind of form something is, it naturally gives the same kind of act.'[32] On this fairly agnostic account, any distinction which can be drawn between different kinds of existence thus depends entirely on independent reasons which we might have for distinguishing different types of form. The reply to Henry's version of (A.2) makes it quite clear that we can find no *explanatory* reason for the fact that some forms are essential, whilst others are accidental, other than that the respective forms are the kind of forms that they are.[33] Scotus goes on to give some

---

[31] Scotus, *Ord.* 4. 11. 3, n. 46 (Wadding edn., viii. 649). For Scotus on the identity of essence and existence, see Allan B. Wolter, 'Is Existence for Scotus a Perfection, Predicate, or What?', in his *The Philosophical Theology of John Duns Scotus*, ed. Marilyn McCord Adams (Ithaca, NY, and London: Cornell University Press, 1990), 278–84; also, usefully, A. J. O'Brien, 'Duns Scotus' Teaching on the Distinction between Essence and Existence', *New Scholasticism*, 38 (1964), 61–77; W. Hoeres, 'Wesen und Dasein bei Heinrich von Gent und Duns Scotus', *Franziskanische Studien*, 47 (1965), 121–86; W. O'Meara, 'Actual Existence and the Individual According to Duns Scotus', *Monist*, 49 (1965), 659–69; Ludger Honnefelder, *Ens Inquantum Ens: Der Begriff der Seienden als Solchen als Gegenstand der Metaphysik nach der Lehre des Johannes Duns Scotus*, Beiträge zur Geschichte der Philosophie und Theologie des Mittelalters, N. F., 16 (Münster: Aschendorff, 1979), 218–67.

[32] Scotus, *Ord.* 4. 11. 3, n. 50 (Wadding edn., viii. 651); see also n. 43 (Wadding edn., viii. 647–8).   [33] Ibid. n. 44 (Wadding edn., viii. 648).

descriptions of the way in which substantial and accidental forms differ.[34] I give an account of these in Chapter 6.

Crucial to Scotus's attack on Henry's position is his attempt to refute (B.1).

(B.1′) Henry argues that neither

> (3) The many forms in a pluriformed composite are produced from one potentiality in matter

nor

> (4) The many forms in a pluriformed composite are produced from many potentialities in matter

is true. Scotus addresses each of arguments (i)–(iv), variously against (3) and (4), in turn.

(i) Although, presumably, Scotus agrees with Henry that (3) entails

> (5) Two forms of the same species actualize one potentiality in matter,

he does not see this as problematic, since he does not regard (5) as false. He does hold that the related principle

> (5*) Two forms of the same order within a species actualize one potentiality in matter

is false. For example, two human bodily forms cannot actualize just one potentiality in matter. But (3) does not entail (5*). We cannot conclude on this basis, therefore that (3) is false.[35]

(ii) Scotus takes issue with the Aristotelian claim

> (C) Distinction of acts is a necessary and sufficient condition for the distinction of potentialities.

Scotus's basic response is that it all depends on what sort of distinction is being made. He reasons that (C) obtains if and only if it is construed as follows:

> (C*) Specific distinction of acts is a necessary and sufficient condition for the numerical distinction of potentialities.

But (C*) presents the adherent to (3) with no difficulties.[36]

(iii) Scotus offers two possible responses to Henry's first attempt to show that (4) is false. The first is that the principle

---

[34] Ibid.   [35] Ibid. n. 41 (Wadding edn., viii. 646).   [36] Ibid.

(D) It is not possible that potentialities are ordered to each other

is just false. The second is that, even if (D) is true, it does not entail

(7) It is not possible that the forms in a pluriformed composite are ordered to each other,

since it is perhaps not the case that the ordering of forms presupposes that their potentialities are ordered to each other: there may be other ways in which the ordering of forms can be explained.[37]

(iv) Scotus argues that there is no reason to accept

(E) Anything which includes a number of different potentialities has merely accidental unity.

He gives an example. Air and water can both be generated from fire, such that fire has two different potentialities: one for becoming air and one for becoming fire. But by (E), it would follow that fire exhibits merely accidental unity: a conclusion which all the scholastics would regard as false.[38] The net result of these four arguments is that Scotus does not decide between (3) and (4). It seems to me, however, that Scotus *should* accept (3). I will give my evidence for this claim in the next section. (I have not been able to find any unequivocal evidence that Scotus *does* accept (3).)

Scotus, as we shall see, accepts Henry's claims (9) and (F), which form his argument (**B.2**), as long as (9) and (F) are correctly understood. So Scotus has no problems with (**B.2**). I discuss his position below.

(**C.1′**) Henry's argument (**C.1**) attempts to show that

(11) It is not possible that two created agents simultaneously and directly produce one substance

is true. (11) is of course inconsistent with Scotus's conclusion

(15) An animate substance has at least two substantial forms,

since (15) is true of *any* living body, including those produced merely in virtue of the causal powers of created agents. Scotus attempts to refute Henry's argument by claiming that it entails the contradictory conclusions

(16) Actualizing exactly one potentiality in matter is a necessary condition for substantial unity,

[37] Ibid.   [38] Ibid.

and

> (16′) It is not the case that actualizing exactly one potentiality in matter is a necessary condition for substantial unity.³⁹

The argument is of extreme complexity, and since as far as I can see it is unsuccessful, I will not discuss it here. But Scotus's failure here to argue successfully against (C.1) need not concern him, since (C.1) relies on the claim that both (3) and (4), one of which is entailed by the plurality theory, are false. And Scotus's argument (B.1′) shows that there is no reason to suppose that either of these two claims is false.

Finally, Scotus agrees with Henry's argument (C.2), which amounts to a defence of

> (2) A human being has two numerically distinct substantial forms,

a thesis which Scotus holds to be true.

Scotus's arguments (D.1) and (D.2) provide sufficient warrant for accepting the plurality thesis for all animate objects. I suspect that there are good reasons for accepting it for most inanimate objects as well, reasons which will become clear in section 5 of this chapter. Scotus's arguments against those of Aquinas and Henry seem to me to be fair enough. Since we have good grounds for accepting the plurality thesis, we have *eo ipso* good grounds for denying theses which entail the unitarian theory: in this case, Aquinas's account of existence and Henry's claim that neither (3) nor (4) is true.

4. SCOTUS'S THEORY

Scotus is happy to accept (C.2). He also accepts Henry's thesis

> (G) A created agent produces a substantial form just if it produces that form from a potentiality in matter.⁴⁰

³⁹ For the argument, see ibid. n. 40 (Wadding edn., viii. 645).
⁴⁰ On Scotus's account of the plurality of forms, see D. E. Sharp, *Franciscan Philosophy at Oxford in the Thirteenth Century*, British Society of Franciscan Studies, 16 (Oxford: Oxford University Press; London: Humphrey Milford, 1930), 311–15; Prospero Stella, *L'Ilemorfismo di G. Duns Scoto*, Pubblicazione del Pontificio Ateneo Salesiano. II. Testi e studi sul pensiero medioevale, 2 (Turin: Società Editrice Internazionale, 1955), 187–230; Zavalloni, *Richard de Mediavilla*, 376–81; Bernardus Baudoux, 'De forma corporeitatis Scotistica', *Antonianum*, 13 (1935), 429–74, pp. 431–45; Abelardo Lobato, 'El cuerpo human en Duns Escoto y Tomás de Aquino', in Leonardo Sileo (ed.), *Via Scoti: Methodologica ad*

But, as we have seen, he rejects

> (10) For any two agents simultaneously and directly producing some one substance, exactly one of them is God,

and its equivalent

> (11) It is not possible that two created agents simultaneously and directly produce one substance,

as well as a thesis entailed by (10) and (11), namely:

> (2*) Only a human being has two numerically distinct substantial forms.

He argues instead that there is a good reason to suppose that *all* animate substances, not just human beings, have (at least) two substantial forms:

> (15) An animate substance has at least two substantial forms.

As noted above, Scotus consistently distinguishes between (i) the bodily form and (ii) the animating soul. The bodily form is responsible for the form and layout of the body and its parts;[41] the animating soul is responsible for the functions of the body.

I noted above that Scotus is happy to accept Henry's (B.2), along with its claims

> (9) There is one natural mutation in the generation of one substance,

and

> (F) Numerical distinction of naturally produced forms is a necessary and sufficient condition for the numerical distinction of natural mutations.

Scotus also accepts that (9) entails

> (1*) A substance has only one naturally produced substantial form.

But he offers an understanding of (1*) and (9) in this context which

mentem Joannis Duns Scoti. Atti del Congresso Scotistico Internazionale. Roma 9–11 Marzo 1993 (2 vols., Rome: Antonianum, 1995), ii. 951–66. See also, though with caution, Etienne Gilson, *Jean Duns Scot: Introduction à ses positions fondamentales*, Études de philosophie médiévale, 42 (Paris: Vrin, 1952), 490–7, and Simona Massobrio, 'Aristotelian Matter as Understood by St Thomas Aquinas and John Duns Scotus' (unpublished doctoral dissertation, McGill University, 1991), 314–56.

[41] Though see below for a slight modification of this claim.

allows it to be consistent with his also accepting the apparent contradictories of (1*) and (9):

(1*′) For some substance s, s has more than one naturally produced
substantial form,

and

(9′) For some substance s, there is more than one natural mutation in
the generation of s,

both of which seem to correspond to the empirical data of the process
of generation. As we shall see in the next chapter, Scotus argues that
there is a sense in which the quiddity of a material substance is
composed of matter together with one or more substantial forms.
Scotus argues that a whole quiddity, thus conceived, can be labelled
a 'form', and that we can read

(1*) A substance has only one naturally produced substantial form

as

(17) A naturally produced substance has only one whole quiddity.

Scotus holds that (17) is true. There is therefore a sense in which (1*) is
true. Since, as we shall see, Scotus argues that it is possible for a
quiddity to be generated just out of pre-existent parts, he argues
that (9) is true just if it is understood to refer to the mutation which
is responsible for generating the whole quiddity, irrespective of any
other prior mutations in virtue of which the pre-existent parts of the
quiddity are generated.

(18) There is one natural mutation in the generation of one naturally
produced whole quiddity.

Of course, when Scotus accepts (1*′) and (9′), he understands 'form' to
refer to the forms which are *constituent parts* of the whole. Scotus
discusses (18) and (9′) as follows:

It can be granted . . . that there is one mutation by which one natural being is
produced, if we are speaking of the last mutation. And then I concede that the
conclusion—that there is only one form [in a composite]—is true [of the
form] that in itself terminates that mutation. There are, however, many partial
mutations terminated on the preceding partial forms, whether by an order of
duration (if it is posited that one form is induced temporally prior to another),

or by an order of nature (if we posit that all those forms are induced temporally simultaneously).[42]

This passage also makes clear that the lower forms do not have to be
temporally prior to the highest form. Furthermore, the lower forms
will be *naturally* prior to the highest form only if, without the highest
form, they would constitute a being that was essentially *incomplete.*

Scotus argues that there must be one mutation corresponding to
each of the forms in a pluriformed composite. In any animate composite there are at least two forms: the bodily form and the soul. In the
case of a human being, the bodily form is the proper end term of the
act of generation, and the intellectual soul is the proper end term of an
act of divine creation. In the case of non-rational animate things, there
are likewise two different mutations involved, on the grounds that,
between the two forms (whose existence Scotus has demonstrated on
other grounds), there is an order of perfection:

It can be posited, with respect to any animate thing, that it has two agents, or
quasi two. Although any living form is simply more excellent than any mixed
form (and thus, whatever produces a living form must be more perfect than
itself (or than some other [agent]) precisely as it produces the mixed form),
and, although the mixed form in a plant or brute [animal] is generated by the
same [agent] as that by which the soul is produced, nevertheless there the
[agent] is like two agents, since [it is an] agent containing in itself the *ratio* of a
more perfect [agent] and of a less perfect agent.[43]

We should bear in mind that even in a pluriformed composite such as
a human being, in which one of the forms fails altogether to be
produced by a natural agent, criteria related to (17) and (18) will apply.
A composite such as a human being has only one whole quiddity, as we

[42] Scotus, *Ord.* 4. 11. 3, n. 41 (Wadding edn., viii. 645). Immediately after the passage
quoted, Scotus refers to his own questions on Aristotle's *Metaphysics*, where he argues
that there is no mutation to the quiddity of the whole, thus offering a different view from
the one he holds in the quoted passage. In the *Metaphysics* questions, Scotus reasons that
the generation of a form or quiddity can be labelled a mutation only if there is some
temporal succession involved in the generation of the form or quiddity (*In Metaph.* 9. 9,
n. 2 (Wadding edn., vi. 780ᵇ)). The generation of a whole quiddity will not satisfy this
condition, since Scotus's position on the question of substantial unity (which I describe
in the next chapter) entails that there is no temporal sequence between the generation of
all the *parts* of a composite quiddity and the generation of the *whole* composite quiddity
itself. But the difference between the *Metaphysics* account and the *Ordinatio* account is
merely verbal—a quibble about the correct usage of the word translated 'mutation'—
with, as far as I can see, no corollaries in the realm of metaphysics.
[43] Scotus, *Ord.* 4. 11. 3, n. 45 (Wadding edn., viii. 648).

shall see in the next chapter, and this quiddity will be produced in virtue of just one mutation: perhaps as a concomitant result of the divine action of creating the human soul.

One of the advantages of the unitarian positions is that they allow for a fairly straightforward account of the *unity* of a material composite. Scotus's position will not, prima facie, provide such an clear account. But this does not mean that Scotus's position is inconsistent with the claim that a material substance exhibits some kind of unity. When replying to Aquinas's (A.2), Scotus notes that there is no a priori way of distinguishing a substantial form from an accidental one. But important for Scotus's account, as we shall see in Chapter 6, is that there is such a distinction, and that it results in a distinction between different kinds of unity: add a substantial form to some item, and you get a substantial unity; add an accidental form to some item, and you get an accidental unity. Both of these unities—which I discuss in more detail in the next two chapters—are spelled out by Scotus in terms of potentiality and actuality. Thus, a necessary condition for either type of unity is that one of the parts is in some sense potential, and the other in some sense actual. The sense of 'potentiality' operative here is subjective potentiality, and the sense of 'actuality' is that actuality which is the correlative of subjective potentiality.[44] I shall label these respectively 'S-potentiality' and 'S-actuality'.

As Scotus understands this, any material composite can be split up into two parts: the part which instantiates S-potentiality and the part which instantiates S-actuality. Thus, in the case of a composite of matter and (one) substantial form, matter instantiates S-potentiality, and form S-actuality. In the case of a composite with two substantial forms, matter and the lower substantial form constitute a composite. This lower-order composite instantiates S-potentiality for the higher substantial form. The higher substantial form instantiates S-actuality. This latter S-potentiality and S-actuality are such that the lower-order composite and the higher substantial form can constitute some higher-order composite. We thus have a pattern of hierarchically arranged composites, each satisfying a unity requirement, since each can be analysed into two parts, one instantiating S-potentiality and the other S-actuality.[45] Thus, the higher form actualizes the S-potentiality of the lower-order composite. But Scotus does not make clear what relation

---

[44] On these, see above, Ch. 2.
[45] Scotus, *Ord.* 4. 11. 3, nn. 46, 53, and 56 (Wadding edn., viii. 649, 652–3, and 654).

holds between the S-potentiality of the lower-order composite and the S-potentialities of the matter and lower form. It is clearly some S-potentiality which is really distinct from these two S-potentialities. But it is not clear whether or not Scotus would argue that these lower S-potentialities are somehow parts *constituting* the S-potentiality of the lower-order composite.[46]

Scotus labels any item exhibiting S-potentiality for a substantial form a 'material cause'. Thus, both prime matter and lower-order composites are material causes. Prime matter is the material cause of the lowest-order composite; the lowest-order composite is the material cause of the next-highest-order composite; and so on. According to Scotus, relations of material causality are essentially ordered:[47] that is, such that they are (among other things) *transitive* relations.[48] Furthermore, Scotus labels every item exhibiting S-actuality a 'formal cause'. The essential ordering of material causes will entail the essential ordering of relations of formal causality. And Scotus in at least one place makes it clear that the many formal causes in one pluriformed composite are essentially ordered.[49] This fact, I believe, enables us to choose between the relative desirability for Scotus's theory of

(3) The many forms in a pluriformed composite are produced from one potentiality in matter

and

(4) The many forms in a pluriformed composite are produced from many potentialities in matter.

Of these two, (3) looks to me preferable. My reason lies in the nature of an essentially ordered series of causes. Crucially, as just noted, such causal relations are transitive, such that in a pluriformed composite, prime matter is the material cause not only of the lowest-order composite, but also of *all* the higher-order composites in the whole.

---

[46] See ibid. n. 46 (Wadding edn., viii. 649).

[47] See Scotus, *Lect.* 2. 12. un., n. 21 (Vatican edn., xix. 76–7).

[48] See Scotus, *De Primo Princ.* 3. 11 (p. 46/7); *Ord.* 1. 2. 1. 1–2, nn. 48–51 (Vatican edn., ii. 154–5).

[49] Scotus, *Ord.* 2. 37. 2, n. 7 (Wadding edn., vi. 993). For an edited version of the relevant passage based on MS A and two other manuscripts, see Allan B. Wolter, 'Scotus' Paris Lectures on God's Knowledge of Future Events', in *Philosophical Theology of John Duns Scotus*, 285–333, p. 323 n. 95. For information on the manuscripts used by Wolter, see ibid. p. 316 n. 82. See also *Quod.* 7, nn. 21–2 (Wadding edn., xii. 180; Alluntis and Wolter, 176–7 nn. 7. 59–6).

Equally, higher substantial forms will be the formal causes of every lower-order composite. Now, to be the formal cause of a lower-order composite entails actualizing the S-potentiality of the lower-order composite. But granted the transitivity of relations of formal causality, it also entails actualizing the S-potentiality both of every lower-order composite and of prime matter. But it does not entail actualizing any S-potentiality in, say, prime matter which has not already been actualized by the lowest-order form. A higher-order form actualizes matter's S-potentiality *merely* in virtue of actualizing the S-potentiality of the lowest-order composite. We can put the issue more simply by labelling the S-potentiality of the prime matter in a pluriformed composite 'SPM', and the S-potentiality of the lowest-order composite 'SPC'. The lowest-order substantial form actualizes SPM. The next-highest substantial form—call it f—actualizes SPC. But since the relation of actualizing S-potentiality is transitive, f also actualizes SPM.[50] Now, if (4) were true, f would actualize, in addition to SPM, some further S-potentiality in prime matter—call it SPM_1. But this looks wasteful, since it is difficult to think of any metaphysical purpose which could be served in positing the actualization of SPM_1. For example, it would not help to guarantee the unity of a pluriformed composite.

I discuss in Chapter 5 the details of Scotus's account of substantial unity. But the basic unity stipulation at work can be summarized thus:

> (M) A necessary condition for substantial unity between any two parts x
>   and y is that x instantiates S-potentiality for y and that y instantiates
>   S-actuality, consisting in actualizing x's S-potentiality for y.

Scotus accepts that an animate thing has two forms: a bodily form and a soul. But he regards it as 'probable' that there are some other forms as well: 'The more perfect an animate [body] is, the more it requires many organs; and it is probable that [these organs are] specifically different through substantial forms.'[51] Thus:

---

[50] In the text referred to in n. 49, Scotus apparently argues that higher forms do not inform prime matter. But the context makes it clear that Scotus is concerned to show merely that higher causes do not *immediately* inform prime matter. He is not concerned to deny the transitivity of relations of essentially ordered causality. Rather, his argument—that the divine will is a mediate partial cause of human activity—relies on the transitivity of relations of essentially ordered causality. Scotus does not in fact accept that the divine will is a mediate partial cause of human activity: but he does not reject the transitivity of relations of essentially ordered causality. On the whole issue, see Wolter, 'Scotus' Paris Lectures', 323–33; also William A. Frank, 'Duns Scotus on Autonomous Freedom and Divine Co-Causality', *Medieval Philosophy and Theology*, 2 (1992), 142–64, and the literature cited there.   [51] Scotus, *Ord.* 4. 11. 3, n. 46 (Wadding edn., viii. 649).

(N) The organs of an animate body have different substantial forms.

In the *Metaphysics* questions, Scotus makes his reason for (N) plain: 'Why should one form give this perfection to this part of matter, and not that [perfection] which, however, [the form] equally contains?'[52] If (N) were false, we would be faced with the anomalous situation of just one form—which is presumably the same 'all over'—giving heart-shape to this lump of matter, liver-shape to that lump of matter, and so on. Granted (N), Scotus holds that the different substantial forms of the body's organs are ordered to the bodily form. They are all actual with regard to matter, and subjectively potential with regard to the bodily form.[53] But there is a problem here. It is difficult to see how the forms of the different organs are ordered to each other in terms of potentiality and act: they are the forms of *different* parts of the composite. So Scotus, if he accepts that the different organs of an animate body have different substantial forms will have to accept a condition weaker than (M):

(M*) A sufficient condition for substantial unity between any two parts x and y is that both x and y instantiate S-potentiality for some substantial form f, and x and y instantiate S-actuality, consisting in actualizing the S-potentiality of some matter m for both x and y.

In the *Metaphysics* questions, Scotus reasons that the forms of the different organs are (in some sense) really distinct parts of the bodily form.[54] Presumably, they could be parts which instantiate S-potentiality for the whole of which they are parts. Whatever we make of this claim, (M*) seems to mean, as Scotus suggests, that more complex organisms might be less of a unity than less complex ones.[55]

Now, granted this account of the unity of an organic body, the S-actuality of each organic form will actualize a different S-potentiality in prime matter. Thus, in the case of organic forms, Scotus will have to hold

(4*) The many organic forms in a pluriformed composite are produced from many potentialities in matter.

He will thus have to abandon any straightforward commitment to (3), and hold instead

[52] Scotus, *In Metaph.* 7. 20, n. 4 (Wadding edn., iv. 732[b]).
[53] Scotus, *Ord.* 4. 11. 3, n. 41 (Wadding edn., viii. 645).
[54] See Scotus, *In Metaph.* 7. 20, nn. 4–5 (Wadding edn., iv. 732[a]–3[b]).
[55] Scotus, *Ord.* 4. 11. 3, n. 46 (Wadding edn., viii. 649); note that MS A, fo. 215[vb], omits Wadding's 'cum minori compositione'.

(3*) The many hierarchically arranged forms in a pluriformed composite
are produced from one potentiality in matter.

This is not inconsistent with my discussion of the desirability of (3) over
(4) in the case of hierarchically ordered forms. Indeed, accepting (3*) is
equivalent to conceding the desirability of (3) in the case of such forms.

Granted (N), the bodily form itself will just be something like the
form of the flesh and bones, or whatever the basic constituent stuff of a
body is held to be. This claim is confirmed by Scotus's view that the
presence of the organs is *not* necessary for the inherence of the bodily
form.[56] The *arrangement* of the organs could perhaps be attributed to
the bodily form; but Scotus sometimes claims that the arrangement of
the organs in a composite is the result of *quantity*, and not of the
bodily form at all. For example, Scotus sometimes argues that it is in
virtue of the extension of a body that a body's head is distant from its
feet. He claims further that the presence of such extension is perhaps
(*forte*) a necessary condition for a body's being animate.[57]

The highest form which we find in an animate composite is the soul.
Unlike some of his contemporaries,[58] Scotus does not hold it necessary to
posit in a human being separate sensory and vegetative souls, in addition
to the intellectual soul.[59] By the same token, he does not hold that animals
have a vegetative soul in addition to their sensory soul. The soul, then,
exhibits some kind of composition, in virtue of which it can perform a
number of different functions.[60] As Scotus makes clear, the intellectual,
sensory, and vegetative elements of the soul are best described as formally
distinct parts of the soul: something like essential *properties* of the soul.[61]

---

[56] Scotus, *Ord.* 4. 11. 3, n. 56 (Wadding edn., viii. 654).

[57] Ibid., 4. 10. 1, n. 13 (Wadding edn., viii. 504).

[58] For some of these, see Zavalloni, *Richard de Mediavilla*, 319–42, 347–67.

[59] Scotus does not give explicit reasons for this, though presumably the principle of
parsimony could again be invoked. For some hints, see *Ord.* 4. 11. 3, n. 37 (Wadding edn.,
viii. 640–1).

[60] On this, see Allan B. Wolter, 'The Formal Distinction', in John K. Ryan and
Bernardine M. Bonansea (eds.), *John Duns Scotus, 1265–1965*, Studies in Philosophy
and the History of Philosophy, 3 (Washington: Catholic University of America Press,
1965), 45–60, pp. 46–7, repr. in Wolter, *Philosophical Theology of John Duns Scotus*, 27–41,
pp. 28–9; see also Zavalloni, *Richard de Mediavilla*, 379–80.

[61] Scotus, *Ord.* 2. 1. 6, n. 321 (Vatican edn., vii. 156); see also Sharp, *Franciscan
Philosophy at Oxford*, 313–14. One of the propositions condemned by Kilwardby in 1277
states 'That the vegetative, sensory, and intellectual [souls] are one simple form' (proposition 12 'in naturalibus': see *Cartularium Universitatis Parisiensis*, i. 559). The point,
presumably, is that we need to posit distinct souls here. Scotus, of course, refuses to make
this move. Perhaps he would claim that the intellectual soul in humans fails to satisfy the
simplicity criterion stipulated in 1277.

The soul, then, is composite in the sense that it has (in animals) two or (in humans) three different essential and inseparable properties.

In a pluriformed composite, Scotus thus holds that we will find, in addition to matter, a bodily form, an animating soul, and the forms of the various organs. Matter, bodily form and animating soul are arranged hierarchically, such that bodily form, and animating soul actualize just one potentiality in matter. The forms of the different organs actualize different potentialities in matter, and they occupy the lowliest place in the hierarchy of substantial forms.

5. FORM AND THE ELEMENTS

In standard medieval chemistry, there are four (sublunar) elements: earth, fire, air, and water. These elements are, in some sense or another, constituents of all other material substances. Thus, Scotus, following normal medieval usage, often refers to the form of a mixed body, by which he means the form of a body which has two or more of the four elements as constituents. I shall refer to such a substance as a 'compound substance', or sometimes just as a 'compound'. The question I want to look at here is the following: Is it the case that the forms of the elements really exist in a compound substance?[62] A positive answer will entail that a compound substance has, in addition to some or all of the forms just outlined, the forms of the elements as well. Scotus gives a negative reply. He takes his position against the theories of Avicenna and Averroës. According to Avicenna, both the substances and the qualities of the elements really exist in a compound; but whereas the substances exist properly, the qualities have some kind of reduced existence—they are 'remitted' or fragmented.[63]

---

[62] As Norma Emerton notes, theories of mixture 'were really form theories': see her *The Scientific Reinterpretation of Form* (Ithaca, NY: Cornell University Press, 1984), 80. On the existence of the elements in a mixture, see Anneliese Maier, *An der Grenze von Scholastik und Naturwissenschaft: Die Struktur der materiellen Substanz. Das Problem der Gravitation. Die Mathematik der Formlatituden* (Studien zur Naturphilosophie der Spätscholastik, 3), 2nd edn., Raccolta di Studi e Testi, 41 (Rome: Storia e Letteratura, 1952), 3–140; an English translation of pp. 3–22 can be found in Maier, *On the Threshold of Exact Science: Selected Writings of Anneliese Maier on Late Medieval Natural Philosophy*, ed. Steven D. Sargent, The Middle Ages (Philadelphia: University of Pennsylvania Press, 1982), Ch. 6.

[63] Scotus, *Lect.* 2. 15. un., n. 9 (Vatican edn., xix. 139–40); see Avicenna, *Liber Primus Naturalium*, 1. 10 (ed. S. van Riet, Avicenna Latinus (Louvain: Peeters; Leiden: Brill, 1992), 91); also Averroës, *In Cael.* 3. 67 (*Aristotelis Opera cum Averrois Commentaria* (11 vols., Venice, 1550), v. 105rb).

According to Averroës, both the substances and the qualities exist in a compound: but neither exists properly. Rather, they both have reduced existence—they are both remitted.[64]

Of these two theories, I would judge that Avicenna's is more desirable. Averroës' theory is open to the objection that substantial forms cannot admit of degrees. A substantial form cannot be remitted: it either exists fully or not at all. But there is nevertheless good reason for wanting to posit that the elements remain *in some sense* in a compound substance: more precisely,

> (O) The elemental forms are properties of a compound substance.

The Aristotelian arguments which Scotus proposes for (O) turn on the claim that the presence of the elements is necessary to explain certain features of the compound substance.

(E.1) As Aristotle notes, 'In its motion, a compound follows the motion of the predominant element.'[65] For example, earth has a tendency to fall, and a compound which is mainly earth will tend to fall. But this seems to entail that the presence of the element in the compound is necessary to explain the motion of the compound.[66]

(E.2) According to Aristotle, 'Two bodies cannot touch each other in water or in air, unless humidity (which does not exist without water or air) interposes.'[67] Here the presence of an element in the compound is required to explain how a compound can touch another body.[68]

(E.3) According to Aristotle, an animal is corruptible *ab intra*.[69] But, according to the defender of (O), this can be explained only if the animal contains different elements.[70]

Scotus's replies all try to show that the presence of an element is not required to do the relevant explanatory work. The replies cannot really be labelled a success. Scotus's arguments against (E.1) and (E.2) seem to rely on the following, dubious principle:

> (19) The qualities of a compound substance are specifically different from the qualities of the elements.

Scotus argues for (19) on the grounds that

---

[64] Scotus, *Lect.* 2. 15. un., n. 12 (Vatican edn., xix. 141); see Averroës, *In Cael.* 3. 67 (v. fol. 104vb–5va); *idem, In Gen. Corr.* 1. 90 (v. fol. 167rb).

[65] Arist. *Cael.* 1. 2 (169^{a}1–2).   [66] Scotus, *Lect.* 2. 15. un., n. 3 (Vatican edn., xix. 137).

[67] Arist. *De an.* 2. 11 (423^{a}22–7).

[68] Scotus, *Lect.* 2. 15. un., n. 4 (Vatican edn., xix. 137–8).

[69] Arist. *De iuv.* 5 (469^{b}21–3).

[70] Scotus, *Lect.* 2. 15. un., n. 5 (Vatican edn., xix. 138).

(P) The effects of qualities of a compound substance are specifically different from the effects of the qualities of the elements.

(19) entails that the presence of an element cannot explain any of the features of a compound substance, since there are *no* features which the compound substance has in common with an element. So, according to Scotus, the Aristotelian claims in (E.1) and (E.2) are both false.[71] Both (19) and (P) are, of course, extremely implausible principles. On (P), the downwards motion of a heavy compound is *specifically different* from the downwards motion of a lump of earth; and on (19) the heat of (say) living flesh is *specifically different* from the heat of fire. As Scotus puts it: 'Flesh does not have the quality of fire. Hence, animal heat is not fire heat.'[72] But I can see no reason for wanting to accept either of these claims.

On (E.3), the presence of different elements is necessary for corruptibility *ab intra*. Scotus argues that this principle is false, since if it were true, any compound substance would be corruptible *ab intra*. But some such substances—namely, minerals—do not seem to be corruptible in this way. (Scotus, of course, did not know about the decay of radioactive elements, which would seem to be a counter-instance to his claim here.) Scotus instead holds that the presence of different organs in a body is necessary to explain corruptibility *ab intra*. These different organs, according to Scotus, have different predominant qualities. For example, Scotus argues that the brain is naturally cold, and the heart naturally hot. These different qualities have an inimical effect on the bodily organs: the heart tends to heat the brain beyond its natural capacity, and the head tends to cool the heart beyond its. This opposition is ultimately responsible for the internal corruptibility of a body.[73]

Scotus also offers several arguments against (O). The basic one is that (O) is inconsistent with the requirement that a compound substance be just *one* thing: that is, (O) cannot allow for genuine composition at all. On medieval accounts of the elements, it is true that

(Q) An individual elemental form is an individual form of a complete species,

and that

---

[71] Ibid. nn. 39–40 (Vatican edn., xix. 150).   [72] Ibid. n. 40 (Vatican edn., xix. 150).
[73] Ibid. nn. 41–3 (Vatican edn., xix. 150–2).

(R) It is not possible that an individual form of a complete species perfects any other such individual form

(a principle related to one which we encountered in Chapter 2). These two premises entail

(20) It is not possible that an individual elemental form perfects any other such individual form,

which, granted Scotus's standard account of the necessary conditions for two or more items to *constitute* a substance (see Chapter 5 and (M) above), in turn entails

(21) It is not possible that two elemental forms are real constituents, with matter, of one substance.

(21) entails that (O) is false.[74]

Scotus is well aware of Aristotle's belief that there is a sense in which the elements can be said to remain in a compound. Scotus is happy to use this kind of language so long as the sense of the word translated 'remain' is clarified: and he clarifies it in such a way as to exclude any substantial or qualitative presence of the elements in the compound substance. Scotus's basic account of the sense in which the elements can be said to remain is fairly inadequate. He argues that the elements can be said to be present in a compound substance in much the same way as the extreme instances of a mixed quality—say, a shade of pink—exist in the mixed quality. Presumably, the idea is that there is no sense in which the extremes of the quality really exist in the mixed quality. Scotus's reason for adopting this analogy is that, just as in the case of a mixed quality, a compound substance is a *bit like* two or more of the elements—and, indeed, more like the elements than the elements are like each other.[75] But this is not really an adequate

---

[74] Ibid. n. 24 (Vatican edn., xix. 145). Scotus's argument is slightly more complicated, since he takes it as empirically evident that the elemental forms, when existing at their putatively most intense (viz. as instances of earth, fire, air, and water), cannot enter into composition with each other. He uses this to infer that, even if the elemental forms could be remitted somehow, they still could not enter into composition with each other. In the *textus interpolatus* printed in a footnote in the Vatican edition, Scotus's argument omits the problematic inference that, since the elements at their most intense cannot enter into composition with each other, they cannot do so at their least intense (Vatican edn., xix. 143, ll. 19–21). For Scotus's other arguments against (O), see *Lect.* 2. 15. un., nn. 21–3 (Vatican edn., xix. 143–5).

[75] Scotus, *Lect.* 2. 15. un., n. 27 (Vatican edn., xix. 146); see *idem*, *Rep.* 2. 15. un., n. 6 (Wadding edn., xi. 344ᵃ).

account, since Scotus's standard account of a degree D of a quality ϕ, as we shall see in Chapter 10, entails

> (S) All degrees of ϕ less than D (and no greater degrees) actually exist in D.

But when replying to the Aristotelian arguments (E.1)–(E.3), Scotus gives a more satisfactory account, still drawing on the basic intuition, just outlined, that a compound substance is a bit like two or more of the elements. In this discussion, Scotus replaces (O) with a different principle:

> (T) The elements remain 'virtually' in a compound substance, such that their power (*virtus*) is preserved,

which, granted his acceptance of (19), Scotus must understand to mean that the powers of a composite substance are similar to the powers of two or more of the elements.[76]

Scotus, then, argues that a compound does not contain the forms of its components. His basic argument against (O) seems to me to be well taken, clearly drawing attention to a difficulty entailed by (O). In fact, of course, (O) is true. Molecules of water, for example, really do contain atoms of hydrogen and oxygen, and *a fortiori* the forms of hydrogen and oxygen. But Scotus's acceptance of (M*) would allow him to provide an account of the unity of a compound substance even granted the presence of the elements which compose it. So Scotus need not be too troubled by the difficulty in (O) highlighted in his arguments, and should instead be happy to accept it.

Scotus's position, and the position of the pluralists in general, seems rather more defensible than the unitarian alternative. Particularly, Scotus's position on the plurality of forms in plants and animals, as well as in humans, is, as he points out, far simpler and more consistent than Henry's, and should therefore be preferred. Equally, it explains better than Henry's theory the persistence of plant and non-human animal bodies through death. On the other hand, Scotus's claim that the bodily organs have different substantial forms seems to make the unity of organic substances looser on his account than it would perhaps ideally be, forcing Scotus to accept the weaker (M*) instead of (M). But there seems to be an obvious argument in favour of (M*).

---

[76] Scotus, *Lect.* 2. 15. un., n. 38 (Vatican edn., xix. 149–50).

If a dead body is dismembered, its erstwhile parts appear to retain numerical identity; which seems to imply, by analogy with (D.1), that the parts have separate substantial forms. Scotus seems to be right, then, that a more complex body exhibits a lesser degree of unity than a less complex one. Equally, (M*) would allow Scotus to give a clear account of the unity of a whole which contains different elements.

5

Composite Substance

As we saw in Chapters 2–4, Scotus holds that the essential constituents of a material substance are prime matter and one or more substantial forms. In what sense do prime matter and substantial form, when united, constitute material substance?[1] Scotus does not usually distinguish between two different but importantly related senses that could be given to this question. (i) In what sense do individual prime matter and individual substantial form constitute an individual material substance? (ii) In what sense do prime matter as such and substantial form as such constitute composite essence?[2]

In this chapter, I shall attempt to give Scotus's answers to both these questions. Since my task is primarily exegetical, it will not always be possible to keep these two questions separate, and I sometimes deliberately choose ways of speaking which draw attention to the fact that Scotus is in at least some passages providing an answer to both of the questions.

---

[1] Brief accounts of some of the issues I deal with in this chapter can be found in Tamar M. Rudavsky, 'The Doctrine of Individuation in Duns Scotus', *Franziskanische Studien*, 59 (1977), 320–77, and 62 (1980), 62–83, pp. 349–52; Costantino Marmo, 'Ontology and Semantics in the Logic of Duns Scotus', in Umberto Eco and Costantino Marmo (eds.), *On the Medieval Theory of Signs* (Amsterdam and Philadelphia: John Benjamins, 1989), 143–93, pp. 156–8; John F. Boler, 'The Ontological Commitment of Scotus's Account of Potency in his *Questions on the Metaphaphysics*, Book IX', in Ludger Honnefelder, Rega Wood, and Mechthild Dreyer (eds.), *John Duns Scotus: Metaphysics and Ethics*, Studien und Texte zur Geistesgeschichte des Mittelalters, 53 (Leiden, New York, and Cologne: Brill, 1996), 145–60, pp. 157–60; also Prospero Stella, *L'Ilemorfismo di G. Duns Scoto*, Pubblicazioni del Pontificio Ateneo Salesiano. II. Testi e studi sul pensiero medioevale, 2 (Turin: Società Editrice Internazionale, 1955), 147–63. For a detailed discussion of the issue, see my 'Duns Scotus's Anti-Reductionistic Account of Material Substance', *Vivarium*, 33 (1995), 137–70.

[2] In the texts which I discuss in this chapter, Scotus uses the terms 'quidditas', 'essentia', 'natura (communis)', and 'quod quid est' interchangeably. I translate all of these terms as 'essence'.

1. SUBSTANCE AND UNITY

Scotus's account of the union of matter and form to constitute material substance (having matter and form as parts) is strongly anti-reductionistic: it is not true, on his account, that a substance is identical with its parts, or that a substance is merely the aggregate of its parts. I shall label Scotus's account 'R''. Scotus opposes his account to four different reductionistic accounts, which I am labelling 'R1'–'R4'. We have already seen how Scotus rejects R1 and R2. He also rejects R3: substance is just the aggregate of matter and form; and R4: substance is just the aggregate of matter, form, and the relation between matter and form. On these two theories a substance will have really distinct parts, existing in some relation or other to the whole. But R3 is distinguished from R4 just because R4, unlike R3, allows that the *relation* between the non-relational parts (matter and form) is itself a part of the whole. As we shall see, Scotus holds that both theories amount to the claim that a material substance is the aggregate of its parts. In the terms I outlined in Chapter 1, both theories amount on Scotus's reading to the claim that a substance exhibits—or is—unity$_1$. Scotus, however, holds that a substance counts as a unity$_4$. The issue that I shall be concerned with here, then, is how to distinguish unity$_1$ from unity$_4$.

As Scotus discusses unity$_4$ in relation to composite substance, it is clear that there are in fact two distinctions at stake. The first is how to distinguish between unity$_1$ and unity$_4$, where satisfying the conditions for unity$_4$ both cannot consist merely in adding some further item to the aggregate of matter and form (and relation) and will include satisfying the condition that the whole is some item really distinct both from its parts and from the aggregate of them. The second distinction is that between an accidental collection of items and a substance: that is, between unity$_3$ and unity$_4$. Scotus is clearly committed to both of these distinctions, though it looks to me as if the first has more metaphysical import. Scotus's discussion of the two distinctions is made rather more obscure by the fact that he (mistakenly) holds that the first distinction entails the second.[3] I deal with the first of these distinctions, that between unity$_4$ and unity$_1$, in this chapter. I deal with the second, between unity$_4$ and unity$_3$, in the next chapter. In

---

[3] Scotus, *Ord.* 3. 2. 2, n. 7 (Wadding edn., vii. 76). The first distinction does not in fact entail the second. Someone could be committed to a distinction between a substance and an aggregate without being committed to the claim that a substance has some of its properties essentially and/or non-essentially.

what follows, I shall indicate if an argument is relevant to the second distinction; otherwise, I shall assume that what is under discussion is the first distinction. Scotus attempts to show both that adopting either R3 or R4 will fail to provide the tools for an account of the distinction between unity$_4$ and unity$_1$, and that there are in any case independent reasons for accepting that such a distinction can be made.

It is worth noting a little about the context of the argument. The discussions mostly occur in the context of a consideration of the unity of a human composite. As we saw in the previous chapter, a human composite, according to Scotus, consists of (at least) prime matter, bodily form, and intellective soul. Scotus's professed aim is to show how body and soul constitute one substance. But, as a perusal of the texts referred to in the notes below shows, Scotus holds that exactly the same problem holds for the unity of matter and form.[4] Since the unity of matter and form is the standard case, obtaining in the case of every material substance, I will concentrate on this issue. But it should be borne in mind that the same kinds of argument hold for the non-standard case of the unity of a pluriformed composite. In this case, as Scotus makes clear, the arguments will apply to the unity of the higher-order composite, composed of body (i.e. matter and lower form) and higher form. Presumably, the arguments also hold for the unity of the lower-order composite (viz. matter and lower-order form) within the pluriformed whole; but Scotus does not make this point explicitly. Thus, what is at issue is the way in which an item exhibiting S-potentiality and an item exhibiting S-actuality can unite to form a composite whole.

2. R3: MATERIAL SUBSTANCE AS THE AGGREGATE OF ALL ITS NON-RELATIONAL PARTS

According to Scotus, adherents of R3 make the following sorts of claim: 'Even though the whole is other than the parts, or from each part separately, it is not however other than all the parts at once,'[5] and, 'The whole is [not] a being other than all the parts conjunctively.'[6]

---

[4] Furthermore, perusal of the quoted texts makes it quite clear that Scotus is concerned with *prime* matter. The forms of air and fire are common examples of forms employed by Scotus in his discussions, and the forms of such elements were held to inhere directly in prime matter.

[5] Scotus, *Ord.* 3. 2. 2, n. 6 (Wadding edn., vii. 75).

[6] Ibid. n. 7 (Wadding edn., vii. 76).

Scotus attributes this opinion to Averroës.[7] The parts at issue are non-relational parts: specifically, matter and form. The central R3 claim is thus:

> (A) An individual material substance is merely the aggregate of all its individual absolute parts.

(I follow Scotus in labelling non-relational parts and properties 'absolute' parts and 'absolute' properties, respectively. I discuss the reasons for this designation in the next chapter.) Scotus consistently discusses R3 as though it entails that the conjunction of the non-relational parts does not add any further item to these parts. In fact, R3 could be developed in a number of ways, some of which depend upon what exactly the *relation* between matter and form should be understood to be. And this will itself depend on a general account of what it is to be a relation. Scotus, for example, understands a relation between two items—say, their union or conjunction—to be itself a thing or entity which would count as part of a whole. A relation is what Scotus would label a 'relational' entity: the kind of entity which is necessarily dependent on the existence of the terms of the relation. (I discuss Scotus's account of relations in the next chapter.) Granted that, necessarily, a relation (say, of union or conjunction) is a thing which would count as part of a whole, R3 should be rejected, since it entails the denial of this claim. On this reading, R3 is contradictory, entailing both that matter and form are united in some way, and that (since there is no relation between them) they are not. As we shall see in the next chapter, Scotus makes use of exactly this claim when arguing for the position that a relation is a thing. But R3 could make perfect sense on a different account of relations. R3 could easily be held by someone who believes a relation to be a mode, or an intention, or indeed anything which cannot be meaningfully called a *part* of some whole, or an item contained within some whole. And there were plenty of possible takers amongst the schoolmen for claims such as these.[8]

Scotus, however, does not capitalize on his account of relations to criticize R3. His arguments are all intended to show merely that union must *in some sense* involve more than just the two (non-relational)

---

[7] Averroës claims, with reference to the material parts of a substance, 'Totum enim nihil aliud est quam congregatio partium': *In Ph.* 1. 17 (*Aristotelis Opera cum Averrois Commentaria* (11 vols., Venice, 1550), iv. 7ᵛᵃ).

[8] See Mark G. Henninger, *Relations: Medieval Theories 1250–1325* (Oxford: Clarendon Press, 1989), for a discussion of a number of different medieval theories.

parts, while remaining neutral on just what needs to be added to the two non-relational parts to allow them to constitute a whole. Scotus's basic argument against (A)—and therefore R3—is that it cannot distinguish a substance, a unity$_4$, from an aggregate, a unity$_1$.[9] The adherent of R3 would presumably have no difficulty with this failure of his position, however, since his point is just that substances are in fact no more than aggregates.

Scotus's next three arguments suppose that some of the properties of the whole are necessarily different from the properties of any of the parts. R3 cannot allow for this, since on this understanding a material substance is no more than an aggregate of matter and form, and hence cannot have any non-trivial properties which are not either properties of matter or properties of form.[10] Scotus argues, by an appeal to the resurrection of the body (in which, on medieval accounts, a composite is generated from two individual pre-existent parts: its body and its soul),[11] that

(1) The end term of generation is neither individual matter nor individual form.

Scotus argues, however, that (1) is inconsistent with (A) (since (A) entails the contradictory of (1)), and hence with R3.[12] Secondly, Scotus argues that

(2) It is possible for an individual material substance to be destroyed while both its parts still exist,

where the relevant parts are matter and form. Scotus's reasons for (2)

---

[9] Scotus, *Ord.* 3. 2. 2, n. 7 (Wadding edn., vii. 76). See my 'Duns Scotus's Anti-Reductionistic Account', 145–6.

[10] A trivial property would be, for example, 'is a part of x', or 'is composed of parts', the first of which would be (trivially) false of any whole which is not a part of some further object, and the second of which would be (trivially) false of any whole which does not have parts of its own. We can easily distinguish such properties from properties like 'has a causal influence on x', or 'has the capacity to smile'. These last are the sorts of thing I have in mind by 'non-trivial property' here.

[11] As shown above, Scotus holds that it would be logically possible for a non-subsistent form to be kept in existence separately from any matter; and presumably that it could be united with some existing matter. Scotus could appeal equally well to this claim in order to justify his argument here.

[12] Scotus, *Ord.* 3. 2. 2, n. 7 (Wadding edn., vii. 76). As shown above, Scotus argues that both matter and form can exist independently of each other. Elsewhere (e.g. *Lect.* 1. 17. 2. 4, nn. 231–3 (Vatican edn., xvii. 255–6); *Ord.* 2. 1. 4–5, n. 209 (Vatican edn., vii. 105)) Scotus uses this argument to show that the relation between matter and form must be a thing over and above matter and form. I discuss the argument in the next chapter.

are loosely Aristotelian. Aristotle argued that the two letters 'a' and 'b' of the syllable 'ab' can remain even if the syllable itself no longer exists.[13] And Scotus holds that the same is true for the matter and substantial form of a composite. (2) is inconsistent with (A), which should therefore be rejected.[14]

Both of these arguments would present the adherent of (A) with some difficulties. But Scotus's final argument is even more interesting. He reasons that, on R3,

It would follow . . . that there would be no being in which in itself proper passion, proper operation or any proper accident inhered, since these do not inhere in matter or form or both of these together (except inasmuch as they are one in some whole in itself), though they do inhere in the species [of the whole].[15]

So Scotus accepts

> (B) Proper passion, operation, and accident do not inhere in individual matter alone, or in individual form alone, or in any aggregate of these two parts.

He reasons that (B) is inconsistent with (A), and hence that it entails that (A) should be rejected. All three of Scotus's arguments turn on at least some of the non-trivial properties of the whole being different from any of the properties of the parts. (B), in fact, turns out to be central to Scotus's own position (R'), and I will return to this claim below.

3. R4: MATERIAL SUBSTANCE AS THE AGGREGATE OF ALL ITS NON-RELATIONAL AND RELATIONAL PARTS

R4 is held by William of Ware.[16] William reasons that, if R3 were true, then it would be impossible to give an account of the union of the

---

[13] Arist. *Metaph*. 7. 17 (1041^{b}11–19).

[14] Scotus, *Ord*. 3. 2. 2, n. 7 (Wadding edn., vii. 76).

[15] Ibid. MS A, fo. 144va reads: 'Sequeretur quinto quod nullum ens esset cui per se inesset propria passio et propria operatio, vel quodcumque accidens proprium, quia ista insunt speciei, nec insunt materiae nec formae eius nec utrique simul nisi ut sunt unum in aliquo toto per se.'

[16] When citing William's *Sentence* commentary, I note in square brackets the question numbers given in A. Daniels, 'Zu den Beziehungen zwischen Wilhelm von Ware und Johannes Duns Scotus', *Franziskanische Studien*, 4 (1917), 221–38, pp. 230–8.

parts of a composite substance.[17] He argues that, for matter and form to be united, some further item over and above the two absolute entities is necessarily required.[18] This claim, of course, is inconsistent with (A), which, according to both William and Scotus, is entailed by R3. William reasons, however, that the required further component cannot itself be an absolute entity. He gives two arguments for this, both *reductiones ad absurdum*.

(R4.1) If there is some absolute form (F_1) required to explain the unity of matter and substantial form (F), then F_1 is the highest form in the composite. But accepting

(C) Higher forms are more perfect than lower forms,

an adherent of the existence of F_1 would have to infer

(3) F_1 is more perfect than F.

But, according to William, (3) is false, since the substantial form is the most perfect form in the composite. Hence, there cannot be such a form (F_1) required to explain the unity of matter and substantial form.[19]

(R4.2) William argues for

(4) If it is the case that an absolute form can make a *per se* unity with some other entity only in virtue of some further absolute form, then there is an infinite regress of forms,

on the basis of the general principle

(D) If, for any absolute form F, a further absolute form F_1 is required in order to explain the unity of the absolute form F with any other entity, then *a fortiori* such an absolute form will be required to explain the unity of F_1 with F: and so on, *ad infinitum*.

But William reasonably enough holds

(E) An infinite regress of forms is impossible.

---

[17] For a more detailed account of William's position, and of his rejection of R3, see my 'Duns Scotus's Anti-Reductionistic Account', 148–53.

[18] William, *In Sent.* 3. 2. 2. [qu. 164] (MS F, fo. 165ᵛ): 'Quod partes non dicant actualem unionem nec separationem praecise, patet: quia si dicerent actualem unionem praecise non possent separari actualiter; si dicerent actualem separationem non possent uniri, et ideo ista repugnant de partibus'.

[19] Ibid.: 'Omnis forma ulterior est perfectior, quia forma ulterior continet in unitate alias praecedentes sicut intellectiva continet in se vegetativam et sensitivam. Si igitur esset alia forma compositi ultra intellectivam, esset perfectior quam intellectiva.'

(4) together with (E) entails

> (5) It is impossible that an absolute form makes a *per se* unity with some
>   other entity in virtue of some further absolute form.[20]

In both (R4.1) and (R4.2), William is supposing that the added absolute entity would be some form which somehow perfects or informs
the matter and substantial form, and thereby causes their unity. This
unifying absolute form would still be a part of some whole; the other
parts would be the matter and substantial form which the unifying
absolute form informs.

Since a composite, according to William, is not just identical with its
matter and form (i.e. William rejects R3), and since a composite is not
identical with matter, substantial form and some further unifying
absolute form (from (R4.1) and (R4.2)), William reasons that a whole
material substance must consist of matter and substantial form
together with a *relation* between these two absolute components.
William argues that, when a substance is generated, the only new
entity involved is a new relation between matter and form. Likewise,
he reasons, when a substance is corrupted, the only entity which ceases
to exist is the relation existing between the two absolute parts:

The parts [of a composite] are prior to their being combined: nevertheless, the
whole composite is said to be generated. But the whole differs really from the
parts only in virtue of the relation which results from the union of the parts.
Likewise, corruption results only from the separation of the natural union [of
the parts]—which is a relation. And thus, a relation is the end term of the
corruption.[21]

Since on this account the composite is no entity other than matter,

[20] Ibid.: 'Si totum addat aliquid reale super partes, accipio illam formam compositi
quam tu das et materiam suam. Illa forma et ista materia sunt partes alicuius compositi.
Igitur oportet per te quod forma istius compositi differat realiter ab istis partibus et
iterum accipio illam formam compositi et materiam suam. Cum sint partes (habent
unum compositum), oportet quod illa forma compositi differat ab istis partibus, et sic in
infinitum.'
[21] Ibid.: 3. 5. 5 [qu. 172] (MS F, fo. 172ʳ). 'Prius sunt partes antequam componantur, et
tamen totum dicitur generari et totum non differt realiter a partibus nisi secundum
relationem quae accidit ex unione partium. Et similiter corruptio accidit ex sola separ-
atione naturalis unionis quae est relatio: et ita relatio est terminus corruptionis.' See also
ibid. 3. 2. 2 [qu. 164] (MS F, fo. 165ᵛ): 'Cum dicitur quod mutatio, quod est generatio,
terminatur ad aliquid absolutum, nego, quia non oportet quod terminetur ad aliquid
absolutum sed ad realem relationem'; the same point—that the whole does not differ
from the absolute parts except in virtue of a relation—is made in ibid. 3. 6. 2 [qu. 175]
(MS F, fo. 174ʳ).

85

form, and relation, I take it that William is committed to the following variant of (A):

(A*) An individual material substance is merely the aggregate of all its individual absolute and relational parts.

Crucial to a correct understanding of William's theory is some notion of William's account of relations. As I have shown elsewhere, William holds that a relation is a thing, having an essence over and above the essence of its foundation.[22] (The foundation of a relation is that in virtue of which two related terms are related.) In the case of the (substantial) unity of matter and form, William argues that the foundation of the relation is just the matter and form.[23] William does not think, however, that it is necessary to posit any further form in virtue of which a relation is united to its foundation. If it were, of course, William would *prima facie* be committed to an infinite regress along the lines of that rejected in (R4.2), such that, in a relation R between two items a and b, it would be necessary to posit some further item R_1 to explain the relation between R and (a and b); and so on, *ad infinitum*. William argues instead that the addition of a relational entity to an absolute one does not itself produce a composite whole. Rather, there is just what William labels 'apposition' between the two entities. And, presumably, whatever this apposition is, it is not the kind of state of affairs which requires any further ontological explanation.[24]

Scotus argues against R4 in much the same way as he argues against

---

[22] See my 'Duns Scotus's Anti-Reductionistic Account', 153. William puts the point as follows (*In Sent.* 1. 33. 3 [qu. 99] (MS F, fo. 83ᵛ)): 'In creaturis autem non solum sunt diversae rationes reales ratio fundamenti et ratio relationis, immo ipsa relatio est alia res a re fundamenti'. Items which are distinct *rationes reales*, but not distinct *res* (things), are distinct in a way related to Scotus's formal distinction: see Gedeon Gál, 'Gulielmi de Ware, O.F.M. Doctrina Philosophica per Summa Capitula Proposita', *Franciscan Studies*, 14 (1954), 155–80, 265–92, p. 176.

[23] William, *In Sent.* 3. 2. 2 [qu. 165] (MS F, fo. 165ᵛ): 'Fundamentum autem huius relationis ad quod terminatur generatio est corpus et anima'. William is here referring to body and soul; but his remarks hold, *mutatis mutandis*, of matter and form also.

[24] William, *In Sent.* 1. 33. 3 [qu. 99] (MS F, fo. 83ᵛ): 'Nec tamen ex hoc quod est alia relatio a fundamento est ibi proprie compositio (ut puta non est compositius album simile[m] quam sit album), nisi appellando compositionem materialem, quia ibi sunt plures essentiae quam ante: est enim ibi nunc essentia absoluta et essentia respectiva, et prius fuit ibi solum essentia absoluta. Unde non est ibi proprie compositio sed appositio magis, quia plures essentiae'. (I use square brackets here to indicate a proposed deletion from the text.) Scotus too believes that it is possible to block the proposed infinite regress. He achieves this by claiming that a relational entity is not really distinct from its relation of inherence: see Henninger, *Relations*, 90–1; also my discussion in section 3 of the next chapter.

R3. He reasons that R4, just like R3, cannot distinguish between a substance and an aggregate. According to Scotus, (A*) entails

> (6) Unity$_4$ consists merely in two absolute parts and the relation between them.

But on Scotus's understanding of unity$_1$, the predicate in (6) could be truly applied to unity$_1$. So (A*) will not allow us to distinguish between unity$_4$ and unity$_1$.[25]

Scotus further argues that R4 will not allow that a material substance could have non-trivial properties distinct from those which inhere in its parts (viz. matter, form, and relational entity). So, he reasons, (A*) entails

> (7) The end term of generation is a relational entity,

> (8) The end term of corruption is a relational entity,

and

> (9) Proper passion, action, and absolute accidents inhere in a relational entity,

all of which, according to Scotus, are false. I return to these arguments below.[26]

4. SCOTUS'S ANTI-REDUCTIONISTIC ACCOUNT OF MATERIAL SUBSTANCE

Scotus claims that a whole composite substance is an absolute entity really distinct from all of its parts. He construes this claim carefully to preclude the view that this absolute entity is itself a part of some (further) whole. Thus, Scotus cites with approval William's arguments (R4.1) and (R4.2).[27] He also agrees with William that, if matter and

---

[25] Scotus, *Ord.* 3. 2. 2, n. 8 (Wadding edn., vii. 79). As Scotus words his argument, it looks as though he is giving an account of the distinction between unity$_4$ and unity$_3$ (not unity$_1$). Since, however, it would be possible to give an account of this second distinction without giving an account of the first, I take this to be a mistake—and one which Scotus himself rectifies in a later discussion, clearly identifying R4 with the failure to give an account of the distinction between unity$_4$ and unity$_1$: see ibid. 3. 22. un., n. 18 (Wadding edn., vii. 451). On this, see also Scotus's analogous rejection of R3.

[26] Ibid. 3. 2. 2, n. 8 (Wadding edn., vii. 79). For two additional arguments against R4, see my 'Duns Scotus's Anti-Reductionistic Account', 155–6.

[27] Scotus, *Ord.* 3. 2. 2, n. 8 (Wadding edn., vii. 79).

substantial form are to be actually united, it is necessary that there exist a relation between them.[28] Like William, Scotus holds that a relation itself counts as a *thing*.[29] Given that a relation counts as a thing, Scotus is committed to the claim that the relation of the two absolute parts adds some further entity over and above the absolute parts. But, as we have seen, Scotus holds that (A*), entailed by William's theory R4, is not a sufficient description of a material substance. (A*), according to Scotus, is an accurate description not of unity$_4$, but merely of unity$_1$.

Scotus puts the claim that essence is a composite of form as such and matter as such as follows:

If the form of the whole is understood not [to be] something constituting a whole, but rather [to be] the whole nature itself as quiddity, then it can be rightly conceded that the form of the whole is different from the partial form, and that nature or quiddity can be called 'form'. This is clear from Aristotle, *Metaphysics* 5. 2.[30] . . . With respect to what is [viz. the form of the whole] a form? I reply by saying that [it is a form] with respect to the whole composite—not an informing form [i.e. a further form added to the whole composite], but the form in virtue of which the composite is a quidditative being. And in this way the whole being is formally a form, just as white is said to be white by whiteness—not that the form of the whole is a quasi-cause of itself, causing a quasi-whole with matter and the partial form. Rather, it [viz. the form of the whole] is the whole itself considered just in the way which Avicenna speaks of in *Metaphysics* 5:[31] 'horseness is just horseness'.[32]

In this passage, 'partial form' (*forma partis*) refers to substantial form. The point of the passage is that essence is more than just its really distinct components: essence is *really distinct* from its really distinct components. The components constitute some essence over and above the essence of the components. Assuming (A*) to entail that a whole is just identical with the aggregate of its parts, R' entails that (A*) is false. Since essence, as understood by Scotus, is not some new *part* of some further entity, Scotus's claim that the essence is a new absolute does not fall victim to William's arguments—(R4.1) and (R4.2)—against

[28] Ibid. n. 11 (Wadding edn., vii. 80).

[29] On Scotus's account of relations, see next chapter.

[30] Arist. *Metaph.* 5. 2 (1013^{b}22–3).

[31] Avicenna, *Metaph.* 5. 1 (ed. S. van Riet, Avicenna Latinus (3 vols., Louvain: Peeters; Leiden: Brill, 1977–83), 228).

[32] Scotus, *Ord.* 3. 2. 2, n. 9 (Wadding edn., vii. 80); the version in MS A, fo. 144va, on which I base this translation, differs in insignificant detail from the version in the Wadding edition.

essence as some further absolute part. Of course, essence understood
as a whole, rather than as a part, does not have any parts that are not
either matter as such, form as such, or matter–form relation: but on
Scotus's non-reductionistic account, it is nevertheless still not identical
with its parts, or with the aggregate of them.

The same is true of individual composite substance. Scotus tends to
slip fairly readily between these two different points, and he often uses
the word translated 'composite' ambiguously, not making it clear
whether he is talking about composite essence or an individual composite. But the context makes it quite clear that what he is saying about
the unity of a composite applies to an individual composite as much as
to composite essence. The discussion of R3, R4, and R′ takes place
within a consideration of the union of Christ's human nature to the
Second Person of the Trinity in the hypostatic union. Scotus is quite
clear that Christ's human nature is itself an individual substance,
individuated without reference to its union with the Second Person
of the Trinity.[33] In our text, Scotus makes the following remarks about
this individual substance (viz. Christ's human nature): 'The whole
nature out of parts . . . is a certain third being, different from each of
its parts, and from both together or separately.'[34] It is also worth noting
that a whole substance on R′ will be *really* distinct from its parts. Some
of Scotus's arguments against R3 and R4 make this clear: for example,
'"ab" is really different from "a" and "b".'[35] Equally, the parts of the
whole are really separable from the whole, since, as Scotus supposes, the
absolute parts can continue in existence even if the whole does not
exist. (Separability is a sufficient condition for real distinction.[36]) Thus,
the whole is really distinct from its absolute and relational parts.[37] We
can formulate the basic claim of the theory as follows:

> (A′) An individual material substance is an absolute entity really distinct
> from matter, form, relation, and any aggregate of two or more of
> these parts.

(A′) should be understood to exclude the claim that there could be any

---

[33] See e.g. Scotus, *Ord.* 3. 1. 1, nn. 6, 17 (Wadding edn., vii. 12, 25).
[34] Ibid. 3. 2. 2, n. 11 (Wadding edn., vii. 80).
[35] Ibid. n. 7 (Wadding edn., vii. 76).
[36] On the separability condition for real distinction, see Ch. 1.
[37] A puzzling note placed in the margin by the scribe in MS A seems to suggest
otherwise: 'Nota quod totum non est aliud realiter quam partes vel coniunctim vel
divisim acceptae' (fo. 144va). In light of Scotus's unequivocal claims in the main text, I
assume this to be a mistake.

parts other than matter, form, and relation. (A') should also be under-stood to entail that substance exhibits unity$_4$.[38]

As we have seen, Scotus argues that matter and form are individ-uated independently of each other. According to (A'), an individual substance is more than the sum of its parts. What account does Scotus give of its individuation? Specifically, we need to see whether Scotus regards the individuation of this composite whole as something *additional to* the individuation of its matter and form, something which cannot be explained just by the individuation of its matter and form. It seems likely, in my view, that Scotus does believe this to be the case. In *Ordinatio* 2. 3. 1. 5–6, n. 187,[39] quoted in Chapter 2, Scotus seems to argue that the composite substance constituted by individual prime matter and individual form is individuated independently of the indi-viduation of its parts; and this seems to be a supposition made throughout Scotus's discussion of the individuation of composite substance. The reason is that the essence of a composite substance is a quiddity, and 'every quiddity is communicable'.[40]

---

[38] Scotus's discussion of composite substance at *In Metaph.* 8. 4, which I do not discuss here, is *prima facie* rather different from that in *Ord.* 3. 2. 2. I have analysed the *Metaphysics* text at length elsewhere, however, arguing that the *Metaphysics* discussion is in fact con-sistent with the *Ordinatio* account: see my 'Duns Scotus's Anti-Reductionistic Account', 166–70. In *Ord.* 3. 2. 2, Scotus considers a possible objection to his theory. How can an absolute item (viz. a whole composite substance) depend on, or in some sense presuppose, a relational entity? (see ibid. n. 11 (Wadding edn., vii. 81)). In response, Scotus argues that, generally, any natural causal activity entails spatial proximity; *a fortiori*, then natural causal activity resulting in the production of a substance or absolute accident entails spatial proximity. But spatial proximity, in Scotus's Aristotelian account of place, is itself merely a relation, as we shall see in Ch. 11. Hence, the natural production of some substance or absolute depends on a relation. Analogously, then, there is no difficulty in the case of a whole depending upon the relation between its parts: see ibid. n. 10 (Wadding edn., vii. 80).

[39] Vatican edn., vii. 483; Spade, 106–7.

[40] Scotus, *Ord.* 2. 3. 1. 7, nn. 227–8 (Vatican edn., vii. 500); on this, see also Allan B. Wolter, 'Reflections about Scotus's Early Works', in Honnefelder *et al.* (eds.), *John Duns Scotus*, 37–57, p. 52. If Scotus really means that a composite substance is individuated independently of its parts, then he would seem to have made a mistake. It is surely impossible for something which is composed of non-repeatable parts to be a repeatable essence. Thus, I would argue that the individuation of the parts is a sufficient condition for the individuation of the whole. Perhaps Scotus's point is just that a whole composite essence is a quiddity, and that, as such, it requires some kind of individuation, where this individuation could be completely accounted for by the individuation of its parts. In my 'Identity, Origin, and Persistence in Duns Scotus's Physics', *History of Philosophy Quarterly*, forthcoming, I argue on the basis of some consideration suggested in Scotus, *Ord*, 4. 43. 3, n. 14 (Wadding edn., x. 55), that the individuation of *matter* is explanatorily prior to the individuation of form and composite. Thus, Scotus believes that the individuation of matter explains the identity of a substantial form of such and such a kind united to it, and that the identity of matter and form in turn explain the identity of the whole composite.

Does Scotus provide us with good reason for wanting to accept (A′)—over against William's (A*), for example? He does not provide an unequivocal argument in favour of the desirability of (A′). But I think that we can find an important hint as to the sort of answer he would give. Some answers clearly will not do. It is clear that neither matter nor form can be the end term of generation and corruption. But the relation between them, as William of Ware would hold, could be. It is clear, however, that there are some other non-trivial properties of a substance that can inhere in neither matter alone, form alone, nor the relation between them. Perhaps the capacity to smile would be an example. So William's theory—at least as he develops it—cannot account for the fact that substances have such properties.

But this alone is not sufficient for the truth of Scotus's (A′). After all, it could be the case that the capacity to smile inheres in the *aggregate* of matter, form, and relation that, according to William, we must hold to be what a substance is. But Scotus provides us with the tools for seeing what might be wrong with this answer. What sort of answer would we need? At the very least, we would have to claim that the properties which inhere in an aggregate—but not the properties which inhere in a substance—are the *same in kind* as the properties which inhere in one or more of the parts of the aggregate. So the properties which inhere in a whole substance will be *different in kind* from the properties which inhere in any of its parts. If we could identify such properties, we would indeed have a principled way of distinguishing substances from aggregates.

Scotus never explicitly claims that the properties which inhere in a whole substance are unlike the properties which inhere in an aggregate in that they are different in kind from the properties of parts of that substance. It may be that Scotus regarded this as so obvious as not to need spelling out—though clearly William would not agree with him about this. But I think Scotus provides a hint that will lead us to what I would take to be the correct solution here. To see what it is, we need to look again at an important passage quoted above:

It would follow [on R3] . . . that there would be no being in which in itself proper passion, proper operation or any proper accident inhered, since these do not inhere in matter or form or both of these together (except inasmuch as they are one in some whole in itself), though they do inhere in the species [of the whole].[41]

---

[41] Scotus, *Ord.* 3. 2. 2, n. 7 (Wadding edn., vii. 76); for the text in MS A, followed here, see n. 15 above. See also *Ord.* 2. 8. un., n. 4 (Wadding edn., vi. 587), and *Ord.* 4. 10. 7, n. 2 (Wadding edn., viii. 560), for a similar (Aristotelian) claim that the subjects of sensory experience are necessarily composites of body and soul. Neither body alone nor soul alone could be the subject of such experience.

Scotus expressly notes that this argument, although directed against R3, is sufficient to refute R4 as well.[42] So Scotus accepts

(F) It is not possible that proper passion, operation, and accident inhere in individual matter alone, or in individual form alone, or in relational entity alone, or in some aggregate of two or more of these parts.

But the passage also signals Scotus's reason for accepting (F). The properties of a whole substance can inhere in the *species* of the whole, even though at least some of them do not inhere in any of the parts or any aggregate of the parts. In other words, the species of the whole is the right sort of thing for the properties to inhere in. And plausibly, this can only be because the properties themselves are the right sort of things to inhere in the whole, but not the right sort of things to inhere in any of the parts or any aggregate of the parts. And this is just the sort of solution I think we should be looking for. We distinguish a unity$_4$ from a unity$_1$ on the grounds that a unity$_4$, unlike a unity$_1$, has properties different in kind from the properties of its parts. Unlike Scotus's position, William's cannot allow for this. So I take it that Scotus's position is preferable.

This account might make it look as though Scotus has an *explanatory* account of the distinction between a unity$_4$ and a unity$_1$: we explain the difference by appealing to the different sorts of property that these different unities can instantiate. But I do not think that Scotus would regard his as a very explanatory account. Scotus sometimes asks whether there is an *explanation* for the fact that matter and substantial form can be united in such a way as to constitute a whole which exhibits unity$_4$. His most important reply gives what looks like a standard Aristotelian response to the question:

A composite of matter and form is one, because 'this one is act, and that one potentiality', as Aristotle says there: [43] for just as there is no medium between matter and its being a cause in its genus, and none between form and its being a cause, therefore these two constitute a substantial [*per se*] unity.[44]

---

[42] Ibid. 3. 2. 2. n. 8 (Wadding edn., vii. 79): with regard to his rejection of R4, Scotus notes: 'Hoc etiam concludunt rationes factae ad prmum articulum.'

[43] Arist. *Metaph.* 7. 6 (1045^{b}17–21).

[44] Scotus, *Lect.* 2. 12. un., n. 50 (Vatican edn., xix. 89). See also *idem, Ord.* 3. 2. 2, n. 10 (Wadding edn., vii. 80); *Lect.* 2. 12. un., n. 67 (Vatican edn., xix. 95); *Ord.* 4. 11. 3, n. 53 (Wadding edn., viii. 652–3). Note that by labelling matter 'potential', Scotus does not mean that matter is pure potentiality, or that it somehow fails to be an entity or thing in its own right. He consistently claims that matter is potentiality merely in the sense of being a subject capable of recieving (substantial) forms, or in which forms can inhere. As we saw in Ch. 2, Scotus labels this type of potentiality 'subjective potentiality'. As we saw

According to this passage, matter and substantial form are united immediately to each other as potentiality and actuality: matter is immediately potential to form, and form is immediately actual to matter. For this reason, a composite of matter and form is one *in itself*. Thus, the explanation of the fact that matter and substantial form unite to constitute an item which exhibits unity$_4$ is just that matter and substantial form are the types of thing that they are. There is no further explanation to be sought. So Scotus cannot, on his own admission, explain why it is that substantial form can endow a substance with certain properties that differ from those of any of its parts (including the properties of the form itself). This is perhaps indicative of the general inability of substantial form to do any genuinely explanatory work. Scotus's frank admission of this fact perhaps shows him at his least Aristotelian. But it seems to be the only philosophically principled answer that can be given to the question of the explanatory value of a theory of substantial form.

Scotus's account of the unity of matter and substantial form is in fact non-explanatory. This does not entail that Scotus cannot give a *principled* account of the distinction between unity$_4$ and unity$_1$. Indeed, I have just attempted to sketch out what I think this distinction would look like in Scotus. An item exhibits unity$_4$ just if it has some properties which are different in kind from any of the properties of its parts. But what Scotus cannot answer is: What is it about matter and substantial form in virtue of which they unite to constitute an item which has some properties which are different in kind from any of the properties of its parts? Put slightly differently, in virtue of which properties of matter and form do matter and form unite to constitute a whole exhibiting unity$_4$? Scotus's anti-reductionistic account of material substance is thus, in my sense, non-explanatory.[45]

---

in Ch. 4, subjective potentiality is not a property that can be instantiated only by prime matter. Scotus believes that some composite substances contain two (or more) essential forms. Since the significant claim here is that matter and lower forms are subjectively potential to higher forms, R′ can, *mutatis mutandis*, be used to give an account of the substantial unity of any composite exhibiting unity$_4$, irrespective of the number of hierarchically arranged forms which, with matter, compose it.

[45] Scotus's concern with this question is reflected in recent scholarly discussion of the passage which he cites from Aristotle. Modern commentators fall roughly into two camps: those who hold that Aristotle had an explanatory account of the way in which matter and form unite to make up an individual composite substance, and those who hold that Aristotle had a non-explanatory account of this unity: see David Charles, 'Matter and Form: Unity, Persistence, and Identity', in T. Scaltsas, D. Charles, and

Scotus defends an account of material substance according to which no such substance is simply reducible to the sum of its parts. He clearly distinguishes between a substance and an aggregate, and criticizes those of his predecessors who fail to make such a distinction. While this anti-reductionistic view was almost certainly the majority view in the High Middle Ages, Scotus, as far as I know, is not only the only thinker to offer a detailed defence of it, but also the only thinker to make it clear that the account should be generalized to include all material substances. Scotus correctly highlights the implications of R3 and especially R4. Whether we are persuaded by his arguments will depend on the extent to which we believe that a reductionistic account of material substance has anything to recommend it. On my account, William of Ware and other reductionists would have to deny that a material substance has any non-trivial properties which are different in kind from the properties of any of its parts. (Hence, for example, William's claim that the property of being generated, far from belonging to a composite substance, merely belongs to the relation between the substance's matter and form.) William's claim that a material substance does not have any non-trivial properties which are different in kind from the properties of any of its parts does not look very plausible to me, though I cannot think of a way to show that it is false.

M. L. Gill (eds.), *Unity, Identity, and Explanation in Aristotle's Metaphysics* (Oxford: Clarendon Press, 1994), 75–105, pp. 76–80, and the literature which Charles cites. Scotus aligns himself roughly with those holding the non-explanatory view. But does not quite fit into the taxonomy proposed by Charles, and there are elements of the explanatory account too. Charles argues that a thoroughgoing non-explanatory account of the unity of matter and substantial form would be committed to the claim that matter and form are 'one and the same' (ibid. 76). But Scotus, as we have seen, wants to give a somewhat different account of the unity of a composite substance, according to which matter and substantial form are two individual objects which unite in some unexplained way to constitute a substance exhibiting unity$_4$.

6

Accidents and Accidental Unity

In his *Categories*, Aristotle proposed a general scheme for classifying the kinds of predicates which can apply to subjects. He listed these predicates as substance, quantity, quality, relation, place, time, position, state, action, passion.[1] All but the first are *accidental categories*. As the medievals understood the purpose of Aristotle's categories, these nine accidental categories provide a means for classifying the *non-essential properties* of a substance: that is, those which it can be without, or which it has contingently. In this chapter, I shall be concerned first with some of the general claims which Scotus makes about the accidental categories, and secondly with his discussion of relations. In subsequent chapters, I shall look in more detail at the categories of quantity, quality, place, position, and time. I shall also look at the concept of motion, a concept which, according to Scotus, can apply across more than one of the categories.

For reasons which will become clear through this chapter, Scotus divides the list of accidents into two significant groups: non-relational accidents and relational accidents. Quantity and quality belong to the first group; the remaining seven accidents to the second group. The set of relational accidents is further divided into two groups: intrinsic relational accidents and extrinsic relational accidents. Accidents in the category of relation are classified as intrinsic relational accidents; accidents in the remaining six categories are classified as extrinsic relational accidents. Scotus holds that all of these accidental properties count as *things*, arguing that they are individuated independently of the subjects to which they are united. In what follows, I discuss (i) Scotus's reasons for thinking that accidents are individuated independently of the subjects to which they are united, (ii) Scotus's account of non-relational accidents and accidental unity, (iii) Scotus's general

---

[1] Arist. *Cat.* 4 (1^{b}25–7).

account of relations, and (iv) Scotus's distinction between intrinsic and extrinsic relational accidents.

1. THE INDIVIDUATION OF ACCIDENTS

As Scotus understands accidents, it is clear that they count as individual things. In one important passage he makes the point explicitly:

In every categorical hierarchy there can be found something intrinsically individual and singular of which the species is predicated—or at least there can be found something not predicable of many.[2]

(For Scotus's use of 'categorical hierarchy', see below. The basic sense of the phrase here is just 'category'.) So Scotus accepts

(1) An accident is an individual item.

Scotus makes the point rather less explicitly elsewhere:

In the second sense of this first member [i.e. 'being' or 'thing' taken in its broadest sense], however, we say a thing is what can have entity outside the soul. Avicenna[3] seems to have this sense in mind when he says that 'thing' and 'being' are common to all genera.[4]

As is the case with a substantial form, one plausible alternative account to Scotus's would be that accidents are *abstracta*, or repeatable properties. Scotus, however, offers an argument for (1). His basic intuition about accidents is that, in order to perform the roles expected of them in Aristotelian science, they must count as (individual) *things* or *beings*:

It is clear that accidents are principles of acting, and are principles of knowing a substance, as is clear from *De Anima* 1,[5] and that they are in themselves objects of the senses. But it would be absurd to claim that something that does

---

[2] Scotus, *Ord.* 2. 3. 1. 4, n. 90 (Vatican edn., viii. 434; Spade, 80). Spade notes that the role of the last clause is unclear. The Vatican editors suggest that Scotus might have had in mind the heavenly spheres, which have just one individual for each species. But, as Spade notes, 'it is hard to see how that is relevant here'. Perhaps Scotus is unhappy with an unqualified identification of accidents as *subjects* of predication, and wants to argue that even an individualized accident is (standardly) in some sense not an ultimate subject of predication.

[3] Avicenna, *Metaph.* 1. 5 (ed. S. van Riet, Avicenna Latinus (3 vols., Louvain: Peeters; Leiden: Brill, 1977–83), i. 33).

[4] Scotus, *Quod.* 3, n. 2 (Wadding edn., xii. 67; Alluntis and Wolter, 62 n. 3. 10).

[5] Arist. *De an.* 1. 1 (403^a3–10).

not have any formal entity is a principle of acting, either of real action in matter, or of intentional action in the senses or the intellect; for [if it were such a principle], it should be claimed that a chimera acted, or was sensed.[6]

There is an exegetical difficulty with this passage, which seems to suggest two quite different arguments. (i) Supposing that 'principle of acting' can be glossed as 'property in virtue of which something is an agent', the first argument runs as follows:

(A) If x is a property in virtue of which y is an agent, then x is a thing,

(B) An accident is a property in virtue of which a substance is an agent,

which jointly entail (1). (ii) Supposing that 'principle of acting' can be glossed as 'efficient cause', the second argument is:

(A*) If x is an efficient cause, then x is a thing,

(B*) An accident is an efficient cause,

which jointly entail (1). In favour of the first reading—a reading which I believe is far more likely to be the correct one—is Scotus's explicit formulation of his premises in the passage quoted. In favour of the less likely second reading is Scotus's chimera example. (A*) makes existence necessary for being an efficient cause. The falsity of (A*) will thus plausibly mean that existence is not necessary for being an efficient cause, and hence that (for example) a chimera could be an efficient cause. I can understand what it would be for a chimera to be the sort of thing that could be an efficient cause; I cannot understand what it would be for a chimera to be the sort of thing that could be a property in virtue of which something is an agent. So Scotus's chimera example is evidence in favour of (A*), not (A), and thus for the second way of reading the argument.

Neither argument is successful. The first fails because, although (B) looks true, (A) seems to be question-begging. It presupposes what it is supposed to prove: namely, that properties are individual things. The

---

[6] Scotus, *Ord.* 4. 12. 1, n. 16 (Wadding edn., viii. 720); the text in MS A, fo. 218vb, on which I base this translation, differs slightly, in unimportant ways, from that in the Wadding edition. Scotus's claim that accidents have 'formal entity' might look to be consistent with the claim that an accident is an abstract property—perhaps that it is a formally distinct property of a substance. But the passages quoted above make it clear, I hope, that Scotus would reject this interpretation. Scotus does not usually label form-alities 'things'; but he is happy so to label accidents.

second fails because, although (A*) looks true, (B*) looks false. We usually think of substances, not their properties, as efficient causes.[7]

Of course, the claim that accidents are individual things does not entail any one account of how accidents are individuated. One plausible account of the individuation of accidents would accept

(C) An accident is individuated by its substance.

Scotus holds, however, that (C) is false, and argues instead for

(2) An item belonging to a category is individuated without reference to any other category.

As he puts it: 'In every categorical hierarchy the singular or individual is not established through anything belonging to any other hierarchy.'[8] (2), of course, entails that quantities, qualities, relations, and all the remaining Aristotelian accidents are individuated independently both of each other and of the substance in which they inhere.

Scotus's arguments for (2) all make use of a concept which Scotus labels 'categorical hierarchy' (*coordinatio praedicamentalis*). The basic idea is that each of the Aristotelian categories admits of subdivision in terms of genus and species along the lines suggested by Porphyry for the category of substance. In his *Isagoge*, Porphyry argues:

In each category, some things are most general and again others most specific, and yet others are between the most general and the most specific. The most general is that above which there is no other genus that transcends it. The most specific is that after which there is no other, subordinate, species. What are between the most general and the most specific are all the others. These, the same things, are both genera and species, taken in relation to one another.[9]

What Porphyry has in mind is a hierarchy from most general to most specific. He uses the category of substance to show what he has in mind:

Let us clarify the above statement for just one category. Substance is itself a genus. Under this is body, and under body animate body, under which animal, under animal rational animal, under which man. Under man are Socrates and

[7] When discussing his claim that *relational* accidents are things, Scotus appeals to the principle that there is no change without the production and/or destruction of an individual thing, which I discussed in Ch. 3. (I discuss his argument below.) In fact, there seems to me no reason why he could not use the principle to support (1).

[8] Scotus, *Ord.* 2. 3. 1. 4, n. 89 (Vatican edn., vii. 434; Spade, 80).

[9] Porphyry, *Isag.* (ed. Adolfus Busse, Commentania in Aristotelem Graeca, iv/1 (Berlin: Georgius Reimer, 1887), 4, ll. 15–20; Spade, 4 n. 21).

Plato the particular men. Of these, substance is the most general and the one that is only a genus. Man is the most specific, and the one that is only a species. Body is a species of substance but a genus of animate body. Animate body is a species of body but a genus of animal. Again, animal is a species of substance but a genus of rational animal. Rational animal is a species of animal but a genus of man. Now man is a species of rational animal, but no longer a genus—of particular men. Instead, it is a species only. Everything prior to individuals and predicated of them is a species only, no longer a genus.[10]

Porphyry clearly suggests, in the first sentence of the first passage, that similar hierarchies can be constructed for each category. Scotus draws on this suggestion, and argues that each category will contain a hierarchy of common essences. But Scotus adds the further claim, which he attributes to Aristotle, that each category will contain the individual instantiations of natures classified in the category.[11] Particular men, for example, belong to the category of substance; particular white things (i.e. patches of white, not the substances in which on this account such patches inhere) to the category of quality, and so on.

Scotus gives four arguments for (2) from the concept of categorical hierarchy. The first argument infers (2) directly from the account just given. But there is a problem with this inference, which the remaining three arguments attempt, in very similar ways, to overcome. The problem is that the account of categorical hierarchy just given does not entail that the different categories are self-contained: that is, are such that none of the features of one category can be explained by a feature of another category. Of course, if we deny that each category is self-contained in this sense, we cannot infer (2). In this case, (2) might still be true; but the concept of categorical hierarchy alone is not sufficient for the truth of (2).

Scotus's remaining three arguments defend the claim that each category is, in the relevant senses, self-contained. I give two of the arguments here. First, Scotus argues that

> (D) For every individual x belonging to a category c, and every property F belonging to the categorical hierarchy of c, if x is F, then x is necessarily F,

[10] Ibid. (p. 4, l. 21–p. 5, l. 1; Spade, 4 nn. 22–3).
[11] Arist. *An post.* 1. 20 (82ª21–3): see Scotus, *Ord.* 2. 3. 1. 4, n. 89 (Vatican edn., vii. 434; Spade, 79). The Aristotelian claim is that there can be only a finite number of stages between a most general predicate term and an individual subject. The text does not in fact give sufficient warrant for supposing that it supports Scotus's far more specific claim.

and

> (E) For every individual x and every property F, if x is a unity$_3$, then it is not the case that x is necessarily F,

entail

> (3) It is not the case that, for every individual x belonging to a category c, x is a unity$_3$.

But, given that

> (F) For every individual x belonging to a category c, if x is individuated with reference to a category other than c, then x is a unity$_3$,

(3) entails (2).[12] (F), according to Scotus, is Aristotelian,[13] and in any case seems plausible. (D) and (E) are both interesting claims. (D) makes it clear that individual categorical items (e.g. an individual cat or an individual patch of blackness) belong to their categories essentially—a claim which I can see no reason to deny. The crucial premiss for Scotus's argument is (E): an accidental whole does not have any essential properties. (E) looks to be false. We might think that the properties of an accidental whole were *all* essential to it. It is certainly true *de dicto* that it is impossible that any two items composing a unity$_3$ fail to compose a unity$_3$; and no unity$_3$ can survive the decomposition of its parts. For example, a black cat is a unity$_3$. But if Felix the cat stops being black, the unity$_3$ composed of Felix and his blackness ceases to exist. This makes it look as though the items composing a unity$_3$ are essential to that unity.

So Scotus's first argument fails, I believe, because (E) seems to be false. Scotus attempts a further defence of (2) by stipulating that

> (G) The features of a category c are not sufficient to account for the individuation of an item belonging to some other category d.

Hence some features contained under d must be necessary for the individuation of an item belonging to d.[14] The conclusion here is not quite strong enough to allow a defence of (2). (G), after all, does not exclude the possibility of a feature of c being *necessary* for the individuation of an item belonging to d. And in any case it does not seem clear to me that there is any reason to accept (G).

---

[12] Scotus, *Ord.* 2. 3. 1. 4, n. 91 (Vatican edn., vii. 434–5; Spade, 80).
[13] Scotus refers to Arist. *Metaph.* 7. 6 (1015^{b}16–36).
[14] Scotus, *Ord.* 2. 3. 1. 4, n. 92 (Vatican edn., vii. 435–6; Spade, 80–1).

The point of Scotus's two arguments is that an accident is individuated independently of its subject. I discuss in the last section of this chapter a possible reason for wanting to accept this claim. The claim that an accident is individuated independently of its subject is necessary—though not sufficient—for the truth of an even more controversial Scotist claim: namely, that some accidents are essentially non-relational or *absolute* items. (I look at Scotus's arguments for this claim, and what the claim amounts to, in the next section.) Since the claim that some accidents are absolute items entails (2), Scotus's arguments, if successful, would give further warrant for accepting (2). On the other hand, if (2) is false, so too is Scotus's claim that some accidents are absolute items.

2. NON-RELATIONAL ACCIDENTS AND ACCIDENTAL UNITY

Scotus argues that the non-relational accidents of quantity and quality are absolute items: more precisely, given that the only sort of composite whole a non-relational accident can be part of is a unity$_3$,

(4) For every non-relational accident *a*, it is possible that, for every whole *w*, *w* is a unity$_3$ and *a* is not a part of *w*.

Scotus's argument for (4) presupposes the following secure thesis

(H) A whole including either quantity or quality is a unity$_3$.

He argues as follows:

A subject is not of the essence of a [non-relational] accident, for then [if it were] a white man would not be an accidental being, which is contrary to Aristotle in *Metaphysics* 5 and 7.[15] The reason is that, if we add to a thing something which is essential to it, we do not get an accidental entity.[16]

The final sentence here makes it clear that Scotus subscribes to the following rather unexpected principle:

(I) For every whole *w* and its parts *p*, *q*, . . . and *n*, *w* is a unity$_3$ only if being parts of *w* are non-essential features of *p*, *q*, . . . and *n*.

In other words, the parts of a unity$_3$ are all non-essentially parts of that whole. ((I) is different from (E). (E) makes the properties of a unity$_3$

---

[15] See Arist. *Metaph.* 5. 30 (1025^{a}19–21), 7. 5 (1030^{b}20–1).
[16] Scotus, *Ord.* 4. 12. 1, n. 9 (Wadding edn., viii. 717).

accidental to it; (I) makes it accidental to the properties that they are parts of a unity$_3$.) (H) and (I) entail the following two claims:

(5) A quantity is non-essentially a part of a unity$_3$,

and

(6) A quality is non-essentially a part of a unity$_3$.

Now, by definition, an accident cannot be part of a substantial unity (unity$_4$), and I take it that Scotus would subscribe to the claim that the parts of an aggregate and a merely ordered whole (i.e. unity$_1$ and unity$_2$) are non-essentially parts of these wholes. Hence, (5) and (6) amount to the claim that there is no whole *w* such that it is essential for quantity or quality to be parts of *w*. Scotus concludes that (5) and (6) entail (4).

In fact, Scotus's argument does not successfully yield (4). Rather, it entails the weaker

(4*) For every non-relational accident *a* and every whole *w*, it is possible both that *w* is a unity$_3$ and that *a* is not a part of *w*.

(4*) does not entail that a non-relational accident could exist without any substance at all, which is what (4) amounts to. (4*) could be satisfied by a non-relational accident's moving from substance to substance. Neither does (4) entail (4*). (4) will be accepted for *theological* reasons by anyone who accepts the doctrine of transubstantiation. According to the doctrine of transubstantiation, in the Eucharist the quantities of bread and wine exist without any substance at all. Scotus clearly accepts (4). He also accepts (4*), since he seems to accept that accidents can, at least under certain circumstances, move from subject to subject.[17]

How plausible is (4)? Scotus sometimes attempts to defend it by appealing to divine omnipotence:

(J) Anything which can be brought about by a created cause can be brought about directly by God.[18]

A substance is in some sense a 'cause' of its accidents. So (J) entails (4).

---

[17] See ibid. 4. 12. 6, n. 12 (Wadding edn., viii. 782). Scotus clearly supposes that an accident can move from subject to subject only by divine power. In ibid. 2. 3. 1. 4, n. 118 (Vatican edn., vii. 451; Spade, 89–90), he denies that it is naturally possible for an accident to move from substance to substance.

[18] Ibid. 4. 12. 1, n. 9 (Wadding edn., viii. 717).

But (J) is a *theological* principle for Scotus, not one which can be known by natural reason,[19] and is thus no help in establishing (4) *philosophically*: though, of course, given (4) and divine infinite power,[20] I take it that God can bring it about that an accident exists separately from any subject whatsoever. In default of any cogent argumentation for (4), I would suggest that there are no compelling philosophical reasons to accept it.

(4*) might be accepted by someone who thought that some bodies fail to retain numerical identity through death. For example, if we thought that the rose-body on my desk was numerically different from the rose that was in my garden this morning, we might nevertheless think that its *redness* is the same. But the medievals would generally have denied the *natural* possibility of an accident's moving from subject to subject, and Scotus is in any case committed to the continuity of bodies through death.[21]

Crucial to Scotus's argument is his principle

> (I) For every whole *w* and its parts *p*, *q*, . . . and *n*, *w* is a unity₃ only if being parts of *w* are non-essential features of *p*, *q*, . . . and *n*.

Whether or not we accept (I) will again probably depend on our prior intuitions about the possibility of accidents moving from subject to subject. We might want to claim that, for Scotus's white man, for example, being a part of this whole is accidental for the man, but *essential* for the whiteness: if the whiteness is Peter's, we would want to claim that it is not possible for it to be Paul's. On the other hand, there could be circumstances under which we would allow one and the same accident to exist successively in two different substances. It might be the case that the size or colour of a body remains constant over the decay of the body; and on any account of bodily decay, there comes a point when what was the body is a body no longer. If we accept the latter intuition—that accidents can move from subject to subject—then we will probably be happy to accept Scotus's (I). If we accept

---

[19] See ibid. 1. 42. un, nn. 8–9 (Vatican edn., vi. 342–4); Scotus, *Quod*. 7, nn. 4, 32 (Wadding edn., xii. 169, 185; Alluntis and Wolter, 162 n. 7. 8, 184–5 nn. 7. 89–90).

[20] For God's infinite power, see the passages cited in the previous note.

[21] Given this, Scotus could have argued (though he did not) for the continuity of a body through death on the basis of its capacity for supporting the *same* qualities. The redness of my rose is thus a good reason for supposing that its body is numerically the same as the rose-body that was in my garden this morning.

the former intuition—that accidents cannot move from subject to subject—then we would want to affirm

> (K) For every whole w and its parts p, q, . . . and n, w is a unity$_3$ only if exactly one of p, q, . . . and n is non-essentially a part of w,

in place of (I). ((K) captures the claim that exactly one of the parts of a unity$_3$ is a substance.)

Whichever of (I) or (K) we opt for, neither principle gives *sufficient* conditions for accidental unity (unity$_3$). The reason is that both would be satisfied by an *aggregate*: a whole exhibiting unity$_1$. How does Scotus distinguish unity$_3$ from unity$_1$? He suggests that 'accident' and 'inherent' are synonyms, from which, I take it, we can infer that a necessary condition for unity$_3$ is that one part of the whole *inheres in* another.[22] This criterion would be sufficient to distinguish a unity$_3$ from a unity$_1$, since I take it that the parts of a unity$_1$ do not inhere in each other.

The inherence stipulation would also, in fact, be sufficient to distinguish a unity$_3$ from a unity$_4$. Scotus never speaks of substantial form 'inhering' in matter or a lower-order composite. So Scotus accepts the following:

> (I*) For every whole w and its parts p, q, . . . and n, w is a unity$_3$ if and only if both being parts of w are non-essential features of p, q, . . . and n, and w includes a subject and its inhering properties.

I will return to the inherence stipulation below.

How much store we set by the distinction between unity$_3$ and unity$_4$ will depend on the extent to which we think that a plausible distinction can be made between the essential and the accidental properties of a thing: in other words, on how committed we are to *essentialism*.[23]

---

[22] Scotus, *Ord.* 4. 12. 1, n. 6 (Wadding edn., viii. 711); see also ibid. 1. 2. 2. 1–4, n. 403 (Vatican edn., ii. 356), where Scotus claims that unity$_3$ adds to unity$_2$ the stipulation that one part (accidentally) *informs* the other. In ibid. 3. 2. 2, n. 7 (Wadding edn., vii. 76), Scotus argues that the inherence stipulation is sufficient for a unity$_3$ to count as one thing (*unum aliquid*). I discuss the relation of inherence in more detail below. For a discussion of the same issues, centring on Scotus's treatment at *In Metaph.* 7. 1, nn. 1–6 (Wadding edition, iv. 672–4), see Berthold Wald, '*Accidens est Formaliter Ens*: Duns Scotus on Inherence in his *Quaestiones Subtilissimae* on Aristotle's *Metaphysics*', in John Marenbon (ed.), *Aristotle in Britain during the Middle Ages*, Société Internationale pour l'Étude de la Philosophie Médiévale: Recontres de Philosophie Médiévale, 5 (Brepols, 1996), 177–93. (Note that Wald occasionaly relies on the inauthentic *Expositio super Metaphysicam*.)

[23] For a modern discussion of essentialism, see Alvin Plantinga, *The Nature of Necessity*, Clarendon Library of Logic and Philosophy (Oxford: Clarendon Press, 1974), ch. 5. For essentialism in Aristotle, see S. M. Cohen, 'Essentialism in Aristotle', *Review of Metaphysics*, 31 (1977–8), 387–405.

Scotus, of course, was strongly committed to essentialism. Furthermore, I hope to show that Scotus has a principled way of drawing the
distinction between unity$_3$ and unity$_4$. But oddly, it is not one which
Scotus himself notices in his 'official' accounts of this distinction.
Prima facie, Scotus's claim that a non-relational accident can exist
independently of any substance makes it hard for him to give an
account of the relevant distinction. After all, one standard Aristotelian
way of distinguishing a substance from an accident is to claim that a
substance has existence in itself, whereas an accident has existence in
something else: an accident, unlike a substance, has *inesse*.[24] Unsurprisingly, Scotus replaces this Aristotelian distinction with a different
one, constructed around the modalities of the relation of inherence.
Scotus argues that a non-relational accident has a *natural tendency* to
inhere in a substance, whereas a substance does not have such a natural
tendency. This natural tendency does not mean that the inherence of
an accident in a subject is logically necessary; just that it is naturally
necessary.[25]

In his 'official' account, Scotus is in fact quite explicit about the
impossibility of an explanation for the fact that accidents cannot be
united with some other entity so as to constitute a whole which
exhibits unity$_4$:

There is no reason why this entity is substantial [*per se*] act with respect to that
entity, whereas another is only accidental [*per accidens*] [act] with respect to
some further entity, except that this [kind of] entity is this [kind of] entity.[26]

Nevertheless, although Scotus claims that the *metaphysics* of the distinction between unity$_3$ and unity$_4$ is obscure, he argues that there are
some good *a posteriori*, non-explanatory grounds on the basis of which
we can distinguish accidental forms from substantial ones. He notes
that philosophers have in times past proposed a number of such
principles: (a) accidental forms, unlike substantial forms, have contraries; (b) accidental forms, unlike substantial forms, admit of degrees;
(c) accidental forms, unlike substantial forms, are the kind of thing in
virtue of which something can change state. But Scotus argues that
there is a clearer criterion than any of these: that when a substantial

[24] See Scotus, *Ord.* 4. 12. 1, n. 1 (Wadding edn., viii. 702); the reference to Arist., *Ph.* 1. 3
(186^{b}7–9) is not found in MS A (fo. 218ra), though it is of course clearly presupposed.
[25] Scotus, *Ord.* 4. 12. 1, n. 23 (Wadding edn., viii. 724–5).
[26] Ibid. 3. 2. 2, n. 10 (Wadding edn., vii. 80). See also ibid. 4. 11. 3, n. 43 (Wadding edn.,
viii. 647–8); Scotus, *Lect.* 2. 12. un., n. 50 (Vatican edn., xix. 89).

form informs some lower-order composite substance, the new substantial form will be *more perfect* than the substantial form of a lower-
order composite; whereas when an accidental form inheres in some
other accidental form, the inherent form will be *less perfect* than the
accidental form in which it inheres. For example, the (substantial)
human soul is more perfect than the bodily form; whereas a relation
inherent in a quality (e.g. the similarity of this whiteness to that) is less
perfect than the accident in which it inheres.[27] Accepting this criterion
requires an acceptance of orders of perfection; something which is, I
suspect, easier for the schoolmen than it is for us. But Scotus's acceptance of the criterion is also puzzling, since he elsewhere argues both
that quality inheres in quantity and that quality is *more* perfect than
quantity.[28]

I claimed above that Scotus has a principled way of drawing the

---

[27] Scotus, *Ord.* 4. 11. 3, n. 44 (Wadding edn., viii. 648).

[28] Scotus is quite clear that quantity inheres directly in substance. But he sometimes
seems to suggest that quality inheres in substance only via quantity. The evidence here is
suggestive rather than conclusive, and there is at least one passage where Scotus clearly
denies that quantity is a material cause of quality (*De Primo Princ.* 2. 36 (p. 29/30)), which
I take it is at least related to a denial of the claim that quality inheres in quantity. At any
rate, here is the evidence in favour of the claim that quality inheres in quantity. (i)
Quality depends on quantity, though it depends even more essentially on substance
(Scotus, *Ord.* 4. 12. 2, n. 9 (Wadding edn., viii. 731)). (ii) Quantity is closer than quality to
substance in terms of 'being a subject for other things: which includes receiving other
things, and being perfected by them' (ibid. n. 12 (Wadding edn., viii. 732)). (iii) An
accident can be the subject of another accident; and in the Eucharist, it is 'probable' that
the quantity of the bread is the subject of its quality: 'quality . . . is received into what is
extended' (ibid. n. 15 (Wadding edn., viii. 734)); (iv) 'When . . . [quality] is separated
from substance, it is however in quantity, or has extension, just as [it did] before [its]
separation from [its] substance' (ibid. 4. 12. 3, n. 17 (Wadding edn., viii. 745); the last
clause (from 'just as') is lacking in MS A, fo. 221rb). The point is that Scotus regards it as
at least probable that in the Eucharist, quality is received by quantity; and this last
passage—at least in the Wadding version—makes it clear that the same state of affairs
obtains outside the Eucharist. In his *Metaphysics* questions, however, Scotus is more
explicit: 'Quantity is prior to the other accidents, because it is more immediately in a
substance than any other accident [is]': *In Metaph.* 4. 2, n. 12 (Wadding edn., iv. 583).
While none of this is an explicit affirmation of the thesis that quality inheres in substance
via quantity, this thesis is clearly suggested by all of the evidence taken together. Given
this, we could explain the troublesome contrary evidence from *De Primo Princ.* by
suggesting that Scotus wishes to restrict the use of the term 'material cause' to substances
alone. If Scotus does think that quality inheres in substance via quantity, he would
presumably want, for reasons of parsimony, to claim that relations of inherence, rather
like relations of material causality in substances, are *transitive*. Scotus could in this way
explain the inherence of quality in substance merely by invoking the inherence of quality
in quantity and the inherence of quantity in substance. But all of this is of course highly
speculative. For five arguments in favour of quality's being more perfect than quantity,
see *Ord.* 4. 12. 2, nn. 9–10 (Wadding edn., viii. 731).

distinction between unity$_3$ and unity$_4$. One plausible candidate here would be the Scotist stipulation that an accident, unlike a substantial form, *inheres in* its subject. The way in which Scotus describes the relation of inherence, however, means that this proposed way for distinguishing accidental from substantial forms turns out to be vacuous. Scotus pin-points two features necessary for the relation of inherence:

One is that of form to the informable; here substance is the recipient and the potential term . . . . The other is the accident's dependence upon the substance; here substance is essentially prior and the accident naturally posterior.[29]

(Note that the relevant kind of potentiality here is S-potentiality.) Thus described, there seems to be no difference between the relation of inherence and the relation which holds between a substantial form and its matter. (I describe a number of features of this relation in Chapter 2, section 2, and Chapter 4, section 4.) In fact, as I have noted, Scotus does not want to claim that a substantial form inheres in its subject. But he gives us no further guidance as to the relevant description of inherence. I take it, therefore, that the stipulation that an accident inheres in its subject does not give us any explanation for the distinction between substantial and accidental forms, or for the distinction between a unity$_4$ and a unity$_3$.

In one short but important passage, however, Scotus outlines what I take to be a fairly clear principle for the relevant distinction: a unity$_3$ (unlike a unity$_4$) has no non-trivial properties distinct from those of its parts. As Scotus makes clear, a white man, for example, has no properties which are not either whiteness or the essential properties of a man.

The inherence of whiteness in a man does not make any added reality; and however, when whiteness is in a man, then the white man is one, and not when they are separated.[30]

(I am reading 'does not make any added reality' to mean 'does not constitute a property different in kind from the properties of the parts'.)

This might allow a principled Scotist account of the distinction between unity$_3$ and unity$_4$ (and thus a defence of essentialism), though it is not one which Scotus seems to have spotted. Whether or not

[29] Scotus, *Quod.* 19, n. 13 (Wadding edn., xii. 502–3; Alluntis and Wolter, 428 n. 19. 40); see *Ord.* 3. 1. 1, n. 3 (Wadding edn., vii. 6).
[30] Scotus, *Lect.* 1. 17. 2. 4, n. 239 (Vatican edn., xvii. 258).

Scotus's position here would *entail* the further claim that a unity$_3$ (say, a white man) is some further item over and above its two parts, such that a unity$_3$ would count as a *numerically discrete* item, is not clear. In one important passage, however, Scotus makes it quite clear that a unity$_3$ counts as one thing (*unum aliquid*). So I take it that he supposes that a unity$_3$ is numerically distinct from its parts.[31] This claim gives rise to a distinct problem. Scotus seems to hold that numerically discrete items require individuating independently of their parts (see Chapter 5, section 4, for this claim). I do not know what solution Scotus would propose here, and the problem does not seem to have occurred to him.

I have tried here to outline Scotus's claim that non-relational accidents are absolute items, and to lay bare the sorts of unity conditions which underlie this claim. We should note that Scotus's (I) entails the claim that accidents are individuated independently of their subjects. And if we accept that accidents can move from subject to subject, we might well want to accept (I) and the individuation principle it entails. Furthermore, Scotus does not give an explanatory account of the distinction between unity$_3$ and unity$_4$. But I have suggested that implicit in what Scotus writes is an appeal to the failure of a unity$_3$ to instantiate properties different in kind from the properties of its parts.

3. RELATIONAL ACCIDENTS

Not all relations, according to Scotus, are accidents. Non-accidental relations are those which an item cannot be without. Scotus labels such relations 'transcendental' relations. The relation between a creature and God is Scotus's standard example of a transcendental relation.[32] Since transcendental relations are necessary features of their subjects, Scotus reasons that they are really identical with their subjects. But such relations are not *defining properties* of their subjects. They are therefore formally distinct from their subjects.[33]

---

[31] Scotus, *Ord.* 3. 2. 2, n. 7 (Wadding edn., vii. 76).

[32] Ibid. 2. 1. 4–5, nn. 261–2 (Vatican edn., vii. 129). See Mark G. Henninger, *Relations: Medieval Theories 1250–1325* (Oxford: Clarendon Press, 1989), 78–82. On relations in general in Scotus, see ibid. 68–97; Jos Decorte, '"Modus" or "Res": Scotus' Criticism of Henry of Ghent's Conception of the Reality of a Real Relation', in Leonardo Sileo (ed.), *Via Scoti: Methodologica ad mentem Joannis Duns Scoti. Atti del Congresso Scotistico Internazionale, Roma 9–11 Marzo 1993* (2 vols., Rome: Antonianum, 1995), i. 407–29, pp. 425–9.

[33] Scotus, *Ord.* 2. 1. 4–5, n. 272 (Vatican edn., vii. 135); see Henninger, *Relations*, 82–5.

Scotus's account of transcendental relations does not have much bearing on his physics, and I will not discuss his theory further. Scotus's account of categorical (i.e. accidental) relations is strongly *realist*: he holds that a real relation between two non-relational items is an accident inhering in a subject. Thus he accepts

> (L) For every non-relational item *x* and every non-relational item *y*, *x* is really categorically related to *y* only if a relational property *R*, really distinct from *x* and *y*, inheres in *x*.[34]

(I talk of 'relational properties' here to stress the difference between medieval and modern accounts of relations. A relation, for the medievals, is a property inhering in its subject. Today we tend to *distinguish* relations from properties.) What (L) amounts to can be seen if we look at some examples. Suppose we can claim that 'Plato is similar to Socrates' is true in virtue of their both being white. In this case, on (L) a real relation of similarity will inhere in Plato. Similarity, in fact, is a symmetrical relation, so on (L) another real relation of similarity will inhere in Socrates. (Scotus would refer to Socrates' whiteness as the *foundation* for his relation of similarity to Plato; likewise Plato's whiteness is the foundation for his relation of similarity to Socrates.) Furthermore, Socrates' whiteness is a non-relational accident of Socrates. On (L) a relation of inherence inheres in Socrates' whiteness. But a relation of inherence necessarily corresponds on a one-to-one basis with a relation of being-inhered-in. So on (L) a relation of being-inhered-in inheres in Socrates. (The relation of inherence itself is a relational item, and so is not covered under the scope of (L). I discuss later in this section the relation between a relational property and its subject.)

On (L), then, relational properties are distinct from their subjects. Scotus is also quite clear that such relational properties count as individual things.[35] Presumably, given Scotus's arguments in the first section of this chapter, a relation is individuated independently of both its subject and its foundation.

Scotus offers five arguments in favour of

> (7) For every real relation *R* and its non-relational foundation *F*, *R* is a thing really distinct from *F*,

---

[34] Scotus, *Ord.* 2. 1. 4–5, nn. 200, 205 (Vatican edn., vii. 101–4).
[35] See e.g. Scotus, *Quod.* 6, n. 33 (Wadding edn., xii. 166; Alluntis and Wolter, 156–7 n. 6. 82); *idem, Ord.* 1. 31. un., n. 6 (Vatican edn., vi. 204).

of which I give the two most interesting. (Two are in any case theological, and so of little help in establishing (7) on philosophical
grounds.[36])

The first exploits the separability criterion for real distinction.
Accepting

> (M) If *x* is really distinct from *y*, then it is possible for *x* to exist without *y*,

and the empirical generalization

> (N) For every categorical relation *R* and its foundation *F*, it is possible for
> *F* to exist without *R*,

Scotus concludes that (7) is true.[37] The kind of identity Scotus wants to
reject is *real* identity; so his conclusion is that *R* and *F* are *really*
distinct. Built into Scotus's argument is the presupposition that real
distinction and separability always obtain between individual things,
and never, for example, between a thing and a (positive) *mode* of
existence. If a categorical relation were just a mode of existence, its
subject according to Scotus could never be without it. How plausible
we regard this presupposition will probably depend on how plausible
we regard Scotus's whole programme of reifying accidental properties.[38]

The second argument bears a close relation to arguments considered
in Chapter 5. It makes use of Aristotle's example of 'a' and 'b' forming
the syllable 'ab'. As the example was used in the arguments considered
in Chapter 5, it makes the point that a whole must be more than just
the aggregate of its absolute and relational parts. Here, Scotus uses the
example to show that (7) is true: that is, he uses it to show that,
whatever the nature of a whole composite, it must be the case that
its parts are united by a real relational entity. Scotus reasons that, if (7)
is false, it will follow that

> (8) A whole composite is identical with its absolute parts.

But (8) is equivalent to

> (9) A whole composite is merely the aggregate of its absolute parts.

(9) is contradictory, and therefore necessarily false. The inference from
the falsity of (7) to (8) could plausibly be rejected by someone who

---

[36] For the two theological arguments, see Scotus, *Ord.* 2. 1. 4–5, nn. 207 and 208
(Vatican edn., vii. 104–5), discussed in Henninger, *Relations*, 74–6.

[37] Scotus, *Ord.* 2. 1. 4–5, n. 200 (Vatican edn., vii. 101–2).

[38] For an excellent discussion of the whole argument, see Henninger, *Relations*, 71–4.

held that relations were modes: and it is difficult to see how Scotus's argument could dislodge this commitment. Scotus uses his principle

(O) It is not possible that change occurs without the production and/or destruction of a thing

to show that (9) is contradictory. Since it is possible for the parts of a substance to continue to exist even if the substance no longer exists, it must be the case that something is produced or destroyed to account for the change. But if (9) is true, there is no such thing. So (9) is false.[39]

Generally, Scotus's arguments will appeal only to someone who accepts his reifying account of accidental properties. Someone adopting an ontology according to which accidental properties are *abstracta* really distinct from their subjects, for example, could deny Scotus's claim that relations are things without finding herself committed to the absurd consequences highlighted in Scotus's arguments. On the other hand, Scotus's approach can be seen most fairly if we look at its context. Scotus uses his arguments to oppose a claim, made by Henry of Ghent, that relations are modes intentionally (not really) distinct from their subjects.[40] Henry's intentional distinction is a near relative of Scotus's formal distinction.[41] I take it that modes will count as some sort of *abstracta*; so the position Scotus opposes is committed to the view that accidental relations are *abstracta* formally distinct from their subjects. Given Scotus's separability criterion for real distinction, according to which separability is sufficient for real distinction, Henry's position is incoherent. (It entails that no accidental (and therefore separable) property is in fact separable from its subject.) And Scotus's arguments are, I think, certainly sufficient to show this.

As we have seen, Scotus holds that it is possible for non-relational accidents to exist without a subject. He does not hold that the same is true for relational accidents. Scotus repeatedly affirms, in fact, that it is impossible for a relational property to exist without a subject: 'There

---

[39] Scotus, *Ord.* 2. 1. 4–5, n. 209 (Vatican edn., vii. 105); see Henninger, *Relations*, 76–7. The argument also appears in Scotus, *Lect.* 1. 17. 2. 4, nn. 231–3 (Vatican edn., xvii. 255–6). For the final argument, which I do not discuss here, see Scotus, *Ord.* 2. 1. 4–5, n. 210 (Vatican edn., vii. 105–6), and the discussion in Henninger, *Relations*, 77–8.

[40] For Henry's position on relations, see Henninger, *Relations*, 52–8, and the passages referred to by Henninger; see also Scotus, *Ord.* 2. 1. 4–5, nn. 192–3, 195–9 (Vatican edn., vii. 96–101), and Decorte, '"Modus" or "Res"', 409–25.

[41] See Jean Paulus, *Henri de Gand: Essai sur les tendances de sa métaphysique*, Études de philosophie médiévale, 25 (Paris: Vrin, 1938), 88–92; J. Wippel, *The Metaphysical Thought of Godfrey of Fontaines* (Washington: Catholic University of America Press, 1981), 80–5.

Accidents and Accidental Unity

is a contradiction that there be similarity which is unrelated either to
its foundation or to its term.'[42] So Scotus accepts

> (P) The existence of both the foundation and the end term of a relation *R*
> are necessary for the existence of *R*.

(P) seems to be true: it is certainly difficult to see what could be
involved in the existence of a relation without its *relata*. (P) is consistent with (8), since the existence of a categorical relation is not
necessary for the existence of its foundation.

Given that a relation inheres in its foundation, Scotus argues that
(P) entails

> (10) It is not possible for a relation to exist without its inherence in its
> foundation,

which on Scotus's account of real identity entails

> (11) A relation is really identical with its relation of inherence in a
> foundation.

On (11), the inherence in Plato of Plato's relation of similarity to
Socrates is identical with Plato's relation of similarity; and the inherence in Plato of the inherence of Plato's whiteness in Plato is really
identical with the inherence of Plato's whiteness. Presumably Scotus
would want to argue for a formal distinction between a relation and its
relation of inherence. As Henninger puts it,

The formal notion of similarity does not logically imply the formal notion of
its inhering in something (as most philosophers today would concede, one
need not conceive of similarity as an inhering accident).[43]

Accepting (11) allows Scotus to block a potentially damaging objection to his claim (7). If the inherence of an absolute accident in a
subject is a relation, and if relations inhere in their subjects, it might
look as though we would have an infinite regress of inherence relations: an absolute accident inheres in its subject; the absolute accident's
relation of inherence inheres in its subject; the relation's inherence
inheres in its subject, and so on, *ad infinitum*. Accepting (11) allows
Scotus to block the regress:

That relation without which it is a contradiction for the foundation to exist is

[42] Scotus, *Quod.* 3, n. 15 (Wadding edn., xii. 82; Alluntis and Wolter, 74 n. 3. 47), cited
in Henninger, *Relations*, 90–1; see also Scotus, *Ord.* 2. 1. 4–5, n. 239 (Vatican edn., vii. 119);
Ord. 4. 12. 1, n. 8 (Wadding edn., viii. 716).   [43] Henninger, *Relations*, 92.

the same as its foundation. This inherence of inherence is of this type, since it is a contradiction for the inherence of whiteness in a surface to be actual, and yet not actually inhere, or for it not to have the inherence.[44]

Accepting (11) leads, however, to a rather odd anomaly, which Scotus does not seem to have spotted. The anomaly arises in Scotus's account of what it is to be a unity₃. On (11), it is a necessary property of a relation that it be united to a subject. (11) entails

> (12) It is a necessary property of a relation R that it is a part of a whole including at least R and its foundation.

But this whole cannot be a unity₃, since it fails to satisfy the requirement in (I):

> (I) For every whole w and its parts p, q, . . . and n, w is a unity₃ only if being parts of w are non-essential features of p, q, . . . and n.

By the same token, no unity₃ can include the inherence relations which, on (I*) distinguish a unity₃ from a unity₁ (i.e. an aggregate). But the whole including both the parts of a unity₃ and their inherence relations will not count as some type of unity₄, since it includes items which inhere in a subject, and none of the parts of a unity₄ inhere in any other item. There is nothing contradictory about Scotus's account here, although he should add a further division to his classification of the types of unity given in Chapter 1: namely, a unity which includes both unity₃ and the inherence relations of the accidents in their subject. But it is surely odd that a unity₃ cannot include just those parts whose presence is necessary to distinguish it from an aggregate. This seems to me to be a further argument in favour of the implausibility of (I) and (I*).

4. INTRINSIC AND EXTRINSIC RELATIONS

As I have noted, Scotus holds that properties belonging to the last seven of Aristotle's categories (relation, state, place, time, position, action, passion) are *relational* properties. But he believes that there is an important difference between properties belonging properly to the category of relation and properties belonging to the remaining six 'relational' categories. Properties belonging to the category of relation

---

[44] Scotus, *Ord.* 4. 12. 1, n. 17 (Wadding edn., viii. 720); *idem, Quod.* 3, nn. 15–16 (Wadding edn., xii. 81–2; Alluntis and Wolter, 73–4 nn. 3. 46–3. 47).

are classified as *intrinsic* relations; properties belonging to the remaining six relational categories are classified as *extrinsic* relations.[45] Adams summarizes the distinction as follows:

A relation is said to be intrinsic, if it is logically possible for the extremes not to exist and the relation and/or its co-relation not to obtain. But a relation is extrinsic, if it is logically possible for the extremes to exist and the relation and its co-relation not to obtain.[46]

As we have seen, Scotus holds that the existence of the *relata* is necessary for the existence of their relation. So the characteristic feature of an intrinsic relation is that the *relata* are necessary and sufficient for the existence of their relation. One of Scotus's favourite examples of such a relation is the property of similarity. It is impossible for two white things to exist and for them not to be similar. An extrinsic relation, on the other hand, is one for which the existence of the *relata* is a necessary but not sufficient condition. As Henninger puts it:

The relation does not necessarily arise given the relata and their foundations, but an additional extrinsic factor is required. For example, the existence of the agent and the patient and the foundations, i.e. the active and passive potencies, though necessary is not sufficient for an action and passion. In addition, some extrinsic factor is necessary, e.g. volition in a free agent, the lack of impeding factors, or spatial proximity.[47]

In subsequent chapters, I discuss in detail the extrinsic relations of

[45] Scotus, *Ord.* 3. 1. 1, n. 15 (Wadding edn., vii. 23), *Ord.* 4. 6. 10, nn. 3–4 (Wadding edn., viii. 351–2); *Ord.* 4. 13. 1, nn. 9–11 (Wadding edn., viii. 793).
[46] Marilyn McCord Adams, *William Ockham*, Publications in Medieval Studies, 26 (2 vols., Notre Dame, Ind.: University of Notre Dame Press, 1987), i. 217. Scotus draws just this distinction in the texts cited in the previous note.
[47] Henninger, *Relations*, 105. When outlining the criteria that must be satisfied by a real relation—i.e. an entity in the category of relation—Scotus includes that 'such a relation itself should follow from the nature of the extremes without the operation of another power comparing one extreme to the other': *Ord.* 1. 31. un., n. 6 (Vatican edn., vi. 204). Categorical relations are thus necessarily *intrinsic* relations. Scotus's distinction between intrinsic and extrinsic relations seems to me both reasonable and sensibly drawn. Adams has argued, however, to the contrary: 'It is true *de dicto* that it is logically impossible for two white things to exist and not be similar, and this fact makes it plausible to identify similarity as an intrinsic relation. But it is not true *de re* that it is logically impossible for two white things to exist and not be similar, since it is logically possible for one of them to be white while the other is black. It is the *de dicto* impossibility that Scotus and Ockham relied on in classifying relations as extrinsic or intrinsic. But this criterion could be trivial unless some restriction is put on the sort of descriptions that occur in the *dictum*, since it is logically impossible *de dicto* for any two things related by R-ness not to be related by R-ness' (Adams, *William Ockham*, i. 217 n. 5). But something has gone wrong here. Clearly, *x*'s being related to *y* by R-ness and *x*'s

place and time. But it should be clear that the relations between matter and form and the inherence of non-relational accidents also count as extrinsic relations.[48] Scotus's arguments for the separability of matter, form, and non-relational accidents all entail that the existence of the *relata* fails to be sufficient for the existence of their relations; and therefore that the relations are extrinsic. Scotus holds that any extrinsic relation belongs to one of the last six categories. He does not explicitly discuss which category the relations between form and matter belong to. But he does discuss the correct categorization of relations of inherence. He does not come to a firm conclusion about this. But he narrows the choice of correct category down to two: inherence is an instance either of action or of passion. If inherence is an instance of passion, then passion properly picks out the fact that the subject passively receives its accident; if inherence is an instance of action, then action properly picks out the fact that an accident actively informs its subject.[49] Scotus could plausibly claim that relational properties inhere in both terms in the relation—that is, the accident and its subject—and hence that the correct categorization of the accident's relation would be action, and the correct categorization of the subject's relation would be passion. Presumably, Scotus would want to categorize the relations between form and matter in the same way.[50]

---

not being so related are not *compossible*. But this does not entail that all non-transcendental relations are *intrinsic*. As Scotus describes the distinction, it is best captured as follows:

For every x and every y, if x is F, y is G, x is categorically related to y by R, and F and G are the foundations for R, then R is intrinsic if and only if it is not possible that x is F, y is G and x is not related to y by R,

and

For every x and every y, if x is F, y is G, x is categorically related to y by R, and F and G are the foundations for R, then R is extrinsic if and only if it is possible that x is F, y is G and x is not related to y by R.

And this way of putting the distinction does not seem to be open to Adams's objection, since it does not entail the compossibility of x's both being related to y and not being related to y.

[48] For the relation between matter and form, see Scotus, *Ord.* 3. 1. 1, n. 14 (Wadding edn., vii. 23). For the inherence of accidents, see ibid. 4. 12. 1, n. 6 (Wadding edn., viii. 711). [49] Ibid. 4. 12. 1, n. 6 (Wadding edn., viii. 711).

[50] As we saw above, Scotus holds that the inherence relations of relational properties are identical with their properties. As such, I take it that they fail to count as categorical relations at all, since they satisfy instead the requirements for transcendental relations. So Scotus need not give an account of the correct categorization of such inherence relations.

I do not find Scotus's arguments in favour of

(1) An accident is an individual item

convincing. On the other hand, there may be good metaphysical reasons for wanting to claim that existing accidents are individual items (and not, say, *abstracta*). After all, it seems at least prima facie plausible to claim that the redness of a substance can survive the demise of its substance; and it is not obvious that an abstract property could do this.[51]

If Scotus is right, that accidents are individuals, then we might want to ask about their individuation. If we claim that accidents are individuals on the grounds that they can survive the demise of their substances, then we should probably claim that they are individuated independently of their substances. This does not entail, of course, Scotus's stronger claim that absolute accidents can exist without any substance whatsoever. Scotus's account of accidental unity is interesting, not least because it lays bare an assumption—namely, (I)—which has to be made by anyone who accepts that accidents can survive the demise of their substances. Equally, Scotus seems to have a principled way of drawing the distinction between unity$_3$ and unity$_4$. On the other hand, his distinction between unity$_1$ and unity$_3$ in terms of the presence or absence of inherence relations is convincing only for someone who holds that at least some of a substance's properties are 'cemented' to their substance by means of inherence relations—a claim which I would judge not to be very popular today.

---

[51] For a discussion of some of these issues, see Christopher Hughes, *On a Complex Theory of a Simple God: An Investigation in Aquinas' Philosophical Theology*, Cornell Studies in the Philosophy of Religion (Ithaca, NY, and London: Cornell University Press, 1989), 10–20. Hughes argues that there is no need to posit individualized properties.

7
Quantity and Continuity

1. QUANTITY AND EXTENSION

In the *Categories*, Aristotle includes number, speech, extension, time, and position under the general classification of quantity.[1] Here I am concerned merely with *extension* and *position* (the layout of parts in an extended whole). Scotus distinguishes position in this sense from the position which is a separate Aristotelian category (the relation between the parts of a body and the parts of its place). I deal with this latter sort of position in Chapter 11. In Chapters 12 and 13 I look at time.

The most noteworthy feature of Aristotle's list is the absence of *mass*, perhaps the first property we would be inclined to think of when considering a thing's quantity. Much the same absence exists in Scotus's thoughts on quantity. (I shall examine an inchoate account of mass, which I believe we can find in Scotus's thought, in Chapter 9. Crucially, as we shall see, Scotus does not seem to think that this mass is properly an instance of categorical quantity.) In this chapter, my aim is to explicate how Scotus conceives of a body's extension.

A body's extension is closely connected with the space that the body occupies. Indeed, we could plausibly identify extension of a body with the extension of the space occupied by the body. According to Scotus, however, such an identification would be mistaken. The extension of a body pertains to the category of *quantity*, whereas the relation of the body to the space it occupies pertains to the category of *place*. And, as we have seen, Scotus is adamant that to interpret one category in terms of another is mistaken. (I discuss Scotus's account of place in Chapter 11.)

Extension, according to Scotus, entails an order of parts in a whole, such that one part exists 'outside' other parts:

---

[1] See Arist. *Cat.* 6 (4^b22–5).

Part outside part . . . is required for the position which is a difference of quantity, if 'outside' refers just to the parts of the body.[2]

It is not easy to understand how something could be a *quantum* with dimensions unless we can designate, in the whole, an order of this part to that part according to quantity or position between the two.[3]

Crucially, Scotus argues that 'part outside part' in turn entails Aristotle's standard definition of quantity:

'Quantum' means that which is divisible into two or more constituent parts, each of which is by nature a 'one' and a 'this'.[4]

'Part outside part' thus entails *divisibility*. Given this, it is easy to see that there will be (at least) no *conceptual* blocks to the potentially infinite divisibility of a quantum. However small a quantum we have, we can always divide it further. Dividing—identifying points on a continuum, or partitioning the continuum into segments—is on this view a process which can be continued infinitely. According to Aristotle, however, it is not a process which can be completed. A quantum is *potentially*, not actually, infinitely divisible.[5] Part of Aristotle's motivation for this view lies in his claim (which I will discuss briefly below) that it is impossible for anything to be *composed of* unextended points. Underlying this claim are two different intuitions, either one of which would be sufficient to show that it is not possible for a quantum to be composed of unextended points. The first is Aristotle's claim that a set of unextended points would itself be unextended.[6] The second is his claim, which I discuss in detail below, that it is not possible for points to be continuous with each other. Scotus accepts both of these intuitions,[7] and, like Aristotle, therefore accepts that a quantum is potentially, but not actually, infinitely divisible. When I refer below to

---

[2] Scotus, *Ord.* 4. 10. 1, n. 17 (Wadding edn., viii. 506).

[3] Ibid. n. 14 (Wadding edn., viii. 505); see ibid. 2. 2. 2. 5, n. 343 (Vatican edn., vii. 304–5).

[4] Arist. *Metaph.* 5. 13 (1020^{a}7–8); see Scotus, *Ord.* 2. 2. 2. 5, n. 342 (Vatican edn., vii. 304); 2. 3. 1. 4, n. 72 (Vatican edn., vii. 424; Spade, 75); for the entailment see ibid. 2. 2. 2. 5, n. 343 (Vatican edn., vii. 304–5). Scotus holds that different quantities are *specifically different* from each other: they are different sorts of thing (see ibid. 2. 3. 1. 4, n. 107 (Vatican edn., vii. 445)). As far as I can see, not much turns on this claim; though see Ch. 10 n. 2 for a possible difficulty.   [5] Arist. *Ph.* 3. 7 (207^{b}12–13).

[6] Arist. *Gen. corr.* 1. 2 (316^{a}30–5); for a discussion of this passage, see Michael J. White, *The Continuous and the Discrete: Ancient Physical Theories from a Contemporary Perspective* (Oxford: Clarendon Press, 1992), 12–14.

[7] For the first, see Scotus, *Ord.* 2. 2. 2. 5, nn. 319, 343 (Vatican edn., vii. 292, 304–5). For the second, see below.

infinite divisibility, I mean to pick out this Aristotelian sense: *potentially* infinite divisibility. Equally, on this view, a quantum contains *potentially* infinitely many points or indivisibles; it does not contain them *actually*.[8] In the next section of this chapter, I give Scotus's attempts to show that the Aristotelian account is correct.

While it is clear that, on this account, there can be no *conceptual* blocks to infinite divisibility, there could be *physical* blocks to divisibility. For example, a quantum could be composed of extended atoms which cannot for physical reasons be further divided.[9] In the third section of this chapter, I will consider Scotus's objections to the position that there are physical (though not conceptual) blocks to infinite divisibility. In the fourth section, I consider Scotus's position regarding the surfaces and boundaries of quanta.

2. EXTENSION AND ATOMISM

Scotus is fiercely opposed to any sort of atomism. For reasons already outlined, an indivisible on Scotus's standard understanding is a geometrical *point*, lacking any extension at all. An indivisible, on this understanding, has zero size, or zero extension. Scotus spends some time considering the arguments of an opponent who believes that quanta are composed of such indivisibles. Both Scotus and his opponent suppose that any such putative quantum would have to be composed of indivisibles along with *gaps*. Since the indivisibles have zero extension, the gaps are required to allow the indivisibles to 'spread out' to form a quantum. So, on this view, a quantum would be composed of *discrete* (i.e. discontinuous) indivisibles. The basic structure of the argument of Scotus's opponent runs as follows. Accepting

(1) If *x* is a quantum, then *x* is composed of indivisibles,

[8] See Arist. *Ph.* 3. 6 (206^{b}17–20); *idem*, *Gen. corr.*. 1. 2 (316^{a}10–317^{a}12). For a discussion of Aristotle's potential infinite, see Richard Sorabji, *Time, Creation and the Continuum: Theories in Antiquity and the Early Middle Ages*, (London: Duckworth, 1983), 210–13. In Scotus's terminology, we would want to claim that the points contained potentially in a continuum exhibit *objective* potentiality: they do not (but can) exist.

[9] By 'physical blocks to divisibility', I mean to refer to the properties of atoms which are such that, given the physical constitution of the actual world, there is no process which could be used to divide them; not to atoms which could not be divided by any active power at all.

and

(2) If x is composed of indivisibles, then it is not the case that x is a continuum,

Scotus's opponent infers

(3) If x is a quantum, then it is not the case that x is a continuum.[10]

Scotus, as I have noted, accepts (2), and argues from its contrapositive

(2^*) If x is a continuum, then it is not the case that x is composed of indivisibles,

coupled with

(4) If x is a quantum, then x is a continuum,

to infer

(5) If x is a quantum, then it is not the case that x is composed of indivisibles.

Before I look at these two arguments in detail, I want to explore further some of the reasons for accepting (2) and (2^*), which both Scotus and his opponent are happy to affirm. The reasons behind (2) and (2^*) are Aristotelian, and they are cited by Scotus.[11] Aristotle argues for (2^*) by showing that it is impossible for two points to be in any sense next to each other. He considers three possible ways in which two points could be next to each other. They could be (i) continuous, (ii) in contact, (iii) in succession.

(i) According to Aristotle, two items are *continuous* if and only if their edges 'are one'.[12] As Aristotle notes, points have no parts, and *a*

---

[10] Scotus, *Ord.* 2. 2. 2. 5, nn. 286–8 (Vatican edn., vii. 279). The argument is designed to show that *motion* cannot be continuous. But, as Scotus discusses the position and his response to it, it becomes clear that the argument would be equally applicable to any extended magnitude: see in particular ibid. n. 317 (Vatican edn., vii. 291). For reasons which I shall make clear below, (1) and (2) are to be understood as referring to a *finite* number of indivisibles.

[11] In ibid. n. 319 (Vatican edn., vii. 292), Scotus cites Aristotle's arguments to support (4). But in n. 287 (Vatican edn., vii. 279), he uses them to support (2), and in *Lect.* 2. 2. 2. 5–6, n. 348 (Vatican edn., xviii. 205) he sees that they support (2^*) (see also ibid. n. 261 (Vatican edn., xviii. 179)). Scotus has his own arguments, which I shall consider in a moment, in favour of (4). As we shall see, it is possible to see the relevant Aristotelian discussion as supporting both (2^*) and (4). This fact perhaps explains Scotus's vacillation. But Scotus's argument in the *Ordinatio* requires support for (2^*), and Aristotle's discussion would supply the relevant support.

[12] Arist. *Ph.* 6. 1 (231^{a}22); see also 5. 3 (227^{a}10–17).

fortiori no edges. So, on this Aristotelian definition of 'continuous', things with no edges cannot be continuous.[13]

(ii) Continuity is a subset of being in contact:

One thing can be in contact with another only if whole is in contact with whole or part with part or part with whole. But since indivisibles have no parts, they must be in contact with one another as whole with whole. And if they are in contact with one another as whole with whole, they will not be continuous: for that which is continuous has distinct parts, and these parts into which it is divisible are different in this way, i.e. spatially separate.[14]

The idea is that two points touching 'in their entirety' would be in exactly the same position as each other, and hence, as Scotus points out, would not constitute a magnitude at all.[15]

(iii) Contact is itself a subset of being *in succession*. Two items are in succession if and only if there is 'nothing of their own sort between them'.[16] Since two points cannot be in contact, it is possible for them to be in succession only if there is something of a different sort between them. But Aristotle reasons that any such thing would itself be infinitely divisible—and hence a continuum.[17] (It is not clear how successful we can regard this third step in Aristotle's argument. Perhaps Aristotle is relying on an infinite regress argument here, such that sooner or later in the process of singling out points in succession, we would have to identify two points with a (non-atomic) continuum between them.) The argument against two points being in succession could be used to support (4). But the remaining two arguments, against continuous or contiguous points, clearly support (2) and (2*): a quantum could be composed of points with *gaps* between them, but not of continuous or contiguous points.

Scotus and his opponent, however, disagree about (1) and (4). Scotus defends his position by showing, first, that his opponent's argument for (1) fails, and secondly that there are good reasons for accepting (4). Scotus's opponent defends (1) as follows. Accepting

(A) For every quantum *q* and every point *p* on *q*, it is possible that *q* is divided at *p*

---

[13] Ibid. 6. 1 (231[a]26–9).   [14] Ibid. (231[b]1–6).

[15] Scotus, *Ord.* 2. 2. 2. 5, n. 319 (Vatican edn., vii. 292).

[16] Arist. *Ph.* 5. 3 (227[a]1); see also 6. 1 (231[b]8–9).

[17] Ibid. 6. 1 (231[b]13–16). For an excellent discussion of the whole set of texts, see White, *Continuous and the Discrete*, 28–31.

(i.e. a quantum is divisible at any point), Scotus's opponent infers

(6) For every quantum q, it is possible that, for every point p on q, q is divided at p

(i.e. a quantum is divisible at every point). But

(B) For every quantum q, if it is possible that, for every point p on q, q is divided at p, then q is composed of points

(i.e. a quantum which is divisible at every point is composed of points). (6) and (B) entail (1). Scotus does not offer, on his opponent's behalf, any argument for (B), although, as we shall see below, Scotus is happy to accept a principle closely related to (B). Scotus's opponent attempts to justify his inference from (A) to (6) by appealing to the (clearly true) Aristotelian claim that what is impossible 'in the process of becoming' (*in fieri*) is impossible 'in the state of having become' (*in facto esse*).[18] If, for example, it is impossible for me to write a scholarly book on Mozart's piano concertos, then it is evidently—even if regrettably—impossible for me to be in a state of having written such a book.

Although Scotus does not discuss this Aristotelian claim, it is evidently of little help in buttressing an inference from (A) to (6). Equally, as Scotus is quick to point out, the inference from (A) to (6) involves an obvious fallacy in scope: 'Singular propositions concerning the possible, taken absolutely, do not entail a universal proposition concerning the possible.'[19]

Having shown that his opponent offers no good reasons for accepting (1), Scotus attempts to defend (4). He does this by invoking two geometrical arguments, the second one of which he borrowed from Roger Bacon.[20] The point of both these arguments is that denying (4)

---

[18] Scotus, *Ord.* 2. 2. 2. 5, n. 288 (Vatican edn., vii. 279–80). The reference is to Arist. *Ph.* 6. 6 (237^b19–20); see also *idem, Metaph.* 3. 4 (999^b11); *idem, Gen. corr.* 2. 11 (337^b14–25).

[19] Scotus, *Ord.* 2. 2. 2. 5, n. 366 (Vatican edn., vii. 316); for Scotus's whole argument, see nn. 362–75 (Vatican edn., vii. 314–21)). I have expressed (A) and (6) in a way that makes the fallacy obvious. It is just the same mistake as Scotus makes in his attempt to show that matter can exist without form, and that accidents can exist without their subjects. The inference from (A) to (6) is perhaps found in an opponent of Aristotle's: see Arist. *Gen. corr.* 1. 2 (317^a4–5) and the discussion in William Charlton, 'Aristotle's Potential Infinites', in Lindsay Judson (ed.), *Aristotle's Physics: A Collection of Essays*, (Oxford: Clarendon Press, 1991), 129–49, pp. 135–6. Aquinas argues similarly when commenting on this Aristotelian passage: see *In Gen. corr.* 1. 5, n. 41 (ed. Raymundus M. Spiazzi (Rome and Turin: Marietti, 1952), 340^b), and the proposed correction in Scotus, *Ord.* 2. 2. 2. 5, n. 356 (Vatican edn., vii. 312–13).

[20] For the argument, see Roger Bacon, *Op. Maius*, 4. 9 (ed. John Henry Bridges (3 vols., London, Edinburgh and Oxford: Williams and Norgate, 1900), i. 151–2). The

will lead to absurd results. On the proposed scenario, we are to suppose that a quantum is composed of a finite number of discrete (i.e. discontinuous) *unextended* points.[21] (I will set out my reasons for holding the finitude of these points on the proposed theory in a moment.)

(i) The first argument runs as follows (see Figure 7.1). Suppose we have two concentric circles, and that we draw a straight line from the centre *o* to a point *a* on the outer circle *B*. If our circles are composed of discrete points, we should be able to draw another straight line from *o* to a point *b*, on *B*, next in succession to *a*. The two lines *oa* and *ob* will both bisect the inner circle *D*, either at different points or at the same point on *D*. In the former case, *B* and *D* will include the same number of points. But, as Scotus notes, 'It is impossible for two unequal things to be composed from parts equal in size and number.'[22]

argument also crops up in Ibn Mattawayh's report of an anti-atomistic argument by the Islamic theologian Naẓẓām (d. *c.*846): see Sorabji, *Time, Creation and the Continuum*, 391–3. The argument does not appear among the six mediated to the West via Ghazālī's *Metaphysics* (though it has some obvious similarities to the fourth of these), and it is not clear to me whether Bacon could have known of Naẓẓām's argument. (For the arguments in Ghazālī, *Metaphysics*, 1. 1. 2, see *Algazel's Metaphysics: A Medieval Translation*, ed. J. T. Muckle, St Michael's Medieval Series (Toronto: St Michael's College, 1933), 10–13; for the fourth argument, see ibid. 12.) On the connections between Ghazālī, Bacon, and Scotus, see J. M. M. H. Thijssen, 'Roger Bacon (1214–1292/97): A Neglected Source in the Medieval Continuum Debate', *Archives internationales d'histoire des sciences*, 34 (1984), 25–34, esp. 28–30.

[21] In *Lect.* 2. 2. 2. 5–6, nn. 355–8 (Vatican edn., xviii. 208–10) Scotus uses the arguments to support (5) directly. There are in fact some exegetical problems with the arguments as they appear in the *Ordinatio*. Scotus is professedly attempting to show that it is not possible for a quantum to be composed of discrete points. But when laying out his two geometrical proofs, which I discuss in a moment, he consistently talks of points *immediate* to each other. Harris takes this as indicating that Scotus supposes the points to be *contiguous* (and therefore not discrete): see C. R. S. Harris, *Duns Scotus* (2 vols., Oxford: Clarendon Press, 1927), ii. 128 n. 2. More recently, Thijssen has adopted the same interpretation: see 'Roger Bacon', 30. I am taking it that, in this context, Scotus means points with nothing (of the same kind?) in between: i.e. points which satisfy merely Aristotle's definition for being next in succession. I am aware that this is a forced reading of 'immediate'. On the other hand, I do not see how else the argument can support (4), which Scotus expressly invokes it to support. Compared with the earlier *Lectura* discussion, which has a slightly different structure, the *Ordinatio* discussion seems rather sloppily put together. Nevertheless, the overall structure of the *Ordinatio* account is clearer, and in any case represents Scotus's more mature thought on the issue. One possible alternative reading to mine would be to claim that Scotus simply identifies the continuous with the non-atomic. On this reading, putatively contiguous points would in fact turn out to be continuous. But this makes the geometrical arguments otiose, and in *Ord.* 2. 2. 2. 5, n. 318 (Vatican edn., vii. 291), Scotus claims that if, *per impossibile*, a quantum were composed of immediate indivisibles, it would be a continuum.

[22] Scotus, *Ord.* 2. 2. 2. 5, n. 321 (Vatican edn., vii. 293).

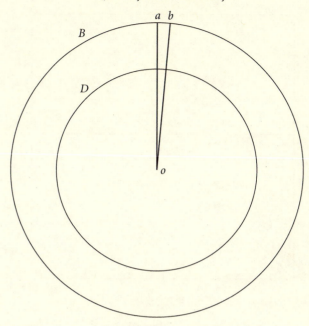

Figure 7.1

If, on the other hand, *oa* and *ob* bisect *D* at the same point, then at least one of *oa* and *ob* will fail to be a straight line, which is contrary to the supposition. So the claim that a quantum could be composed of discrete points is false.[23]

(ii) Scotus's second argument turns on the incommensurability of

---

[23] Ibid. nn. 320–6 (Vatican edn., vii. 292–5). This argument seems to be original. But one not dissimilar to it can be found in Avicenna, *Liber Primus Naturalium*, 3. 4: 'The existence of indivisible atoms entails that there can be no circle, . . . for in the case of the circle, the outer perimeter will be greater than the inner perimeter with which it is in contact. But what is in contact must equal that with which it is in contact': Avicenna, *al-Shifā' al-Tabī'iyyāt: al-Samā' al-Tabī'ī* ed. S. Zāyid (Cairo, [1985]), 190; trans. in Alnoor Dhanani, *The Physical Theory of Kalām: Atoms, Space, and Void in Basrian Mu'tazilī Cosmology*, Islamic Philosophy, Theology and Science: Texts and Studies, 14 (Leiden, New York, and Cologne: Brill, 1994), 172. I am grateful to Fritz Zimmermann for drawing my attention to this, and for providing translations from the Arabic of other relevant parts of Avicenna's *Liber Primus Naturalium*. The standard twelfth-century Latin translation breaks off at the beginning of the third *tractatus*. But there was a later medieval translation of the rest of the third *tractatus*. It is just possible, therefore, that this is the source of—or at least the inspiration for—Scotus's first geometrical argument.

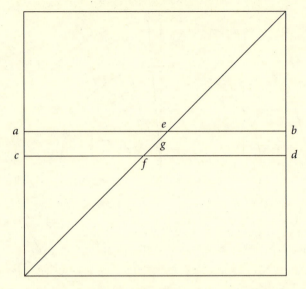

Figure 7.2

the diagonal and the side of a square (see Figure 7.2).[24] Suppose we draw a straight line, parallel to the base of a square, from a point *a* on one side of a square to a point *b* on the opposite side, and another line, parallel to *ab*, from a point *c* next in succession to *a*, to a point *d* next in succession to *b*. *ab* bisects the diagonal at point *e*, and *cd* bisects the diagonal at point *f*. Either *f* is next in succession to *e*, or there is another point *g* in between *e* and *f*. If the former, then there will be as many points on the diagonal as there are on the side, which is absurd. If the latter, then we could draw a line from *g*, parallel to *ab* and *cd*, in between *ab* and *cd*. In this case, *a* and *c* would fail to be adjacent, which is contrary to the supposition. So the claim that a quantum could be composed of discrete points is false.[25]

Scotus's two geometrical arguments for (4), given his opponent's claim that a quantum will be composed of a finite number of discrete unextended points, seem fair enough. What Scotus's arguments do not exclude, however, is the sort of position espoused by his eminent

---

[24] As Scotus points out, this incommensurability was known to Euclid: see *Ord.* 2. 2. 2. 5, n. 327 (Vatican edn., vii. 296). He claims that the whole of the tenth book of Euclid shows that, if lines were composed of points, there could be no lines of irrational length.
[25] Ibid. nn. 327–30 (Vatican edn., vii. 296–8).

Oxonian predecessor Robert Grosseteste. According to Grosseteste, a quantum is composed of an infinite number of unextended points.[26] Grosseteste appeals to the possible inequality of infinites to explain the empirically evident difference in size between different quanta.[27] Scotus was aware of the possibility of an appeal to unequal infinites, and in a passage which has not been noticed in the literature argues that such an appeal can legitimately be made by someone anxious to defend the eternity of the world.[28] Given this, Scotus cannot have believed his arguments to be effective against a quantum's being composed of an infinite number of points; from which we can infer that he did not attribute this view to his opponent here.[29] In any case, interpreting Scotus's arguments as relevant to an infinite number of points is excluded by (2) and (2*)—accepted by both sides in the debate—since it would presumably be difficult for anyone to suppose that a quantum could be composed of an infinite number of *discontinuous* points. (There would, in such a scenario, be an infinite number of extended gaps; so any such quantum would be infinite in extent.)

But how plausible are (2) and (2*)? Aristotle, as we have seen,

---

[26] Grosseteste, *De Luce* (ed. Clements Baeumker, Beiträge zur Geschichte der Philosophie des Mittelalters, Texte und Untersuchungen 9 (Münster: Aschendorff, 1912), 52; for a discussion, see conveniently Adam Wodeham, *Tractatus de Indivisibilibus: A Critical Edition with Introduction, Translation, and Textual Notes*, ed. Rega Wood, Synthese Historical Library, 31 (Dordrecht, Boston, and London: Kluwer, 1988), 5–6; also James McEvoy, *The Philosophy of Robert Grosseteste* (Oxford: Clarendon Press, 1982), 153–4, 175.

[27] Grosseteste, *De Luce*, 52–3.

[28] Scotus, *Ord.* 2. 1. 3, n. 171 (Vatican edn., vii. 87). The Vatican editors notice a similar view taken by Thomas Sutton, *Qu. Ord.* 29 (Merton College, Oxford, MS 138, fo. 324ra). Doubtless the arguments were well known after Grosseteste, at least in Oxford.

[29] A. W. Moore therefore wrongly understands Scotus's arguments to be opposed to the possibility of a quantum's being composed of an infinite number of points: see his *The Infinite*, The Problems of Philosophy. Their Past and their Present (London: Routledge, 1990), 50. It is not clear, in fact, who Scotus's opponent is. According to John Murdoch, the only fourteenth-century thinker to hold that a quantum could be composed of a finite number of indivisibles was Walter Chatton: see John E. Murdoch, 'Infinity and Continuity', in Norman Kretzmann, Anthony Kenny, and Jan Pinborg (eds.), *The Cambridge History of Later Medieval Philosophy* (Cambridge: Cambridge University Press, 1982), 564–91, p. 576 n. 36. On Chatton, see more particularly J. E. Murdoch and E. Synan, 'Two Questions on the Continuum: Walter Chatton (?), O.F.M. and Adam Wodeham, O.F.M.', *Franciscan Studies*, 26 (1966), 212–88; for a continuum's being composed of a finite number of points, see nn. 63–5 of the Chatton(?) question edited by Murdoch and Synan (ibid. 248–9). Chatton was not active in theological and philosophical debate until the 1320s. So unless Scotus's opponent is a straw man, there must have been an earlier Oxonian defender of the sort of view later taken by Chatton.

supposes that two items are continuous only if there is nothing between them. This supports his claim that two indivisibles cannot be continuous. But modern conceptions of continuity are rather different from this, and inconsistent with it. On the modern account, if x is a continuum, then between any two points on x there is always a third.[30] On this view, a continuum is composed of an infinite set of continuously ordered points. No two points are adjacent; but all the members of the set are nevertheless 'actually there'. The set is not potentially, but actually, infinite.[31] On this sort of view, (2) and (2*) are both false.

Given this account, we might be able to accept Scotus's opponent's

 (6) For every quantum q, it is possible that, for every point p on q, q is divided at p

(i.e. a quantum is divisible at every point)—though not, of course, the opponent's attempt to derive (6) from (A). Given that the relevant sorts of quanta are composed of an infinite set of points, we could replace (6) with a principle which (on the modern account) it entails,

 (6*) For every continuous quantum q composed of an actual infinity of points, it is possible that, for every point p on q, q is divided at p.

On the account I am now sketching, (6*) entails that a quantum can be divided into an infinite number of points. Scotus's opponent would probably not understand (6) to entail (6*), since the only sort of set of points he considers is a finite set of discrete points. But some of Scotus's near contemporaries understood (6) in a way related to the modern sort of understanding, and thus allowed that it entailed (6*). I have already noted Grosseteste in this regard. Henry of Harclay likewise held that a continuum was composed of an infinite number of indivisibles. Contrary to the modern conception, however, Henry held that the indivi-

---

[30] For a classic statement of this conception of continuity, see Richard Dedekind, *Essays on the Theory of Numbers* (Chicago: Open Court, 1901), 7–12. The account just offered is not sufficient for the modern conception of continuity, which includes irrational numbers as well as rational ones: i.e. a set of continuously ordered points will be such that both between any two points there is always a third, and there are no gaps in the series (e.g. corresponding to irrational numbers). A series satisfying merely the first of these conditions (viz. that between any two points there is always a third) is said to be not continuous but *dense*.

[31] This conception is paradoxical: the points are continuous even though none is adjacent to any other. But Aristotle's potential infinite here is just as paradoxical: the points on a continuum can be identified, but they do not exist—they are not 'actually there'—until we (or something) identify them.

sibles composing a continuum were immediately adjacent to each other.[32] Scotus's account seems to me to be much stronger than either Grosseteste's or Harclay's. All three thinkers would accept a basically Aristotelian conception of continuity (viz. two items are continuous only if there is nothing between them). And given this conception, we should, I think, be convinced by Aristotle's arguments for (2*), given above. Both (2*) and (2) exclude the possibility of a continuum's being composed of indivisibles, whether finite or infinite in number. And, as I noted above, it is difficult to see how a quantum could be composed of an infinite number of discontinuous indivisibles.[33]

One sort of atom which could easily enough satisfy Aristotle's continuity criterion would be an *extended* atom. Scotus in several places considers such atoms. But we need to make a distinction. One sort of extended atom could be indivisible into parts of the same sort, but divisible into parts of a different sort. Such atoms were usually labelled 'minima': minimal homoeomeric parts.[34] Scotus discusses such minima. I examine his account in the next section. But Scotus also uses the term 'minimum' for a different sort of item: a physical (extended) atom which is *conceptually* indivisible.[35] At one point he notes:

It is not intelligible that something should be a quantum unless it is out of parts; neither [is it intelligible] that it is out of parts unless a part is less than the whole; and thus it is not intelligible that something should be [both] a quantum [and] indivisible, such that there is nothing in it, less than it, existing in it.[36]

---

[32] On Harclay see John E. Murdoch, 'Henry of Harclay and the Infinite', in A. Maierù and A. Paravicini Bagliani (eds.), *Studi sul xiv secolo in memoria di Anneliese Maier*, Raccolta di Studi e Testi, 151 (Rome: Storia e Letteratura, 1981), 219–61. On the immediate adjacence of Harclay's infinite indivisibles, see p. 230; also Murdoch, 'Infinity and Continuity', 577 n. 39.

[33] Scotus's geometrical arguments are sufficient to show that a quantum will include points corresponding to irrational numbers as well as rational numbers. For example, if the line *ab* in Scotus's second argument cuts the side of the square exactly half-way along, it will cut the diagonal at $(n \times \sqrt{2})/2$, where n = the length of the side. And this point will correspond to an irrational number.

[34] On this sort of minimum, see Norma Emerton, *The Scientific Reinterpretation of Form* (Ithaca, NY: Cornell University Press, 1984), 76–105.

[35] We need to be careful with our terminology here. The idea with such minima is that they have *essential* properties which are such that it would be logically impossible for them to be divided. No active power could possibly divide them. This is why I suppose them to be conceptually indivisible. We can, of course, always *imagine* smaller items.

[36] Scotus, *Ord.* 2. 2. 2. 5, n. 343 (Vatican edn., vii. 304–5).

Scotus's point is that there could be no indivisible quantum such that the blocks on divisibility are *conceptual* (rather than, say, physical). After all, Aristotle's definition of 'quantum' entails that there are no conceptual blocks to infinite divisibility—irrespective of the possibility of physical blocks to divisibility.

Scotus provides a geometrical argument to show that, even if, *per impossibile*, there were (conceptually indivisible) extended indivisibles, no quantum could be composed of a set of such indivisibles. The argument is presumably intended to be effective both against a quantum's being composed of continuous extended indivisibles, and against its being composed of extended indivisibles. Suppose that every quantum is composed of such extended indivisibles (I shall label them 'Q-indivisibles').[37] On this supposition, a circle *C* is composed of Q-indivisibles (see Figure 7.3). Now, a Q-indivisible clearly has edges. So any Q-indivisible forming part of *C* has edges. We can thus draw a straight line from the centre (*o*) of *C* to one of the edges of a Q-indivisible *I* forming part of *C*: and we can likewise draw a straight line from *o* to the opposite edge of *I*. The problem which Scotus considers with this scenario is similar to one already encountered. Suppose there is a circle (*D*) smaller than *C* and concentric with it. Where do the two lines from *o* to *I* pass through *D*? There are two possibilities. Either the lines pass through *D* at the edges of one of the Q-indivisibles composing *D*, or not. In the former case, it will be evident that *D* is composed of the same

[37] Scotus's term for Q-indivisible is 'minimum'. Confusingly, he also uses the word 'minimum' in a further sense, to refer to unextended indivisibles. Pierre Duhem suggests that the Scotist distinction between indivisibles and minima is between 'discontinuous atoms separate from one another' and atoms 'continuously welded one to another' (Pierre Duhem, *Le Système du monde: histoire des doctrines cosmologiques de Platon à Copernique* (10 vols., Paris: Hermann, n.d.–1959), vii. 20–1, trans. in Duhem, *Medieval Cosmology: Theories of Infinity, Place, Time, Void, and the Plurality of Worlds*, ed. Roger Ariew (Chicago and London: University of Chicago Press, 1985), 18). This distinction does not seem to me to be correct. As I shall show below, Scotus's argument against the existence of Q-indivisibles is effective whether or not these Q-indivisibles are continuous or discrete. There are some good reasons for supposing that Scotus does not make a clear systematic distinction between indivisibles and minima at all. Crucially, in *Ord.* 2. 2. 2. 5, nn. 342–3 (Vatican edn., vii. 304–5), Scotus describes an indivisible as a minimum, and a minimum as an indivisible. Furthermore, in ibid. n. 291 (Vatican edn., vii. 280–1), Scotus's opponent gives an argument to show that a minimum cannot be part of a continuum. So Scotus's opponent, at least, does not understand a minimum in Duhem's way. But Scotus's opponent here is probably a straw man; so in default of any further evidence, there seems no reason to expect his understanding of the term 'minimum' to be different from Scotus's.

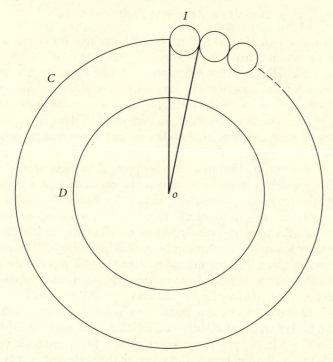

Figure 7.3

number of Q-indivisibles as *C*, and thus (given that the Q-indivisibles are the same size) that *C* and *D* are equal: which is contrary to the supposition. In the latter case, Scotus argues that the two lines would have to cut *D* at exactly the same point, and thus not be straight lines, which is again contrary to the supposition.[38] (To understand the second disjunct here, bear in mind that Scotus is supposing that any putative Q-indivisible is *conceptually* indivisible; and presumably that it is therefore impenetrable even by a geometrical line.)

This all seems reasonable enough. Scotus's arguments are, after all, geometrical: and it is difficult to see why there should be conceptual blocks on the divisibility of a geometrical magnitude. On the other hand, there may be *physical* blocks to infinite divisibility. It is to a discussion of Scotus's attempt to reject this possibility that I now turn.

---

[38] Scotus, *Ord.* 2. 2. 2. 5, n. 332 (Vatican edn., vii. 298–9).

3. ATOMISM AND NATURAL OBJECTS

One plausible objection to Scotus's programme here is that his arguments are relevant merely to geometrical objects, not to real physical
bodies. We might concede, with Scotus, that there are no conceptual
barriers to infinite divisibility, but nevertheless wish to hold that there
are *physical* barriers to infinite divisibility. Scotus was well aware of this
possible objection to his position, and attempts to show that considerations relevant to geometrical bodies are just as relevant to physical
bodies.

Of course, just to claim that there are physical barriers to indefinite
divisibility would not in itself allow us to conclude that a physical
object is *composed* of atoms, the barriers to whose divisibility are
purely *physical* (not conceptual). To get this conclusion, we would
have to add the premiss—closely related to (B) above, and seemingly
accepted by Scotus—that what can be divided into indivisibles must be
composed of them. This premiss gains some plausibility if it is the case
that the barriers to infinite division are all physical: there would be
physical particles *blocking* further division.

Giles of Rome argues that there are physical barriers to infinite
divisibility. He argues that there could be minimal parts in the first
sense outlined in the previous section: minimal homoeomeric parts,
such that their division fails to yield parts of the same sort as they are.
(Given this, Giles does not accept that bodies are composed of indivisibles.) He holds that magnitude might be considered in three ways: (i)
as a mathematical abstraction, (ii) as realized in an unspecified material
substance, (iii) as realized in a specified material substance. In the first
two ways, a magnitude is infinitely divisible. But in the third way—say,
the division of a cubic foot of water—a point is reached at which the
divided water ceases to be water and becomes something else. Giles
holds that we can divide a continuum infinitely according to its quantity, but that we cannot do this in so far as the continuum is a natural
entity (he gives the examples of water and air). The reason is that,
following an argument of Aristotle's against Anaxagoras's atomism, we
will eventually reach a smallest part of the natural object, such that if we
divide further, we will not have the same natural object, but something
different. On this view, it is not legitimate to argue from the infinite
divisibility of a line to the non-atomic nature of natural objects.[39]

---

[39] For the whole discussion, see Giles of Rome, *Quod* 4. 6 ((Venice, 1504), 66va–7ra).

Scotus argues strongly against this position. He agrees that if we divide a natural substance, we will eventually reach a point (not an indivisible point, but a *quantum*) at which the natural substance will be corrupted and become something else. But this, he claims, is not the result of any intrinsic property of the substance. It is, rather, the result of the way in which a physical object is related to its natural environment. And this relation, Scotus argues, is a *contingent* state of affairs.

Scotus's argument is difficult, and I am not sure that I understand all its stages. But before I assess Scotus's position, I will try to give at least some idea of the contours of his argument. Scotus attempts to argue that the presence of quantity is *sufficient* for infinite divisibility, such that none of the other intrinsic physical properties of a natural substance could block infinite divisibility.[40] Scotus tries three different strategies to make his point, none of which is really satisfactory.

(i) The first, if I understand it correctly, is clearly unsound:

To be divided into such extended integral parts of the same sort pertains to nothing except formally in virtue of quantity [and does] not [pertain] to a natural maximum any more than to a minimum. Therefore, since [divisibility] pertains to a minimum in virtue of this feature [viz. quantity], it pertains [to it] simply, just as [it does] to a maximum.[41]

This is evidently a mistake. I take it that the first clause of the last sentence of the quotation means that quantity is *sufficient* for divisibility. Scotus clearly supposes that this clause is equivalent to the claim made in the first sentence of the quotation. But this is not so. The first sentence makes quantity *necessary*, but not sufficient, for divisibility.

(ii) Scotus's second strategy is to claim that any proposed physical block to divisibility is in fact reducible to a conceptual block. He reasons that if a natural form is a (physical) block to infinite divisibility, then that form is sufficient to block the presence of quantity in the first place.[42] This is clearly question-begging. Whether or not there are any physical blocks which are *irreducible* to conceptual blocks is just what we need to find out.

(iii) Scotus's most successful strategy is to note that, in effect, the

---

[40] Put like this, it is clear that the sort of physical indivisibility which Scotus has in mind is just the sort I outlined above, according to which there is no *process* which a body could go through in order to be divided, not that there is no active power which could divide the body. Crucially, Scotus tries to show that such physical blocks on divisibility are contingent features of a body, not an intrinsic part of its structure.

[41] Scotus, *Ord.* 2. 2. 2. 5, n. 341 (Vatican edn., vii. 304).

[42] Ibid. n. 342 (Vatican edn., vii. 304).

defender of physical blocks to divisibility should be able to pin-point the physical features of a natural substance which prevent divisibility. As he puts it, 'What pertains naturally to quantity is not blocked by concurrent natural features.'[43] Scotus's point is that it is difficult (impossible?) to pin-point features which are sufficient to prevent infinite divisibility. Clearly, it is relatively easy for the defender of the claim that natural substances are composed of Q-indivisibles to appeal to physical blocks on infinite divisibility. But Scotus's opponent here, Giles of Rome, like Scotus, does not accept that natural substances are composed of Q-indivisibles. So, like Scotus, he accepts that (homoeomeric) substances are in every sense the same all over, composed throughout of matter and form. Given this, Scotus reasons, there can be no plausible structural feature of such substances which could possibly act as a physical block to infinite divisibility.[44] This seems correct. The defender of Q-indivisibles can perhaps find plausible physical blocks to infinite divisibility, but it is difficult to see how a convinced anti-atomist could.

According to Scotus, then, none of the essential properties of a substance is a sufficient physical block to infinite divisibility. Nevertheless, Scotus is happy to concede that it is a fact of the natural world that the four elements naturally corrupt each other, and hence that if you have just a little of one of them, it will be corrupted by a greater quantity of another of them. For example, a minute amount of water will automatically be corrupted into air by the air which surrounds it. But Scotus argues that this fact is explained by contingent *relational* properties of such a substance. To show this, Scotus proposes a thought-experiment. Imagine that there is nothing except water in the universe, and therefore that there is no other element which will naturally corrupt it. In this case we could carry on dividing the water indefinitely; and each smaller part would still be water, since there is no intrinsic or extrinsic reason preventing it from existing as an instance of water.[45] Thus, Scotus clearly does not regard a natural form as in any way preventing quantitative division.[46]

[43] Ibid. n. 344 (Vatican edn., vii. 305).   [44] Ibid. n. 347 (Vatican edn., vii. 306).
[45] Ibid. n. 349 (Vatican edn., vii. 308).
[46] Nevertheless, Scotus does believe that there is a smallest part of a natural thing in so far as that natural thing can be naturally *generated*. The reason for this is that a natural generator requires some determined quantity in the material substrate of generation. According to Scotus, however, a natural thing can be produced directly by God, and if this were to occur, God could generate a natural substance however small: see ibid. nn. 389, 391 (Vatican edn., vii. 325–7).

Scotus holds, then, that there are no physical blocks (essential to a natural substance) to infinite divisibility. His arguments are mixed, and even the least questionable of them (the third) seems overly optimistic. Whether or not there are physical blocks to infinite divisibility is in any case an empirical matter, not one which can be solved conceptually in the sort of manner attempted by Scotus.

4. INDIVISIBLES ARE THINGS

The majority view during the thirteenth and fourteenth centuries was that quanta are infinitely divisible, and hence that quanta are not composed of indivisibles. This view does not, of course, entail a theory which has been labelled 'non-entitism': that is, the theory that indivisibles do not exist at all. Some fourteenth-century divisibilists accepted non-entitism—Ockham, Adam Wodeham, and John Buridan are good examples.[47] But with the exception of Peter John Olivi,[48] no thirteenth-century thinker accepted it. Scotus simply defends the majority thirteenth-century view on this point. According to this view, the *limits* of a continuum are things really distinct from the continuum of which they are the limits. Now, all the medievals are agreed that the limits of things are indivisibles. So any one accepting the existence of limit entities accepts that at least some indivisibles count as things or entities. Furthermore, given that (as Scotus supposes) continua in the physical world reflect mathematical continua, it follows that indivisibles exist in the physical world. And this is exactly the view Scotus defends.

Generally, rejecting the non-entitist view makes it easier to provide solutions to a number of important limit-decision problems. We shall see some of these in later chapters.[49] Here, I want to deal with a more limited question: Why does Scotus accept the existence of limit

---

[47] For a good discussion of these three thinkers, drawing out consequences of their non-entitism, see Jack Zupko, 'Nominalism Meets Indivisibilism', *Medieval Philosophy and Theology*, 3 (1993), 158–85.

[48] See Olivi, *In Sent.* 2. 31 (ed. Bernardos Jansen, Biblioteca Franciscana Medii Aevi, 4–6 (3 vols., Quaracchi: Collegium S. Bonaventurae, 1922–6), i. 554, 557). Olivi claims to derive his view from Avicenna: see Avicenna, *Liber Primus Naturalium*, 2. 5 (Venice edn., i. 27vb); 2.9 (Venice edn., i. 31$^{ra–vb}$).

[49] For a discussion of a further instance, see Zupko, 'Nominalism Meets Indivisibilism', 164.

entities? Scotus's reasons have nothing to do with the appeal of the entitist position in solving limit-decision problems.

On the non-entitist position which Scotus rejects, it is not the case that the (unextended) limit of a continuum C is an item really distinct from C. It is, rather, merely the *property* of being unextended:

It is claimed that an indivisible is nothing other than the lack of a continuum, such that an instant is, formally, nothing other than the lack of continuous succession; and thus a point is the lack of length, and implies nothing positive.[50]

The idea seems to be both that the limit of a continuum is unextended, and that it fails to be an item distinct from the continuum of which it is the limit. The view, put thus, is rather difficult to understand. We can capture this by asking which thing instantiates the property of being a limit. Clearly, not the continuum; but there are no other possible contenders here. So the property of *being a limit* does not seem to be a property of anything. On the other hand, the non-entitist would want to deny that anything has the property of being a limit. As Ockham, who defends this view, was quick to point out, it is easy enough to gloss talk of indivisibles in terms of a body's being 'no further extended'.[51]

Scotus has a number of criticisms of this non-entitist position. One is that there are some properties which a limit, however understood, should be able to instantiate; and that a limit as understood on this non-entitist position cannot instantiate these properties. The examples which Scotus gives are colour and shape. For example, the colour of a substance inheres in its surfaces. On a non-entitist account of limits, however, there is no (real) surface for the colour to inhere in. The idea is that a surface is just a negative property—a privation—and colours cannot inhere in privations.[52] Scotus's opponent could plausibly reply, however, that such properties inhere in the *body*, without thereby

---

[50] Scotus, *Ord.* 2. 2. 2. 5, n. 376 (Vatican edn., vii. 321). Put in this way, it is not clear that Olivi is Scotus's opponent here. Olivi does not claim that a limit is a *negation*, merely that it is not an item distinct from the continuum which it bounds: see *In Sent.* 2. 31 ad 4 (i. 557).

[51] William of Ockham, *De Quant.* 1. 1 (*Op. Theol.*, ed. Juvenalis Lalor *et al.* (10 vols., St Bonaventure, NY: St Bonaventure University Press, 1967–86), x. 22); see Marilyn McCord Adams, *William Ockham*, Publications in Medieval Studies, 26 (2 vols., Notre Dame, Ill.: University of Notre Dame Press, 1987), i. 203. For an excellent discussion of Ockham's position, see Eleonore Stump, 'Theology and Physics in *De Sacramento Altaris*: Ockham's Theory of Indivisibles', in Norman Kretzmann (ed.), *Infinity and Continuity in Ancient and Medieval Thought* (Ithaca, NY, and London: Cornell University Press, 1982), 207–30.

[52] Scotus, *Ord.* 2. 2. 2. 5, n. 385 (Vatican edn., vii. 324).

committing himself to the inherence of such properties in a (real) surface.

The non-entitist position, as Scotus understands it, has some odd (though not necessarily false) consequences. The most interesting is that it seems to entail that all talk of limits is reducible to talk about *bodies*. Moore puts the point as follows:

> Points are, precisely, where lines do such things as stop. Lines themselves, for that matter, are where surfaces do such things as stop; and surfaces where bodies do such things as stop. . . . By extending this principle we might eventually be led to the somewhat Hegelian thought that only the whole is non-derivatively real.[53]

Scotus was aware of this sort of difficulty with non-entitism (though, unlike Moore, he was not happy with the consequence):

> The same would follow . . . that a line will be only the lack of width, and a surface will be only the lack of depth. And then there will be only one dimension, which is posited [to be] body.[54]

How we assess Scotus's worry here will of course depend wholly on whether we are happy with the consequence that all talk of limits (or dimensionality, in Scotus's account) is reducible to talk about bodies.[55]

One consequence of Scotus's position is that a whole quantum is not uniform throughout. While the quantum is made up of infinitely divisible parts, its limits are indivisible entities.[56] Scotus thus holds that a limit is an indivisible entity, really distinct from the continuum of which it is the limit. His opponent raises a series of objections to this view, of which I give two. Scotus does not explicitly reply to these objections.

(i) Scotus's position leaves it unclear exactly how a limit and a continuum could together instantiate any kind of unity. They cannot instantiate unity$_4$. Necessary for unity$_4$ is that one of the components be potential, and the other actual: and neither the limit nor the continuum is actual or potential with respect to the other. On the

---

[53] Moore, *Infinite*, 158.   [54] Scotus, *Ord.* 2. 2. 2. 5, n. 383 (Vatican edn., vii. 323).
[55] It may be thought that I have jumped too quickly from Scotus's dimensionality to talk about limits. But as Scotus understands dimensionality, it is clear that he regards it as reducible to talk about limits: 'These three dimensions are distinguished by imagining three lines, intersecting each other in the same point' (ibid.). The point of the whole passage, presumably, is that the three lines need to be analysable as *real* limits if our talk of dimension is to be possible at all.   [56] Ibid. n. 388 (Vatican edn., vii. 324–5).

other hand, they cannot instantiate unity$_3$, since it is an essential feature of a continuum that it has limits.[57]

(ii) Scotus's position entails that items can be naturally produced without undergoing a process of generation. Suppose we split a continuum into two parts. Each part is bounded by an indivisible at each end. The indivisibles thus produced will be individual items, and at least one of them cannot have existed prior to the split, since otherwise a continuum would have two adjacent indivisibles. The new indivisible will thus be produced without generation.[58] I am not sure how Scotus should reply to this. Since there is no new form, it is difficult to see how a new substance could be generated. In the next chapter, I consider Scotus's discussion of some related issues which might cast some light on at least the first of these objections.

Rejecting non-entitism makes explicit a question which all divisibilists need to face. Given that a limit is an indivisible (whether this is conceived entitatively or not), and given that it is impossible for an indivisible to be adjacent to any other item, will it not be the case that, necessarily, there is a *gap* between a limit and the continuum of which it is the limit? Scotus, of course, answers negatively, claiming that a continuum and its limit are *immediate* to each other (i.e. that there is no gap between them). He justifies his answer by trying to distinguish between two ways in which things could be immediate to each other:

'Immediate' can be understood in two ways. In one way, [it means] that there is no medium between something which is in itself a whole and another thing; in the other way, it means that something which is in itself a whole is immediately with or after another one.[59]

The first meaning merely entails that there is no gap between two items *a* and *b*. The second entails both that there is no gap between *a* and *b* and that the *whole* of *a* is immediate to the *whole* of *b*. (Scotus would presumably want to construe this second claim to allow that exactly one part of *a* could be immediate to exactly one part of *b*.) Scotus reasons that a limit and a continuum can be immediate in the first sense, since the first sense does not entail that any one part of the continuum is immediate to its limit. As Scotus puts it, 'It follows the indivisible part by part, to infinity.'[60] On the other hand, as Scotus notes, it is not possible for a limit and a continuum to be immediate in

---

[57] In formulating this objection, I have conflated two Scotist arguments: see ibid. nn. 377–8 (Vatican edn., vii. 321–2).   [58] Ibid. n. 378 (Vatican edn., vii. 322).
[59] Ibid. n. 410 (Vatican edn., vii. 337).   [60] Ibid.

the second sense, since no one part of the continuum is immediate to the limit. Scotus's claim that a limit and a continuum are immediate does not violate his Aristotelian claim that nothing can be immediately adjacent to an indivisible. The relevant sense of 'immediate' to catch the intuition that nothing can be immediately adjacent to an indivisible is the second one: nothing can be such that the whole of it (or any one part of it) is immediately adjacent to an indivisible. Scotus's claim that there is no gap between a limit and a continuum does not violate this stipulation.

Scotus is strongly opposed to any theory claiming that things could be composed of atoms. His arguments, like those of Aristotle, clearly aim to show that no genuine continuum can be composed of indivisibles (though it might, of course, *contain* indivisibles—for example, at its limits). Like Aristotle, Scotus is firmly convinced that his arguments apply to the real world. But he goes further than Aristotle in buttressing this second claim with an explicit discussion of the objection (found in Giles of Rome) that there might be physical blocks to divisibility. (Giles's argument would, of course, count as an argument in favour of (physical) atomism only for someone who accepted that anything which can be divided into indivisibles must be composed of them.) He also rejects the theory that continua could be composed of extended, conceptually indivisible items (the things I am labelling 'Q-indivisibles').

How we assess Scotus's arguments for the Aristotelian claim that it is not possible for a continuum to be composed of atoms will largely depend on how sympathetic we feel to the Aristotelian conception of the infinite as opposed to the modern set-theoretic one. On the modern view, Scotus's arguments are of course deficient. But we should not be too harsh on Scotus here. Given the Aristotelian claim that continuity entails immediate adjacence, it is difficult to see how Scotus could have avoided claiming that a continuum is (at best) *potentially* infinitely divisible. Nor is it clear that he should have done so; though this again depends on our intuitions about the infinite. Scotus's view certainly seems to me more appealing than its (slightly later) major rival: Henry of Harclay's claim that a continuum could be composed of an actually infinite number of points such that each point is immediately adjacent to another.

Whether or not we are convinced by Scotus's arguments against non-entitism will depend, rather, on some other metaphysical presuppositions we might have about the reducibility or irreducibility of a limit to a *body*. I do not see a way of deciding the issue here. On the other hand, as we shall see, Scotus's stance against non-entitism allows him to come to some principled answers to certain limit-decision problems. If we think that the ability to make principled decisions here is important, we might well favour Scotus's position over that of the non-entitists.

8

The Metaphysics of Continuity

1. INTRODUCTION

In previous chapters, we have considered various sorts of part–whole relationships: substantial, organic, accidental, and aggregative. In this chapter, I want to look at a further such relationship: the constitution of items—namely, continua—whose parts are distinguished *merely* by their extension. The basic question is: How should we most perspicaciously describe the unity of a continuum composed of homogeneous parts? (Scotus's Aristotelian (anti-atomistic) account of continuity in fact allows for genuine homogeneity. Any continuum on this account will be homogeneous.) Here, I am concerned not with continua which might count as processes, but merely with those continua which have all their parts *at once*.[1] Homoeomeric substances[2] are perhaps the most obvious example of the sort of continua I have in mind. A stone, for example, will count, on Scotus's anti-atomistic account of such substances, as such a continuum, as will a puddle of water. Scotus's term for the relevant kind of unity is 'unity of homogeneity'.[3] I label this sort

---

[1] I deal with the nature of time and motion in subsequent chapters. It might be thought that nothing (except perhaps God) has all its parts at once. But Scotus's point here is that substances, unlike processes, do not have *temporal* parts. The medievals' label for something lacking temporal parts is a 'permanent', and for something including temporal parts a 'successive'. Very few medievals thought that substances had temporal parts (for an example of one see the author of the Abelardian *Fragmentum Sangermanense* (in Peter Abelard, *Ouvrages inédits d'Abélard*, ed. V. Cousin (Paris: Imprimerie Royale, 1836), 514), discussed in Desmond Paul Henry, *That Most Subtle Question (Quaestio Subtilissima): The Metaphysical Bearing of Medieval and Contemporary Linguistic Disciplines* (Manchester and Dover, NH: Manchester University Press, 1984), 247–8). I look at the permanent–successive distinction in Ch. 13. Here I am interested in the metaphysics of a permanent continuum.

[2] i.e. individual substances divisible into parts of the same sort: see Arist. *Gen. corr.* 1. 1 (314^{a}18–20), 1. 10 (328^{a}10–12); *idem*, *Top.* 5. 5 (135^{a}20–^{b}6).

[3] Scotus, *Lect.* 1. 17. 2. 4, n. 226 (Vatican edn., xvii. 253). Curiously, the unity of homogeneity does not appear in Scotus's list of the different sorts of unity in *Ord.* 1. 2. 2. 1–4, n. 403 (Vatican edn., ii. 356–7). But Scotus does consider the issue in the *Ordinatio*:

of unity 'H-unity'. The parts of an H-unity are labelled by Scotus 'integral parts'.[4]

Scotus's account of homogeneity does not apply merely to homoeomeric substances. Chunks or amounts of matter are conceived of in this way, even if (as is, according to Scotus, logically possible) they are unextended. These 'amounts' of matter have some similarity to what we call 'mass'. (I examine this in the next chapter.) The quantity in virtue of which something is extended is homogeneous too. Scotus's account of the different degrees of a quality (different shades of blue, for example) involves seeing such degrees *quantitatively*. The unity of such-and-such a shade of blue, for example, composed of degrees of lesser intensity than itself, is analogous to the unity of a homogeneous whole. (I look at this issue in detail in Chapter 10.)

As we have seen, Scotus's account of the structure of continua is strongly divisibilistic or anti-atomistic. Excepting the limit entities of a continuum, it is not possible that even the simplest parts of a continuum are indivisible. Underlying this account of continuity is the intuition that a continuum is infinitely divisible, such that in principle any of its parts is really separable from any other of its parts. But Scotus, as we shall see, holds that we can plausibly regard a continuum as *one* object. Given this, Scotus clearly needs some account of how the various parts can unite to form any sort of whole. In the next section of this chapter, I try to spell out just what Scotus's account of this is. In the third section I examine some possible objections to Scotus's theory, and in a fourth section I look in a bit more detail at some of the contexts in which Scotus applies his account. In the fifth section I consider Scotus's discussion of a biological counter-instance to his account—the problem of nutrition. As we shall see, Scotus does not hold that his standard account of H-unity obtains in the case of living homoeomeric substances. In the final section, I discuss whether or not Scotus might try to apply his account too generally.

Unfortunately, Scotus's account of the matter in the *Ordinatio* is incomplete, and most of the important material is found either in the *Lectura* or in the *Reportatio Parisiensis*. Moreover, the account in the latter of these is by no means extended. This means, of course, that Scotus might later have wanted to change the account found in the

see *Ord.* 2. 3. 1. 4, n. 106 (Vatican edn., vii. 443–4; Spade, 85), and *Ord.* 4. 44. 1, which I discuss below.

[4] Scotus, *Ord.* 2. 3. 1. 4, n. 106 (Vatican edn., vii. 443–4; Spade, 85).

Lectura; as he notes there, '"Unity" is one of the most difficult words in philosophy',[5] and the *Lectura* discussion is not one of the easiest parts of the Scotist *corpus*.

2. CONTINUITY AND H-UNITY

An H-unity, as understood by Scotus, has some rather odd features. Some of these, as we shall see, are entailed by Scotus's Aristotelian account of continuity. But one such feature is not so entailed. Scotus is quite clear that the (homogeneous) integral parts of an H-unity cannot be analysed in terms of potentiality and actuality. No part of an H-unity is potential to another. But Scotus is adamant that an H-unity is *composed of* its parts. For example, suppose that we join together two magnitudes A and B. The resultant magnitude, according to Scotus, is *composed of* A and B, even though neither A nor B is potential to the other.[6] Scotus expressly notes that having parts exhibiting respectively S-potentiality and S-actuality[7] is not a necessary condition for composition:

For this reason the proposition which states universally that for everything composed of diverse things, one is potentiality and the other act, such that all the constituents of some whole are related to each other such that one is potentiality, and the other act, should be denied. This [proposition is] true only when the constituents are of a different sort [from each other], and not of the same sort.[8]

In the case of an H-unity, Scotus thinks of the parts as *all* actual.[9]

As we have seen, Scotus explains unity₃ and unity₄ by means of an analysis in terms of potentiality and actuality. I have indicated that such an analysis turns out to be more or less vacuous as an explanation of unity, and I have indicated that Scotus was aware of this. As Scotus sees, his account of H-unity as a whole composed of actualities is equally non-explanatory:

[A degree of the theological virtue of] charity is composed of its parts of the same sort, and one thing is made from them, not as from potentiality and act,

---

[5] Scotus, *Lect.* 1. 17. 2. 4, n. 238 (Vatican edn., xvii. 257).
[6] Ibid.; see also ibid. n. 230 (Vatican edn., xvii. 254).
[7] For this terminology, see Ch. 4.
[8] Scotus, *Lect.* 1. 17. 2. 4, n. 229 (Vatican edn., xvii. 254); *idem, Rep.* 1. 17. 6 (MS M, fo. 86ᵛ). [9] Scotus, *Lect.* 1. 17. 2. 4, n. 238 (Vatican edn., xvii. 257).

neither as from material parts, but as from accidental parts: and they make one thing from themselves. Whence we should not ask in virtue of what they make one thing, because they make one thing in themselves.[10]

Elsewhere, Scotus is seemingly a little less agnostic: 'When there is one actuality from parts, we should not ask how the whole is one, except as one form.'[11] But Scotus offers no further clarification of the mysterious 'except as one form', so I take it that Scotus holds that we cannot find features of the parts of a homogeneous whole which genuinely *explain* how the parts form an H-unity. In both the *Lectura* and the *Ordinatio*, Scotus speaks of the parts 'integrating' the whole.[12] Again, this seems to me to be intended as a non-explanatory description of the way in which its integral parts compose an H-unity.

Scotus explicitly distinguishes H-unity from both unity$_1$ and unity$_4$. What he has to say about unity$_3$ makes it clear how he would distinguish this from H-unity too, although Scotus does not discuss this distinction explicitly. As we saw in Chapter 6, it is a necessary feature of a unity$_3$ that it can be analysed in terms of potentiality and actuality. So no H-unity is a unity$_3$. And, as just noted, Scotus explicitly distinguishes H-unity from unity$_1$ and unity$_4$. Necessarily, no unity$_1$ is a composite of its parts. But, as Scotus notes, necessarily an H-unity is a composite. So an H-unity clearly fails to satisfy a necessary condition for unity$_1$.[13] Equally, Scotus expressly distinguishes H-unity from unity$_4$:

For this reason, although the parts [of a degree of the theological virtue of charity] remain when separated, and the whole charity does not remain, nevertheless it does not follow that there was something in the charity beyond those parts (just as water is composed of parts of water of the same kind, and it does not follow that the water is anything else beyond the separated parts of water).[14]

[10] Ibid. n. 221 (Vatican edn., xvii. 252).

[11] Ibid. n. 238 (Vatican edn., xvii. 257). In ibid. n. 223 (Vatican edn., xvii. 252) Scotus claims that, naturally, all discrete homogeneous wholes of a given kind will compose just one thing (see also here ibid. n. 214 (Vatican edn., xvii. 250); Scotus, *Rep.* 1. 17. 6 (MS M, fo. 86^v)). Physically, then, what requires explaining is division, not unity. He makes the point in response to a query about the explanation of H-unity. But the answer is insufficient. The sort of explanation that Scotus should be looking for is a *metaphysical* one, not a physical one. It may well be the case that, physically, homogeneous wholes have a natural tendency for unity with each other. But this does not explain what it is for the parts to be parts of an H-unity.

[12] Scotus, *Lect.* 1. 17. 2. 4, n. 238 (Vatican edn., xvii. 257); *idem*, *Ord.* 2. 2. 2. 5, n. 353 (Vatican edn., vii. 311).

[13] Scotus, *Lect.* 1. 17. 2. 4, n. 232 (Vatican edn., xvii. 255–6).

[14] Ibid. n. 238 (Vatican edn., xvii. 257).

The idea is that the parts of an H-unity are all the same sort of thing as the whole. (This is hardly surprising. An H-unity is homogeneous, such that definitionally it is the same sort of thing as its parts.) But, as I have argued in Chapter 5, Scotus's account of unity$_4$ entails that, necessarily, a unity$_4$ is different in kind from its parts.

The passage quoted might suggest that an H-unity is nothing over and above its parts. But Scotus clearly thinks that an H-unity is *numerically distinct* from its parts:

When a new [part of] charity comes, it does not remain as *this*, and another pre-existed which likewise does not remain as *this*, but [they remain] as parts of the [new] whole charity which they make [to be] one thing from themselves as formal parts.[15]

(This, of course, is wholly consistent with Scotus's claim that an H-unity is a composite whole.) So Scotus accepts

(A) If two homogeneous items x and y form an H-unity z, then z is numerically distinct from x, y, and any aggregate of x and y.

It might be thought here that I have generalized too quickly from Scotus's example, charity, to every H-unity. But Scotus also talks about homoeomeric substances in much the same way, so I take it that he intends his account to obtain for all homogeneous items.[16] Importantly, (A) is equivalent to the claim that the addition of a homogeneous item x to a homogeneous item y (where x and y are the same sort of thing) entails that the new whole formed thereby is numerically distinct from both x and y. For example, the addition of a drop of water to a puddle entails that there exists a new puddle which is a numerically distinct substance from the original puddle. (This account of things like puddles looks remarkably similar to Joseph Butler's claim that material objects like trees fail to persist through changes in their material composition. But, as we shall see in section 5 of this chapter, Scotus denies that this sort of account could be true of *living* things such as trees, though he is happy to accept it for inorganic homoeomeric substances like puddles.[17]) The claim that the addition of a drop of water to a puddle is sufficient for the existence of a new puddle

---

[15] Ibid; see also ibid. n. 234 (Vatican edn., xvii. 256).

[16] See ibid. n. 238 (Vatican edn., xvii. 257) and Scotus, *Ord.* 1. 17. 2. 1, n. 232 (Vatican edn., v. 251).

[17] See Joseph Butler, *The Analogy of Religion* (Oxford: Clarendon Press, 1874), first dissertation.

looks implausible to me, at least when applied to some sorts of homogeneous stuff. I will outline my reasons for this below, and I shall label the problem the 'identity problem'.

The passage also signals Scotus's commitment to a different principle

> (B) If two homogeneous items x and y form an H-unity z, z necessarily has x and y as parts

(i.e. it is an essential feature of z that it have x and y as parts). More generally:

> (B*) For every H-unity z and every set of homogeneous parts P, if z is P, then z is necessarily P.

Scotus offers explicit support for (B*) in an important passage:

'More' is an individual condition, not a signed one, like 'this', but vague, since there can exist the same grade which is not *this* [individual, but a different one], but not vice versa: this individual could not exist unless it were of this grade.[18]

(A), (B), and (B*) are of course consistent. (B*) entails (B), but (A) is independent of the other two. Scotus's account of the increases that can obtain in the case of homogeneous items entails all three principles, since the addition of two homogeneous items entails both that each item fails to retain its haecceity, and that any new item composed of them has its haecceity in virtue of having just those parts which compose it.

I shall discuss Scotus's acceptance of (A), (B), and (B*) and its desirability below. His motivation for accepting (A), (B), and (B*) lies in the claim (accepted by both Scotus and his opponent, Godfrey of Fontaines, as we shall see in the next chapter) that the end terms of a change must be *incompossible*. This means that it is not possible that the end terms of a change are identical; more precisely,

> (C)(i) It is not possible that the end terms of any increase are identical, and (ii) it is not possible that the end terms of any decrease are identical.

(A) is sufficient (though not of course necessary) for (Ci), and (B)

---

[18] Scotus, *Ord.* 1. 17. 2. 1, *textus interpolatus* (Vatican edn., v. 245, ll. 14–16). The passage is marked as being in Scotus's own hand. Note that Scotus uses the word 'vague' in a rather different sense from that in which I use it below.

likewise for (Cii). But they are not necessary, and we might think that a more economical way of guaranteeing incompossibility would be to allow that one item x, persisting over a change, could gain or lose parts. On this sort of picture, the fact that x gains or loses parts would be sufficient for the incompossibility of the end terms of the change: before the change, x has n (quantity of) parts; after the change, x has m (quantity of) parts, where 'having n parts' and 'having m parts' are incompossible properties.[19] On Scotus's account, (C) is guaranteed by claiming that a whole, x, which has n (quantity of) parts, is incompossible with another whole, y, which has m (quantity of) parts, where x and y are the end terms of a change.

Clearly, the parts of an H-unity will be related to the whole of which they are parts. The rather attenuated *Ordinatio* account makes this quite evident, speaking of a relation between the parts and their whole.[20] Scotus uses this claim to distinguish an H-unity from its parts. An H-unity is a homogeneous magnitude which additionally satisfies a merely privative (negative) condition: it *fails* to be related to any other homogenous magnitude as part to whole:

To be a distinct act adds to that absolute grade [of the theological virtue of charity]—as it remains—nothing except the privation [*praecisionem*] which is

---

[19] I shall later on suggest that we might think that the spatial and temporal boundaries of some homogeneous items are in fact fuzzy. Both my proposal here and Scotus's (A), (B), and (B*) would want to avoid this fuzziness. And *this* seems to be a reason for rejecting both proposals (Scotus's and mine). Scotus might find reasons for preferring his (A), (B), and (B*) to my proposal here by appealing to the fact that an H-unity does not seem to have any parts relevant for establishing identity other than its homogeneous ones. (On my proposal, the identity of an H-unity is determined *prior* to its having n or m number of parts.) My proposal as it stands is in fact less plausible than Scotus's. It is clearly the case that if we add or subtract *enough* parts, we get a new item. Unlike Scotus's position, my proposal cannot allow this. So it must be false.

[20] Scotus, *Ord.* 1. 17. 2. 1, n. 231 (Vatican edn., v. 251). Oddly, the *Lectura* account tends to blur this point. In this account, Scotus repeats several times that, although an H-unity is something over and above its homogeneous parts, there is nevertheless nothing in an H-unity which is not a homogeneous part: see e.g. Scotus, *Lect.* 1. 17. 2. 4, n. 234 (Vatican edn., xvii. 256); also n. 238 (Vatican edn., xvii. 257). On the other hand, when discussing unity$_4$ in the same passage, Scotus likewise claims that there is nothing in a unity$_4$ which is not either matter or form: ibid. nn. 232–4 (Vatican edn., xvii. 255–6). Since in ibid. 2. 1. 4–5, n. 192 (Vatican edn., xviii. 63), Scotus expressly claims that a unity$_4$ contains a relation in addition to its absolute parts, I take it that, in the book 1 discussion, Scotus intends us to understand 'parts' as 'absolute parts': there is no further absolute part in a unity$_4$ beyond its matter and form. So the passage cannot be taken as evidence that, in the *Lectura* discussion, Scotus intends us to understand that an H-unity does not contain relations between itself and its parts. Unfortunately, Scotus does not discuss the question in the *Reportatio*.

existence in another (as part in a whole), and thus to posit an end term [of an increase in homogeneous parts] is to posit [something] formally under the negation of a relation.[21]

So Scotus's account of H-unity commits him to the following principle:

> (D) A homogeneous item is an H-unity only if it fails to be a homo-
> geneous part of any homogeneous item.[22]

Clearly, on Scotus's account of H-unity, there is a sense in which the parts of an H-unity are really distinct from the whole of which they are parts. Scotus argues, however, that the parts do not themselves count as individuals. For a homogeneous item, being an H-unity is a necessary condition for being an individual. Furthermore, Scotus holds that the division of an H-unity into parts is sufficient for its division into items having their own haecceities.[23] So I take it that being an H-unity is sufficient for having a haecceity (which is in turn, of course, sufficient for being an individual). In the *Ordinatio* account, Scotus uses (D) to explain how a part can both exist and fail to count as an individual. He argues that a necessary condition for numerical discreteness (and presumably for non-repeatability) is failing to be part of an H-unity. Scotus distinguishes two relevant ways in which things can have existence: (i) they can have the general sort of existence which belongs to anything which has been the end term of a process of generation; (ii) they can have the sort of existence which belongs uniquely to discrete items. The integral parts of an H-unity satisfy the first, but not the second, of these descriptions.[24] We can put this differently by claiming that the integral parts of an H-unity satisfy the first description, and that they have objective

---

[21] Scotus, *Ord.* 1. 17. 2. 1, n. 231 (Vatican edn., v. 251); see also nn. 232–3 (Vatican edn., v. 251–2). The insight is Henry of Ghent's: 'Number or discrete quantity adds nothing to a continuum except for the notion [*rationem*] of a negation or a relation of the parts to each other': *Quod.* 7. 1 (ed. R. Macken *et al.*, Ancient and Medieval Philosophy, De Wulf-mansion centre, Series 2 (Leuven: Leuven University Press; Leiden: Brill, 1979–), xi. 10). In *Rep.* 1. 17. 3 (MS M, fo. 83ʳ), Scotus refers to this privation as a 'mode of being'.

[22] Given that all sorts of things, as we shall see, are homogeneous, I use the word 'item' as a suitable neutral term to cover all these cases. I mean it to refer here to whole discrete homogeneous continua, not the (potential) parts of such continua.

[23] Scotus, *Ord.* 2. 3. 1. 5–6, n. 199 (Vatican edn., vii. 489; Spade, 110); see also *Ord.* 2. 3. 1. 4, n. 106 (Vatican edn., vii. 443–4; Spade, 85).

[24] Ibid. 1. 17. 2. 1, nn. 232–3 (Vatican edn., v. 251–2); Scotus, *Rep.* 1. 17. 3 (MS M, fo. 83ʳ).

potentiality to the sort of existence which satisfies the second description. They can be (but are not) discrete individuals.[25]

This seems quite right: the parts of an H-unity exist, but since an H-unity is infinitely divisible (such that we can divide it up however we like), the parts count as discrete items only after the process of division. As Scotus points out elsewhere, it is possible for the parts of an H-unity to exist as discrete individuals.[26] And of course parts which are actually divided will satisfy the criterion set out in (D). This account entails, as Scotus points out, that being a discrete item is a *contingent* property of any given chunk of homogeneous stuff.[27] And we would have no non-arbitrary way of dividing up a genuinely homogeneous whole into different individuals.

Scotus's account of H-unity is nuanced. But it suffers from too little explanation: it could not really count as a *theory* of H-unity. Scotus does not, for example, show us how H-unity might be distinguished from *contact*.[28] Perhaps it would be difficult to achieve a principled distinction here without a fairly sophisticated account of chemical bonding. (A), (B), and (B*) look prima facie to be reasonable enough, though I will suggest that Scotus tries to apply them far too widely. In the next section I examine an objection to (D) which I consider to be fatal, and suggest a principle which should replace it.

3. PROBLEMS AND APORIAS

Scotus's account of H-unity, despite its intuitive appeal, is not free of problems. The most damaging runs something like this.[29] According to Scotus, failing to be part of a homogeneous item is necessary for H-unity. Now on Scotus's metaphysic such a privative property is not in any

---

[25] It is not clear to me whether this claim is consistent with Scotus's claim that an H-unity is *composed of* its integral parts. Perhaps the claim that an H-unity is composed of its integral parts is supposed to pick out only the way in which some H-unities are formed: a puddle, for example, is formed out of (= (loosely) composed of) the raindrops that fell into it.

[26] Scotus, *Ord.* 2. 2. 2. 5, n. 340 (Vatican edn., vii. 303); see also n. 346 (Vatican edn., vii. 306). In ibid. 2. 3. 1. 5–6, n. 198 (Vatican edn., vii. 489; Spade, 110), Scotus notes that a quantity contains its extended parts 'confusedly' ('confuse').

[27] Ibid. 1. 17. 2. 1, n. 233 (Vatican edn., v. 251).

[28] Scotus clearly sees that such a distinction can plausibly be made: see e.g. ibid. 4. 44. 1, n. 13 (Wadding edn., x. 113).

[29] I owe this objection to a similar one noticed in a rather different context by Alfred J. Freddoso: see his 'Human Nature, Potency, and the Incarnation', *Faith and Philosophy*, 3 (1986), 27–53.

sense a *thing* really distinct from its subject (or even a reality formally distinct from its subject). But, given that any homogeneous stuff satisfying the conditions for H-unity does so only *contingently*, will it not be the case that Scotus's account of H-unity violates Leibniz's law? (I shall take Leibniz's law to be the conjunction of the following two relatively uncontroversial principles: (i) if there is no property which *x* has and *y* lacks, or vice versa, then *x* and *y* are identical; and (ii) if *x* and *y* are identical, then there is no property which *x* has and *y* lacks, or vice versa.[30])

To see why Scotus's account of H-unity should violate Leibniz's law, consider the following. Suppose we have a discrete homogeneous magnitude *A*. *A* is a discrete homogeneous item, and therefore satisfies the privative condition set out in (D)—that of failing to be a homogeneous part of a homogeneous whole. We could appropriately name this individual 'Chip'. Since satisfying a privative condition, according to Scotus, adds no real entity to *A*, it is clear by Leibniz's law that *A* and Chip are identical. But, according to Scotus, *A* could become part of a new larger homogeneous whole *B*. On this scenario, according to Scotus, Chip would no longer exist, because *A* would now be a part of *B*, and therefore no longer a discrete individual. By Leibniz's law, if Chip no longer exists, neither does *A*, since Chip is identical with *A*. But Scotus's account entails that, on the proposed scenario, *A* exists (as part of *B*). So Scotus's account violates Leibniz's law.

The basic point of this objection is that there can be no two discrete items which are distinguished merely in virtue of *privative* contingent properties. Whether or not a sufficiently nuanced account of privative properties would be sufficient to rebut this objection head on is unclear to me, though I am fairly sure that Scotus's hypostatizing account of contingent properties does not contain the relevant metaphysical equipment. But at least prima facie the objection highlights a clear problem in Scotus's account of H-unity. Given that there can be no privative contingent properties without corresponding non-privative contingent properties, Scotus's claim that a privative contingent property is sufficient for the H-unity of a homogeneous item must be a mistake.[31] But

---

[30] The first of these principles is often referred to as 'the identity of indiscernibles', and the second as 'the indiscernibility of identicals'. The two principles are in fact independent, though the sorts of reasons which would make us want to accept the one are much the same as the sorts of reasons which would make us want to accept the other. Both principles seem to me to be true.

[31] Freddoso's objection here in fact has wide-ranging consequences for a number of medieval accounts of privative properties. For example, Aquinas, as is well known, holds

perhaps Scotus is being a bit disingenuous when he claims that for a homogeneous item to have H-unity is merely a privative property. Having H-unity entails having all sorts of non-privative properties. For example, it certainly entails that an H-unity instantiates certain relations to its parts. My objection does not mean that an H-unity will not have some privative contingent properties. But it does mean that it cannot have such properties unless it also have some non-privative contingent properties. Scotus should therefore replace (D) with something like

> (D*) A homogeneous item is an H-unity only if it both fails to be a homogeneous part of any homogeneous item and it instantiates some contingent relation to its parts not possibly instantiated by a homogenous part.

(D*) is extremely unsatisfactory, however, since the second criterion, as it stands, is vacuous. But it is not clear to me how the second criterion in (D*) should be tightened up. (I leave this task to the reader. If there are no properties which could plausibly be substituted for the second criterion, I take it that there can—for good metaphysical reasons—be no genuine H-unities.)

Moreover, Scotus's account is not free of further difficulties. His Aristotelian account of the infinite divisibility of a continuum raises a rather puzzling problem. Clearly, the parts of an H-unity exist in the first sense of existence outlined above, though they fail to count as individuals and therefore as H-unities. But any of these parts is *potentially* an H-unity. The parts of a continuum exist, but are only potentially discrete individuals. But Scotus's (plausible) claim that the parts of an H-unity all have *real* relations to their whole seems to raise a difficulty here. Given the infinite divisibility of a continuum, a continuum potentially has an infinite number of parts. These parts cannot all actually have real relations to the whole of which they are parts, since I take it that a real relation must have real relata, and none of the parts are discrete individuals. So there must be a way in which these real relations can exist merely potentially. But the claim that a real thing can exist potentially violates Scotus's basic account of potentiality discussed in Chapter 2. I shall label this worry the 'potentiality problem'. Given Scotus's account of potentiality, the only move available to him would be the undesirable one of conceding that homogeneous items are composed of indivisibles.

that blindness is a (merely) privative property. But blindness is also a contingent property. Freddoso's objection renders Aquinas's position here untenable.

In the previous chapter, I considered two objections which Scotus raises to his rejection of non-entitism: (i) it is unclear how limit entities can be united to a continuum; (ii) the rejection of non-entitism entails that limit entities can be produced and destroyed without undergoing a process of generation or corruption. We are now in a position to answer the first of these, which entails that potentiality and actuality are jointly necessary for composition. The account of H-unity just described entails that it is *not* necessary for a composite whole that it have parts analysable in terms of potentiality and actuality. On the other hand, Scotus does not offer a positive account of the unity exhibited by a continuum together with its limit entity. (It clearly cannot be H-unity, since such unity entails having parts of the same sort, and Scotus holds, as we have seen, that a point is not the same sort of thing as a continuum.[32])

But Scotus's account of H-unity is no help in solving the second of these two problems. Indeed, it tends to exacerbate the problem, since the account of H-unity seems to entail non-entitism. According to Scotus, if two homogenous magnitudes A and B are added together to compose a larger whole C, A and B lose nothing, but gain relations to C. This entails that there are no limit entities at the ends of A and B (which are joined together in the process of forming C). But given Scotus's rejection of non-entitism, there will be two limit entities, one belonging to A and one belonging to B which (supposing an H-unity to be a genuine continuum) are in fact destroyed. Scotus's discussion of H-unity does not provide the tools for a solution to this problem.

4. APPLICATIONS

What sort of things can count as H-unities? According to Scotus, the most obvious example of an H-unity is the accident of quantity (continuous extension).[33] Certain qualities can be homogeneous (and thus possibly count as H-unities) in two ways: as extended and as more or less intense in *degree*.[34] Equally, instances of homogeneous substances will count as H-unities.[35] One of Scotus's favourite exam-

---

[32] See also Scotus, *Lect.* 1. 17. 2. 4, n. 228 (Vatican edn., xvii. 254): 'A point is not a unity of continuity.'   [33] Ibid. n. 222 (Vatican edn., xvii. 252).
[34] Ibid. n. 218 (Vatican edn., xvii. 251); for the latter, see nn. 220, 221, 238 (Vatican edn., xvii. 252, 257). I discuss Scotus's account of the degrees of a quality in Ch. 10.
[35] Ibid. n. 218–19 (Vatican edn., xvii. 251–2).

ples of an H-unity is a (drop of) water.[36] Scotus consistently supposes
that any instance of a homogeneous substance such as water is an H-
unity. Given Scotus's claim that any change in the amount of homogeneous stuff in an H-unity entails a change in identity, if we, for
example, add one further raindrop to a puddle of water P, we will have
a new puddle P_1, where P_1 is numerically distinct from P. (Almost all of
P_1's parts will, of course, have been parts of P.[37]) As we have seen, having
such-and-such an amount of homogeneous stuff is necessary for the
identity of an H-unity, such that a variation in amount entails a change
in numerical identity. This claim raises the identity problem which I
mentioned in section 2 of this chapter. We might well want P and P_1 to
count as the same puddle—though we might want to regard the addition
(say) of a whole *bucket* of water to P to be sufficient to bring about a new
puddle P_2. We might well think that the identity and persistence conditions governing things like puddles are fairly vague, in the loose sense of
things like puddles having *fuzzy* spatial and temporal boundaries.[38]
Scotus's account seems to entail too much.

Sufficient for homogeneity is having parts of the same sort. Importantly, Scotus does not believe that satisfying this condition entails
being spatially extended. A homogeneous substance has parts of the
same sort irrespective of the inherence of quantity.[39] The same is true
of some of the essential parts of material substances. Significantly,
matter is invariably homogeneous (again, irrespective of the inherence of quantity), and a chunk of matter is an H-unity.[40] Again,

---

[36] See e.g. ibid. n. 238 (Vatican edn., xvii. 257); Scotus, *Ord.* 1. 17. 2. 1, n. 232 (Vatican edn., v. 251).

[37] Scotus is quite clear that things like puddles count as substances. Scotus labels discrete chunks of homoeomeric substance 'supposita' (see *Lect.* 1. 17. 2. 4, n. 227 (Vatican edn., xvii. 253)), a term which he reserves for individual instances of substances (see *Ord.* 4. 12. 3, n. 1 (Wadding edn., viii, 739)); an accident, according to this passage, has the *mode* of a *suppositum*.

[38] On fuzziness in the relevant sense, see e.g. Timothy Williamson, *Vagueness*, The Problems of Philosophy. Their Past and their Present (London and New York: Routledge, 1994), 255–7. In the final section of this chapter, I examine the concept a bit more closely. More complex puzzles concerning vagueness arise when we try to spell out what happens in the case of certain continuous changes. I deal with these cases in Ch. 12. Here, my concern is with discrete changes of clearly fixed amounts: the addition of a raindrop to a puddle, for example, or the snapping of a stick.

[39] Scotus, *Lect.* 1. 17. 2. 4, n. 230 (Vatican edn., xvii. 254); see also *idem, Rep.* 1. 17. 6 (MS M, fo. 86ᵛ): 'Substantia ante quantitatem habet virtualiter partes homogeneas, et unius rationis non a unitate compositionis sed homogeneitatis.'

[40] Scotus, *Lect.* 1. 17. 2. 4, n. 230 (Vatican edn., xvii. 254); see also *idem, Rep.* 2. 12. 2, n. 7 (Wadding edn., xi. 322ᵃ⁻ᵇ); *idem, Ord.* 2. 3. 1.4, n. 114 (Vatican edn., vii. 447; Spade, 87).

some substantial forms will count as H-unities.[41] The numerical divisibility of (extended) chunks of substantial form of course entails Scotus's
thesis (discussed in Chapter 3) that substantial forms are individuals.

Scotus clearly regards the unity$_4$ exhibited by a material substance as
unnecessary for the H-unities of, respectively, matter and form:

Scotus's claim that matter has proper parts 'prior to its being understood to be perfected
by form' turns out to be central to the inchoate account of *mass* which I shall argue we
can find in Scotus's works. Simona Massobrio argues that Scotus believes matter to be
extended prior to the inherence of the accident of quantity: see 'Aristotelian Matter as
Understood by St Thomas Aquinas and John Duns Scotus' (unpublished doctoral dissertation, McGill University, 1991), 208–17. This seems to me to be mistaken. On
Massobrio's account, matter in itself has unspecified extension; quantity gives the matter
precise or fixed extension. Her interpretation is based on a passage from the *Quodlibet*,
where Scotus argues: 'Extension cannot be separated from the aptitude or potentiality to
be in a place' (*Quod.* 11, n. 4 (Wadding edn., xii. 263; Alluntis and Wolter, 259 n. 11. 8)).
According to Scotus, matter without the accident of quantity exhibits the potentiality to
be in a place: see e.g. *Rep.* 2. 12. 2, n. 7 (Wadding edn., xi. 322^{a-b}). So, Massobrio reasons,
matter, even without the accident of quantity, must have extension. I think that we
should be wary of this interpretation, not least since there is a relevant argument from
silence: Scotus never explicitly claims that matter has extension of its own prior to the
inherence of quantity. But there is a stronger reason against Massobrio's reading. She
clearly understands the passage in *Quod.* 11 to be an *identity* statement, such that
extension is identical with the potentiality to be in a place; hence:

(α) Both (i) it is impossible for extension to be separated from the potentiality to
be in a place, and (ii) it is impossible for the potentiality to be in a place to be
separated from extension.

But Scotus's account in *Quod.* 11 does not entail (α). Scotus claims merely that extension
is inseparable from the potentiality to be in a place, not that the potentiality to be in a
place is inseparable from extension. So Scotus's account entails (αi); i.e.

(αi) It is impossible for extension to be separated from the potentiality to be in a
place.

Massobrio's interpretation, however, crucially requires that (αii) is true; i.e.

(αii) It is impossible for the potentiality to be in a place to be separated from
extension.

(On (αii), anything which exhibits the potentiality for being in a place will have
extension.) Since (αii) is not entailed by Scotus's account in *Quod.* 11, I take it that there
is no reason to accept Massobrio's reading of Scotus's position. And in this case the
argument from silence gains much greater force. Nothing Scotus says implies that he
would accept that matter has extension of its own prior to the inherence of quantity. So
we should not accept Massobrio's reading. This makes it harder to understand Scotus's
claim that matter is an H-unity prior to the inherence of quantity. But it makes complete
sense of his claim that matter without form exists in a place *definitively*; i.e. such that,
unlike an extended body, the whole of matter exists in each of its parts (see e.g. *Rep.* 2. 12.
2, n. 7 (Wadding edn., xi. 322^{a-b}); on definitive presence, see Ch. 11 below).

[41] Scotus, *Lect.* 1. 17. 2. 4, n. 228 (Vatican edn., xvii. 254); see also *idem, Ord.* 4. 11. 3, n.
37 (Wadding edn., viii. 641); 4. 44. 1, nn. 6, 7, 11 (Wadding edn., x. 104, 107, 112).

The unity of homogeneity is prior to the unity of composition from essential parts, because, if the separation of a unity of composition (from essential parts) is completed down to the last [stage], the unity of composition according to homogeneous parts remains in both end terms (as when a composite is reduced to matter and form, matter is whole by a unity of homogeneity from parts of the same sort (since it is not whole under a whole quantity and whole under each part, as the intellective soul exists in a whole)—and it is similar for a form which was previously extended: therefore the unity of homogeneity can exist without the unity of composition from act and potentiality.[42]

The idea is that the matter and form of a substance are themselves homogeneous, and that their homogeneity is not dependent upon their being united to compose a substance. This seems entirely unobjectionable.

Whatever we make of the metaphysics of Scotus's account of H-unity, we might well feel that Scotus applies his doctrine too widely. Specifically, there might be some sorts of homogeneous thing whose spatial and temporal boundaries might be fuzzy in the sort of way I hinted at above. I will return to this in the final section of this chapter, where I consider the philosophical lessons we might want to draw from Scotus's account of H-unity. In the next section, I consider Scotus's account of the biological process of digestion, which forces him to deny that all discrete homogeneous items are H-unities.

5. A BIOLOGICAL COUNTER-INSTANCE

As Scotus understands the process of digestion, it is *prima facie* a counter-instance to (A). According to Scotus, human digestion involves a change from foodstuff to human flesh. Flesh on most Aristotelian accounts is a homoeomeric substance.[43] Throughout the process the stuff undergoing the process remains (at best) in contact with the flesh of which it is to become a part. But at the conclusion of the process, the newly produced flesh becomes a part of the pre-existent flesh. So, for example, when Felix the cat eats his mouse, the end of the process of digestion will bring it about both

---

[42] Scotus, *Lect.* 1. 17. 2. 4, n. 228 (Vatican edn., xvii. 253–4). Scotus uses these observations to defend the claim that an H-unity can be a composite even though its parts cannot be analysed in terms of actuality and potentiality. I do not see how the observations can support this conclusion.

[43] See e.g. Scotus, *Ord.* 4. 44. 1, n. 3 (Wadding edn., x. 98).

154 The Metaphysics of Continuity

that the matter that was the mouse receives a newly produced form of cat flesh,[44] and that the newly generated cat flesh becomes a part of Felix's flesh. Scotus puts the point as follows:

> [The generation involved in the process of nutrition] can be called 'adgeneration', since [it is] the generation of something which (by generation) becomes the same as some pre-existent thing to which it is adgenerated. Or it can be called 'ingeneration', because [it is] the generation of a part in a whole of which it was not a part.[45]

If flesh can count as an H-unity, this will look to be a counter-instance to (A). On (A), we would expect the new cat flesh, F, and the flesh that already belonged to Felix, F_1, to compose a lump of flesh numerically distinct from both F and F_1. But what in fact happens in nutrition, according to Scotus, is that F somehow becomes a part of F_1. If flesh can count as a discrete homogeneous item, Scotus will here be committed to:

> (B′) For some discrete homogeneous item x, some of the homogenous parts of x are accidental to x,

which is inconsistent with (B), and therefore with (B*). But if flesh can count as an H-unity, Scotus's account seems to entail a stronger (and contradictory) claim:

> (E) If two homogeneous items x and y form an H-unity z, then, if z is caused by nutrition, x is identical with z.

The reason is that by both (B) and (B*) none of the parts of an H-unity is accidental to it; and on Scotus's account of nutrition, the resultant whole 'becomes the same as the pre-existent thing'.

(E) is false. If y is a part of z, then, by Leibniz's law, y is a part of x: but the antecedent of (E) entails that x and y are numerically distinct, such that neither is a part of the other. (E) is also a contrary of

> (A) If two homogeneous items x and y form an H-unity z, then z is numerically distinct from x, y, and any aggregate of x and y.

---

[44] The claim that the form which belongs to the newly generated cat flesh is itself newly produced is directed against a claim of Henry of Ghent. According to Henry, Felix's process of digestion consists in the (pre-existent) form of Felix's flesh beginning to be the form of the matter which prior to the process belonged to the mouse: see Henry of Ghent, *Quod.* 2. 10 (Macken edn., ii. 74), cited in Scotus, *Ord.* 4. 44. 1, n. 5 (Wadding edn., x. 103–4). In support of Henry's view, Scotus (though not Henry) appeals to an important part of Aristotle's account of nutrition: see Arist. *Gen. corr.* 1. 5 (321^{b}33–4).

[45] Scotus, *Ord.* 4. 44. 1, n. 7 (Wadding edn., x. 107). The process (as opposed to the result) admits of a fairly complicated description which we do not need to discuss here.

(According to (E), *z* will be identical with *x*.) So if Scotus believes that flesh is an H-unity, his account of nutrition is inconsistent with two of the pivotal features of his standard account of H-unity. I take it, however, that (A) is true, from which we should conclude that the flesh of an organic substance does not count as a genuine H-unity (despite initial appearances to the contrary). If this is correct, then the following is true:

> (D**) A homogeneous item is an H-unity if and only if (i) it fails to be a homogeneous part of any whole, (ii) it instantiates some contingent relation to its parts not possibly instantiated by a homogeneous part, and (iii) it is not caused by a process of nutrition.

(D**) gives the complete list of conditions necessary for H-unity. (Note that condition (ii) is mine, not Scotus's; I gave my reasons for accepting it in the previous section.)

It is not clear to me whether Scotus would in fact regard flesh as an H-unity (and hence (D**) as preferable to (D*)). He certainly speaks consistently of flesh as a *whole*,[46] and the flesh of Felix the cat seems to have some claim to be a discrete item (I can easily distinguish it both from the flesh of Felix's sister Polly and from the other parts of Felix's body). But suppose that Scotus (correctly) holds that flesh is not a genuine H-unity. Does he have a way to distinguish it from genuine H-unities? *Prima facie*, it is difficult to see why the case of nutrition should be significantly different *metaphysically* from the sorts of case considered above. Flesh seems analogous to water, a homogenous substance which, according to Scotus, can exhibit H-unity. Unless Scotus can find some principled way of distinguishing nutrition from standard increases, it seems to me that he should take nutrition as a good reason for rejecting his principles (B) and (B*).

But it seems to me that Scotus can in fact reasonably distinguish flesh from his genuine H-unities. Scotus's account of nutrition gives no reason to reject (A), since the principle inconsistent with (A)—namely, (E)—which the nutrition account would entail if flesh were an H-unity, is false. So, if we reject the clearly false (E), nutrition is not a counter-instance to (A). But could Scotus offer any principled reasons for holding that flesh fails to count as an H-unity? Flesh, of course, is (on Scotus's view) homogeneous. So what Scotus needs is a principled way of determining which sorts of homogeneous parts can unite to

---

[46] See e.g. ibid. nn. 7–10 (Wadding edn., x. 106–8).

form an H-unity. Scotus suggests three ways in which nutrition differs from standard cases of the increase of homogeneous parts. First, nutrition for Scotus paradigmatically involves the *replacement* of one part by another, such that the overall amount of stuff remains much the same.[47] Secondly, the relevant increase involved in nutrition is *instantaneous*.[48] Thirdly, according to Scotus, nutrition is a process whose agent is the pre-existent flesh. In my example of Felix the cat, Felix's pre-existent flesh *brings it about* that, at the last stages of decay of the mouse, Felix's new flesh comes into existence.[49]

The first of these differences is no use here, since standard instances of an increase in homogeneous parts could satisfy the condition. Neither is the second of any help, for just the same reason. But the third of these principles might be some use. Scotus could claim that

(F) For every two homogeneous items x and y, if x causes y, it is not possible for x and y to form an H-unity.

Note that (F) does not preclude x and y being united, and even being united to form a discrete homogeneous item. (F) entails merely that x and y cannot form an H-unity. In Scotus's account, as we have seen, not all discrete homogeneous items count as H-unities.

Philosophically, this is an important move. If Scotus is right about (F), he has a useful way of distinguishing genuine continuants—trees, for example—from the sorts of items which might satisfy Butler's description (according to which a change in material composition is sufficient for the existence of a new object)—puddles, for example. It will be difficult for Scotus to find a principled way of undergirding (F). But this does not mean that there might not be a suitable criterion available. *We* might want to claim, for example, that flesh fails to count as an H-unity on the grounds that the sorts of chemical changes which occur in nutrition are significantly different from the sorts of chemical changes which occur in, say, the conjunction of two drops of water. Scotus's principle will show that, in such complex cases, (A) is inapplicable—and hence that flesh is not an H-unity. On the other hand, I shall argue in the next section that there is no real reason for accepting that any putatively homogeneous substance is in fact an H-unity at all.

---

[47] Ibid. nn. 13–14 (Wadding edn., x. 112–13).
[48] Ibid. n. 14 (Wadding edn., x. 113). The idea seems to be that the acquisition of a new lump of flesh is instantaneous: it is instantaneously joined to the pre-existent flesh.
[49] Ibid. n. 8 (Wadding edn., x. 107).

6. H-UNITY AND SUBSTANCE

Does Scotus really need an account of H-unity? Scotus's account of H-unity is central (and probably required) for his theory of the degrees of a quality, which I examine in Chapter 10. It is required for his theory of continuous quantity, as I will show in the next chapter. But is it required for a theory of substance? I want here to argue that it is not, and that Scotus is far too cavalier in the sorts of things he allows to count as H-unities. If we look at Scotus's account of nutrition, it is clear that, on (B'), Scotus holds that there are some homogeneous items whose parts are *non-essential* for the identity of the whole. The parts of Felix the cat's flesh are not essential for his identity; and I take it that there is no complex organic substance whose homogeneous parts are necessary for identity. Should Scotus hold that there are *any* substances whose homogeneous parts are necessary for their identity? A drop of water or a puddle composed of many such drops might seem to be such a substance. But it seems to me far more plausible to claim, on the basis of the identity problem outlined above, that such substances *per accidens* (as some writers knew them) are not genuine H-unities at all. Such things seem to me to count as substances (I would, for example, suppose that a puddle is more than an *aggregate* of water molecules), but they do not count as H-unities (in Scotus's sense of H-unity). The reason for this is that drops of water do not exhibit any real sort of *fixity*: they can be combined in infinitely more or less arbitrary ways. So a substance will not satisfy the conditions in the antecedent of (B). On this sort of account, I doubt that (A) applies to substances either. Having a set of homogeneous parts does not look to be sufficient for the substancehood of a homogeneous substance.

Scotus's account of H-unity is clearly necessary for some of the unities which he discusses, and it is to his credit that he attempts to sketch a theory of H-unity. The problems which I have tried to outline are twofold. First, it seems to me that the potentiality problem constitutes an aporia which can be solved only on the supposition that homogeneous items are composed of genuine indivisibles (be they physically or conceptually indivisible). Secondly, Scotus is too hasty in wanting to classify homogeneous *substances* as genuine H-unities. I indicated above that the spatial and temporal boundaries of substances *per accidens* could be fuzzy. I also suggested that we could plausibly account for some sorts of change by appealing to the possibility of some substance retaining its identity and gaining or losing homogeneous parts. We could in fact combine these two claims to argue both that, if a substance gains or loses *enough* homogeneous parts, it becomes a new substance, and that there is no principled way of designating *how much* stuff we would need to add or subtract. This claim could, of course, be satisfied in two rather different ways. First, it could be the case that the boundaries between two substances are genuinely (ontologically) fuzzy; secondly, it could be the case that the boundaries are in fact precise, but that there is no empirical way of discerning their location. The second of these looks to me to be preferable (and more Scotistic). If we adopt the first, we will have to sacrifice a whole series of claims about identity which we might not want to lose.

9

Quantity: Change and Mass

Given Scotus's account of H-unity, it is quite clear that some changes—those which happen to things which count as H-unities—can be sufficiently explained in terms of the addition or subtraction of homogeneous parts. Scotus's puddle example, discussed in the previous chapter, could not be bettered here. Scotus, however, holds that both quantity and the degrees of a quality can be construed as H-unities. His reason is that if changes in the identity of homogeneous items can be explained in terms of the addition or subtraction of homogeneous parts, those items will count as H-unities. I will look at this inference more closely in the next chapter, where I examine different models for explaining changes in degrees of a quality. In this chapter, I am interested in one sort of quantitative change: condensation and rarefaction (a change which Scotus characterizes as the sort of change resulting from an increase in extension without a corresponding increase in the amount of substance). There is another sort of quantitative change too: augmentation and diminution (the sort of quantitative change resulting from the addition of more bits of substance). But this second kind of change does not seem to present any particular physical or metaphysical points of interest for Scotus over and above the sorts of thing discussed in the previous chapter, so I will not discuss it further here.[1]

I examine the process of condensation and rarefaction in the first section of this chapter. In the second section I examine the extent to which Scotus's account of condensation and rarefaction seem to imply some cognizance on his part of what we now label 'mass'. I shall argue that Scotus does indeed have an inchoate account of mass, though it is an account which locates mass not in the category of quantity but in the category of substance. As we shall see, one of Scotus's predecessors

---

[1] For a discussion of these sorts of change, see Scotus, *Ord.* 4. 12. 4, nn. 25–6 (Wadding edn., viii. 769–70).

and several of his successors have an account of mass. But, unlike Scotus, they locate mass in the category of quantity, not substance. I shall also discuss what I take to be the relative merits of these two ways of categorizing mass.

1. QUANTITATIVE CHANGE

Scotus claims that condensation and rarefaction are the result of prior changes in quality.[2] Obviously, condensation and rarefaction involve at least two sorts of change: one in extension and one in density. A change in density is a qualitative change; so we might be tempted to think that what Scotus has in mind is that a change in density explains the change in extension. But Scotus cannot in fact mean this, since at one point he argues that a change in extension explains the change in density (and not vice versa).[3] Presumably the prior qualitative change that Scotus has in mind is something like a change in temperature. If we heat at least some sorts of substance, they increase in size and decrease in density; and if we cool them, the opposite changes occur.

Scotus tries to use his addition and subtraction model to describe the changes in extension which occur in condensation and rarefaction. He opposes two other accounts. (i) The first of these involves the claim that the quantitative changes involved in condensation and rarefaction can be explained only by positing the complete corruption of one quantity and the complete generation of another. (ii) On the second theory opposed by Scotus, the rarefaction of a substance x is explained in terms of the juxtaposition of less dense substance(s) throughout x; presumably condensation is explained in terms of the removal of such less dense juxtaposed substance(s).

(i) Scotus seems to have constructed the first theory—the generation and corruption theory—from arguments considered variously by Godfrey of Fontaines and Walter Burley.[4] Scotus presents two arguments in favour of the first theory.

---

[2] Such a change is described as 'a change in quantity which concomitates a change in quality' (ibid. n. 19 (Wadding edn., viii. 766)): which I take it means that the presence of such a quantitative change is a necessary indicator of the presence of an (explanatorily prior) qualitative change.   [3] Ibid. n. 22 (Wadding edn., viii. 768).

[4] The editors of the Wadding edition are wrong in ascribing this theory to Godfrey and Walter: see Wadding edn., viii. 760, discussed rather misleadingly in Anneliese Maier, *Die Vorläufer Galileis im 14. Jahrhundert* (Studien zur Naturphilosophie der Spätscholastik, [1]), Raccolta di Studi e Testi, 22 (Rome: Storia e Letteratura, 1949), 46 n. 20.

(B.1) Accepting

(A) The end terms of motion are incompossible,[5]

Scotus infers

(1) It is not possible that one of the end terms of motion includes the other as a part,

which entails the generation and corruption theory of quantitative change.[6]

(B.2) Scotus argues secondly as follows:

[a] Each part of a rarer thing is rarer. Therefore [b] each part of a rarer thing is greater according to quantity. Therefore [c] each [part] is a quantum in virtue of a new quantity.[7]

---

[5] For the meaning of this, see above, Ch. 8, axiom (C).

[6] Scotus, *Ord.* 4. 12. 4, n. 4 (Wadding edn., viii. 761). The argument was proposed in a rather different context by Godfrey of Fontaines, though not used to defend a generation and corruption theory of condensation and rarefaction. I discuss Godfrey's argument in its context in the next chapter.

[7] Ibid.; I have followed the text in MS A, fols. 222[vb]–3[ra]: 'Quaelibet pars rarioris est rarior. Ergo quaelibet pars rarioris est rarior secundum quantitatem. Igitur quaelibet est quanta nova quantitate.' This argument is found in Burley as part of an attempt to show that it is not possible to account for condensation and rarefaction in terms of quantity at all. Burley has two arguments for this. The first is that quantity is really identical with matter. In condensation and rarefaction, the amount of matter remains unchanged; so the quantity must be unchanged too. The second is that the argument I have labelled **(B.2)** has absurd results. Having given **(B.2)**, Burley suggests that it has the absurd result that the generation and corruption theory will entail that the two quantities (the one generated, the other corrupted) will exist simultaneously (though presumably so only for an instant). (For both arguments see *In Ph.* 4. 86 ((Venice, 1501) 123[ra]).) Burley gives no reason why **(B.2)** should entail this, and I cannot think that it is right. Burley holds instead that condensation and rarefaction are correctly explained in terms of the inherence of different qualities, where the qualities he has in mind are just 'dense' and 'rare': see *In Ph.* 4. 86 (p. 123[ra–rb]). Burley's version of **(B.2)** is almost verbatim the same as Scotus's. The relevant parts of Burley's second *Physics* commentary, however, date from 1324–7. On Burley, see C. Martin, 'Walter Burley', in R.W. Southern (ed.), *Oxford Studies Presented to Daniel Callus*, Oxford Historical Society, NS 16 (Oxford: Clarendon Press, 1964), 194–230; on the dates of the last version of Burley's *Physics* commentary, see ibid. 212–13; also Rega Wood, 'Walter Burley's *Physics* Commentaries', *Franciscan Studies*, 33 (1984), 275–327, p. 293. The first edition of Burley's *Physics* commentary probably dates from 1300–7: see Martin, 'Walter Burley', 203–4. Wood dates this version before 1316: 'Walter Burley's *Physics* Commentaries', 283. Unfortunately, the discussion is lacking in this first edition, and the manuscript has a blank page where we would expect the treatment of these matters to be found (see MS G, fo. 311). In this early version of his commentary, Burley merely signals his support for Aristotle's claim (accepted by Scotus too) that condensation and rarefaction cannot be explained by invoking the existence

Scotus defends the inference from (b) to (c) by showing the impossibility of both (b) being true and (c) being false. He reasons that, if (c) were false, it would follow that some of the quantity of a rarefied substance pre-existed in the denser substance. Let Q be the pre-existing quantity, and x the subject in which it inheres. All sides accept

> (B) In the condensation or rarefaction of a substance x, x retains all its homoeomeric parts, and gains no new ones,

and

> (C) It is not possible for an accident to move from subject to subject, or from one part of a subject to another part of a subject.

(B) and (C) together entail

> (2) In the condensation or rarefaction of a substance x, Q continues to inhere in the whole of x.

(If (2) were false, then Q would somehow have slipped across its substance, violating (C).) Given that, for example, x is bigger than it was before, x must have some further quantity in addition to Q. But this is impossible, since no whole can be extended by two quantities such that at least one of them inheres in the whole of it.[8]

Scotus holds that there is good reason to reject the generation and corruption theory. One argument is that the generation and corruption theory is inconsistent with the view—held, according to Scotus, by his opponent here—that quantity individuates substances. On this view, the corruption of a quantity will entail the corruption of the substance which it individuates.[9] This argument, however, is effectively an argument against individuation by quantity, rather than an argument against the generation and corruption theory. It would be possible to abandon the individuation claim but retain the generation and corruption theory.

Scotus offers a far more damaging criticism of his opponent's position, however.

> (B′) He argues that his opponent's position violates (C). Scotus

---

of a vacuum, since 'quaelibet pars rari est rara et quaelibet pars densi est densa': see Burley, *In Ph.* [1st edn.] 4. 82 (MS G, fo. 310^a).

[8] Scotus, *Ord.* 4. 12. 4, n. 4 (Wadding edn., viii. 761).
[9] Ibid. n. 10 (Wadding edn., viii. 763).

accepts that quantity is the subject of the other accidents.[10] He argues that it is empirically evident that qualities such as colour do not (necessarily) change in condensation and rarefaction. But, given his opponent's claim that the quantity inhering in a condensed or rarefied substance is completely new, it will follow that, if this view is true, accidents such as quality can move from subject to subject—which violates (C).[11] If his opponent insists that the qualities are in fact new, Scotus has a reply. The new qualities must be produced by an agent. But it is not always the case that an agent responsible for condensation and rarefaction is also the sort of agent which could bring about instances of all the relevant qualities. Suppose we rarefy a blue liquid by heating it. We would have to conclude on the generation and corruption theory that a flame could bring about instances of blueness. And this might not be all that plausible.[12]

If the generation and corruption theory is false, so too must be the arguments in its favour.

(B.1') Scotus accepts (A), but denies that it entails (1). He argues that it is sufficient for the incompossibility of the end terms of a motion that the end terms are not *in all respects* the same. And this is consistent with the claim that one of the end terms could be a part of the other.[13] We will return to an objection and reply similar to these when considering qualitative change in the next chapter.

Scotus does not offer a reply to (B.2). This seems to me unfortunate, since, as we shall see, (B.2) looks fatal for his own theory. All Scotus suggests when considering (B.2) is that the first premiss of the argument (viz. each part of a rarefied thing is rarer) might be false. The falsity of this claim, as Scotus notices, would entail that no rarefied substance is of equal density all over, a claim which, as we shall see, is made by the second theory opposed by Scotus. The claim is, of course, extremely implausible. Doubtless some rarefied substances fail to be of

---

[10] The discussion in *Ord.* 4. 12. 4 is about the separated accidents in the Eucharist, which were generally held to inhere in quantity (see *ibid.* 4. 12. 2, n. 15 (Wadding edn., viii. 733–4)). But, as we saw in Ch. 6, Scotus holds that, generally, quality inheres in quantity: and most of the remaining accidents of a substance inhere in it in virtue either of quantity or of quality.

[11] Scotus, *Ord.* 4. 12. 4, n. 8 (Wadding edn., viii. 762).

[12] Ibid. nn. 9–10 (Wadding edn., viii. 762–3). Note that Scotus probably supposes, as we saw in Ch. 6, that quality inheres in substance via quantity.

[13] Ibid. n. 11 (Wadding edn., viii. 763).

equal density all over; but I do not see that, necessarily, all rarefied substances are like this.

Scotus's arguments against the generation and corruption theory highlight difficulties in consistency in the theory. But I am not sure that any of Scotus's arguments could be regarded as fatal. I shall return to this again once I have examined both the other theory Scotus opposes and his own theory.

(ii) The second theory opposed by Scotus explains the condensation and rarefaction of a body *B* in terms of juxtaposition: less dense bodies are added to or removed from proximity to *B*:

> Rarefaction is not to some quality uniform in the whole altered thing and each of its parts. Rather, the rarefying agent generates from some parts of the rarefactible substance some bodies less dense than the rarefactible body. For this reason, since these [less dense bodies] cannot exist in the same place [*simul*] as the other parts which remain here in their original species (since two bodies cannot exist in the same place), [the new parts] expel the other parts from their place, and consequently the whole body occupies a larger place. Thus to be less dense is just to have many less dense bodies mixed in this way with its parts thus remaining in [their] proper form.[14]

Scotus's main objection to this theory is that the agent responsible for rarefaction would have to be able to generate new substances. And this does not look very plausible.[15]

Scotus argues that the correct model for understanding condensation and rarefaction is a version of his addition and subtraction theory. The substance does not gain or lose any parts, but its *quantity* is increased or decreased by the addition or subtraction of homogeneous parts of quantity:

> It is said . . . that in rarefaction, the quantity is new: not all, but a part in the same subject; [and] that the change of rarefaction (by which there is accidentally some new grade of quantity) is in quantity as in a subject.[16]

On this account, *part* of the quantity is new; it is added to the pre-existent quantity, and the two quantities together explain the greater

[14] Ibid. n. 12 (Wadding edn., viii. 763). The text found in MS A, fo. 223ra, which I follow in my translation here, differs marginally, but not significantly, from that found in the Wadding edition.   [15] Ibid. n. 20 (Wadding edn., viii. 766).
[16] Ibid. n. 22 (Wadding edn., viii. 767–78). MS A, fo. 223vb, which I follow here, has: 'Aliter dicitur, tenendo in isto membro communem opinionem—quod scilicet in rarefactione quantitas sit nova, non tota, sed pars in eodem subiecto—quod in quantitate ut in subiecto est motus rarefactionis, per quem per accidens est aliquis gradus quantitatis novus.'

extension of the rarefied substance. Quantity here counts as an H-unity, and, given the properties of an H-unity, Scotus's account will not entail his rejecting the clearly true claim

(A) The end terms of motion are incompossible.

The reason is that seeing quantity as an H-unity will allow Scotus to accept (A) without being forced to accept

(1) It is not possible that one of the end terms of motion includes the other as a part.

The nature of an H-unity is such that it can contain parts quantitatively smaller than itself without being numerically identical with such parts.

But Scotus's theory seems deeply problematic. He himself recognizes his failure to respond to the crucial (B.2), an argument effectively against the possibility of appealing to addition and subtraction to explain condensation and rarefaction. As I have indicated, in attempting to respond to (B.2), Scotus appeals to the juxtaposition theory as a (the only?) plausible alternative to the generation and corruption theory.[17] According to (B.2), the addition and subtraction theory entails that a quantity can migrate from subject to subject. And as we have seen, Scotus's (B′) rejects the generation and corruption theory on the grounds that it violates

(C) It is not possible for an accident to move from subject to subject, or from one part of a subject to another part of a subject.

But Scotus's position contradicts (C) as well.[18] So perhaps Scotus should reject (C). As we saw in Chapter 6, Scotus in fact (whether intentionally or not) espouses a principle which allows for the migration of accidents. He could therefore replace (C) with

(C*) It is not naturally possible for an accident to move from subject to subject, or from one part of a subject to another part of a subject.

But (C*) is not much help either, since Scotus's addition and subtraction theory of quantitative change must allow that accidents can

---

[17] Ibid. n. 12 (Wadding edn., viii. 763).
[18] For Scotus's rejection of (C), see ibid. nn. 4, 8–10 (Wadding edn., viii. 761–3).

migrate naturally from subject to subject (unless, of course, Scotus were to explain all occurrences of condensation and rarefaction by appealing to divine intervention, a move which he certainly would not want to make). Of course, rejecting (C) does not mean accepting the generation and corruption theory. On the other hand, accepting (C) is the strongest reason Scotus has for rejecting the generation and corruption theory.

In the *Lectura*, Scotus tries a different tack from the one I have suggested. He argues that a dense substance has some *substantial* parts which fail to be extended. In rarefaction these parts begin to receive a new part of a quantity:

It is necessary to claim that those parts [of a substance] which are now under parts of quantity were previously in the substance according to the proper unity of substance from its parts of the same sort.[19]

This claim seems puzzling, though if it were true, it would presumably allow Scotus to retain (C) and avoid the damaging argument—(B.2)—against him. The parts in which the new quantity inheres were previously the subject of *no* quantity; so there is no question of the pre-existing quantity slipping across the subject in the manner suggested in (B.2).

2. SUBSTANCE AND MASS

How close was Scotus to discerning, through his account of condensation and rarefaction, the concept of mass? The medievals clearly had a concept akin to that of *weight*. They labelled it 'gravitas' or 'ponderositas'. *Gravity* is a quality: the tendency of some bodies to fall.[20] But Scotus also seems to have an inchoate account of *mass*. In this section, I will examine the evidence for this claim, and try to see what Scotus's position might amount to.

Scotus was not the first person to see that we might talk about mass.[21] Giles of Rome, for example, worked out a fairly sophisticated

[19] Scotus, *Lect.* 1. 17. 2. 4, n. 218 (Vatican edn., xvii. 251).
[20] Ibid. n. 210 (Vatican edn., xvii. 248). On *gravitas* and *ponderositas*, see Ernest A. Moody and Marshall Clagett, *The Medieval Science of Weights* (Scientia de Ponderibus): *Treatises Ascribed to Euclid, Archimedes, Thabit ibn Qurra, Jordanus de Nemore and Blasius of Parma* (Madison: University of Wisconsin Press, 1952), 374. Scotus uses 'ponderositas' instead of 'gravitas' in *Rep.* 1. 17. 6 (MS M, fo. 86^{r-v}).
[21] For a history of ancient and medieval conceptions of mass, see Max Jammer, *Concepts of Mass in Classical and Modern Physics*, Harper Torchbacks Science Library (New York, Evanston, Ill., and London: Harper and Row, 1964), chs. 2–4.

account of what he labelled 'quantitas materiae': a quantity with non-fixed dimensions which inheres in prime matter prior to any other form.[22] Some of Scotus's successors clearly held similar ideas. Francis of Marchia uses 'quantitas molis' to refer to the 'amount' of a substance.[23] Scotus uses the term 'quantitas molis' too; but he uses it to refer not to mass but to extension. Giles and Francis agree in locating mass in the category of quantity. Giles, for example, argues like Aquinas that prime matter is pure potentiality, and hence that its quantity must be some kind of form.[24] Is Giles's *quantitas materiae* a primitive concept of mass? This rather depends, I think, on what sort of conception of mass we are looking for. Giles introduces *quantitas materiae* to explain what remains constant over the processes of condensation and rarefaction. As the medievals knew, condensation and rarefaction involve changes in both volume and density. So Giles's conception of what remains constant in such changes must at least be related to Newton's definition of mass as a constant relating volume and density, even if he did not come up with the relevant quantitative formula $m = \rho V$ (where m is the measure of mass, ρ the measure of density and V the measure of volume).[25]

---

[22] See Maier, *Die Vorläufer Galileis*, 29–46; in particular her discussion of Giles's early theory on pp. 31–6, commenting on Giles, *Th. de Corp. Christi* 44 ((Venice, 1554), 31^{rb}B-32^{rb}D). 'Quantitas materiae' is of course the Latin phrase which Newton used to refer to mass: see Isaac Newton, *Principia Mathematica Philosophiae Naturalis*, in his *Opera*, ed. S. Horsley (5 vols., London: John Nichols, 1779), ii. 1.

[23] See his *In Sent.* 4. 13. 1: the relevant passage is printed in Anneliese Maier, *Metaphysische Hintergründe der spätscholastischen Naturphilosophie* (Studien zur Naturphilosophie der Spätscholastik, 4), Raccolta di Studi e Testi, 52 (Rome: Storia e Letteratura, 1955), 206.   [24] Giles, *Th. de Corp. Christi* 44 (31^{rb}C–D).

[25] See Isaac Newton, *Mathematical Principles of Natural Philosophy*, trans. by Andrew Motte, ed. Florian Cajori (2 vols., Berkeley, Los Angeles, and London: University of California Press, 1971), i.1 (from definition 1). Newton adds that mass thus construed is known only in proportion to weight. André Goddu has argued on the basis of this that an account of *quantitas materiae* which fails to define it in terms of weight fails to be a concept of mass at all: see André Goddu, *The Physics of William of Ockham*, Studien und Texte zur Geistesgeschichte des Mittelalters, 16 (Leiden and Cologne: Brill, 1984), 106. But this conclusion seems over-hasty. An intuitive account of mass as relative to volume and density can easily be grasped without appealing to weight. In fact, although Newton was probably not aware of this, the concepts of mass and weight are independent, and Newton's use of weight in his account of mass is in some senses merely accidental. Mass is proportional to weight just because weight is reducible to the product of the mass of a body b and b's acceleration in free fall: see Jammer, *Concepts of Mass*, 74. But there are other ways of measuring mass. For example, it is possible (even using Newtonian principles from the beginning of *Principia*) to quantify mass as a constant that relates force to acceleration (see Newton, *Mathematical Principles*, i. 1. 13–14 (from definition

Scotus seems to me to have a conception of something very similar to Giles's *quantitas materiae*. So he too has an inchoate account of mass. But there are differences between the two accounts. In particular, Scotus locates the property I want to label 'mass' in the category of substance, not that of quantity.

Scotus introduces his conception via a consideration of the physics of rarefaction. As the *Lectura* passage just quoted makes clear, Scotus holds that, even though in rarefaction there are new parts of quantity, there are no new parts of substance. The idea is that a substance has a certain fixed amount of stuff prior[26] to its extension. Scotus reasons that a substance has S-potentiality for extension, and that, as such, it must have parts of a kind which can (but need not?) be extended.[27] Note that Scotus is not suggesting that the substance is extended in any way prior to its having quantity. Divisibility into parts of the same sort, such that one part is *outside* another, pertains to a substance if and only if it has quantity. But substances, according to Scotus, have parts of the same sort *prior* to the inherence of quantity.[28] In fact, as we saw in Chapter 8, Scotus argues that prime matter, substantial form, and composite substance all have homogeneous parts prior to the inherence of quantity. But, following a hint from Aristotle, Scotus argues that the crucial component here is *matter*. In the *Physics* Aristotle explains condensation and rarefaction by appealing to the potentiality which matter

2, law 2, and law 3)), a concept that we now know as *inertial mass*. So whether or not Goddu is right that the concept of *quantitas materiae* cannot be identified as a concept of mass, his reason for this assertion seems to be wrong. In fact, Newton's whole discussion at the beginning of *Principia* has been the cause of some controversy. Newton appears to treat *density* as his basic explanatory category in defining mass. But attempts to define mass quantitatively as the product of measures of density and volume turn out to be vacuous, since measures of density are ultimately explained only in terms of measures of mass and volume (such that $\rho = m/V$). As later commentators have noted, we would probably want to treat force and acceleration as explanatorily prior to mass. But it is not clear that Newton saw this. For a useful discussion of the whole set of issues, see Jammer, *Concepts of Mass*, 64–74; also the comments by Cajori in his appendix to Newton, *Mathematical Principles*, ii. 638.

[26] Logically, not temporally, prior.
[27] Scotus, *Lect.* 1. 17. 2. 4, n. 219 (Vatican edn., xvii. 251–2).
[28] Ibid. n. 230 (Vatican edn., xvii. 254); Scotus, *Ord.* 2. 3. 1. 5–6, n. 166 (Vatican edn., vii. 473; Spade, 101). For Simona Massobrio's claim that matter has extension prior to the inherence of quantity, see her 'Aristotelian Matter as Understood by St Thomas Aquinas and John Duns Scotus' (unpublished doctoral dissertation, McGill University, 1991), 208–17. I gave reasons for supposing this interpretation to be mistaken in the previous chapter: see Ch. 8. 41.

has for this or that extension.[29] Scotus argues that this Aristotelian claim entails the further (not so Aristotelian) claim that matter gains or loses no parts in condensation and rarefaction. He concludes: 'It is necessary for matter to have proper parts from which it is one.'[30] In the *Ordinatio*, Scotus makes the same point. He reasons that, whether or not the parts of matter are actually divided up into different chunks by the inherence in them of numerically discrete quantities, matter will have really distinct parts all its own.[31] By using the (pseudo-)quantitative term 'divisibility', Scotus makes it clear that he has in mind some (constant) amount of matter. But by refusing to categorize this 'amount' as quantity, Scotus seems to be wanting to categorize it as a part of substance. Given that this amount remains constant over changes in volume and density, it seems to me that we can reasonably think of it as akin to the Newtonian conception of mass.

Locating mass in the category of substance presumably entails that the mass of a substance is essential to it, such that a change in mass will result in a change in the *identity* of a substance. It would certainly entail this if we bear in mind that, according to Scotus, the matter of a substance is an H-unity. It cannot be correct, therefore, that the matter of a substance is an H-unity, since it would lead to protean variations in substantial identity. On the other hand, given Scotus's account of accidental unity, it is clearly not open to him (as it seems to be to Giles of Rome) to locate mass in the category of quantity. For Scotus, this would entail that matter plus mass form a unity₃, and thus that each could exist without the other. And what Scotus wants to preserve is that matter, whether extended or not, *always* has mass. And this, at least, seems to be correct.

Explaining condensation and rarefaction will be problematic for anyone who thinks that extension is an absolute accident over and above substance. Scotus was aware of these difficulties, and I think realized his failure to come up with a satisfactory account. In particular, (C) remains problematic for his theory, and he does not attempt to reply to the argument—(B.2)—which could be used to exploit (C)

---

[29] Arist. *Ph.* 4. 9 (217ᵃ20–ᵇ20; esp. ᵃ31–3, ᵇ8–11). Presumably, Scotus was aware of Giles's account of *quantitas materiae*, which likewise isolates *matter* as the significant component of a composite substance here.

[30] Scotus, *Lect.* 1. 17. 2. 4, n. 240 (Vatican edn., xvii. 258).

[31] Scotus, *Ord.* 2. 3. 1. 4, n. 114 (Vatican edn., vii. 447; Spade, 87–8).

against him. The *Lectura* account, discussed at the very end of section 1, might be more promising here. But this account seems to entail the odd claim that, for any material substance x, some parts of x's matter exist without any quantity at all. And this would seem to imply, wrongly, that x is not equally dense all over.[32]

---

[32] Indeed, given that $\rho = m/V$, the *Lectura* account would imply that some parts of a body are of infinite density: which is, I take it, necessarily false. Goddu argues that an analogous oversight in Ockham supports his claim that Ockham fails to have even a basic concept of mass. But this oversight is hardly sufficient to show that Ockham—or Scotus— did not have a concept of mass of the sort that I have been trying to outline. It is also worth noting in this context Scotus's account of the possible motion of a body in a vacuum. Scotus is clear that the speed of a body moving in a vacuum would be finite. But this is not because he has a concept of mass as providing some sort of *intrinsic* resistance. (On the significance of intrinsic resistance here, see Pierre Duhem, *Le Système du monde: histoire des doctrines cosmologiques de Platon à Copernique* (10 vols., Paris: Hermann, n.d.-1959), viii. 18–20, trans. in Duhem, *Medieval Cosmology: Theories of Infinity, Place, Time, Void, and the Plurality of Worlds*, ed. Roger Ariew (Chicago and London: University of Chicago Press, 1985), 378–81, referring to Aquinas, *In Ph.* 4. 12, n. 536 (p. 258[b]).) Rather, he claims that the limit on speed follows from the *spatial* extension of the mobile thing, such that local motion requires the successive occupation of different places. He seems in fact to suppose that motion necessarily takes time. He discusses this by referring to the 'essential succes- sion' of motion, by which he means some sort of (unfixed) speed. Further qualification in terms of speed is attributed to the (accidental) presence of the (extrinsic) resistance of the medium through which the mobile thing moves. A body moving through a vacuum will have essential succession without the further qualification resulting from the resistance of the medium (since a vacuum can offer no resistance): see Scotus, *Ord.* 2. 2. 2. 5, n. 435 (Vatican edn., vii. 348–9). Scotus's failure to use his inchoate conception of mass in this context is disappointing, but not fatal for the issue of whether he had such a conception.

10

Quality: Unity, Degree, and Change

Scotus holds that a degree of a quality—say, a shade of blue—counts as an H-unity, exhibiting the features of such unities outlined in Chapter 8. Scotus's reasons for this claim are tied up with his account of the way in which qualities undergo changes in degree or intensity (say, a change in the quality blue, from light blue to dark blue). In particular, Scotus holds that any degree of a quality Q is a discrete homogeneous item, containing lower degrees as parts, and that changes in degree can be explained by the addition or subtraction of homogeneous parts of Q. These two claims together entail that any degree of Q is an H-unity. I shall discuss both Scotus's account of changes in degree and his claim that a degree of Q is an H-unity. The account of change is, of course, directly relevant to a discussion of Scotus's physics. The account of degrees will help to clarify some of the metaphysical presuppositions which inform Scotus's account.

1. THE SHAPE OF THE ARGUMENT

Scotus considers, and rejects, three possible pairs of theories concerning the degrees of a quality and their changes. In summary:

(I) (a) A difference in degree of a quality Q is explained by each degree of Q being a *species* of Q.

   (b) A change from one degree D to another E is explained by the complete corruption of D and the complete generation of E (such that no part of D is a part of E).

(II) (a) A difference in degree of a quality Q is explained by the degree of participation in Q by a substance x.

   (b) A change from one degree D to another E is explained by x's having a greater or lesser degree of participation in Q.

(III) (a) A difference in degree of a quality Q is explained by the
degree of Q's actualization.

(b) A change from one degree D to another E is explained by an
increase or decrease in Q's actualization.

(Ib)is espoused by Godfrey of Fontaines and Walter Burley. (I have not
been able to find anyone who accepts (Ia), though, as we shall see,
Scotus holds that it is entailed by (Ib).) The second theory is adopted
(loosely) by Aquinas. The third exists in two different versions. Both
accept (IIIa), but draw on different ways of understanding (IIIb):

(IIIb1) A change from one degree D to another E is explained by an
increase or decrease in Q's actualization, such that the higher
degree contains actual parts which existed merely potentially in
the lower one;

(IIIb2) A change from one degree D to another E is explained by an
increase or decrease in Q's actualization, such that the whole
higher degree existed merely potentially in the lower one.

(IIIb1) is accepted by Henry of Ghent, (IIIb2) by an unidentified
opponent.

Scotus rejects all of these theories, and proposes his own:

(IV) (a) A difference in degree of a quality Q is explained by the
amount of the quality present, such that a degree of Q is an
H-unity.

(b) A change from one degree D to another E is explained by the
addition and subtraction of (homogeneous) parts of Q.

As Scotus understands the first theory, its two claims, (Ia) and (Ib), are
logically equivalent (each entails the other). According to Scotus, the
change thesis (IIb) of the second theory entails the degree thesis (IIa);
likewise, each of (IIIb1) and (IIIb2) entails (IIIa). Scotus's theory consists of two equivalent claims, (IVa) and (IVb). Scotus argues that the
conjoint falsity of (Ib), (IIb), and (IIIb) entails (IVb); and that (IVb)
entails (IVa). But I take it that, given some of Scotus's presuppositions
here, the conjoint falsity of (Ia), (IIa), and (IIIa) would likewise entail
(IVa). We need now to look in more detail at these four theories.[1]

---

[1] For an extensive discussion of medieval theories of the degrees of a quality, see
Anneliese Maier, *Zwei Grundprobleme der scholastischen Naturphilosophie: Das Problem
der intensiven Grösse. Die Impetustheorie* (Studien zur Naturphilosophie der Spätscholastik, 2), 3rd edn., Raccolta di Studi e Testi, 37 (Rome: Storia e Letteratura, 1968), 3–109.

2. THEORY (I): GODFREY OF FONTAINES AND WALTER BURLEY

Scotus proposes two arguments for

(Ib) A change from one degree *D* to another *E* is explained by the complete corruption of *D* and the complete generation of *E* (such that no part of *D* is a part of *E*).

The first, which I label '(I.1)', shows that (Ib) is entailed by

(Ia) A difference in degree of a quality *Q* is explained by each degree of *Q* being a *species* of *Q*,

The second, which I label '(I.2)', appeals directly to an account of the nature of motion. The second of these is found in Walter; the first seems to be a construct of Scotus's, though one based on a number of passages found in Godfrey.

(I.1) Neither Godfrey nor Walter expressly accepts (Ia). Scotus, however, provides an argument for it. He reasons that

(A) More perfect species are less composite than less perfect species

entails

(1) It is not possible that the intension of a more perfect species includes a less perfect species,

which in turn entails

(2) It is not possible that an individual instantiating a less perfect species is part of an individual instantiating a more perfect species.[2]

But since

(B) Degrees of a quality exhibit a hierarchy of perfection,

---

[2] Oddly, (2), which Scotus does not explicitly reject, has some consequences which would be fatal for Scotus's claim, noted in Ch. 7, that different quantities are specifically different from each other. Scotus accepts that a quantity is an H-unity, such that any instance of a given quantity includes (potentially) all lesser quantities. But given (2), the claim that a quantity is an H-unity is inconsistent with the claim that different quantities are different species. On the other hand, nothing in Scotus's theory entails that he accept (2). Hence (2) need not present Scotus's account of quantity with any real problems. For (A), see Godfrey, *Quod.* 7. 7 (ed. M. de Wulf and J. Hoffmanns, Les Philosphes Belges: Textes et Études, 3 (Louvain: Instit Supérieur de Philosophie de l'Université, 1914), iii. 360–2). Godfrey does not infer (1) or (2) from (A).

(2) entails (Ia).[3]

Given (Ia), Scotus attempts to show that it entails (Ib). His argument is loosely based on one proposed by Godfrey. The starting-point is the Aristotelian comparison of a species with a number.[4] According to Aristotle, a number is indivisible in the sense that addition or subtraction will yield a *different* number. A species is similarly indivisible: the addition or subtraction of defining features will yield a different species.[5] Following a hint in Godfrey, Scotus argues that the Aristotelian

    (C) A species is indivisible,[6]

coupled with (Ia), entails (Ib).[7] Scotus, as we shall see, does not attack

---

[3] Scotus, *Ord.* 1. 17. 2. 1, n. 200 (Vatican edn., v. 235). As we shall see below, Scotus holds that (Ib) entails (Ia).

[4] Arist. *Metaph.* 8. 3 (1043^b32–1044^a14).   [5] Ibid. (1043^b36–1044^a2).

[6] For (C), see Godfrey, *Quod.* 2. 10 (ed. M. de Wulf and A. Pelzer, Les Philosophes Belges: Textes et Études, 2 (Louvain: Institut Supérieur de Philosophie de l'Université, 1904), 140, 145).

[7] Scotus, *Ord.* 1. 17. 2. 1, n. 200 (Vatican edn., v. 235). Scotus's argument bears some relation to the following passage in Godfrey: 'Since more and less in qualities cannot be applied according to the notion of species (since [species] consists in an indivisible), it is necessary that it is applied according to the notion of individuals. And since also the existence of an individual, in so far as it is an individual, is simple, [it follows that] if there is a change according to more or less in an individual, there is also a change of the individual itself': *Quod.* 2. 10 (de Wulf and Pelzer edn., 145). The passage continues: 'though the species remains the same'. So Godfrey does not hold that (Ib) entails (Ia). For Walter Burley's acceptance of (Ib), see *De Int.* 4 ((Venice, 1496), 10va); also *De Inst.* (ed. Herman and Charlotte Shapiro, *Archiv für Geschichte der Philosophie*, 47 (1965), 157–83, p. 171). Burley's *De Intensione* dates from 1319–27: see C. Martin, 'Walter Burley', in R.W. Southern (ed.), *Oxford Studies Presented to Daniel Callus*, Oxford Historical Society, NS 16 (Oxford: Clarendon Press, 1964), 194–230, pp. 208–9. The treatise thus post-dates Scotus's work by a considerable number of years. *De Instanti* dates from 1326–7 (ibid. 209–10), so is again rather too late to have been known to Scotus. Perhaps Burley had formulated his views as early as his years as a Master of Arts at Merton College (1300/1–1306/7), in which case Scotus could have known his views. More likely perhaps, given Burley's claim in *De Instanti* that (Ib) was propounded by others (*De Inst.*, p. 171: presumably at least Godfrey of Fontaines), we should assume that the Parisian Godfrey, and not Burley, is the source for Scotus's argument. Like Godfrey, Walter rejects (Ia). He argues: 'One form can be more intense than another of the same species' (*De Int.* 4 (p. 11va)), and, like Godfrey, that any individual form is indivisible, such that the indivdual cannot remain over any increase or decrease (see *De Int.* 6 (p. $14^{ra–b}$)). Walter's reason for this is that 'no quality remains in two instants, whereas that which is increased must remain' (*De Int.* 4 (p. 11rb; see also p. 10va)). Walter's position is thus, as far as I can see, indistinguishable from Godfrey's. For recent discussions of Walter's acceptance of (Ib), see Edith Sylla, 'Medieval Concepts of the Latitude of Forms: The Oxford Calculators', *Archives d'histoire doctrinale et littéraire du moyen-âge*, 40 (1973), 223–83, pp. 233–8; Marilyn McCord Adams, *William Ockham*, Publications in Medieval Studies, 26 (2 vols., Notre Dame, Ind.: University of Notre Dame Press, 1987), ii. 700–9.

this inference from (Ia) to (Ib). But he attacks (Ia) in a way which entails rejecting (C)—and presumably (A) as well.

(I.2) The second argument infers (Ib) directly from the claim (accepted by all sides in the debate) that

(D) The end terms of motion are incompossible.

Scotus reasons that (D) entails

(3) It is not possible that one of the end terms of motion includes the other as a part,

which entails (Ib).[8]

Scotus argues that theory (I) is false. He rebuts it with a total of six arguments, of which I shall give four here. I label these '(I′.1)'–'(I′.4)'. The point of the first three of these is that (Ib) cannot explain all possible changes in degree. The fourth serves to show that (Ia) is false, and that the falsity of (Ia) entails the falsity of (Ib). Scotus also offers rebuttals of (I.1) and (I.2), which I label respectively '(I.1′)' and '(I.2′)'.

(I′.1) On (Ib), the generation and corruption theory, a change in degree from degree D to degree E entails that D is completely corrupted and E is completely generated. Scotus argues that this theory is incapable of allowing for genuinely *continuous* changes. In a genuinely continuous change, it is not possible that any degree persists for a period (however short).[9] But neither can any degree exist merely instantaneously (i.e. such that the degree does not persist at all). If a degree in a continuous change existed instantaneously, a continuous change would be composed of indivisible steps or stages.[10] And, as we shall see in Chapter 12, Scotus (following Aristotle) thinks that much the same arguments can be marshalled against motion's being composed of indivisibles as can be marshalled against a spatial magnitude's being composed of indivisibles.[11] In the *textus interpolatus* of the *Ordinatio*, Scotus notes further that any putative continuous change composed of indivisible stages would have to be composed of an *infinite* number of such indivisibles, which is (for the same reason) impossible.[12] I do not

---

[8] Scotus, *Ord.* 1. 17. 2. 1, n. 199 (Vatican edn., v. 235). See also (B.1) in the previous chapter. The argument is found in Burley, *De Int.* 1 (p. 4$^{ra–va}$). For (D), see also Godfrey *Quod.* 14. 5 (ed. J. Hoffmanns, Les Philosophes Belges: Textes et Études, 5/3–4 (Louvain: Institut Supérieur de Philosophie de l'Université, 1935), 415–16).

[9] I discuss this claim in detail in Ch. 12.

[10] Scotus, *Lect.* 1. 17. 2. 1, n. 143 (Vatican edn., xxvii. 226–7).

[11] I have discussed this latter impossibility in Ch. 7.

[12] Scotus, *Ord.* 1. 17. 2. 1, *textus interpolatus* (Vatican edn., v. 244, ll. 18–23).

see a way for the adherents of (Ib) to reply to this, and Burley is later happy to admit it as a (harmless) consequence of his theory.[13]

(I′.2) The second of Scotus's arguments raises an interesting problem which I will return to later. He argues that in the case of at least some qualitative changes, an increase in the overall degree of a quality—say from a degree D to a higher degree E—can be explained by the action of an agent a which could never by itself produce E. But on (Ib) the change from D to E involves the complete generation *de novo* of E. So on (Ib) a by itself will produce E, which is contrary to the supposition that a by itself cannot produce E. The conclusion is that (Ib) cannot provide a complete theory of qualitative change.[14] The argument raises a number of metaphysical questions so central to Scotus's position here that I will return to a detailed discussion of them below.[15]

(I′.3) The third argument against (Ib) is similar, again drawing on the incapacity of (Ib) to explain some sorts of qualitative change. The changes here pertain to those qualities which admit of contraries. Scotus's examples are heat and its contrary, coldness. Suppose we gradually cool an object x exhibiting a degree of heat E by applying a cold object c to it. On any account, x will exhibit lesser degrees of heat before it finally becomes cold. Scotus reasons that, on (Ib), new degrees of heat, less than E, will be generated *de novo*. But the only possible agent for the generation of these degrees of heat will be c. Scotus argues that in this case c—*qua* cold—would be the cause of heat. And this is impossible.[16]

---

[13] Burley, *De Int.* 6 (p. 14[va]).

[14] Scotus, *Ord.* 1. 17. 2. 1, nn. 208–9 (Vatican edn., v. 239–40). Burley raises this objection to his own position. He replies that it is a problem for any account of the intensification and remission of qualities. (Scotus, I believe, has good reason to suppose that it is not an objection to his own position. I discuss this reason below.) Burley argues that a lesser degree of a quality can produce a degree greater than itself during the process of remitting some quality: cold water added to a hot bath, for example, produces a heat far greater than itself. He concludes that the capacity of a quality to produce a degree greater than itself is a relational capacity, not an absolute one: a capacity, in other words, which depends on the sort of patient the quality acts on: see *De Int.* 6 (p. 13[va]). A more satisfactory solution would be to see the quality and the (putative) patient as, in some cases, joint causes of the effect. The hot water *and* the cold water are the causes of a warm bath.   [15] See pp. 189–90.

[16] Scotus, *Ord.* 1. 17. 2. 1, n. 212 (Vatican edn., v. 243); see *idem, Lect.* 1. 17. 2. 1, nn. 139–41 (Vatican edn., xvii. 225–6). Burley replies that there is no problem in an agent producing a contrary form, just so long as that form is part of a process towards the production of the form naturally produced by the agent: in my example, C can produce degrees of heat less than E just so long as the degrees of heat produced by C are part of a process the end result of which is the production of coldness. See *De Int.* 6 (p. 13[rb]). The reply looks to me to be no more than stipulative.

These three arguments try to show that (Ib) is false. Scotus has a fourth argument, directly against (Ia).

(I′.4) Scotus argues in two steps. (i) (Ib) entails (Ia); (ii) (Ia) is false. The second of these two steps is not found in the *Lectura*, the *Ordinatio*, or the *Reportatio*, though it is found in the *textus interpolatus* of the *Ordinatio*, marked as an addition 'manu Scoti'—in Scotus's own hand. Unfortunately, Scotus's attempt to show the first of these claims—namely, that (Ib) entails (Ia)—cannot be counted a success. So the argument will not be effective against (Ib). On the other hand, the second step—that (Ia) is false—seems reasonable enough.

(i) Scotus's argument for the first of these two claims is extremely compressed. To understand it, we must recap the basic (Ib) claim: namely, that changes in degree are explained by the total generation and corruption of degrees, such that different degrees have no real parts in common. Scotus supposes that this view of a change in degree is inconsistent with any theory of the degrees of a quality which would allow a 'quantitative' account of the degrees of a quality (such as, for example, Scotus's own (IVa), which I discuss in the section 5 below). The argument to (Ia) relies on the following principle:

(E) For every nature F and every instance x of F, if (a) x is necessarily F, (b) F is a unified composite concept, and (c) F is indivisible, then F is a species.

(b) and (c) here require a bit of explanation. For a nature to be a 'unified composite concept' means that the nature is not an accidental unity. (It will presumably mean, additionally, that the nature is not an aggregate, though Scotus does not spell this out. Perhaps he thinks (understandably) that no aggregate has sufficient unity to count as a nature.) By a nature's being *indivisible*, Scotus means that it cannot be composed of lower degrees, or divided up into lower degrees. Scotus supposes, as we have just seen, that (Ib) entails that a quality is in this sense indivisible. (The reason is that (Ib) entails that different degrees can have no real parts in common; which is presumably much the same as claiming that different degrees are indivisible.) Scotus reasons that (Ib) entails

(4) For every degree D of a quality Q, and every instance x of $(D + Q)$, x is necessarily $(D + Q)$, $(D + Q)$ is a unified composite concept, and $(D + Q)$ is indivisible.

(4) and (E) entail

(5) $(D + Q)$ is a species,

which is equivalent to (Ia).[17] (E) looks reasonable enough. Any property which satisfies (a), (b), and (c) will surely count as a natural kind. (Note, however, that (E) commits neither Scotus nor his opponent to the claim that satisfying any of (a), (b), and (c) is *necessary* for a property to count as a species; and, as we shall see, Scotus does not believe that satisfying (c) is necessary for a property to count as a species.) Why accept that (Ib) entails (4)? Scotus unfortunately does not offer any reasons on behalf of his opponent here. Presumably, Scotus would want to claim that (Ib) is inconsistent with any *quantitative* account of difference in degree. Perhaps he would argue that (Ib) entails that different degrees have no parts in common. But the crucial

(1) It is not possible that the intension of a more perfect species includes a less perfect species

seems to entail, but not be entailed by, (Ib). So I do not see how Scotus defends the inference from (Ib) to (5). I conclude that the first step of (I′.4) fails to show that (Ib) entails (Ia).

(ii) The second step takes issue with (Ia). And it seems to me that this step is successful. So while (I′.4) leaves (Ib) unassailed, it seems to give good reason to reject (Ia). According to Scotus, the only possible account of the degrees of a quality is a 'quantitative' account (such as his own (IVa)). And such a quantitative account entails that (Ia) is false. Scotus's reason for this last claim is that an amount (such as is entailed on the quantitative account) does not have sufficient *quidditative* content to serve as a differentiating feature of the type relevant for determining sortal differences.[18] Scotus refers us to a passage in *Ordinatio* 1. 8, where he tries to show why an amount cannot serve as a specific difference. He argues that the concept 'quality + degree' is no more composite than the concept 'quality'.[19] Presumably, Scotus's

[17] Scotus's discussion focuses on an attempt to defend (E): 'Whatever [concept] is predicated in itself [*per se*] and quidditatively [*in quid*] of individuals, and [the concept] is in itself one thing, is their [viz. the individuals'] species. A nature in a determinate degree—of this or that sort [of degree]—is predicated quidditatively of the individuals, and is in itself one thing. The reason is that the nature according to this degree belongs essentially to those things which have the nature in such a sort of degree, and the grade adds no accident to the nature. It is therefore clear that the nature in such a grade is a species': *Ord.* 1. 17. 2. 1, n. 214 (Vatican edn., v. 245). But presumably Scotus will want to defend the inference from (E) to (5) too.

[18] Scotus, *Ord.* 1. 17. 2. 1, *textus interpolatus* (Vatican edn., v. 245, ll. 22–3).

[19] Ibid. 1. 8. 1. 3, n. 108 (Vatican edn., iv. 202–3).

point is that simply specifying 'how much' of a quality we have does not add anything to the *definition* of the quality. On this account, the concept 'quality + degree' fails to be a composite concept. Now, according to (E), being a composite concept is one of a sufficient set of conditions for being a species. But in fact, it is clear that being a composite concept is also *necessary* for being a species. A species, according to standard Aristotelian accounts, is a composite of genus and difference.[20] And on this account, being a composite concept is necessary for being a species.

I think I can get some glimmer of what Scotus is trying to say in denying that a quantity could serve as a specific difference. We might well want to hold that different degrees of, say, blue are the same sort of thing as each other, and that they are different from each other in a different way from that in which, say, blue and red are. Whatever we make of Scotus's attempt to refute (Ia), I think it is clear that an account of the degrees of a quality that appeals to a quantitative model has far more *explanatory* power than (Ia). Scotus's opponent would, I suspect, be at a loss to give some sort of account of the features which *do* differentiate different degrees of a quality.

In the *Ordinatio*, Scotus makes no attempt to refute (I.1). But in the *Reportatio* and *Additiones Magnae* we can find an argument against it.

(I.1′) Scotus reasons that it is not possible to infer (Ia) from

> (2) It is not possible that an individual instantiating a less perfect species is part of an individual instantiating a more perfect species,

since it is not the case that a grade of a quality is a species; that is, since

> (5) $(D + Q)$ is a species

is false (where D = any degree of any quality Q). In effect, Scotus claims just that (I.1) would be relevant to the question at issue only if (5) were true; but in fact (5) is false.[21]

(I′.2) Given that (Ib) is false, Scotus needs to reply to the attempt to infer (Ib) from

> (D) The end terms of motion are incompossible,

a claim accepted by Scotus. Scotus reasons that (D) does not entail

---

[20] See e.g. Arist. *Top.* 1. 4 (101^{b}17–23).
[21] Scotus, *Rep.* 1. 17. 3 (MS M, fo. 83^r), conveniently summarized in *Add. Mag.* 1. 17. 3, n. 6 (Wadding edn., xi. 99^a).

(3) It is not possible that one of the end terms of motion includes the other as a part.

He argues that necessary for the incompossibility of the end terms (*D* and *E*) of a motion is just that the end terms are not *in all respects* the same. And this is consistent with the claim that *D* could be a part of *E*, or vice versa[22]—a claim which, as we shall see, Scotus accepts.

Scotus's arguments against theory (I) are a mixed bag. (I'.1)–(I'.3), directed against (Ib), all seem to me to have some value. And if we accept that (Ib) is entailed by (Ia), these three arguments are sufficient to refute (Ia) as well. It is difficult to know what to make of (I'.4), Scotus's argument against (Ia). Perhaps we should concede the minimal claim that theory (I) is incapable of providing an *explanation* of differences in degree.

3. THEORY (II): THOMAS AQUINAS

According to the second theory, changes in degree of a quality *Q* are paradigmatically explained by the degree of a subject's participation, or *inesse*, in *Q*. This is Aquinas's basic model for non-complex qualities.[23] Godfrey of Fontaines also holds that changes of some qualities can be explained in terms of participation—specifically, those where we might need to appeal to the *disposition* of a subject for a species of a quality.[24] I could, in an example Godfrey gives, participate to a greater or lesser degree in whiteness in virtue of my having a greater or lesser disposition for whiteness. But, as I discuss in a moment, Godfrey is quite clear that such changes are ultimately reducible to changes that can be described according to some other theory (perhaps (Ib) or (IVb)).[25]

---

[22] Scotus, *Ord.* 1. 17. 2. 1, nn. 226–7, 230–1 (Vatican edn., v. 249–51).
[23] *ST* 1–2. 52. 1 (ed. Petrus Caramello (3 vols., Turin and Rome: Marietti, 1952–6), i. 229ᵃ-31ᵇ). By 'non-complex qualities' I mean qualities which, in Aquinas's words, 'are not predicated according to an order to something else' (i. 230ᵇ). Heat and colours are examples of such qualities. Qualities such as habits will not satisfy this description: they 'receive their species from the thing to which they are ordered' (i. 230ᵃ). Aquinas allows a quantitative account for degrees of such qualities. I can, for example, *know* an (extensively) large number of propositions. But the quantitative account is not, according to Aquinas, a complete account. My friend can know the same set of propositions 'more easily and clearly' (*ST* 1–2. 52. 2 (i. 231ᵇ)), and he does this by participating more greatly in the relevant habit.
[24] Godfrey, *Quod.* 2. 10 (de Wulf and Pelzer edn., 141–2, 146).
[25] Ibid. (de Wulf and Pelzer edn., 142–3).

Clearly, the claim that changes can be explained in terms of degrees of participation—namely, (IIb)—entails (IIa), the claim that differences in degree can be explained in terms of participation.

As Scotus understands (IIb), it entails that numerically one quality instance Q will survive unchanged over any number of changes in degree. These changes are in turn explained in terms of more basic changes in the degree to which a subject x participates in Q. This degree of participation is in turn explained by the degree to which x is *disposed* to receive Q.[26] Given that (IIb) entails (IIa), as just noted, Scotus employs two strategies against Aquinas's theory. The first is to attack (IIb) directly; the second is to attack (IIb) by showing that (IIa) is false.

(II′.1) Scotus's major argument against (IIb)—and the only one I discuss here—is that it violates his principle

(F) It is not possible that change occurs without the production and/or destruction of an individual thing,

a principle we encountered in Chapters 3 and 6, and which is central to Scotus's natural philosophy. On (IIb), in a change from one degree D to another E, D and E are numerically identical. But on this showing a change can occur which does not involve the production and/or destruction of anything.[27]

(II′.2) Scotus's most devastating criticism of (IIa) is that it turns out to be *reducible* to a different theory: specifically, to Scotus's (IVa), which I discuss below. As Scotus understands (IIa), it involves talk of degrees of participation, or *inesse*, in a subject. And these degrees of participation themselves require explaining:

Greatness with regard to *inesse* is attributed [by the adherents of the participation theory] either [i] to the greater disposition of the subject, or [ii] to the greater removal of the opposing indisposing [quality].[28]

[26] Scotus, *Ord.* 1. 17. 2. 2, n. 241 (Vatican edn., v. 254–5); see also *idem, Lect.* 1. 17. 2. 2, n. 207 (Vatican edn., xvii. 247). That Scotus should explain participation in terms of disposition shows that it is Godfrey's version of the theory, rather than Aquinas's, which is his immediate source. But Aquinas is a far worthier target, since he supposes (with Scotus's objector) that there are some changes for which the most basic explanation is participation.

[27] Scotus, *Ord.* 1. 17. 2. 2, n. 243 (Vatican edn., v. 256); see also *idem, Lect.* 1. 17. 2. 2, n. 162 (Vatican edn., xvii. 232).

[28] Scotus, *Ord.* 1. 17. 2. 2, n. 241 (Vatican edn., v. 255).

Scotus later adds a third: (iii) degrees of *inesse* can be explained by degrees of a quality's *rootedness* (*radicatio*) in a subject.[29]

(i) Scotus reasons that degrees of a disposition can be explained only in one of two ways. First, the disposition of a subject x for a quality Q could itself be a further quality of x. Secondly, the degree of disposition of x for Q could itself be the *result* of a degree of a more basic quality Q_1 of x. For example, dryness is a disposing quality for heat: so degrees of heat could be explained by invoking degrees of dryness. Scotus argues, however, that both of these two explanations for degree ultimately rely on some quality whose degrees cannot be explained merely in terms of disposition.[30]

(ii) Scotus's strategy against the second explanation is similar. The opposing indisposing form proposed in this explanation must, Scotus reasons, admit of degrees; and these degrees cannot be explained simply by invoking a further opposing indisposing form. We cannot explain the degrees of the indisposing quality Q', opposed to Q, by appealing to degrees of Q, since degrees of Q are supposed to be explained by degrees of Q'.[31]

(iii) Scotus rejects the third option, rootedness, by proposing a dilemma. Either (a) rootedness is an absolute property, or (b) it is a relational property (presumably, a relation between the subject and its inhering quality). If (a), then degrees of rootedness must be explicable in terms of some further quality. If (b), then degrees of rootedness would have to be explained by degrees exhibited by the foundation of the relation.[32] The first of these consequences seems clear enough, and its fatally non-explanatory nature evident. But the second is rather opaque. Presumably, Scotus would argue that a relation R between a subject x and an absolute property Q is ontologically dependent on both x and Q, such that R cannot be used to explain features of either x or Q. And of course, a degree of Q is a feature of Q.

Whatever we make of this last argument, it seems clear to me that

[29] Ibid. n. 247 (Vatican edn., v. 259). This position was adopted by William of Auxerre: see *Sum. Aur.* 3. 16. 4 (ed. Jean Ribailler, Spicilegium Bonaventurianum, 16–19 (4 vols., Paris: CNRS; Grottaferrata: Collegium S. Bonaventurae ad Claras ad Aquas, 1980–6), iii. 317–18). Aquinas later discusses and rejects the theory, which he regards as equivalent to (and hence unable to explain) the theory that differences in degree can be explained by degrees of *inesse*: see *ST* 2–2. 24. 4 ad 3 (ii. 120[b]).

[30] Scotus, *Ord.* 1. 17. 2. 2, n. 245 (Vatican edn., v. 256–8). Godfrey argues similarly: see *Quod.* 2. 10 (de Wulf and Pelzer edn., 142–3).

[31] Scotus, *Lect.* 1. 17. 2. 2, n. 171 (Vatican edn., xvii. 235).

[32] Scotus, *Ord.* 1. 17. 2. 2, n. 247 (Vatican edn., xvii. 259).

the participation theory cannot survive Scotus's attack. Perhaps in any case we should not regard participation as anything more than a metaphor. And in this case, any explanatory value it might have would have to be spelled out in terms of an appeal to those real features of a thing which admit of non-metaphorical description.

4. THEORY (III): HENRY OF GHENT

Henry's theory—and Scotus's refutation of it—raises rather deeper metaphysical questions than either of the two we have considered so far. The basic claim is

> (IIIb) A change from one degree D to another E is explained by an increase or decrease in Q's actualization.

(IIIb) in turn entails

> (IIIa) A difference in degree of a quality Q is explained by the degree of Q's actualization.

Underlying (IIIa) is a claim, deriving from Simplicius, that a quality has a certain 'latitude' (*latitudo*). Henry interprets this claim as entailing that any lesser degree contains potentially all greater degrees. As Henry understands his position, it involves the claim that any *individual* quality instance (except for instances of the maximal degree of a quality) contains the potentiality for increasing. The individual quality instance is thus susceptible of degrees. Henry uses this to explain (IIIb): increases can be explained by the actualization of parts—or of whole quality instances—which exist potentially in the lower degree. Since the parts (or quality instances) already *exist*, they are not generated. Rather, they are *actualized*.[33]

How is this process of actualization to be understood? Given that lower degrees contain higher ones only potentially, one plausible reading would be to claim that a quality instance is the *subject* of an increase in degree: the quality instance, in other words, is what is

---

[33] Scotus, *Lect.* 1. 17. 2. 3, n. 189 (Vatican edn., xvii. 241), with reference to Henry, *Quod.* 5. 19 ((2 vols., Venice, 1613), i. 291^{va-vb}). For the Simplicius reference, see *In Cat.* 'De Qualitate' (ed. A. Pattin, W. Stuyven, and C. Steel, Corpus Latinum Commentarium in Aristotelem Graecorum, 5 (2 vols., Louvain: Publications Universitaires; Paris: Béatrice–Nauwelaerts 1970 [vol. i]; Leiden: Brill, 1975 [vol. ii], ii. 300, 325), referred to by Henry in *Quod.* 4. 15 (i. 184rb).

increased. Proponents of (IIIb), however, would not want to accept such a simple account, mainly because it seems to contradict the widely accepted Boethian claim that, 'forms cannot be subjects'.[34] As we saw, Scotus notes two possible versions of (IIIb). Neither of them looks to me to avoid the claim that a quality instance is (in some sense or other) the subject of a change, though they both deny that a quality instance *qua* individual is the subject of a change. I have labelled the two versions '(IIIb1)' and '(IIIb2)'.

On (IIIb1), proposed by Henry of Ghent, the denial of the claim that a quality instance is the subject of an increase entails the following:

> (G) It is not the case that lower degrees of a quality Q exhibit S-potentiality for higher degrees.

Henry cryptically argues instead that a quality instance has a potentiality for change not in virtue of its being a subject but rather 'in virtue of its nature and essence'.[35] It is difficult to see what all this amounts to.

On (IIIb2), proposed by an unknown opponent, (G) is understood to entail

> (6) Lower degrees of a quality Q exhibit objective potentiality for higher degrees;

such that, Scotus explains, '[the lower degree], as imperfect, can become perfect'.[36] Scotus's use of the phrase 'objective potentiality' here is confusing, and it evidently is not to be understood in Scotus's normal sense. In Scotus's normal usage, objective potentiality is a property exemplifiable only by *non-existent* items. On this view, a degree E of a quality is capable of existing first potentially and then actually, such that E contains no parts not found in D; D just has the capacity for 'getting bigger'. Presumably 'having actual existence' and 'having potential existence' are *accidental* properties of D and E.

Why should anyone want to accept (IIIb) in either of its versions?

[34] Boethius, *De Trin.* 2 (*The Theological Tractates: The Consolation of Philosophy*, ed. H. F. Stewart, E. K. Rand, and S. J. Tester, Loeb Classical Library (Cambridge, Mass.: Havard University Press; London: Heinemann, 1978), 10), referred to in Scotus, *Lect.* 1. 17. 2. 3, n. 187 (Vatican edn., xvii. 230) and Henry, *Quod.* 5. 19 obj. 1 and ad 1 (Venice edn., i. 291[va–vb]). The gist of Boethius's claim is that forms are *universals*, and as such cannot be *instances* of properties. The point of the Scotist objection, presumably, is that forms cannot be in potentiality to further modifications.

[35] Henry, *Quod.* 5. 19 ad 1 (Venice edn., i. 291[vb]); see Scotus, *Lect.* 1. 17. 2. 3, n. 190 (Vatican edn., xvii. 241–2).

[36] Scotus, *Lect.* 1. 17. 2. 3, n. 191 (Vatican edn., xvii. 242).

Given that (Ib) and (IIb) are false, Henry argues that (IVb)—the position that an increase involves the addition of completely new parts—is false too. To show this, he gives an example. Suppose we mix together two equally tepid objects. If the addition theory were true, the resultant substance should be twice as hot as its components. And experience shows that this is obviously false. So addition cannot be sufficient to explain an increase in intensity.[37] And Henry obviously regards his proposed alternative theory as sufficient to account for increase.

Scotus is convinced, for some fairly deep metaphysical reasons, that (IIIb) is false. As we shall see, he accepts (IVb), according to which increase and decrease should be explained by the addition and subtraction of parts. I discuss his theory below, as well as his proposals for rebutting Henry's empirical objection to the addition and subtraction theory, just outlined. Scotus marshals arguments against both (IIIb1) and (IIIb2). He thinks that (IIIb1) will turn out to be indistinguishable from a theory explaining increase in terms of the addition of new parts. According to (IIIb1), an increase involves the actualization of parts which pre-exist potentially in a lower degree of the quality. But, Scotus reasons, if the parts begin to have actuality, and if the lower degree is somehow in potentiality to these parts, it will follow that the lower degree in fact exhibits S-potentiality for the higher one. This violates (G); so (IIIb1) is contradictory.[38] Given the incomprehensibility of the theory as Henry puts it, I can only assume that Scotus's criticism is a fair one.

(IIIb2) is a far more interesting account, and likewise Scotus's attempt to refute it. The proponent of this theory is happy to allow a sense in which a whole item can exist potentially. As we saw in Chapter 3, Scotus does not think that such a claim could possibly make any sense. Scotus tries to apply his model of objective potentiality—where objective potentiality is the sort of potentiality exhibited by non-existent objects—to his opponent's theory. Not surprisingly, he comes up with absurd results.[39] But Scotus also offers two attempts at substantive criticisms of the theory. The attempts reveal clearly the metaphysical gulf between Scotus and his opponent. On (IIIb2), a higher degree *E* contains no parts not found in *D*, the lower degree from which *E* was actualized. So, Scotus reasons, *E* and *D* are identical. In this case, given Scotus's principle

---

[37] Henry, *Quod.* 5. 19 (Venice edn., i. 291^{va-vb}); see Scotus, *Lect.* 1. 17. 2. 3, n. 188 (Vatican edn., xvii. 240–1).
[38] Scotus, *Lect.* 1. 17. 2. 3, nn. 195–6 (Vatican edn., xvii. 243).
[39] Ibid. n. 194 (Vatican edn., xvii. 242.)

(F) It is not possible that change occurs without the production and/or destruction of an individual thing,

an increase—from *D* to *E*—will entail that the same thing (*D/E*) is produced twice over: 'once through creation,[40] and once through augmentation'.[41] Scotus's opponent would presumably reject (F) here. But even given this, it is difficult to see how *D* and *E* could possibly be really identical, as (IIIb2) seems to entail. They do not appear to have *all* the same properties.

Scotus's second argument against (IIIb2) exploits his worry that nothing can *exist* first potentially and then actually. He reasons that if an object exists at *t* (in whatever sense of 'exists'), there is no way in which it could be held to come into existence at t_1. Scotus uses the example of a part: if a part exists potentially at *t*, there is no way in which it can begin to exist actually at t_1.[42] The adherent of (IIIb2) could argue that Scotus has conflated 'existing potentially' and 'existing actually'. But it is easy to be sympathetic to Scotus's claim that nothing is such that it can exist potentially. We probably would not want a universe ontologically dense with non-actual existents, particularly if, as seems to be the case on (IIIb2), actual existence is an accidental property of these items.

5. THEORY (IV): DUNS SCOTUS

Given that (Ib), (IIb), and (IIIb) are false, Scotus reasons that the only possible explanation for a change in the degree of a quality is

(IVb) A change from one degree *D* to another *E* is explained by the addition and subtraction of (homogeneous) parts of *Q*.

Scotus describes his position as follows:

In this increase there is some change, otherwise charity would not be increased. Therefore it is necessary to posit some new reality, which previously did not exist, in the end term of the change; otherwise, the same thing would receive existence twice over. But the whole reality in the end term of this change is not new, because then the prior [term] would be corrupted. So the whole end term of the production is not new (as it is in creation). Therefore a partial end

---

[40] Scotus's example here is the theological virtue of charity, a quality which he holds to be created directly by God.

[41] Scotus, *Lect.* 1. 17. 2. 3, n. 192 (Vatican edn., xvii. 242).

[42] Ibid. n. 193 (Vatican edn., xvii. 242).

term will be new (just as in generation something pre-existed and something is newly acquired). Therefore in the end term of mutation something new is acquired, such that the whole is said to be new in virtue of a part.[43]

Scotus goes on to give examples of the sort of quality which can be changed in the sort of way described: light, heat, and weight (*gravitas*).[44] Crucially, the parts which Scotus is talking about are all of the same sort (*ratio*) as each other. They are thus *homogeneous*—not in the sense of being extended, but in the sense that *degrees* of a quality contain lesser degrees, such that all the degrees are the same sort of thing. So (IVb) entails (IVa).[45] Scotus explains the way in which the parts are united to form one quality instance by appealing to his model of H-unity:[46] indeed, Scotus proposes the H-unity model primarily to explain the unity of the homogeneous parts of a degree of a quality. Consistent with this, Scotus (as we have seen) rejects the view that a degree of a quality could be a composite of potentiality and actuality.[47] Equally, he rejects (Ia), the claim that each degree is a different species. As we saw above, Scotus argues that a degree of a quality *Q* is an *intrinsic mode* of *Q*. Hence all instances of *Q*, whatever their degree, are exactly the same sort of thing.[48]

The point of all this is that Scotus rejects

(C) A species is indivisible.

As Scotus understands species, a species of quality could be *divisible* into different quantitative grades. This does not, of course, entail that Scotus reject

(E) For every nature *F* and every instance *x* of *F*, if (a) *x* is necessarily *F*, (b) *F* is a unified composite concept, and (c) *F* is indivisible, then *F* is a species.

The satisfaction of (a), (b), and (c) is probably, as I indicated above, sufficient for *F*'s being a species. (Rejecting (C) just means that satisfy-

---

[43] Ibid. 1. 17. 2. 4, n. 208 (Vatican edn., xvii. 248).

[44] Ibid. n. 210 (Vatican edn., xvii. 248–9).

[45] Scotus's (IVa) is inconsistent with a claim he makes in the *Lectura*, discussed in Ch. 4, that intermediate degrees of a quality are composites of the maximal and minimal degrees of that quantity: see ibid. 2. 15. un., n. 24 (Vatican edn., xix. 145). As I suggested in Ch. 4, we must suppose that Scotus's claim here is inadequate.

[46] Ibid. 1. 17. 2. 4, n. 214 (Vatican edn., xvii. 249–50).

[47] Ibid. 1. 17. 2. 3, n. 196 (Vatican edn., xvii. 243).

[48] Ibid. 1. 17. 2. 2, nn. 178–9, 185 (Vatican edn., xvii. 237–9); see also Scotus, *Ord.* 1. 17. 2. 2, n. 252 (Vatican edn., xvii. 261).

ing (c) of (E) is not necessary for F to count as a species.) Equally, Scotus clearly rejects

> (4) For every degree D of a quality Q, and every instance x of $(D + Q)$, x is necessarily $(D + Q)$, $(D + Q)$ is a unified composite concept, and $(D + Q)$ is indivisible.

The reason is that $(D + Q)$ fail to satisfy the second of these criteria: that is, they fail to count as a unified composite concept. And the reason for this is that $(D + Q)$ fail to be a *composite* concept at all. So accepting (E) does not commit Scotus to

> (5) $(D + Q)$ is a species.

And in fact, as we saw above, Scotus regards his account of degrees as intrinsic modes as inconsistent with (5).

Given that a degree of a quality is an H-unity, it is clear that a change in degree entails a change in identity. But this does not mean that a degree is responsible for individuating a quality. We could have two individuals of exactly the same degree. As we saw in Chapter 8, an H-unity is individuated not by its quantity but by its haecceity. As Scotus notes, the intrinsic mode of a quality is a necessary but not sufficient condition for individuality: '"More" is an individual condition, not signed, like "this" [*haec*], but vague, since there could be the same degree but not the same "this" [*hoc*].'[49]

Underlying Scotus's claim that a degree of a quality is not only a discrete homogeneous item but also an H-unity is a supposition that (permanent or enduring) degrees of a quality cannot be vague (in our sense, not Scotus's) objects. Just as we saw in the case of quantity and homoeomeric substances, the addition or subtraction of a discrete amount of homogenous stuff brings about a *new* object.[50] Scotus is probably correct that enduring quality instances of any degree D are not vague objects. Even if we cannot always discriminate between close different degrees, I think we would want to claim that the degrees are genuinely ontologically different from each other.

But given that quality instances are not vague objects, will it not be the

[49] Scotus, *Ord.* 1. 17. 2. 1, *textus interpolatus* (Vatican edn., v. 245, ll. 14–15). Edith Sylla somewhat misleadingly claims that, according to Scotus, an individual quality is individuated by its grade: see 'Medieval Concepts of the Latitude of Forms', 230. My observations in Ch. 8 are, I hope, sufficient to show why this account must be false.

[50] In the case of an increase, some of the parts of the newly generated quality existed in the pre-existent quality; in the case of a decrease, all of the newly generated quality existed as a part of the pre-existent quality.

case that Scotus's theory is open to the same sort of objection as Scotus levels against the first theory in (I′.1)? On (I′.1), (Ib) is not capable of allowing for genuinely continuous change. (Ib) entails the generation of an infinite number of intermediate degrees—an impossible state of affairs on the Aristotelian account of continuity accepted by Scotus. The adherent of (Ib) could argue, however, that given Scotus's claim that an individual degree of a quality is an H-unity, Scotus's account will equally fail to allow for a continuous change of degree. Scotus, however, unlike the adherents of (Ib), is not committed to the generation of *complete* degrees to explain a change. On Scotus's account, a gradual increase in the degree of a quality can be explained by the gradual addition of more of a quality, such that the new parts of the quality do not themselves need to be discrete items. Scotus, unlike the adherents of (Ib), could claim that there is never a time when, for example, any part of the sky during a sunset is just one (discrete) shade of red. Its redness in the example is *continuously* added to. So the degree of redness of the sky at night might be, on Scotus's account, a genuinely vague object. (And, as we shall see in Chapter 12, Scotus makes just this sort of claim about all continuous changes. Their parts exist at best (objectively) *potentially*, not actually (i.e. the whole change exists; its parts do not exist unless we actively demarcate them).) But the redness of the sky during a sunset cannot be a vague object on (Ib), since (Ib) requires an analysis in terms of discrete actual slices. So (IVb) is preferable to (Ib).

In the previous section I discussed an argument proposed by Henry of Ghent to show that (IVb) must be false. According to Henry, (IVb) is empirically false: the addition of two tepid items, for example, does not make a hotter item. Generally, the addition of different degrees of a quality seems to result in their 'averaging out'; we run hot and cold water to get a warm bath, and we might mix light and dark blue paints to get sky-blue. (Much the same point is made in Burley's proposed reply to Scotus's (I′.2), discussed in n. 14 above.) This objection evidently caused Scotus some difficulties,[51] though it does in fact admit of a straightforward answer which he gives in both his early *Lectura* and the *Reportatio*. The problem with Henry's argument, according to Scotus, its that it supposes that the two qualities exist (roughly) *side by*

---

[51] For example, in a cancelled passage in the *textus interpolatus* of the *Ordinatio* (Vatican edn., v. 240, ll. 31–p. 241, l. 14) Scotus tries unsuccessfully to argue (drawing on Arist. *Ph.* 8. 10 (266ª24–6)) for the evidently false claim that the addition of different degrees of a quality Q via the juxtaposition of two substances exhibiting Q will necessarily result in a greater degree of Q.

side—just like, say, hot and cold water mixing in a bath do. It is of
course empirically obvious that a hot thing and a cold thing placed
contiguously will tend to average out. But Scotus is not interested in
changes which can be explained *extensively*. He is interested in changes
which can be explained *intensively*. If something gets hotter, for example, without gaining any additional extended parts, then the increase in
heat can be explained by the addition of degrees of heat:

> Sometimes a tepid [degree] added to a tepid [degree] in diverse subjects does
> not increase [heat]; [but] this is accidental, on account of the extension and
> dispersal of the parts. If [the new tepid degree] were in the same [extended]
> part of a subject with the pre-existing tepidness, then [the subject] would
> certainly be increased, and be hotter.[52]

In the *Ordinatio*, Scotus attempts to address the *causal* question lying
behind Henry's concern. The problem with Henry's example is that the
two tepid objects x and y are *the same sort of thing* as the tepid object z
which they constitute. All three objects are tepid, such that the tepidness
of x and y causes the tepidness of z. In scholastic terminology, the cause
and effect are *univocal*. And Scotus suggests that such univocal causes
can never cause the sort of increase which he is proposing. Thus, Scotus
does not hold that the degrees D and E of a quality Q are the *causes* of
degrees of Q greater or lesser than D and E. He argues, however, that
increases or decreases in degree of Q can be caused by an agent which is
not itself Q. The scholastics would label such causes 'equivocal' causes.
Scotus argues that in at least some cases where increases or decreases can
be causally *explained* in terms of the action of an equivocal agent, the
increases or decreases can be *described* in terms of (but not caused by)
the addition or subtraction of degrees of Q:

> It could be said that a univocal agent does not increase its more intense form
> found in the patient, but rather vice versa. An equivocal agent however
> increases [the form], since it naturally acts on this [viz. the patient], and
> does not undergo [any change] from this [viz. the patient].[53]

The idea is that an equivocal cause is not the sort of thing whose action
entails any relevant change in itself. The electricity causing the heat of
a convection heater, for example, is made neither hot nor cold by the
heat which it causes. So Henry's example does not count as an empirical counter-instance to (IVb).

---

[52] Scotus, *Lect.* 1. 17. 2. 4, n. 241 (Vatican edn., xvii. 258–9); see *idem, Rep.* 1. 17. 6 (MS M,
fo. 86ʳ).   [53] Scotus, *Ord.* 1. 17. 2. 1, n. 211 (Vatican edn., v. 242).

Scotus's account of the degrees of a quality, and the changes which can pertain to them, draws on his account of H-unity just as much as does his account of quantitative change, discussed in the previous chapter. Given his 'quantitative' account of the degrees of a quality, this is not perhaps surprising. So Scotus's theories here have the virtue of consistency. They also have the virtue of simplicity. I would judge that Scotus's account—at least in its basic contours—is more straightforward than its rivals. It clearly invokes fewer entities than the generation and corruption theory. But it also denies the non-actual existents of the actualization theory. Equally, given that a degree of a quality counts as a discrete homogeneous item, I have indicated that Scotus is probably right to regard it as an H-unity (i.e. as failing to count as a vague object).

Scotus's quantitative account of qualities had a fair amount of historical significance. The Mertonian mathematicians of the first half of the fourteenth century regarded velocity as the *quality* of a motion. Seeing degrees of qualities in quantitative terms allowed them to quantify velocity, and thence to formulate the famous proof that 'the space traversed in a given time by a body moving with uniformly accelerated velocity [is] equal to . . . the total time of moving multiplied by the mean of the initial and final velocities',[54] first found sometime before 1335 in the works of William Heytesbury, Richard Swineshead, and John Dumbleton.[55] According to Pierre Duhem, whose assessment here seems to me eminently reasonable, Scotus's account of degrees of qualities as H-unities was what allowed for such a quantitative account of qualities.[56] Scotus's account of qualities is

---

[54] A. C. Crombie, *Augustine to Galileo: The History of Science A.D.* 400–1650 (London: Falcon Educational Books, 1952), 261. Sylla, in 'Medieval Concepts of the Latitude of Forms', provides an excellent account of some of these developments, and shows clearly the links between discussions of qualitative change and discussions of velocity: see in particular pp. 251–2, 264, on Dumbleton.

[55] Heytesbury's *Regulae Solvendi Sophismata*, which contains a discussion of the crucial definition, is dated 1335 in an Erfurt manuscript (Stadtsbibliothek, MS Amplon. F. 135, fo. 17^r): see Anneliese Maier, *An der Grenze von Scholastik und Naturwissenschaft: Die Struktur der materiellen Substanz. Das Problem der Gravitation. Die Mathematik der Formlatituden* (Studien zur Naturphilosophie der Spätscholastik, 3), 2nd edn., Raccolta di Studi e Testi, 41 (Rome: Storia e Letteratura, 1952), 266 n. 26. For an accessible series of relevant texts with commentary, see Marshall Clagett, *The Science of Mechanics in the Middle Ages*, Publications in Medieval Science, 4 (Madison: University of Wisconsin Press; London: Oxford University Press, 1961), 255–329.

[56] See Pierre Duhem, *Le Système du monde: histoire des doctrines cosmologiques de Platon à Copernique* (10 vols. Paris: Hermann, n.d.-1959), vii. 530–3; see also Clagett, *Science of Mechanics*, 252. This interpretation has recently been forcibly challenged. Maurice Clavelin, for example, argues that 'not only is there no single text that entitles one to assert

not, of course, sufficient for all of these developments. But it seems, nevertheless, to have been a necessary condition for them.

This does not mean, of course, that there are not problems in Scotus's account. Clearly, the quantitative treatment of degrees of intensity entails that we can order such degrees linearly; but, as Curtis Wilson has noted, its also entails crucially that such degrees are *additive*: that is, such that we can specify how much one is greater than another:

> On the contrary, in a scale of intensity based on what is immediately perceivable, the numbers lack this quantitative significance; they indicate simply positions in a linearly ordered series. Such a scale is illustrated by the scale of hardness in minerals; a mineral to which is assigned a higher degree of hardness is able to produce a scratch on a mineral to which is assigned a lower degree, but it is operationally meaningless to speak of a degree of hardness of 8 differing from a degree of hardness of 7 *by the same amount* as a degree of hardness of 5 differs from a degree of hardness of 4.[57]

But perhaps it would be unfair to ask too much sophistication of a theory in its early stages of development. After all, our accounts of qualities such as density, temperature, and illumination add to the medieval ones no more than the claim that such qualities are best understood as *quotients* of extensive quantities; but the crucial move to an account according to which (some sort of) *numerical value* can be assigned to qualitative intensities can be reasonably traced to Scotus's insight here.

that the Mertonian and Parisian treatments of changes in speed was in any way influenced by the Scotists, but there is no shred of evidence that their general methods were based on an implicit adoption of Scotist arguments. Duhem's view is based on hindsight': Maurice Clavelin, *The Natural Philosophy of Galileo: Essay on the Origins and Foundations of Classical Mechanics*, trans. A. J. Pomerans (Cambridge, Mass., and London: MIT Press, 1974); see also Maier, *Zwei Grundprobleme*, 86. But, *pace* Clavelin, there is in fact a good deal of evidence that Scotus's quantitative treatment of qualities has—at the very least—a great deal in common with the sorts of concepts utilized in Mertonian kinematics. Of course we cannot prove that the Mertonians based their treatment of acceleration on Scotus's account of the degrees of a quality. But it would be odd if the two sets of concepts sprang up wholly independently of each other, especially given the fact that the works of Scotus were widely read in early fourteenth-century Oxford.

[57] Curtis Wilson, *William Heytesbury: Medieval Logic and the Rise of Mathematical Physics*, Publications in Medieval Science, 3 (Madison: University of Wisconsin Press, 1956), 145; Wilson's italics. Wilson cites Scotus's analogy between an increase in intensity and the addition of water to water as evidence for the claim that thinkers of the early fourteenth century assumed additivity to be a property of degrees of intensity: ibid. 146.

11

Place and Space

As the medievals noticed, Aristotle seems to have had two different conceptions of place. In the *Categories*, Aristotle defends a three-dimensional conception of place: place *runs right through*, or is *coextensive with*, the bodies it contains.[1] In the *Physics*, however, Aristotle argues that place is the two-dimensional surroundings of a body. A body is in a place if it is enclosed by the *surface* of another body.[2] The medievals thought that the *Categories* account expressed the 'vulgar' or 'common' opinion.[3] I shall label the *Physics* conception 'place', and the *Categories* conception 'space'.[4] Confusingly, Scotus does not find this sort of account in the *Categories*, and he sees the differences between the accounts in the *Categories* and the *Physics* to be little more than terminological. In section 1 here, I examine the account Scotus gives of place, basing himself on *Physics* 4; in the second section, I examine his (nearly identical) account based on the terminology found in the *Categories*.

Despite not finding the three-dimensional conception of space in the *Categories*, Scotus does develop such an account. In sections 3 and 4, I examine it, looking first at his account of void (section 3), and

---

[1] Arist. *Cat.* 6 (5^{a}8–14). See also Henry Mendell, 'Topoi on Topos: The Development of Aristotle's Concept of Place', *Phronesis*, 32 (1987), 206–31, pp. 206–10.

[2] See e.g. Arist. *Ph.* 4. 2 (209^{a}31–^{b}1); Mendell, 'Topoi on Topos', 210–12.

[3] See Edward Grant, 'Place and Space in Medieval Physical Thought', in P. K. Machamer and R. G. Turnbull (eds.), *Motion and Time, Space and Matter: Interrelations in the History and Philosophy of Science*, (Columbus, Oh.: Ohio State University Press, 1976), 137–67, p. 138. For this view, Grant cites Siger of Brabant, *In Ph.* 4. 7 (ed. Philippe Delahaye (Louvain: Institut Supérieur de Philosophie, 1941), 153–4); Buridan, *In Ph.* 4. 7 ((Paris, 1509), 73rb); Albert of Saxony, *In Ph.* 4. 1 ((Paris, 1518), 43va).

[4] Mendell argues that, in the *Physics*, Aristotle explicitly rejects his earlier conception. Mendell is accordingly reluctant to use the term 'space' for the *Categories* conception: see 'Topoi on Topos' 207 n. 5, correcting Max Jammer, *Concepts of Space: The History of Theories of Space in Physics*, 2nd edn. (Cambridge, Mass.: Harvard University Press, 1969), 17. But I think that both conceptions can be found in Scotus. So it seems terminologically expedient to give the two conceptions two different labels here.

secondly at his attempts to develop a thorough going account of three-dimensional space, springing from an exegesis of Aristotle's claim in *Physics* 4 that place is *immobile* (section 4).

Scotus's Aristotelian talk about place is rendered more complex than it need have been by a terminological difficulty which, I believe, he inherited from Aristotle. First, two important terms: 'place' and 'position'. Scotus has two words that correspond to 'place': *ubietas* (= 'whereness') and *locus*. Scotus uses the first of these, which I shall render 'ubiety', as his technical term for the category of place. Scotus argues that, like all of the last six categories (place (i.e. ubiety), time, position, state, action, passion), both *ubiety* and *position* are relations. As Scotus understands Aristotle's category of ubiety, for a body b_1 to have ubiety is for it to be enclosed by the surface of a surrounding body b_2.[5] For a body b_1 to have position is for its parts to correspond to the parts of the surface of the body b_2 surrounding b_1.[6] Scotus uses his second word for place, *locus*, when discussing the issues as they are presented in Aristotle's *Physics*. As understood by Scotus, Aristotle's *Physics* gives an account of place which conflates the distinction between ubiety and position found in the *Categories*. So Scotus's use of *locus*—which I shall translate simply as 'place'—is intended to include both ubiety and position.

1. PLACE

In an important passage—which I shall label 'O'[7]—Scotus cites Aristotle's view in the *Physics* that, for a body b_1 to be in a place is for it to be enclosed by the surface of another body b_2, such that the surface of b_2 is the *place* of b_1.[8] As Scotus spells out the account in O, being in a place entails satisfying no fewer than five ordered relational properties:

(i)   Being wholly enclosed by a body,
(ii) Being actually enclosed by a body,
(iii) Being enclosed by a body of equal size,

---

[5] Scotus, *Ord.* 4. 10. 1, n. 16 (Wadding edn., viii. 506); for the Latin text in MS A, fo. 206[vb], see n. 19 below.   [6] Scotus, *Ord.* 4. 10. 1, n. 16 (Wadding edn., viii. 506).

[7] Ibid. 2. 2. 2. 1–2, nn. 216–35 (Vatican edn., vii. 253–60); Scotus, *Lect.* 2. 2. 2. 1–2, nn. 191–211 (Vatican edn., xvii. 161–6).

[8] Scotus, *Ord.* 2. 2. 2. 1–2, n. 219 (Vatican edn., vii. 254), with reference to Arist. *Ph.* 4. 4 (212[a]20–1); see also ibid. 4. 2 (209[a]31–[b]1).

(iv) Being enclosed by a commensurable body,
(v) Being enclosed by just one body.[9]

In **O**, clearly taking its cue from the *Physics* account of place, there is no explicit distinction between ubiety and position: though, as I will try to show in the second section of this chapter, the distinctions Scotus makes in **O** do correspond roughly to distinctions he makes elsewhere between ubiety and position. What is clear is that the **O** account of being in a place entails that a body is in a place if and only if it satisfies all five relational properties listed.

(i) The first of these properties is the one pin-pointed in Aristotle's definition just cited. As Scotus understands this definition, it involves two further Aristotelian claims. The first is that the enclosing surface is two-dimensional: it lacks any sort of thickness, surrounding a body rather than running right through it.[10] The second is that place—the boundary of the enclosing body—is immobile.[11] Both these claims, as Scotus understands them, require further explication. I will return to them in section 4, when I introduce Scotus's discussion of space.

(ii) The second property required for a body b_1 to be in a place is that b_1 is in some sense responsible for displacing the surrounding body—for separating its sides from each other.[12] Following Aristotle, Scotus reasons that a place must be really distinct from the body it locates. Like Aristotle, Scotus argues that if a body b_2 surrounds another body b_1, then it will be the case that the sides of b_2 are separate from each other. Thus, distance between the sides of b_2 logically entails that b_1 and b_2 are distinct objects. (This criterion, of course, will not serve to *explain* the distinction between b_1 and b_2.[13]) The point of labelling this property 'being in an *actual* place' is, I think, that there is a sense in which some of the parts of, say, a continuum are 'sur-

---

[9] Scotus, *Lect.* 2. 2. 2. 1–2, n. 191 (Vatican edn., xviii. 161); *idem, Ord.* 2. 2. 2. 1–2, n. 216 (Vatican edn., vii. 253).

[10] Scotus, *Ord.* 2. 2. 2. 1–2, n. 220 (Vatican edn., vii. 255); *idem, Lect.* 2. 2. 2. 1–2, n. 195 (Vatican edn., xviii. 162); see Arist. *Ph.* 4. 4 (211^a3-^b5, 211^b9-29).

[11] Scotus, *Ord.* 2. 2. 2. 1–2, n. 221 (Vatican edn., vii. 255); *idem, Lect.* 2. 2. 2. 1–2, n. 196 (Vatican edn., xviii. 162); see Arist. *Ph.* 4. 4 (212^a14-21).

[12] Scotus, *Ord.* 2. 2. 2. 1–2, n. 232 (Vatican edn., vii. 260); *idem, Lect.* 2. 2. 2. 1–2, n. 207 (Vatican edn., xviii. 165); see Arist. *Ph.* 4. 5 (212^b3-6).

[13] The role of b_1 in 'making [b_2's] sides separate' may be—but need not be—causal. Scotus reasons that the presence of b_1 may be sufficient for the continued separation of b_2's sides, but that it need not be the efficient cause of this separation: *Quod.* 11, n. 15 (Wadding edn., xii. 271; Alluntis and Wolter, 268–9 n. 11. 45); *Ord.* 4. 10. 2, n. 6 (Wadding edn., viii. 511).

rounded' by other of its parts. But we would not want to say that these various parts could correctly be categorized as distinct bodies in different places.

(iii) The third criterion, equality, just means that if a body is in a place, then its place will be equal to it in size.[14]

(iv) For a body to be commensurable with its place is for its parts to correspond to the parts of the surface of the body b_2 surrounding b_1.[15] In the *Ordinatio*, Scotus claims that the commensurability of b_1 and b_2 is entailed by their equality.[16] In the *Lectura*, however, he claims that the human soul instantiates the third property but not the fourth.[17] (The human soul does not have parts which are distinct from the whole.) Presumably the relevant claim made in O is that if a body is equal to its place, then it will be commensurable with its place.

(v) The fifth property again looks trivially true, and Scotus seems to treat it as such in O.[18] We might be inclined to view (i)–(v) as *coextensive* properties of any physical body: if a body instantiates one of these properties, then it will instantiate the others as well. Scotus, however, does not believe that this is the case. In the next section, I will consider another important set of texts in which Scotus offers an account of some of the issues just discussed in terms derived from Aristotle's *Categories*. We shall see that there is substantial overlap between the two accounts. But there are some differences as well— differences which seem to be more than just terminological.

2. UBIETY AND POSITION

In *Ordinatio* 4. 10. 1, which I shall label 'P', Scotus gives a similar— though, as we shall see, not identical—account of the same issues. In P, however, he uses terminology derived from Aristotle's *Categories*:

---

[14] Scotus, *Lect.* 2. 2. 2. 1–2, n. 208 (Vatican edn., xviii. 165); *idem, Ord.* 2. 2. 2. 1–2, n. 233 (Vatican edn., vii. 260).

[15] Scotus, *Lect.* 2. 2. 2. 1–2, n. 209 (Vatican edn., xviii. 165).

[16] Scotus, *Ord.* 2. 2. 2. 1–2, n. 233 (Vatican edn., vii. 260); see also ibid. 4. 49. 16, n. 16 (Wadding edn., x. 619). In this latter passage, Scotus argues that if a body is equal to its place, then it has 'local presence' in its place. But local presence is equivalent to being in a place *commensuratively*. (The version in MS A, fo. 287vb, has: 'Quod est in loco sibi aequali est essentialiter localiter in loco.')

[17] Scotus, *Lect.* 2. 2. 2. 1–2, n. 209 (Vatican edn., xviii. 165).

[18] Scotus, *Ord.* 2. 2. 2. 1–2, n. 234 (Vatican edn., vii. 260); *idem, Lect.* 2. 2. 2. 1–2, n. 210 (Vatican edn., xviii. 165).

specifically, the categories of ubiety and position. His problem, in P, is to explain how Christ's body can be really present in the quantity of the Eucharistic bread despite the fact that Christ's body is considerably bigger than the quantity of the Eucharistic bread. His solution is that Christ's body has ubiety but not position.

Scotus distinguishes ubiety and position as follows:

[The relation] which ubiety is primarily is of a whole [circumscribed item] to the whole of the circumscribing item; but position, which is said [to be] another genus, adds [to ubiety] a relation of the parts to the parts.[19]

He elsewhere describes position as '[t]he coextension of the parts of one [quantum] with the parts of another',[20] where coextension in this context is identified with commensuration: 'Coextension . . . is properly labelled "commensuration", which properly means the simultaneity of part with part.'[21] This discussion has clear points of contact with that found in O. Roughly, the idea would thus seem to be that a body has ubiety if it satisfies conditions (i) and (ii) outlined in O, and that it has position if and only if it both has ubiety and satisfies condition (iv) outlined in O.[22] I shall label ubiety 'U-place', and position 'P-place'. Thus, if a body has ubiety, it has U-place, and if it has position, it has P-place. If it seems that Scotus's remarks in P apply equally to U-place and to P-place, I shall refer just to 'place'. Using this terminology, the account in O, discussed in the previous section, is something like an account of P-place.

Although Scotus does not make the point explicitly, it would seem that, necessarily, any body which has P-place also has U-place. As he puts it, 'position specifies ubiety',[23] and, as we just saw, 'position . . . adds [to ubiety] a relation of the parts to the parts'.[24] But having U-place is not sufficient for P-place:

[19] Scotus, *Ord.* 4. 10. 1, n. 16 (Wadding edn., viii. 506); MS A, fo. 206[vb], reads: 'Ubi primo est totius ad totum circumscribens, sed positio dicta quae est aliud genus superaddit respectum partium ad partes.'
[20] Scotus, *Ord.* 4. 10. 1, n. 14 (Wadding edn., viii. 505).
[21] Ibid. n. 16 (Wadding edn., viii. 506). 'Simultaneity' is being used metaphorically here to pick out that the parts are *spatially* coincident.
[22] Scotus makes it clear that condition (v) from O needs to be satisfied for ubiety. But he also claims that a body has a property closely related to ubiety if (like Christ's body in the Eucharist) it satisfies (i) and (ii) from O, but not (v): see ibid. n. 11 (Wadding edn., viii. 502). Whether this property could properly be labelled 'ubiety' seems to me to be a terminological matter with little or no philosophical import.
[23] Ibid. n. 14 (Wadding edn., viii. 505).
[24] Ibid. n. 16 (Wadding edn., viii. 506): the whole passage was quoted above.

Place and Space

The coexistence of some whole to [another] whole, or to any part [of that other whole] abstracts from that position in virtue of which ubiety necessarily has position: therefore it is simply possible for that coexistence to exist without position.[25]

What would it be for a body to have U-place but not P-place? Scotus is quite clear that a body *b* satisfying this description would be an extended object: *b*'s parts would be spatially distant from each other.[26] And the parts of *b*'s U-place would likewise be spatially distant from each other. But the parts of *b* and the parts of its U-place would not themselves have any spatial relation to each other. None of *b*'s parts, for example, would be spatially coincident with any of the parts of *b*'s U-place. Scotus attempts the following description of a U-place which fails to be a P-place: '[The place is] indivisible, or [is] divisible to such a small extent that there is not one presence to one part, and another to another to which a part is present.'[27] On the second of these two possible conditions, the U-place is really two-dimensional (which, as we saw, both Aristotle and Scotus hold place to be); but in relation to the body it surrounds, it should be thought of as somehow non-dimensional (indivisible).

This position is extremely difficult to understand. But Scotus supposes that, however implausible the position might look, there are reasons for believing it to be true—reasons which are stronger than the obvious arguments against it. Specifically, he clearly supposes that the doctrine of Christ's real bodily presence in the Eucharist demands it.

But Scotus believes there to be a good philosophical argument for his account of P-place too. He believes that he can show that having a P-place is merely an extrinsic relation, distinct from having a U-place. As we saw in Chapter 6, a relation is extrinsic if it is logically possible for its extremes to exist and the relation and its co-relation not to obtain. In the case of a P-place, the two extremes will be the located body and its U-place. Scotus's argument, which I label '(T)', to show that having a P-place is an extrinsic relation runs as follows.

(T) Accepting the empirically evident

> (A) For every body *b* located in a U-place, and for every P-place *p*, *x* is contingently related to *p*

[25] Ibid.   [26] Ibid. n. 14 (Wadding edn., viii. 505).
[27] Ibid. n. 17 (Wadding edn., viii. 506); MS A, fo. 206[vb], reads: '. . . ad aliquod extra indivisibile, vel quantumcumque modicum divisibile, ita quod ibi non est alia praesentia alii parti et alia alii cuius est pars praesens'.

(i.e. it is possible for *b* not to have *p*), and the (controversial)

  (B) For every item *x*, if *x* is contingently related to an individual instance of a genus φ, then *x* is contingently related to φ,

Scotus infers

  (1) For every body *b* located in a U-place, it is possible that, for every categorical position *p*, *b* is not related to *p*

(i.e. it is possible for *b* to lack any position whatsoever).[28]

  (A) is clearly true. Imagine a perfect sphere *S*. Even supposing *S* to have a fixed U-place, the parts of *S* are only contingently related to the parts of *S*'s P-place. *S*, after all, could be rotating about an axis. (B), however, is clearly false, involving just the same fallacy in scope as I noted when discussing (M) in Chapter 2. If (B) were true, we could— using my example from Chapter 2—infer from my being contingently 68 inches tall that I could have no height at all. On the other hand, the inference from (A) and (B) to (1) is clearly valid. And what (1) amounts to is just that a body could have a U-place and still lack any P-place. (Note that the location of *b* in a U-place in (A) and (1) falls outside the scope of the modal operator.) And just this state of affairs, according to Scotus, holds in the case of Christ's body located in the quantity of the Eucharistic bread.[29]

---

[28] Scotus, *Ord.* 4. 10. 1, n. 15 (Wadding edn., viii. 505–6).

[29] It is important to understand that Scotus, unlike Aquinas, holds that Christ's body is genuinely located in the Eucharistic bread: for Aquinas, see *ST* 3. 76. 5 (ed. Petrus Caramello (3 vols., Turin and Rome: Marietti, 1952–6), iii. 459^{b}–60^{a}), discussed in Anthony Kenny, 'The Use of Logical Analysis in Theology', in his *Reason and Religion. Essays in Philosophical Theology* (Oxford: Blackwell, 1987), 3–20, pp. 19–20. Scotus also rejects the view, which would be held a few years later by Ockham, that Christ's body is present *definitively* in the quantity of the bread; where 'definitive' presence is defined as the presence of an item whose parts fail to be spatially extended: see Ockham, *Rep.* 4. 6 (*Op. Theol.*, ed. Juvenalis Lalor *et al.* (10 vols., St Bonaventure, NY: St Bonaventure University Press, 1967–86), vii. 78–81, 88–9); *idem, Quod.* 1. 4 (*Op. Theol.*, ix. 25; Freddoso and Kelley, i. 25); *idem, De Corpore Christi* 7 (*Op. Theol.*, x. 102–5). For Scotus on the nature of definitive presence, see *Ord.* 4. 10. 2, nn. 10 and 15 (Wadding edn., viii. 513, 519); on the rejection of this account of Christ's presence in the Eucharist, see ibid 4. 10. 1, n. 13 (Wadding edn., viii. 503–4). For Scotus's account of transubstantiation, see D. Burr, 'Scotus and Transubstantiation', *Mediaeval Studies*, 34 (1972), 336–60; Marilyn McCord Adams, 'Aristotle and the Sacrament of the Altar', in Richard Bosley and Martin Tweedale (eds.), *Aristotle and his Medieval Interpreters, Canadian Journal of Philosophy*, suppl. vol. 17 (1991), 195–249, pp. 222–35. On Ockham, see Gabriel Buescher, *The Eucharistic Teaching of William Ockham*, Franciscan Institute Publications, Theology Series, 1 (St Bonaventure, NY: The Franciscan Institute, 1950); Adams, 'Aristotle and the Sacrament of the Altar', 236–48.

Of far greater philosophical significance than the metaphysical quagmire of (T) is another Scotist claim: that a body could lack any U-place. I will return to this claim in the next section. But before I do so, a further feature of his account of P-place requires treatment. I have thus far ignored stipulation (iii) in O: that for a body to be in a P-place, it must be *equal* to its place (supposing, as I suggested above, that O gives something like an account of P-place). O and P differ slightly here. Both accept that equality is necessary for being in a P-place.[30] But in O, equality between body and place is sufficient for their commensuration.[31] This is not true in P, where Scotus is committed to the view that equality is not sufficient for commensuration. The reason is that he generally regards *commensuration* as necessary and sufficient for a body located in a U-place to be located in a P-place (see, for example, the first passage quoted in this section). And he clearly accepts (A). But in P, Scotus makes it clear that every relation of size is an *intrinsic* relation: that is, such that it is not logically possible for its extremes to exist and the relation and its co-relation not to obtain: 'Equality or inequality—which are intrinsic relations—follow the posited quantity and the end term.'[32] So on the P account, commensuration cannot entail equality. A body could be equal to its place, and still fail to be commensurate with it. The account in P thus differs from that in O—though, admittedly, not much of philosophical note seems to hang on this difference.

Scotus uses his relational account of P-place to argue both that a body could exist in more than one P-place and that more than one body could exist in one P-place. The basic arguments for these two claims are much the same, both relying on the following premiss:

(2) It is possible that one subject instantiates more than one extrinsic relation of the same sort.

Given that being a P-place is an extrinsic relation, and that being in a P-place is an extrinsic relation, Scotus infers

[30] Scotus, *Ord.* 4. 10. 1, n. 8 (Wadding edn., viii. 499): 'That quantum, viz. the body of Christ, could not be circumscriptively in the place of the bread, since it is bigger than the bread'. I am understanding 'circumscription' in this passage to mean 'commensuration'. If Scotus really means that equality is necessary for *circumscription* in the sense developed above, then his whole account of U-place loses any semblance of coherence. The account of U-place found in P entails both that a body is circumscribed (enclosed) by its U-place and that it is not necessary that a body in a U-place is equal to its place. For O, see above, n. 16.
[31] Scotus, *Ord.* 2. 2. 2. 1–2, n. 233 (Vatican edn., vii. 260); see also ibid. 4. 49. 16, n. 16 (Wadding edn., ix. 619).   [32] Ibid. 4. 10. 1, n. 16 (Wadding edn., viii. 506).

(3) It is possible that one P-place encloses more than one body,[33]

and

(4) It is possible that one body is in two P-places.[34]

(2) is defended by appealing to

(C) It is possible that one subject instantiates more than one intrinsic relation of the same sort,

and

(D) If it is possible that a subject *x* instantiates more than one intrinsic relation of the same sort, then it is possible that *x* instantiates more than one extrinsic relation of the same sort.[35]

Scotus illustrates the sort of relation which would satisfy the condition set out in the antecedent of (C) by appealing to the case of a white object which has two relations of similarity, one to each of two other white things. But there seems to me to be no reason to accept the implication in (D): there seems to be all the difference in the world between the similarity relation instantiated by a white object and the P-place relation instantiated by a located object. Given that (D) leads to such counter-intuitive results, I would judge that it should be rejected.[36]

Scotus's commitment to (3) and (4) has a curious metaphysical consequence the extensive treatment of which is well beyond my modest programme here. No one familiar with Scotus's famous account of haecceity will be surprised to learn that Scotus would not regard spatio-temporal continuity—or at least our ability to trace any

---

[33] Scotus, *Quod.* 11, n. 15 (Wadding edn., xii. 271; Alluntis and Wolter, 268 n. 11. 44).

[34] Scotus, *Ord.* 4. 10. 2, n. 11 (Wadding edn., viii. 513).   [35] Ibid.

[36] For other arguments in favour of the possibility of two bodies in one P-place, see ibid. 4. 49. 16, n. 17 (Wadding edn., x. 620–1). Scotus also holds that it is possible for two bodies to occupy one U-place: see ibid. 4. 10. 1, n. 5 (Wadding edn., viii. 498); and for one body to occupy more than one U-place: see ibid. 4. 10. 2, n. 9 (Wadding edn., viii. 512). Scotus does not need (3) or (4) for any theological purpose. They are not required, for example, for the doctrine of transubstantiation, as understood by Scotus. (As Scotus understands Christ's presence in the Eucharist, Christ's body instantiates one P-place (in heaven) and more than one U-place (see ibid. 4. 10. 1, n. 10 (Wadding edn., viii. 501)); and the quantity of the bread instantiates P-place in the same place as Christ's body instantiates U-place: see ibid. 4. 10. 2, nn. 3–4 (Wadding edn., viii. 528–9).) Scotus mentions the case of Jesus's birth from the Virgin Mary: see ibid. 4. 49. 16, n. 17 (Wadding edn., x. 620–1). (According to some theologians, the Virgin Birth involved the existence of two bodies—Jesus's and part of Mary's—in the same place.)

medium size object through one spatio-temporal route—as *sufficient* for individuation. But (3) and (4) show that Scotus would not regard spatial continuity as *necessary* for individuation either. And this is far less plausible than the claim that spatio-temporal continuity is not sufficient for individuation. In fact, Scotus does not regard temporal continuity as necessary for individuation either. His motivation for this second view is theological. Our resurrected bodies are numerically identical with our bodies here on earth, even though there is no temporal continuity between them.[37] Scotus, for theological reasons, is thus happy to allow both spatial and temporal discontinuity.

3. VOID AND VACUUM

Thus far, I have tried to give an account of a broadly Aristotelian view of place which we find in Scotus. On this view, place is identified as the innermost surface of a container. Without further qualification, this view will not allow empty space. Aristotle famously held that a vacuum is impossible,[38] and that there is nothing at all—neither place nor body—outside the outermost heavenly sphere.[39]

Theologians in the late thirteenth century felt that this sort of account tended to restrict God's power unduly. If there is literally nothing at all—neither place nor body—outside the cosmos, then God cannot create another universe beyond ours: there is nowhere for it to go. Neither could God move our universe. Both of these restrictions on God were felt to compromise God's omnipotence, and were among the positions condemned by Stephen Tempier at Paris in 1277.[40] But there are also more Aristotelian reasons for wanting to modify the theory that a body's place is the innermost surface of its

---

[37] See ibid. 4. 43. 1, n. 13 (Wadding edn., x. 18–19); 4. 43. 3, nn. 9–12, 14, 19 (Wadding edn., x. 44–5, 55, 62); see my 'Identity, Origin, and Persistence in Duns Scotus's Physics', *History of Philosophy Quarterly*, forthcoming.

[38] Arist. *Ph.* 4. 7 (214^{a}16–^{b}11).   [39] Arist. *Cael.* 1. 9 (279^{a}11–18).

[40] See *Cartularium Universitatis Parisiensis*, ed. H. Denifle and E. Chatelain (4 vols., Paris: Delalain, 1889–97), i. 543–55; English trans. in Ralph Lerner and Muhsin Mahdi (eds.), *Medieval Political Philosophy: A Sourcebook* (New York: The Free Press of Glencoe, 1963), 338–54. The relevant propositions are 27: 'That the first cause cannot make more than one world', and 49: 'That God could not move the heaven in a straight line, the reason being that he would leave a vacuum'. For a discussion of the relevance of the condemnations to medieval discussions of place, see Edward Grant, 'The Condemnation of 1277, God's Absolute Power, and Physical Thought in the Middle Ages', *Viator*, 10 (1979), 211–44.

physical surroundings. In the *Physics*, Aristotle held that there is an important sense in which place is *immobile*.[41] This stipulation looks *prima facie* to be at odds with Aristotle's claim, also central to his *Physics* account, that a body's place is the innermost surface of its physical surroundings. As Aristotle spotted, it looks as though the physical surroundings of a body could change without the body moving. But on Aristotle's standard account, a change in physical surroundings ought to be sufficient for a change in the body's place. And this would mean that a stationary body could change place just in virtue of a change in its physical surroundings. Aristotle was aware that this cannot be right. We would surely want to be able to say that the body does not change its place even though its surroundings do.[42] I shall argue that, in giving an account of the immobility of place, Scotus begins to develop an account of space as *dimension*, running right through the bodies it contains.

So Scotus has broadly two reasons for wanting to modify Aristotle's account. The first is that empty place exists; the second is that place is immobile. In this section I will look at the first of these issues; I will examine the second—Scotus's account of *space*—in the next section. In principle the two issues are linked. But they do not entail each other. We could have a conception of empty place—void or vacuum—without having a conception of space as three-dimensional. Empty space could *yield* to body; three-dimensional space could not. But both conceptions are, I think, sufficiently far removed from Aristotle's account of place in the *Physics* to be usefully referred to as conceptions of space.

Scotus argues for the existence—or possible existence—of a void in two ways. The first is to show that there could be extra-cosmic void. The second is to show that even within the universe it is logically possible for there to be a vacuum. Both of these rely on a broadly Aristotelian account of place as the two-dimensional surroundings of a body. As we shall see, the second of Scotus's two arguments is unambiguous in its affirmation of the possibility of a void. The first, however, is less clear, depending rather more on the precise interpretation that we choose to give it. It draws on Scotus's claim that being in a U-place is an extrinsic relation, such that a body could lack any U-place. (A body which lacked every U-place would have to exist *outside* the universe.) Part of Scotus's motivation for supposing that being in a U-place is an extrinsic relation is

---

[41] Arist. *Ph.* 4. 4 (212ᵃ14–16).   [42] Ibid. (212ᵃ14–21).

theological. Christ's body gains a U-place in the Eucharist without any other concomitant change.[43] The claim that being in a U-place is an extrinsic relation, coupled with Scotus's

> (B) For every item x, if x is contingently related to an individual instance of a genus ϕ, then x is contingently related to ϕ,

will entail that a body could lack any U-place whatsoever.[44]

Scotus also holds that there is a good *philosophical* reason for supposing that a body could lack every U-place. In *Quodlibet* 11, which I shall label 'Q', Scotus gives this reason. I shall label the argument '(U)'.[45] (U) He derives

> (5) For every body b, it is possible that, for every U-place u, b lacks u

(i.e. a body could exist without any U-place whatsoever) from

> (E) For every body b and every U-place u, b is really distinct from, and naturally prior to, u

and the separability criterion

> (F) If x is really distinct from, and naturally prior to, y, then it is possible for x to exist without y.[46]

In fact, however, (E) and (F) do not entail (5), but the weaker

> (5*) For every body b and every U-place u, it is possible that b lacks u.

---

[43] Scotus, *Ord.* 4. 10. 1, n. 11 (Wadding edn., viii. 502); see also ibid. 4. 10. 3, n. 5 (Wadding edn., viii. 529).

[44] Scotus did not use this argument, though there is no reason why he should not have done so. On my account here, Scotus's account of transubstantiation, along with his (controversial) (B), is sufficient for the claim that empty space can exist.

[45] There are certain terminological differences between Q and P. In P, as we have seen, 'ubiety' refers to U-place, and a body in a U-place is said to be circumscribed by its U-place. In Q, Scotus seems to use 'ubiety' to refer not to U-place but to P-place, and he denies that a body not in a P-place could be circumscribed by its place: see *Quod.* 11, n. 12 (Wadding edn., xii. 268; Alluntis and Wolter, 265 n. 11. 30); also ibid. n. 17 (Wadding edn., xii. 272; Alluntis and Wolter, 269 n. 11. 47). On the other hand, the parts of Q in which I am interested here aim to show that (i) a body can exist without any physical surroundings, and (ii) that a vacuum can exist. We do not need an account of P-place for either of these claims; an account of U-place is sufficient. Scotus's arguments are thus sufficient to show that a body could lack any U-place—and *a fortiori* lack any P-place. The distinction is important, since the claim that a body could exist without any P-place does not entail that it could exist without any U-place.

[46] Ibid. n. 3 (Wadding edn., xii. 263; Alluntis and Wolter, 258 n. 11. 4). On the possibility of God's creating a stone outside the universe, see Scotus, *Ord.* 2. 2. 2. 1–2, n. 231 (Vatican edn., vii. 259); 4. 10. 1, n. 14 (Wadding edn., viii. 505).

(5^*), of course, does not entail (5); and (**U**) is guilty of the same scope fallacy as we have come across in numerous other contexts.

Scotus's argument could, however, be read more fruitfully—though less faithfully to his intentions—as an attempt to force his opponent to give a reason why it is *not* possible for a body to lack every U-place. In particular, Scotus thinks that the outermost heavenly sphere furnishes a good example of a body which, since it is enclosed by nothing, lacks every U-place.[47] One result of this conclusion is to dissociate the concept of body from the Aristotelian conception of place. Does the discussion also signal Scotus's adherence to the idea of extra-cosmic void or vacuum? At least one of Scotus's predecessors would have thought so. Henry of Ghent argues that, so long as God does not create anything outside the universe, then there is nothing—not even empty space—outside the universe. But if God were to create a body outside—and distant from—the universe, he would also have to create the empty space or void to allow spatial distance between our universe and the extra-cosmic body.[48] In this context, Henry develops the idea of *privative dimension*. Henry supposes—as Scotus does too (as we shall see in a moment)—that actual dimensions require a subject. But he supposes that a vacuum can count *as if* it is a thing, and a subject of properties: it is a quasi-something (*quasi-aliquid*), and can be the subject of 'privative dimension'. As Henry describes the privative dimension of a vacuum, it is logically equivalent to the actual dimension of a body which could be 'received' by the vacuum.[49] So Henry's discussion here clearly signals his adherence to the (possible) existence of extra-cosmic void. Scotus uses the idea of privative dimension when discussing the possibility of an intra-cosmic vacuum. (I discuss his treatment of this in a moment.) But he does not mention Henry's privative dimension when discussing the possibility of extra-cosmic

---

[47] On the location of the outermost heavenly sphere, see Edward Grant, 'The Medieval Problem of Place: Some Fundamental Problems and Solutions', in A. Maierù and A. Paravicini Bagliani, (eds.), *Studi sul xiv secolo in memoria di Anneliese Maier*, Raccolta di Studi e Testi, 151 (Rome: Storia e Letteratura, 1981), 57–79, pp. 72–9; Cecilia Trifogli, 'The Place of the Last Sphere in Late-Ancient and Medieval Commentaries', in Simo Knuuttila *et al.* (eds.), *Knowledge and the Sciences in Medieval Philosophy: Proceedings of the Eighth International Conference of Medieval Philosophy*, Publications of the Luther–Agricola Society (3 vols., Helsinki: Yliopistopaino, 1990), ii. 342–50.

[48] Henry of Ghent, *Quod.* 13. 3 (ed. R. Macken *et al.*, Ancient and Medieval Philosophy, De Wulf-Mansion Centre, Series 2 (Leuven: Leuven University Press; Leiden: Brill, 1979–), xviii. 18). [49] Ibid. (Macken edn., xviii. 16–17).

void. My guess, however, would be that he would be happy to affirm Henry's discussion here. There is certainly no evidence to the contrary.

Of course, on Henry's view, extra-cosmic void exists *only if* God creates it. Scotus would certainly concede that any sort of void would need to be created by God. In an important discussion, Scotus denies that any space existed *before* the creation of the universe.[50] So even if Scotus does admit the possibility of extra-cosmic void, he is by no means committed to the *actual existence* of extra-cosmic void. Elsewhere, Scotus speaks of an imaginary 'outside' of the universe. His point is that there really is *nothing* 'outside' the universe, and no real 'outside' at all.[51] Presumably, this amounts to a denial of (actual) extra-cosmic void.

Scotus also believes that it is possible for a vacuum to exist within the cosmos. He states that an argument for this claim can be constructed from what he says about the possibility of extra-cosmic void. I label the argument, which Scotus never outlines explicitly, '(V)'. (V) As far as I can make out from the relevant passages in Q, Scotus argues for his intended conclusion

> (6) For every concave spherical surface *s*, it is possible that, for every U-place *u*, *s* exists without *u*,

in a manner exactly analogous to the way he attempts to defend (5) in (U). Thus, his premises will be

> (G) For every concave spherical surface *s* and every U-place *u*, *s* is really distinct from, and naturally prior to, *u*,

and the separability criterion (F).[52] (6) and (G) require a word of explanation. The idea is that a concave spherical surface will naturally surround a body, and thus be a U-place. (The surface need not, of course, be spherical: but it must be continuous, lacking any sort of *gap*.) (G) states that being a U-place is a contingent property of such a concave surface. (V), of course, suffers from just the same scope fallacy as (U).

But Scotus believes that he has got empirical evidence in favour of (6). He reasons as follows. The outermost heaven is indestructible in a stronger sense than that in which the elements contained by the outermost heaven are indestructible. The reason for this is that the elements

---

[50] Scotus, *Ord.* 1. 37. un., n. 9 (Vatican edn., vi. 302).
[51] Ibid. 2. 1. 3, n. 174 (Vatican edn., vii. 88).
[52] Scotus, *Quod.* 11, n. 7 (Wadding edn., xii. 265; Alluntis and Wolter, 260–1 n. 11. 16), with reference to ibid. n. 3 (Wadding edn., xii. 263; Alluntis and Wolter, 258 n. 11. 4).

are naturally destructible, whereas the outermost heaven is not. God could annihilate the elements in an instant. If he were to do this, the outermost heaven would not be immediately destroyed, and therefore it would not immediately cease to be a container. This is because for the outermost heaven to cease to be a container, its sides would have to cease to be distant. But for the heaven to collapse in upon itself would involve local movement, and would therefore necessarily take time; and thus, if God destroyed the elements but not the outermost heaven, we would have to allow a certain time for the heaven naturally to collapse in upon itself: 'Nature cannot cause such a transmutation in an instant. Therefore, the concave surface of the heaven could remain and nevertheless contain no body.'[53] The scenario itself, however, seems to me to be question-begging. The elements are the only things, as it were, that keep the sides of the heaven apart. If the elements were destroyed, we could claim perfectly plausibly that the sides would collapse instantaneously: that is, the scenario could more plausibly be seen as showing that, under some circumstances, local movement could be instantaneous.[54]

Scotus raises three objections to his account of the possibility of a vacuum. The gist of the objections is that if there is nothing between the sides of the concave spherical body, then *a fortiori* there can be no distance between the sides. His replies draw on Henry's concept of privative dimension. In the case of a vacuum, there is nothing between the sides of the concave spherical body, so the vacuum contained by it has no actual dimensions. But this does not mean that the vacuum is totally devoid of dimensions. Rather like Henry, Scotus reasons that although a vacuum is nothing, it nevertheless has certain non-trivial physical properties. For example, a vacuum has the capacity to yield to a body should a body be placed where the vacuum is. And it has the capacity to yield to a body of no greater dimension than the vacuum would be were there a body there.[55] This second property clearly

[53] Ibid. n. 7 (Wadding edn., xii. 265; Alluntis and Wolter, 261 n. 11. 17).

[54] Scotus, of course, has an argument to show that local motion cannot be continuous: see above, Ch. 9 n. 32.

[55] See Scotus, *Quod.* 11, n. 8 (Wadding edn., xii. 265; Alluntis and Wolter, 262 n. 11. 21), *idem, Ord.* 2. 2. 2. 5, nn. 431, 435–6 (Vatican edn., vii. 346–9); and Edward Grant, *Much Ado About Nothing: Theories of Space and Vacuum from the Middle Ages to the Scientific Revolution* (Cambridge: Cambridge University Press, 1981), 32, for the first of these two properties; Scotus, *Quod.* 11, n. 9 (Wadding edn., xii. 265–6; Alluntis and Wolter, 262 n. 11. 22) for the second. Note that Aristotle denies that a vacuum could yield to a body: see Arist. *Ph.* 4. 8 (216^{a}26–^{b}2).

entails that a vacuum has a certain size. Since it cannot have actual dimensions, we can refer instead to its having 'privative dimension'.[56]

4. SPACE

Scotus's account of vacuum indicates his distance from Aristotle's account of place in the *Physics*. But Scotus's discussion of the Aristotelian claim that place is *immobile* forces him further away from the Aristotelian conception of place as body-containment. As both Aristotle and Scotus spell out the idea of body-containment, body-containment is *two-dimensional*: place *surrounds* the bodies it contains. When discussing Aristotle's immobility requirement, Scotus begins to sketch out a conception of space as *three-dimensional*, running right through the bodies it contains. Aristotle's claim that place is *immobile* caused both him and his commentators a great deal of trouble.[57] Scotus discusses Aristotle's immobility requirement in O; and it is now time to complete my account of Scotus's five conditions for place outlined in the first section of this chapter.

As I noted above, the problem for Aristotle is that the place of a thing might move while the thing itself remains still. Aristotle's example is a boat moored in a river. Aristotle's solution was to modify his standard account of place to mean that the place of a thing is not necessarily the *surrounding* surface with which it is in contact, but rather the nearest *immobile* surface. Thus, Aristotle argues (as usually interpreted) that the banks and river bed are the place of the moored boat in his example.[58]

The medievals were not at all happy with Aristotle's discussion here. Possibly drawing on a hint in Aristotle's *De caelo* they formulated an account of place as a *distance* relation between a container's surface and some fixed immobile reference point or points: usually the centre and poles of the earth.[59] Giles of Rome labelled this concept 'formal

[56] Scotus, *Quod.* 11, n. 10 (Wadding edn., xii. 266; Alluntis and Wolter, 263 nn. 11. 24–5).

[57] See Grant, 'Medieval Doctrine of Place', 59–65; Richard Sorabji, *Matter, Space and Motion: Theories in Antiquity and their Sequel* (London: Duckworth, 1988), 186–201.

[58] Arist. *Phys.* 4. 4 (212^a14–21); see Sorabji, *Matter, Space and Motion*, 188.

[59] See e.g. Aquinas, *In Ph.* 4. 6, nn. 468 and 471 (ed. P. M. Maggiòlo (Turin and Rome: Marietti, 1965), 227^b–8^a); also Grosseteste, *In Ph.* 4 (ed. Richard Dales (Boulder, Colo.: University of Colorado Press, 1963), 80–1); Bacon, *In Ph.* 4 (ed. Ferdinand M. Delorme and Robert Steele, Opera hactemus inedita a Rogeri Baconi, 13 (Oxford: Clarendon Press, 1935), 193), all cited in Grant, 'Medieval Doctrine of Place', 63–4. For the possible Aristotelian inspiration here, see *Cael.* 2. 13–14 (293^a15–298^a20).

place', in contrast to what he labelled 'material place' (i.e. the standard Aristotelian view of place as the surface of the surrounding body).[60]

The notion of formal place was intended to provide for just one fixed frame of reference. Scotus argues that the conception of formal place, as just outlined, fails to provide such a frame of reference. Formal place is a relation of distance between the material place and some fixed reference points. But relations are accidents, and on standard accounts of accidents—even Scotus's—accidents cannot move naturally from subject to subject. Thus, the identity of an accident is contingent upon the identity of its subject. But, as Aristotle's boat example makes clear, the material place of a body can change. So the accidents of this material place will change too. Since the formal place of a body is an accident of its material place, formal place cannot retain numerical identity. And given this, formal place cannot be immobile.[61]

On the other hand, Scotus is clear that we need an account of the immobility of place. Mobility entails some sort of location. We should be able to say of a mobile object that it was in such and such a place, and will be in some other place. So if place were mobile, it would follow that place must itself be in a place—a potentially vicious non-explanatory regress.[62] To explain just what the immobility of place might entail, Scotus introduces a new concept: the incorruptibility of place 'by equivalence': 'Place has immobility totally opposed to local motion, and incorruptibility according to equivalence in comparison with local motion.'[63] What Scotus means is that the successive places surrounding a stationary body are *indiscernible*, and that they can therefore be thought of as if they are numerically identical:

These relations which are only numerically distinct will seem to be numerically one, since they are as indistinct with regard to local motion as [they would be] if they were just one relation.[64]

---

[60] Giles of Rome, *In Ph.* 4 ((Venice, 1502), 72va); on formal place, see, in addition to Grant, 'Medieval Doctrine of Place', Trifogli, 'Place of the Last Sphere', 348–50.

[61] Scotus, *Ord.* 2. 2. 2. 1–2, n. 222 (Vatican edn., vii. 255–6); *idem, Lect.* 2. 2. 2. 1–2, n. 201 (Vatican edn., xviii. 163).

[62] Scotus, *Ord.* 2. 2. 2. 1–2, n. 225 (Vatican edn., vii. 257); *idem, Lect.* 2. 2. 2. 1–2, n. 203 (Vatican edn., xviii. 163–4). As Scotus notes in the *Lectura*, Averroës held that there is a sense in which place is mobile: see Averroës, *In Ph.* 4. 37 (*Aristotelis Opera cum Averrois Commentaria* (11 vols., Venice, 1550), iv. 64^{ra-va}).

[63] Scotus, *Ord.* 2. 2. 2. 1–2, n. 224 (Vatican edn., vii. 256).

[64] Ibid. n. 227 (Vatican edn., vii. 258). The only recent article on place according to Scotus—Helen S. Lang, 'Bodies and Angels: The Occupants of Place for Aristotle and Duns Scotus', *Viator,* 14 (1983), 245–66, repr. with alterations in her *Aristotle's* Physics

They are, in fact, *specifically identical*, such that equivalent places are specifically distinct from every other place in the universe: 'All places in the universe, howsoever close, differ by species.'[65]

Scotus's theory of the equivalence of place could be no more than a refinement of the earlier idea of formal place. Scotus could be saying that the identity of the places successively surrounding a body is determined by the relation they have to some fixed immobile reference points. But Scotus does not mean this, and adds a further component to his theory which is inconsistent with the idea of formal place, and which makes it clear that we should not interpret Scotus's specific place as a sort of formal place. Scotus argues that the (specific) identity of a place is determined not by its relation to any immobile reference point, but by its relation to the whole universe: that is, presumably, to the whole framework of other (immobile) places. The idea here is that we do not need certain fixed reference points to anchor our talk about all other places—where these 'other places' are *ex hypothesi* unfixed or mobile. Rather, the *whole collection* of places is fixed and immobile; the identity of a place is established merely by its location within this whole.[66] Given this, Scotus's claim that places differ 'by species'

and its Medieval Varieties (Albany, NY: State University of New York Press, 1992)—unfortunately completely misunderstands Scotus's position here. According to Lang, Scotus's claim that place is incorruptible by equivalence should be understood to mean that the place of a body remains the same even if the body moves from location to location. Thus, with reference to Scotus, *Ord.* 2. 2. 2. 1–2, n. 224 (Vatican edn., vii. 256), cited above, Lang writes: 'If a given body of fixed size has moved from place A to place B, it has indeed changed place in the sense of moving from one location to another location; but the body has not changed place in the sense that the two locations are dimensionally equal to each other. . . . Hence, place is "incorruptible" in the sense that a given fixed body must always occupy the same dimension' ('Bodies and Angels', 254; *Aristotle's* Physics *and its Medieval Varieties*, 178). She thus argues that Scotus understands the place of a body to be the dimensions of that body. As far as I can tell from her exegesis of the various Scotist passages we have been looking at, Lang fails to understand that when Scotus talks about the *subject* of a place, he is referring not to the located body but to its immediate physical surroundings: see 'Bodies and Angels', 254–5; *Aristotle's* Physics *and its Medievel Varieties*, 178–9. Lang argues that Scotus's move allows him to sever body from 'its tie to place' ('Bodies and Angels', 257; *Aristotle's* Physics *and its Medieval Varieties*, 179–80). Lang's conclusion here is correct; but it is only fortuitously so, given her misunderstanding of Scotus's position. Scotus's claim that a body could exist outside the cosmos is (as I have tried to show) the result of an odd application of some fairly standard Aristotelian principles.

[65] Scotus, *Lect.* 2. 2. 2. 1–2, n. 204 (Vatican edn., xviii. 164); *idem, Ord.* 2. 2. 2. 1–2, n. 227 (Vatican edn., vii. 258); see also Grant, 'Medieval Doctrine of Place', 67.

[66] Scotus, *Ord.* 2. 2. 2. 1–2, n. 227 (Vatican edn., vii. 258); *idem, Lect.* 2. 2. 2. 1–2, n. 204 (Vatican edn., xviii. 164).

presumably entails that *distance* between places is sufficient for their differentiation. Grant usefully summarizes Scotus's innovations here:

Scotus's doctrine of place by equivalence [challenged] the doctrine of formal place which relied on constant and equal distance measurements to fixed, cosmic termini, such as the center and poles of the world. With Scotus, the immobility of place and of the body it contains is now determined by the essential equivalence of successive material places surrounding the same body. It is as if each place were the exact replica of its predecessor replacing it without interruption. Distance measurements from a given place to fixed termini were thus superfluous to establish immobility. Only the relationship between the containing surface and the body it contained need to be considered.[67]

We might be tempted to think that Scotus's conception of the incorruptibility of place amounts to an explicit doctrine of *space*. Crucially, Scotus claims that a place—construed as a set of sortally identical individuals—is incorruptible: it exists as long as the universe does.

[Place] is not corruptible in itself and according to equivalence, because another body (in which there is a numerically different notion of place from the preceding one: though the same as the preceding according to equivalence in comparison to local motion) necessarily succeeds that body in which that notion of place existed.[68]

The idea here seems to be that whatever the layout of the different bodies in the universe, all places exist. So place exists along with its occupants, and runs right through them. *Prima facie*, this reading looks to be in conflict with Scotus's claim that for a body to be in a place, it must be in an *actual* place: that is, it must actually separate the sides of its container.[69] But Scotus does not here suggest that place as such requires actual body-containment. So my reading does not seem to violate the actuality requirement. Equally, these different places are distinguished by the distances between them.

This looks quite like a conception of space as the three-dimensional container of bodies. But, as I hope my discussion of Scotus on vacuum has made clear, Scotus would not regard space—in this three-dimensional sense—as necessarily extending beyond the boundary of the physical universe. Presumably, it would only extend beyond the boundaries of the universe if God were to create a vacuum outside

---

[67] Grant, 'Medieval Doctrine of Place', 67.
[68] Scotus, *Ord.* 2. 2. 2. 1–2, n. 229 (Vatican edn., vii. 258–9).
[69] Ibid. n. 232 (Vatican edn., vii. 260).

the universe. But Scotus is not explicit even about this, since he does not explicitly suggest that Henry's conception of privative dimension could be used to measure putative distances outside the universe—say, between the boundary of the universe and some extra-cosmic body created by God. Scotus's account generally seems wedded to a view of space as *constituted by* the bodies located in it.

Generally, Scotus's account of space marks a strong move away from the Aristotelian accounts of two-dimensional place which he elsewhere supports. How consistent are these two accounts? It would, I think, be difficult to accuse Scotus of any formal inconsistency. Clearly, we can without confusion operate with a two-dimensional concept of place as the surroundings of a body and a three-dimensional concept of space.

Scotus's accounts of space—as void and as dimension—are not fully integrated into one theory. While the two accounts do not entail each other, Scotus could have used his account of space as dimension to allow for extra-cosmic space *dissociated* from his conception of void as something which would yield to body. Space here would just be dimension; it would not need to be constituted by the bodies located in it. It is doubtful that space, thus conceived, would need to be created by God. It would just be there, existing necessarily. On this view, there would be extra-cosmic space continuous with the space which inter-penetrates the universe.

Modern physicists see the universe as both unbounded and finite: unbounded, such that 'every region of place is . . . surrounded on all sides by other regions of space',[70] and finite, such that 'all the straight lines are closed lines, returning to their starting point'.[71] So they would not generally suppose that much sense could be made of the notion of space that is both outside the universe and immediately adjacent to it. Scotus's conception of extra-cosmic void, however, seems to require that there could be space both outside the universe and immediately adjacent to it. For example, if God were to create a body outside our universe and distant from it, he would, according to Scotus, have to create the space or void between the universe and the extra-cosmic body.

The modern account of space does not, as far as I can tell, mean that there could not be extra-cosmic space. Such spaces on the modern account would need to be *spatially inaccessible* from our universe.

---

[70] Richard Swinburne, *Space and Time*, 2nd edn. (London and Basingstoke: Macmillan, 1981), 26.   [71] Ibid. 107.

(There is in any case no reason to suppose that all places are in fact spatially related to each other: that is, be such that an appropriately powerful and long-lived substance could journey between them.[72]) It might be thought that, in Scotus's account, an extra-cosmic body would satisfy this inaccessibility requirement. But this would be a mistake. An extra-cosmic body certainly looks to be inaccessible from our universe. But it is not *spatially* inaccessible. The physical constitution of the outermost heavenly sphere is such that we cannot pass through it. But God could replace it with a differently constituted sphere—perhaps one with holes in—which would allow us passage out of the universe. So Scotus's Aristotelian cosmology will not provide him with the tools to flesh out a claim that there is extra-cosmic space inaccessible in the relevant sense from our space.

[72] On this, see Anthony Quinton, 'Spaces and Times', *Philosophy*, 37 (1962), 130–47, and the modifications proposed in Swinburne, *Space and Time*, 28–40.

12

Motion, Time, and Continuity

According to Scotus, following Aristotle and the majority scholastic view, both motion (i.e. gradual change) and time are continua. In this Chapter, I shall explore this claim and the way Scotus develops it. In the first two sections, I shall outline Scotus's account of a motion (in the sense of a motion *token* or instance: my journey from Oriel to the Bodleian, for example). In the first section I shall look at Scotus's claim that any motion token is reducible to a succession of forms, and, given this, at the non-atomic structure of motion. In the second section, I shall examine Scotus's claim that the limits of any motion token are entities, and look at Scotus's account of the relation between a motion token and its limiting entities. As we shall see, much of what Scotus has to say about spatially extended continua (discussed above in Chapters 7 and 8) applies generally to motion and time. There are, however, some differences, which I shall note below. In the third section I shall give an account of Scotus on the structure of time, and in the fourth section I shall try to defend the claim that Scotus *reduces* talk of time to talk of motion.

1. MOTION AND CONTINUITY

Aristotle's accounts of motion leave it unclear how motion is correctly to be categorized. Sometimes, he seems to suggest that there is no categorical distinction between motion and a changing form.[1] Elsewhere, however, he seems to imply that motion is an instance of passion,[2] and sometimes even of quantity.[3] Scotus opts broadly for

---

[1] Arist. *Ph.* 3. 1 (200^{b}32–201^{a}3).   [2] Arist. *Cat.* 9 (11^{b}1–2).
[3] Arist. *Metaph.* 5.13 (1020^{a}31–3). For a useful history of medieval interpretations of the Aristotelian material, see Anneliese Maier, *Zwischen Philosophie und Mechanik* (Studien zur Naturphilosophie der Spätscholastik, 5), Raccolta di Studi e Testi, 69 (Rome: Storia e Letteratura, 1958), 61–143; also the (not entirely fair) comments in James A. Weisheipl,

the first of these accounts, arguing that motion is just a succession of forms.[4] On this account, a motion token is held to belong to the category to which the changing forms belong.[5] For example, a change between different shades of blue belongs to the same category (viz. quality) as blueness; a change in extension belongs to the category of quantity; and a change in place belongs to the category of place.

Adopting this sort of account has certain metaphysical consequences. The most important—and the only one which is of interest here—is that a change will consist in the succession of forms which exist in between the two end terms, and will have these successive forms as *parts*. A change from light blue (B_1) to dark blue (B_2), for example, will contain the various shades of blue which exist in between B_1 and B_2. A change of place, from P_1 to P_2—will consist of all the places between P_1 and P_2. But, as we shall see, Scotus holds that this view is compatible with his claim that motion is not in any sense composed of atomic 'stages'. In the rest of this section, I shall try to show why Scotus rejects any atomic account of a motion token.

To understand Scotus's arguments, we need to do a bit of metaphysics. Following a hint in Aristotle, the medievals often distinguished between *successive* things and *permanent* things. The Aristotelian distinction which the medievals drew upon was between the parts of time, or of an utterance, which do not exist 'all at once', and the parts of a line, which do.[6] The distinction in modern terms is roughly between

'Aristotle's Physics and the Science of Motion', in Norman Kretzmann, Anthony Kenny, and Jan Pinborg (eds.), *The Cambridge History of Later Medieval Philosophy* (Cambridge: Cambridge University Press, 1982), 521–36, pp. 527–8. For a briefer summary of Maier's views, see *Die Vorläufer Galileis im 14. Jahrhundert* (Studien zur Naturphilosophie der Spätscholastik, [1]), Raccolta di Studi e Testi, 22 (Rome: Storia e Letteratura, 1949), Ch. 1, trans. in Maier, *On the Threshold of Exact Science: Selected Writings of Anneliese Maier on Late Medieval Natural Philosophy*, ed. Steven D. Sargent, The Middle Ages (Philadelphia: University of Pennsylvania Press, 1982), Ch. 1.

[4] Scotus, *Ord.* 2. 2. 1. 4, nn. 171–2, 181, 183 (Vatican edn., vii. 231–2, 236, 237).

[5] Ibid. 1. 2. 2. 1–4, n. 339 (Vatican edn., ii. 328–9). This passage seems to imply that motion cannot necessarily be categorized merely in relation to its end term, since there are some instances where a motion can result in an end term specifically different from the forms whose succession constitutes the motion: see Maier, *Zwischen Philosophie und Mechanik*, 78–80. But the point of the Scotist passage is not that motion is an item over and above the changing form, just that the *end term* of the motion is not sufficient to locate it in a particular category.

[6] See Arist. *Cat.* 6 (5^a15–37). The relevance of Aristotle's discussion in this context was spotted by Norman Kretzmann: see his 'Incipit/Desinit', in P. K. Machamer and R. G. Turnbull (eds.), *Motion and Time, Space and Matter: Interrelations in the History of Philosophy and Science* (Columbus, Oh.: Ohio State University Press, 1976), 101–36.

those objects which *perdure*, and those which *endure*. A perduring object includes among its components *temporal* parts. An enduring object, by contrast, has no temporal parts. If something endures, such that it 'lasts from one time to another', then there is some object 'existing at one of those times which is literally identical with a[n] . . . object existing at the other'.[7] A motion token—and any process in general—is a perduring object, one which has temporal parts. It is what the medievals would label a 'successive' thing.[8] Perduring or successive objects, according to Scotus, will have (temporally) continuous parts in a way highly analogous to the way in which spatially extended objects have (spatially) continuous parts. Scotus labels these temporal parts 'flowing parts' (*partes fluentes*), and argues that such parts are the proper parts of a successive object:

A part of a successive has no other existence in the whole than to make one part flow before another (which flowing parts integrate the whole); therefore just as for a part to exist in a permanent whole is for a permanent part to exist in a whole, so for a part to exist in a successive whole is for a flowing part to be continued by another [such] part.[9]

Scotus describes the relation between these flowing or temporal parts and their whole in the terms he usually reserves for instances of H-unity. So I take it that a whole motion token is an H-unity, and that it is, as such, a non-vague individual with temporal parts.[10] Given that processes take time, the claim that a process is an H-unity will entail that its identity cannot be fixed until it is *over*, and its end boundary is determined. A change in boundary conditions, as we saw in Chapter 8, is sufficient for a change in the identity of an H-unity.

As we saw in Chapter 7, Scotus denies that the parts of a spatial continuum (with the exception of its limit entities) are atoms. Likewise, he denies that the temporal parts of a successive object can be in any sense atomic. What would it be for the parts of a successive object

---

[7] Trenton Merricks, 'On the Incompatibility of Enduring and Perduring Entities', *Mind*, 104 (1995), 523–31, p. 525. The terminology comes from David Lewis, *On the Plurality of Worlds* (Oxford: Blackwell, 1986), 202.

[8] On the distinction, see e.g. Scotus, *Ord.* 2. 2. 1. 4, n. 168 (Vatican edn., vii. 230–1); 2. 2. 2. 5, n. 317 (Vatican edn., vii. 291). [9] Ibid. 2. 2. 2. 5, n. 353 (Vatican edn., vii. 311).

[10] See also Scotus's explicit statement in *Ord.* 2. 2. 2. 6, n. 484 (Vatican edn., vii. 373): 'This total heavy thing, in so far as it is homogeneous, is from similar parts (and these parts are prior in some way to the whole itself) . . . And a whole motion is composed of parts from partial motions, just as a whole heavy thing [is] from heavy parts.' (Scotus is oddly not quite right about his homogeneous heavy object: some of its parts will be extremely light.)

to be atomic? There are three quite distinct possibilities with regard to motion: (i) Motion is *temporally* discontinuous; (ii) motion is *spatially* discontinuous; (iii) motion is *temporally* and *spatially* discontinuous. On the first option, motion would include *temporal* pauses, where such pauses would intervene between the time atoms which constitute the temporal aspect of the motion token. On the second option, a motion token would include *spatial* jumps, or—in the case of changes in degree—of jumps from one degree to another. On the third, a motion token would consist of both pauses and jumps—which we might label 'jerks'. The third is the standard rejected view on Aristotelian and medieval accounts. On the third view, a motion token consists of 'instantaneous acquisitions of changed states' (*mutata esse*).[11]

There are several ways in which these three models could be interpreted. The motion atoms postulated in them could be extended or unextended; and they could be (I suppose) continuous or discrete. Like Aristotle, Scotus is not always clear which of these options his arguments attack—though it is clear that he would want to reject all of them. Generally, Scotus seems to disregard the possibility of motion atoms forming a continuum. As with the arguments in Chapter 7, Scotus supposes that continuity is equivalent to non-atomicity. And I have the impression that he generally (though perhaps not always) regards the motion atoms he wants to reject as unextended.

Underlying Scotus's arguments is his acceptance of an Aristotelian claim:

The same reasoning applies equally to magnitude, to time, and to motion: either all of these are composed of indivisibles and are divisible into indivisibles, or none.[12]

Aristotle, in fact, fails to provide an argument for this claim which is not question-begging.[13] And Scotus seems to have much the same difficulty. Scotus's basic argument against the claim that a motion

---

[11] For this translation of *mutata esse*, see Norman Kretzmann, 'Continua, Indivisibles, and Change in Wyclif's Logic of Scripture', in Anthony Kenny (ed.), *Wyclif in his Times*, (Oxford: Clarendon Press, 1986), 31–65, p. 37.   [12] Arist. *Ph.* 6. 1 (231^{b}18–20).
[13] 'What is undoubtedly true is that all of Aristotle's arguments for the infinite divisibility of space and time . . . depend on the premiss that motion is continuous': David Bostock, 'Aristotle on Continuity in *Physics* VI', in Lindsay Judson (ed.), *Aristotle's Physics: A Collection of Essays* (Oxford: Clarendon Press, 1991), 179–212, p. 189; see also Fred D. Miller, 'Aristotle against the Atomists', in Norman Kretzmann (ed.), *Infinity and Continuity in Ancient and Medieval Thought*, (Ithaca, NY, and London: Cornell University Press, 1982), 87–111, pp. 102–9.

token could include temporal pauses is a standard Aristotelian one,[14] and, as Scotus notes in the *Lectura*, it is based on the supposition that *speed* is infinitely variable. Suppose that two bodies are to traverse a fixed distance, and grant that the speed of the bodies is infinitely variable. Let 's' = speed, 'd' = distance, and 't' = time. If $s = d/t$, it will follow that time is infinitely divisible.[15] As the argument appears in Aristotle, it could also be utilized against the possibility of spatially discontinuous atoms, since Aristotle also considers a scenario in which two bodies traverse different distances in the same time. Aristotle also uses the argument against the third model—and I can see no sign that Scotus would want to disagree with him. But this inference does not look so reasonable, even given the infinite variability of speed. To show that time is infinitely divisible, we would have to assume that distance is; and to show that distance is infinitely divisible, we would have to assume that time is. All three arguments, of course, stand or fall on the truth of the claim that speed is infinitely variable: a claim which, as Scotus notes, is likely to be denied (wrongly, according to Scotus) by adherents of motion atoms.[16]

Scotus also tries an argument against the first model which does not rely on the infinite variability of speed. The basic argument, if I understand it rightly, goes like this. Spatial continuity entails temporal continuity. But a spatial quantum is a continuum, as we saw in Chapter 7. So an object traversing such a continuum will do so temporally continuously; and hence the first model of the putative atomicity of motion cannot be correct. Why accept that spatial continuity entails temporal continuity? Suppose, Scotus argues, that a spatial magnitude is a continuum, while time is atomic and discontinuous. On this supposition, an object moving along the continuum will have to jump from place to place, its jumps corresponding to time atoms. But in this case, the object will fail to traverse the whole continuum. It will, for example, jump from point a to point b without traversing any of the points between a and b. And Scotus seems to regard this as absurd.[17]

---

[14] For the argument in Aristotle, see *Ph.* 6. 2 (233^b19–32).

[15] Scotus, *Lect.* 2. 2. 2. 5–6, n. 351 (Vatican edn., xviii. 207); see *idem. Ord.* 2. 2. 2. 5, n. 316 (Vatican edn., vii. 290–1).

[16] Scotus, *Lect.* 2. 2. 2. 5–6, n. 351 (Vatican edn., xviii. 207).

[17] Scotus, *Ord.* 2. 2. 2. 5, n. 318 (Vatican edn., vii. 291); *idem. Lect.* 2. 2. 2. 5–6, n. 353 (Vatican edn., xviii. 207–8). The first part of the argument, which I do not discuss here, supposes that if there were *immediate* temporal or spatial indivisibles, such indivisibles would compose a continuum. But, as we saw in Ch. 7, Scotus denies this. So I do not see what the first part of his argument adds to his rejection of any of the models.

Elsewhere, Scotus reasons that if a motion token contains temporal pauses, it will follow that the agent causing the motion will have, during the pauses, to refrain from its action: a scenario which Scotus finds implausible.[18] The argument does not, however, seem sufficient to refute the claim that motion could contain temporal pauses. After all, one plausible reason for positing such pauses would be that time is, as a matter of necessity, discontinuous. But the discontinuity of time will apply equally to the agent and its effect.

What about the supposition that the time atoms could be continuous? Scotus, as we saw in Chapter 7, accepts the Aristotelian view that (putatively) immediate indivisibles would have to be identical. So he reasons that immediate temporal indivisibles (i.e. instants) would be simultaneous; and hence, given the atomicity of time, that any agent could cause the whole of its effect simultaneously. But this conclusion is, as Scotus puts it, 'extremely irrational', given our sound, empirically founded belief that many agents require time to produce their effects.[19] Of course, accepting this argument would rely on an acceptance of Scotus's claim that immediate indivisibles would be identical.

Scotus clearly wants to deny that motion is in any sense composed of atoms. We cannot regard his arguments as successful. The most successful arguments rely on the infinite variability of speed. But the most plausible reason for supposing that speed is infinitely variable is that space and time are infinitely divisible—that is, not composed of atoms. So the arguments seem circular (though perhaps not viciously circular, since there might be other reasons for wanting to hold that speed is infinitely variable). Given that motion is not composed of atoms, Scotus needs to give some account of the structure of a motion token. The rest of this section will be devoted to an account of this.

Scotus makes it clear that he regards a motion token as a non-atomic continuum structured in much the same way as a linear spatial continuum. His arguments for the non-atomic structure of motion, as we have seen, draw on an exact analogy between a motion token and a spatial continuum. As Scotus points out, the Aristotelian account of motion, on which he draws, entails that motion is infinitely divisible: 'Every motion precedes—to infinity—[a state of] having changed.'[20] This passage also makes it clear that (unlike a spatial continuum) a continuous motion token has *direction* as well as order. The same point

[18] Scotus, *Ord.* 2. 2. 2. 5, n. 393 (Vatican edn., vii. 328).   [19] Ibid.
[20] Ibid. n. 392 (Vatican edn., vii. 328); see Arist., *Ph.* 6. 6 (236^b32–237^b22).

is made in an important passage quoted above, where Scotus refers to 'part *before* part'.[21]

Scotus thus denies that a motion token is in any sense composed of atoms. But his position seems to be open to a fatal objection. As we saw in Chapter 10, Scotus objects to the generation and corruption theory for continuous qualitative change proposed by Walter Burley, on the grounds that it involves the generation of an infinite number of things.[22] But Scotus must accept the generation and corruption theory for at least some sorts of change—local motion, for example, which involves the generation and corruption of place relations. And Scotus's account of the infinite divisibility of all motion seems to entail that changes such as local motion involve the generation of an infinite number of things. Scotus would perhaps want to appeal to the standard Aristotelian account of continuity, outlined above in Chapter 7, as merely *potentially* infinitely divisible. But such an appeal would merely serve to show that local motion cannot satisfy a necessary condition for continuity, since it involves the *actual* generation of an infinite number of place relations. I do not know what Scotus could say to this worry.

Whatever we make of this objection, it is clear that changes which take place by addition or subtraction (of the sort discussed in Chapters 9 and 10) involve, on the view just outlined, the claim that forms *undergoing change* are vague objects. Take, for example, a shade of blue. Let us label it 'B_1'. Say we continuously add parts, deepening our shade of blue, starting from B_1, and ending at B_n. We can pick out discernible individuals at will during the change: B_2, B_3, and so on. But we can never pick out two such individuals immediately adjacent to each other. This follows from the infinite divisibility of motion. So we could never pick out all the possible individuals between (say) B_2 and B_3. In fact no *segment* of the change from (say) B_2 to B_3 contains definite individuals. As soon as we isolate an individual degree, we mark off another segment. In this sense, the whole change will in some sense contain (objectively potential) objects whose boundaries are both spatially and temporally vague. On the other hand, the *whole* change, consisting of the conjunction of all of its potential segments, is non-vague. It is, presumably, a kind of H-unity, as I suggested above.

---

[21] Scotus, *Ord.* 2. 2. 2. 5, n. 353 (Vatican edn., vii. 311), my italics; see above, p. 216.
[22] See (I'.1) in Ch. 10.

2. MOTION AND ITS LIMITS

Even though Scotus denies that motion is composed of atoms, he clearly accepts that there are such things as motion atoms. These atoms are limit entities, bounding a motion token at its beginning and end. As we have just noted, there are three possible sorts of motion atoms: (i) temporally indivisible motion atoms, (ii) spatially indivisible motion atoms, (iii) temporally and spatially indivisible motion atoms. As we shall see, Scotus is interested in defending the existence of the third sort of atom.

Given Scotus's basic Aristotelian assumption that there is a close isomorphism between spatial continuity and the continuity of time and motion, it is no surprise to discover that Scotus's account of motion atoms is *entitist*. Scotus firmly rejects the view that motion atoms could be no more than negations. Scotus reasons that if such temporally unextended motion atoms do not exist, it will be impossible to give an account of *instantaneous* change. Aristotle, of course, held that no change could be instantaneous. His reason is that no *process* is instantaneous.[23] Scotus however, in common with many medieval theologians, denies that all changes are processes. His motivation is at least partly theological. For example, in the Eucharist, the bread is changed instantaneously into the body of Christ.[24] But he argues that certain other changes are instantaneous too: in particular, the first light occurring at dawn.[25]

The argument for the existence of real motion atoms at instantaneous changes runs as follows. Suppose for the sake of a *reductio* that motion atoms are just negations. On such an account, it may prima facie be possible to give an account of the limits of continuous changes. The limits of such changes could be described in terms reducible to the continuous changes of which they would be the limits. But there are also clearly motion atoms identifiable with instantaneous

---

[23] See e.g. Arist. *Ph.* 6. 6 (236^{b}20). For Scotus's exposition of Aristotle's claim that no change can be instantaneous, see *Ord.* 2. 2. 2. 5, nn. 398–403 (Vatican edn., vii. 332–5). According to Scotus, Aristotle's claim is just that some seemingly instantaneous changes turn out on closer inspection not to be such.

[24] Scotus, *Ord.* 2. 2. 2. 7, n. 492 (Vatican edn., vii. 376).

[25] Ibid. n. 493 (Vatican edn., vii. 376). Scotus here argues against Aquinas's claim that all instances of seemingly instantaneous change can be analysed as the end results of processes. Dawn, for example, is really the end result of the motion of the sun: see *ST* 1. 53. 3 (ed. Petrus Caramello (3 vols., Turin and Rome: Marietti, 1952–6), i. 265^b). Scotus's example here seems very odd. Dawn, after all, seems to be a continuous process, involving a gradual increase in brightness. But transubstantiation seems a much clearer case.

changes. Such atoms correspond to the temporal instant at which the instantaneous change takes place. Scotus reasons that the motion atom identified with an instantaneous change cannot admit of a description in terms reducible to some *continuous* change, since an instantaneous change is not continuous, and therefore such an atom would not in fact be the limit of such a change. So the atom identified with an instantaneous change—the instantaneous acquisition of a changed state—has to be an entity. It cannot be a mere negation. As Scotus puts it, if this atom is not an entity, it will follow that 'the generation of a substance will be nothing, or at least that it will be *in* nothing [viz. in no instant]'.[26] The point is that an instantaneous change will have to *be* something; and if it is just a negation, it will in fact be nothing at all.

The argument does not, of course, have a direct bearing on the existence of limit entities at the boundaries of a motion token. But, as I shall show below, the way in which Scotus solves certain limit-decision problems entails that he reject non-entitism with regard to the motion atoms bounding a continuous process. The limits of a process are the points where it starts and stops. If we examine Scotus's discussion of starting and stopping, we will get a fairly good idea of his account of the relation between motion atoms and the continua which they limit.[27] Scotus is committed to the existence of instants of starting and stopping. But he insists that these instants are not in any sense *parts* of the motion token they limit. They are *extrinsic* to the motion token they limit. The instant of starting is the last instant *before* the motion token; the instant of stopping is the first instant *after* the motion token. Some quotations: first, starting:

It [viz. the mobile] is under the same form—under which it is at rest—in the instant of mutation. . . . From this instant the mobile begins to move. And [it does] this successively: either because of the parts of the mobile—since no part of the mobile is equally close to the agent, but each part is closer to another part to infinity (only a [putatively] mobile point is completely immediate to its agent, and [such a thing] is not [really] mobile); or because of the parts of the form according to which the motion should take place, of which each is producible before another by the mover present.[28]

[26] Scotus, *Ord.* 2. 2. 2. 5, n. 380 (Vatican edn., vii. 322–3).

[27] For discussion of limit decision problems in the Middle Ages, see Norman Kretzmann's seminal 'Incipit/Desinit'; also *idem*, 'Continuity, Contrariety, Contradiction, and Change', in his *Infinity and Continuity*, 270–96, and the literature cited there.

[28] Scotus, *Ord.* 2. 2. 2. 5, n. 394 (Vatican edn., vii. 329); see also *idem. Lect.* 2. 2. 2. 5–6, n. 395 (Vatican edn., xviii. 221).

Secondly, stopping:

> To change [i.e. to have changed] is to exist differently now from before, where 'to exist differently' is taken for an indivisible, and 'before' is taken for a divisible. Therefore the first existence of the form that terminates the flux is measured in itself by the first [temporal] instant, and the change is properly to this [viz. the first existence of the form].[29]

Thirdly, a limit-decision principle:

> When one [of a] contradictory [pair] is measured by an indivisible, [then] the other is measured by a divisible.[30]

The first passage might make it look as though Scotus is just interested in spatially indivisible motion atoms. But the second passage makes clear that this is not the case, and that Scotus is anxious to defend the existence of both spatially and temporally indivisible motion atoms. The third makes it clear that there could not be two immediately adjacent motion atoms: a conclusion which follows from the isomorphism between spatial and successive continua.

Figure 12.1 captures Scotus's basic model for starting and stopping: *a* and *b* are motion atoms, spatially and temporally indivisible; they are the instants of starting and stopping. According to Scotus, they belong to the periods of stasis, not to the motion. And his reason for this is the good Aristotelian one cited above: 'Every motion precedes—to infinity—[a state of] having changed.'[31] And Aristotle is evidently correct here. Processes necessarily *take time*. As Scotus notes, no real part of a process can be instantaneous.[32]

Figure 12.1 also makes clear that a permanent item has intrinsic limits. Thus, there are, for example, first and last instants at which I am a human being.[33] The medievals usually made a distinction

---

[29] Scotus, *Ord.* 2. 2. 1. 4, n. 181 (Vatican edn., vii. 236).

[30] Ibid. 2. 2. 2. 5, n. 411 (Vatican edn., vii. 337).

[31] Ibid. n. 392 (Vatican edn., vii. 328).

[32] Scotus, *Lect.* 2. 2. 2. 5–6, n. 393 (Vatican edn., xviii. 220). Of course, modern dynamics allows for instantaneous velocity. But Richard Swinburne points out that instantaneous velocity is necessarily analysable in terms of things happening over periods of time: instantaneous velocity is 'not a velocity possessed at an instant discovered via study of limits but rather a limit of velocities possessed over series of periods bounded by that instant' ('God and Time', in Eleonore Stump (ed.), *Reasoned Faith: Essays in Philosophical Theology in Honor of Norman Kretzmann* (Ithaca, NY, and London: Cornell University Press, 1993), 203–22, p. 207).

[33] In Scotus, *Ord.* 1. 19. 2, n. 65 (Vatican edn., v. 297), Scotus puzzlingly claims that at the instant of death the soul no longer informs the body, though it is still spatially 'in' the

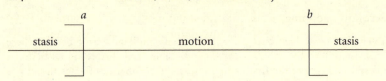

Figure 12.1

between being permanent and being at rest. An *enduring* substance—one which cannot change—is permanent; a form which can be (but is not) changing is at rest. As we shall see in the next chapter, Scotus regards such a form as a successive. But he holds that the periods of stasis surrounding a motion token (the periods before *a* and after *b* in Fig. 12.1) can be occupied equally by a permanent as by something merely at rest. By the same token, the motion atoms *a* and *b* can belong equally to periods of permanence as to periods of rest. Despite the fact that motion and rest both perdure, Scotus is able to pin-point some clear disanalogies between them.[34] But as Figure 12.1 makes clear, Scotus holds that the limits of periods of rest are *intrinsic* to these periods. This is not very Aristotelian. According to Aristotle, a change from rest to motion involves a neutral instant which is both the last instant of the non-being of the motion token and the first instant of the non-being of rest.[35] Scotus's treatment of rest as strongly analogous to permanence allows him to come to a principled rejection of Aristotle's puzzling view. Rest, after all, is not itself a process.

Given that Scotus holds that instantaneous change is possible—change of one substance directly to another without any intervening process—what account can he give of the instant of change in such cases? As far as I can tell, Scotus argues that there is a first instant of the new substance, but no last instant of the old.[36] This may be an arbitrary stipulation; but perhaps Scotus is supposing that we would not be able to identify the instant of change until (at least) *after* the destruction of the first substance.

body. This seems to make the limits of human existence extrinsic to it, and (supposing the departure of the soul from the body to be successive) seems to make the limits of a successive intrinsic. Both of these are inconsistent with Scotus's standard account of limit-decision problems, and seem to be mistaken.

[34] See e.g. Scotus, *Ord.* 2. 2. 1. 4, nn. 173–4, 176–80 (Vatican edn., vii. 232–5).

[35] See Arist. *Ph.* 6. 3 (234ᵃ34–5), discussed in Kretzmann, 'Incipit/Desinit', 114–15.

[36] Scotus, *Ord.* 2. 2. 2. 5, n. 380 (Vatican edn., vii. 322–3); 2. 2. 2. 7, nn. 492–3 (Vatican edn., vii. 376).

Scotus's account of starting and stopping is much the same as Peter of Spain's analysis of propositions about starting and stopping.[37] Generally, the account in both thinkers seems to be exactly right. But, as I hinted above, it seems to me that the account entails rejecting non-entitism. If non-entitism were true with regard to motion atoms, Scotus could have no principled way of denying the existence of adjacent motion atoms, one corresponding to the non-being of motion, the other to the non-being of stasis. The atoms would not *be* anything; so I do not see why they could not be adjacent. The negation of motion could be immediately adjacent to the negation of stasis. So it seems to me that Scotus's basic limit-decision model entails the rejection of non-entitism.

As we saw in Chapter 7, Scotus holds that there is no gap between a spatial continuum and the point which limits it. Scotus argues similarly in the case of motion. There is no gap between a motion token and the atom which limits it. Scotus, as we saw, argues that the lack of a gap between two objects *a* and *b* does not entail that the whole of *a* is immediate to the whole of *b*, or that any single part of *a* is immediately adjacent to *b*. Thus a continuous, infinitely divisible motion token can be immediate to its limit entities without there needing to be any single part of the motion token which is immediate to any one of its limit entities.[38]

Given that Scotus holds that there is no part of a motion token which is atomic, what sort of account can he give of the mid-point of a change? Scotus clearly thinks that all such problems can be analysed fairly straightforwardly. He gives an example. Suppose a hot body

---

[37] Scotus cites Peter of Spain at *Ord.* 2. 2. 1. 1, n. 56 (Vatican edn., vii. 181) and *Lect.* 2. 2. 1. 1, n. 48 (Vatican edn., xviii. 115–16), both times referring to Peter of Spain, *Syncat.* 6. 5 (ed. L. M. de Rijk, trans. Joke Spruuyt, Studien und Texte Geistesgeschichte des Mittelalters, 30 (Leiden, New York, and Cologne: Brill, 1992), 252/3). For Peter's whole discussion, see *Syncat.* 6 (pp. 248/9–254/5). According to Peter, there are first and last instants of the existence of permanent items, but not of successive ones: see *Syncat.* 6. 3 (p. 250/1), where Peter states: 'Permanent things exist at their beginning and their end . . . whereas successive things do not exist at their beginning or at their end.' Kretzmann's analysis in his 'Incipit/Desinit', 110–14, differs from that offered here, but this can easily be explained. When Kretzmann wrote that article, no critical edition of Peter's *Syncategoreumata* was available, and the text of the older editions is extremely flawed. According to the older editions (I looked at that published in Cologne in 1494, p. 48vb), there are no last instants of permanent items, and Kretzmann followed this in his analysis of Peter's position. Scotus's account differs from this, but conforms exactly to that found in the critical edition of Peter's *Syncategoreumata*. So I think we can be fairly sure that Peter is Scotus's source here.

[38] Scotus, *Ord.* 2. 2. 2. 5, n. 410 (Vatican edn., vii. 337).

gradually grows cold. According to his opponent, there will be a point at which the body stops losing heat, and starts gaining coldness. But both motion tokens are continuous. So, for at least one of the motion tokens, it must be the case that a motion atom is part of a continuous change.[39]

The example is, of course, specious, as Scotus is quick to point out. According to Scotus, the body is always *both* losing heat *and* gaining coldness. (We would regard this solution as equally specious, since we would regard cold as just a way of talking about lack of heat. But Scotus seems to suppose that hot and cold are both non-privative properties.) Scotus cites Aristotle's claim that anything undergoing a change 'has something of both extremes'.[40] He reasons that there is no last instant of heat and no first instant of coldness. There is, however, a motion instant at the beginning of the whole process (a last instant at which heat is constant) and one at the end (a first instant at which coldness is constant).[41]

At one point, Scotus does allow that there can be instants *during* a change. But he does so in such a way as to preclude the idea of motion *at* an instant. He allows that we can mark out at will instants during a change, and claims that such instants mark 'the end of one [change] and the beginning of another'.[42] (Putting the point in this way makes it clear that there can be no immediately adjacent instants.) But he is careful in the way he talks about such an instant: it is an instant of 'having reached a certain stage' (*mutata esse*, clearly being used of some point during a change). So the fact that Scotus talks of an instant of having reached such a stage during a change should alert us to the fact that, like Aristotle, Scotus does not have a conception of motion 'at an instant'. Moving takes time.

3. SOME TOPOLOGICAL PROPERTIES OF TIME

In the rest of this chapter, I want to look at Scotus's account of the structure of time: what modern writers label its *topology*.[43] Scotus does

---

[39] Ibid. n. 395 (Vatican edn., vii. 329).

[40] Ibid. (Vatican edn., vii. 330); see Arist. *Ph.* 6. 4 (234^{b}9–20); 6. 10 (240^{b}8–31).

[41] Scotus, *Ord.* 2. 2. 2. 5, n. 396 (Vatican edn., vii. 330). For the general account of motion as involving two corresponding changes, see ibid. 2. 2. 2. 3, n. 272 (Vatican edn., vii. 273–4).   [42] Scotus, *Lect.* 2. 2. 1. 2, n. 91 (Vatican edn., xviii. 128–9).

[43] The only extended account of Scotus on time, C. R. S. Harris, *Duns Scotus*, (2 vols. Oxford: Clarendon Press, 1927), ii. 129–46, is based on the inauthentic *De rerum principio*,

not always clearly distinguish time's topology from its *metric*: time's being a measure of determinate, quantifiable temporal periods. In fact, like Aristotle, Scotus often speaks of topological matters in metrical terms. As one modern commentator notes: 'It is not obvious, I think, to what extent Aristotle realizes that he is dealing with two separate matters here';[44] and the same seems true of Scotus. This does not mean, however, that Scotus does not draw implicitly on the distinction, or that using the distinction will not help us clarify what Scotus wants to say about time. As we shall see, for example, Scotus defines temporal extension independently of any questions of temporal metric.

Scotus's account of the topology of time is by no means complete. But I think he gives us enough information to get clear on at least some of the topological properties of time. I shall argue in the next section that Scotus tends to *reduce* time to motion. In this case, the arguments against motion's being composed of temporally indivisible motion atoms are in effect arguments against time's being composed of instants. (We examined such arguments in the first section above.) And what we find in Scotus's discussions is a clear isomorphism between the structure of time and the structure of motion. Topologically, time—both the whole of time and any part of it—is an ordered linear continuum bounded by instants:

A mobile can be considered in three ways: either as it is under the end terms of the mutations, or as it is under the medium between the mutations, or as it is prior to motion and mutation (though able to receive these). In the first way diverse nows . . . correspond to it; in the second way time—the medium between these two nows—corresponds to it.[45]

Scotus argues that any quantitative indivisible—such as a temporal

now known to be the work of Vitalis of Furno. Harris is followed closely by Edith Wilks Dolnikowski, *Thomas Bradwardine: A View of Time and a Vision of Eternity in Fourteenth-Century Thought*, Studies in the History of Christian Thought, 65 (Leiden, New York, and Cologne: Brill, 1995), 67–72. The best account to date of Scotus on time is still Pierre Duhem, *Le Système du monde: histoire des doctrines cosmologiques de Platon à Copernique* (10 vols., Paris: Hermann, n.d.–1959), vii. 363–8, trans. in Duhem, *Medieval Cosmology: Theories of Infinity, Place, Time, Void, and the Plurality of Worlds*, ed. Roger Ariew (Chicago and London: University of Chicago Press, 1985), 295–9.

[44] Michael J. White, *The Continuous and the Discrete: Ancient Physical Theories from a Contemporary Perspective* (Oxford: Clarendon Press, 1992), 79.

[45] Scotus, *Ord.* 2. 2. 1. 2, n. 110 (Vatican edn., vii. 205); see also nn. 97, 100 (Vatican edn., vii. 199–201); *idem, Lect.* 2. 2. 1. 2, nn. 87–8 (Vatican edn., xviii. 127); 2. 2. 1. 3, n. 115 (Vatican edn., xviii. 137).

instant—is necessarily the end term of a continuum.[46] Furthermore, Scotus probably holds that the ordering of time can be defined in terms of the relations holding between the instants which bound it: 'In one property of the now [Aristotle] claims that by the now before and after in time are made known.'[47] (Talk of 'now' here is, as I shall show in the next Chapter, just a way of talking about a temporal instant.)

Scotus's account of the relation between the instant limiting a time period and the time period itself is exactly the same as the account he offers in the case of motion. Thus, just as in the case of motion, the limits of a temporal period are *extrinsic* to the period. Figure 12.1 thus maps time as well as motion. A problem arises in the case of a temporal instant, however. Aristotle noticed that, if this account of time—according to which 'static' instants limit temporal periods—is correct, we should be able to say just *when* a temporal instant ceases. But, as he points out, no possible answer is satisfactory:

The prior now cannot have ceased to be in itself (since it then existed); yet it cannot have ceased to be in another now. For we may lay it down that one now cannot be next to another, any more than point to point. If then it did not cease to be in the next now but in another, it would exist simultaneously with the innumerable nows between the two—which is impossible.[48]

Given Scotus's firm adherence to the existence of static temporal instants limiting temporal periods, he needs to find some answer to this paradox.

Aristotle's aporetic account of time in *Physics* 4 does not include a convincing solution to the problem of the ceasing instant. But Scotus suggests a solution—one which, incidentally, bears a striking resemblance to a modern solution to the same problem. The *Lectura* account is clearer and more thorough than the *Ordinatio* account. Scotus raises the paradox as follows:

An instant . . . remains the same over the whole of time. The reason is that, if it is corrupted, it is not corrupted while it exists, and it is not corrupted while it

---

[46] Scotus, *Ord.* 2. 2. 1. 2, n. 102 (Vatican edn., vii. 202). Scotus actually claims that an indivisible is necessarily either the end term of a continuum or part of a whole composed of indivisibles. But the second option here is counterfactual. According to Scotus, there can be no whole composed of indivisibles. So any temporal instant is necessarily the boundary of a temporal continuum.

[47] Scotus, *Lect.* 2. 2. 1. 2, n. 88 (Vatican edn., xviii. 127); see also *idem, Ord.* 2. 2. 1. 2, n. 97 (Vatican edn., vii. 199–200): see Arist., *Ph.* 4. 11 (219[b]23–5).

[48] Arist. *Ph.* 4. 10 (218[a]17–22).

does not exist (for it will exist neither in a mediate now, nor in an immediate [now]).[49]

Scotus notes that there is a proposed solution to this in *Metaphysics* 3: we do not need to concern ourselves with the paradox, since it arises only in the case of an item which is *corrupted*; and an instant is not this kind of thing.[50]

This Aristotelian solution seems, however, to be no more than *ad hoc*. According to Richard Sorabji, Aristotle proposes another, far more satisfactory solution in the same passage of *Metaphysics* 3. According to Sorabji, Aristotle argues that the correct solution to the paradox is that it can never be true to claim that an instant 'is ceasing', just that, for any instant after its cessation, we can claim that it 'has ceased'.[51] Michael Inwood suggests, however, that both Aristotle and Sorabji are too hasty here. He reasons that while it is objectionable to refer to the now ceasing by means of *continuous* present and past tenses

the non-continuous present and past tenses ('It ceases, ceased to be 6 o'clock at 6 o'clock') are not similarly objectionable. Normally events and times are not said to start, occur and stop at the same time. . . . But this is because they do not normally start, occur and cease simultaneously rather than because their doing so would be intrinsically contradictory: 'It stopped being 6 o'clock at 6 o'clock' does not obviously entail 'It was not 6 o'clock at 6 o'clock'.[52]

Inwood's solution—that we can correctly assert that an instant ceases—is very close to that proposed by Scotus, though Scotus does not claim to find even hints of this solution in Aristotle's *Metaphysics*. Scotus formulates the solution on the basis of a reading of Peter of Spain. The solution turns on the reading of the verb translated 'cease' which obtains when talking about the cessation of permanents. Peter argues that when we speak of a permanent item ceasing, what we mean is that the item 'is now for the last time . . . and will no longer be'.[53] On this reading, it would be correct to claim that a permanent item ceases in the last instant of its existence: roughly, that there is a last instant of its existence, and no first instance of non-existence.[54] In the *Ordinatio*,

---

[49] Scotus, *Lect.* 2. 2. 1. 2, n. 83 (Vatican edn., xviii. 126–7).

[50] Ibid.; see Arist., *Metaph.* 3.5 (1002ª32–ᵇ7).

[51] Richard Sorabji, *Time, Creation and the Continuum: Theories in Antiquity and the Early Middle Ages* (London: Duckworth, 1983), 10.

[52] Michael Inwood, 'Aristotle on the Reality of Time', in Judson (ed.), *Aristotle's* Physics, 151–78, p. 164.   [53] Peter of Spain, *Syncat.* 5 (p. 252/3).

[54] Scotus, *Lect.* 2. 2. 1. 1, n. 48 (Vatican edn., xviii. 115–16); idem., *Ord.* 2. 2. 1. 1, n. 56 (Vatican edn., vii. 181).

Scotus adds (again following Peter of Spain) that the opposite state of affairs obtains in the case of the cessation of a successive item. When we use the verb 'cease' in the present tense, referring to a successive item, we mean that the item existed, but now no longer exists: roughly, that there is no last instance of its existence, but a first instance of its non-existence.[55] Since a (static) instant is a permanent item, lacking temporal parts, the first reading of the verb 'cease' is relevant: an instant ceases in the instant of its existence; that is, it ceases 'in itself'.

Scotus's solution is thus rather different from the one which, according to Sorabji, can be found in Aristotle. But the point of both solutions is that there is no first instant of the non-existence of some instant. Scotus's rather different account of the semantics of the solution is based on the reading of the verb 'cease' which he derives from Peter of Spain. But the solution seems correct, and I think represents a significant attempt to provide a reasonable solution to an Aristotelian aporia.

4. TIME AND MOTION: MODAL REDUCTIONISM

According to Aristotle, time is relative to motion.[56] Scotus follows Aristotle in this view. Adopting a relativist theory of time does not entail adopting a stronger *reductionistic* theory of time, according to which time is in some sense reducible to motion. But I shall argue here that Scotus does make just this reductionistic move.

We can get some idea of what Aristotle and Scotus—and, for that matter, most medieval thinkers—mean when they claim that time is relative to motion by drawing on a distinction made by Newton. Newton distinguishes 'absolute, true and mathematical time', which 'of itself and from its own nature flows equably without relation to anything external', from 'relative, apparent, and common time', which is the 'sensible and external (whether accurate or inequable) measure of duration by the means of motion'.[57] By 'time', medieval thinkers mean something like Newton's *relative* time. They do not generally have a conception of *absolute* time.[58] Scotus clearly holds not only that

---

[55] Scotus, *Ord.* 2. 2. 1. 1, n. 56 (Vatican edn., vii. 181); see Peter of Spain, *Syncat.* 5 (p. 252/3).

[56] See e.g. Aristotle's definition of 'time' at *Ph.* 4. 11 (219^{b}1–2); there is a vast amount of evidence in *Physics* 4 for this claim.

[57] Isaac Newton, *Mathematical Principles of Natural Philosophy*, trans. A. Motte, ed. F. Cajori (2 vols., Berkeley, Los Angeles, and London: University of California Press, 1973), i. 6.

[58] I note an exception to this claim in the next chapter.

the existence of time is entailed by the existence of natural processes, but also that time does not exist apart from natural processes.[59]

In what follows, I shall argue that the position which Scotus espouses is one which has been labelled 'modal reductionism': the view that 'all assertions about time and the temporal aspects of things can be parsed as assertions about relations between actual and possible events'.[60] But before I do this, I will offer some initial evidence in favour of my claim that Scotus does not accept the existence of absolute time. (This evidence seems to me conclusive; but I shall discuss below other evidence which some might be inclined to regard as defending the absolutist claim.)

If Scotus wanted to defend the existence of absolute time, he would have to appeal to the existence of time in a universe containing merely *permanent* things. (A permanent thing is one for which change is logically impossible.) The reason is that such a universe would uniquely contain items which *could not* change; that is, it would be such that it contained neither actual nor possible events or processes. So the temporality of permanent items would be sufficient for the existence of absolute time. But the proper metric for a permanent item, according to Scotus, is the *aevum*.[61] The *aevum* is a durational measure quite different from time. The difference is best spelt out topologically. Topologically the *aevum* has the properties not of a continuum, but of an *instant*.[62] So in a static universe (one composed merely of permanent things) there would be no time—no periods of time—at all.[63] Scotus thus rejects any account of absolute time.

---

[59] See e.g. Scotus, *Ord.* 2. 2. 1. 2, n. 111 (Vatican edn., vii. 205–6); 2. 2. 1. 3, nn. 138–40 (Vatican edn., vii. 216–17); *idem, Lect.* 2. 2. 1. 3, nn. 109–11, 113 (Vatican edn., xviii. 135–7) for initial confirmation of this claim.

[60] W. H. Newton-Smith, *The Structure of Time*, International Library of Philosophy (London, Boston, and Henley: Routledge and Kegan Paul, 1980), 47. In my 'Duns Scotus on Eternity and Timelessness', *Faith and Philosophy*, 14 (1997), 3–25 n. 33, I suggest that Scotus's position should be labelled 'modal relativism', since he does not argue that time is just *reducible to* motion. But this now seems to me to be mistaken.

[61] See e.g. Scotus, *Lect.* 2. 2. 1. 4, n. 155 (Vatican edn., xviii. 150); *idem, Ord.* 2. 2. 1. 4, nn. 171–4 (Vatican edn., vii. 231–3); *idem, Rep.* 2. 2. 1, nn. 3–5 (Wadding edn., xi. 265[a–b]).

[62] On this, see Ch. 13, sect. 4.

[63] What this means is that in such a universe there would be nothing having any of the significant *topological* properties of time. Nevertheless, Scotus puts this point by noting that, in a static universe, nothing would be *measured by* time: viz. that in such a universe nothing would have the metrical properties of time. So the way in which Scotus discusses his relativist position makes it look as though merely *metrical* issues are at stake: if there were no natural processes, then we would not be able to assign a measurable duration to any existing state of affairs. Richard Swinburne points out that such a claim does not

In the rest of this chapter, I shall try to show that Scotus accepts modal reductionism, examining first his account of the temporality of actually successive items, and secondly his account of the temporality of non-permanent static items (i.e. items *at rest*). Scotus distinguishes actual time and privative time. In a central passage, Scotus argues that something is measured by actual time if it is actually in motion, and that it is measured by privative time if both it is not in motion and it is physically possible for it to be in motion.[64] The distinction, however, is not quite as straightforward as this passage suggests, and elsewhere Scotus makes it clear that the distinction between actual and privative time needs to be spelt out in terms which include the motion of the outermost heavenly sphere. The reason is that he identifies the motion of the outermost heavenly sphere with actual temporal metric. Scotus holds that, after the resurrection of the body, Peter the Apostle will be able to walk around, even though the motion of the outermost heavenly sphere will have ceased. And he suggests that, in this case, Peter's walk will be measured by privative time.[65] Now, Peter himself is clearly in motion: he is walking around. So Scotus's intended distinction between actual and privative time, (Ta) and (Tp), can be captured by the following:

(Ta)   An item x is measured by actual time if and only if both x is in motion and the outermost heavenly sphere is in motion.

(Tp)   An item x is measured by privative time if and only if it is the case that either (i) x is at rest, or (ii) if x is in motion, then the outermost heavenly sphere is at rest.

These definitions are basically metrical. But they have, of course, topological implications. In what follows, I want to establish the following four claims: first, that Scotus reduces the topological properties of actual time to the structure of actual motion; secondly, that he wants to reduce the metrical properties of actual time to actual

---

entail the further claim that if there were no natural processes, there would be no temporal extension at all. On Swinburne's account, there could be temporal extension but no measurable duration: see Swinburne, 'God and Time', 208–11. Scotus's account, however, does not seem to be quite like this, and it is clear that Scotus would regard his account of time as having primarily topological implications, despite the (Aristotelian) way in which he phrases the point.

[64] Scotus, *Ord.* 2. 2. 1. 4, nn. 171–80 (Vatican edn., vii. 231–5). For the distinction between actual and privative time, see also *idem, Quod.* 11, n. 9 (Wadding edn., xii. 266; Alluntis and Wolter, 263, n. 11. 23).

[65] Scotus, *Ord.* 2. 2. 2. 7, n. 502 (Vatican edn., vii. 380–1).

motion; thirdly, that he reduces the topology of privative time to possible motion; and finally, that he wants to reduce the metric of privative time to possible motion.

First, then, Scotus is happy to reduce the *topological* properties of actual time to the structure of motion. We saw in the previous section that the topology of time—to the extent that Scotus developed an account of this—parallels exactly the non-atomic structure of motion. And given (Ta), actual time is relative to actual motion (i.e. that there is no actual time without motion). This pair of relations between actual time and actual motion makes it probable that Scotus would want to deny that there is any feature of the topology of actual time which cannot be captured in terms of the structure of motion. It seems to me that Scotus makes just this claim with regard to one structural feature of time in the early book 5 of the *Metaphysics* questions:

All motions, because they flow in a linear way, are simultaneous with regard to the present now. . . . For this reason they have the feature of unity of subject in relation to time. For this reason time is one.[66]

Here Scotus seems to hold that time is reducible to the conjunction of all motion tokens. So, on this account, the topology of actual time is reducible to motion.[67]

Does Scotus regard the metric of actual time as reducible to talk about motion? (Ta) makes it clear that, unsurprisingly, actual time has a metric. Clearly, on (Ta), the metric of actual time will be closely bound up with the motion of the outermost heavenly sphere. On one theory, we might want to claim that time is *reducible* to the motion of the outermost heavenly sphere. In this case, it would be false to claim—at least without further qualification—that the motion of the outermost heavenly sphere was itself temporal, or (more precisely) was measured by time. The motion of the outermost heavenly sphere would be our temporal measuring device, a kind of cosmic clock. On a different theory, however, we might want to claim that there was some other (non-physical?) process which measured the duration of motion. In this case we could allow that the motion of the outermost

---

[66] Scotus, *In Metaph.* 5. 10, n. 4 (Wadding edn., iv, 632ª). I shall return to this passage in the next chapter, since the property of time that it entails—viz. that time *flows*—Scotus unequivocally rejects later in his life.

[67] For my glossing of 'subject of' as 'reducible to', see Scotus, *Lect.* 2. 2. 1. 3, n. 107 (Vatican edn., xviii. 134), which I quote below. In this passage, Scotus contrasts '*x*'s being measured by time' and 'time being in *x* as a passion in a subject'. So I take it that time is in some sense reducible to its subject, and measures *other* things.

heavenly sphere was temporal. Scotus notices that the reducibility or irreducibility of time to motion depends on our ability to talk about speed:

> If time differs from motion, the reason for this is that parts of some proportion of some motion are not necessarily equal in number and quantity to parts of the same proportion of time; and no quantity [viz. motion] is the same as another quantity [viz. time] unless the parts in some proportion of it are equal to parts of the same proportion in the other (equal, that is, as much in number as magnitude).[68]

Scotus does not seem easily able to decide about this. In the early *Metaphysics* questions he seems to hold the second theory: namely, that the metric of time is *not* reducible in any sense to motion.

> The quantity by which motion is a quantum is specifically different from [spatial] magnitude and from time; thus there are three species of permanent quantity (viz. body, surface, and line), and there is agreed to be two species of successives (viz. the succession of motion and of time).[69]

Sometimes, however, Scotus seems to accept the stronger, reductionistic theory. On this theory, the metrical properties of actual time are reducible to the motion of the outermost heavenly sphere. In the *Ordinatio*, Scotus argues that the quantity of a *motion* refers to succession without any assignable measure. *Time* merely adds to the quantity of motion two things 'which are required for measurement: i.e. uniformity or regularity, and speed'.[70] Scotus then *identifies* this actual time with the motion of the outermost heavenly sphere. His reason for this is that this motion is regular and has maximal speed, such that other speeds could be measured as subdivisions of its speed.[71] So Scotus here argues that the motion of the outermost heavenly sphere (uniquely) satisfies the conditions required of a temporal metric, and thus that the metric of (actual) time is reducible to the motion of the outermost heavenly sphere.

There is an obvious objection—of which Scotus was aware—to the attempt to reduce the metrical properties of actual time to the motion of the outermost heavenly sphere. As Aristotle spotted, we cannot meaningfully talk of time (unlike the motion of the outermost

---

[68] Scotus, *Ord.* 2. 2. 1. 2, n. 111 (Vatican edn., vii. 205–6).
[69] Scotus, *In Metaph.* 5. 10, n. 1 (Wadding edn., IV, 631[a–b]); see also *idem, Ord.* 2. 2. 1. 2, n. 112 (Vatican edn., vii. 207).
[70] Scotus, *Ord.* 4. 48. 2, n. 12 (Wadding edn., X, 317).   [71] Ibid.

heavenly sphere) as having any speed at all. So we cannot identify time with the motion of the outermost heavenly sphere.[72] In the *Lectura* Scotus replies by offering an argument *in favour* of the identity of time with the motion of this sphere:

> The motion of the first heaven neither is exceeded by time, nor ceases in time, according to Aristotle. Therefore time will not be the measure of the first motion, but will be in it as a passion in a subject.[73]

This argument seems to presuppose that the motion of the outermost heavenly sphere is *everlasting*, a position which Scotus clearly disagrees with elsewhere.[74] But despite this, I think that the evidence generally favours the view that Scotus identifies the metric of (actual) time with the motion of the outermost heavenly sphere. In a passage in the *Ordinatio* parallel to the one just cited from the *Lectura*, Scotus reasons that we could still provide some sort of temporal measure for the motion of the outermost heavenly sphere. Although the whole motion of the heavenly sphere is not 'exceeded by time', nevertheless any given part of this motion is. So presumably the duration of any given part could be measured as a subdivision of the whole motion.[75]

What about privative time, as defined in (Tp)? It is easy enough to show, I think, that privative time is relative to (physically) possible motion; and probably that it is reducible to (physically) possible motion. In both book 2 of the *Ordinatio* and question 11 of the *Quodlibet*, Scotus characterizes privative time as being analogous to a spatial vacuum. In a spatial vacuum, as we saw in Chapter 11, there is spatial extension of a determinate magnitude, though no body to be the subject of this extension. In privative time, there is temporal extension of a determinate magnitude, though no motion to be the subject of this extension. In the *Quodlibet*, Scotus puts it as follows:

> Between any two imagined instants of this duration there could have been an interval of so much movement, and so, if we call time the measure of flow or motion, then this immobile existence would have a time period, although the flow of time would not be actual and positive but only potential and privative. Hence if a mind aware of actual positive time were to use it to measure this period of uniform duration, it would know how long it was,

---

[72] Ibid. 2. 2. 1. 2, n. 85 (Vatican edn., vii. 194); 2. 2. 1. 3, n. 140 (Vatican edn., vii. 217); Scotus, *Lect* 2. 2. 1. 3, nn. 109–10 (Vatican edn., xviii. 135); see Arist., *Ph.* 4. 10 (218^{b}13–18).

[73] Scotus, *Lect.* 2. 2. 1. 3, n. 107 (Vatican edn., xviii. 134).

[74] Scotus, *Ord.* 2. 1. 3, n. 170 (Vatican edn., vii. 86–7).

[75] Ibid. 2. 2. 1. 3, n. 139 (Vatican edn., vii. 216–7).

namely, the positive extent of time that would have elapsed if time had been positive.[76]

This passage seems to me to entail that privative time has both a *topology*, consisting of periods bounded by instants, and a *metric*, since it can measure periods of a determinate quantity.

The passage might suggest, however, that privative time is just imaginary, rather like the merely imaginary space outside the universe, discussed in the previous Chapter. And Scotus elsewhere uses 'imaginary time' as a way of referring to 'before' the universe, where the point is that there is no real 'before' the universe.[77] If this is what Scotus means, then he will be committed to privative time's lacking both metric and topology. This looks to be an immensely implausible claim. But if we look at the context more closely, we discover that Scotus wants to liken privative time not to non-existent extra-cosmic space, but to existent intra-cosmic vacuum. As we saw in Chapter 11, privative dimension is *real* distance.[78] On this analogy, Scotus's 'imaginary' instants in the *Quodlibet* passage are real enough. And a passage in the late *Reportatio* confirms this reading:

'Time' means a relation of measure, not actual but only aptitudinal; neither is the measuring of time in relation to any mobile, or of the heaven [as] actually measured, but aptitudinally consists in some common [mobile] which is measured by time, such that time [taken] aptitudinally does not relate to this body [viz. the outermost heavenly sphere] as measured any more than it relates to another: though it actually (and in some sense accidentally) relates more to the motion of the outermost heavenly sphere.[79]

Here, Scotus identifies privative time with time generally,[80] and argues that time measures potential motion. But crucially he does

---

[76] Scotus, *Quod.* 11, n. 9 (Wadding edn., xii. 266; Alluntis and Wolter, 263, n. 11. 23); see also *idem, Ord.* 2. 2. 1. 4, n. 178 (Vatican edn., vii. 234–5). Modern writers use considerations related to Scotus's to try to show that time is relative to actual *or possible* motion: see famously Sydney Shoemaker, 'Time without Change', *Journal of Philosophy*, 66 (1969), 363–81.

[77] See Scotus, *Ord.* 2. 1. 3, nn. 160–1 (Vatican edn., vii. 80–1).

[78] Ibid. 2. 2. 1. 4, n. 171 (Vatican edn., vii. 234–5); see also Scotus, *Quod.* 11, n. 9 (Wadding edn., xii. 266; Alluntis and Wolter, 262–3, n. 11. 23), quoted in n. 80 below.

[79] Scotus, *Rep.* 4. 48. 2, n. 15 (Wadding edn., xi. 888^b–9^a).

[80] For a similar identification, see Scotus, *Quod.* 11, n. 9 (Wadding edn., xii. 266; Alluntis and Wolter, 262–3 n. 11. 23): 'Without motion there could be rest even in the proper sense of the term. . . . To this uniform immobile existence there corresponds a proper measure, which is time.'

not identify privative time as imaginary, or suggest that it is in any sense mind-dependent.

The identification, in this late *Reportatio* passage, of privative time with time in general allows us to make a suggestion about the reducibility of privative time to possible regular motion. Given that Scotus, on my account, generally wants to reduce time to regular motion, I believe that it is probable, on the basis of the *Reportatio* passage just quoted, that he would reduce privative time to possible motion. This would mean that the physical possibility of regular motion would be identified with privative time, and would measure periods of rest.

This conclusion should not mislead us into thinking that Scotus's privative time is some sort of inchoate absolute time. Privative time corresponds to periods of the *rest* of successive items, not to the duration of permanent items. And, as I argued above, the crucial test for Scotus's putative adherence to absolute time would be a claim (which he does not make) that (privative) time could measure the duration of permanent items, not merely items at rest.[81]

The basic point I have tried to argue in this chapter is that neither time nor motion, according to Scotus, is composed of atoms. This does not mean, of course, that time and motion atoms do not exist. Scotus argues that they exist at the boundaries of motion tokens and periods of time. I have also tried to show that Scotus rejects any sort of Newtonian absolute time, holding instead that time is relative to motion. I have tried to show that Scotus defends a stronger position than this, according to which time is reducible to motion. The sort of

---

[81] Olivier Boulnois argues on the basis of Scotus, *Ord.* 2. 2. 2. 7, n. 502 (Vatican edn., vii. 380–1) that Scotus is committed to the existence of absolute time: see his 'La Présence chez Duns Scot', in Leonardo Sileo (ed.), *Via Scoti: Methodologica ad mentem Joannis Duns Scoti. Atti del Congresso Scotistico Internazionale, Roma 9–11 Marzo 1993* (2 vols., Rome: Antonianum, 1995), i. 95–119, pp. 103–4. This cannot be right. The point of Scotus's example in this passage—of the apostle Peter walking around during the stasis of the outermost heavenly sphere—is that there is in fact motion even though the outermost heavenly sphere is still. So whatever time there is will certainly be relative to motion. Boulnois might have found the *Quodlibet* account more useful. But even here, Scotus does not reject his claim that time is relative to *potential* motion; so it is not clear that the passage just quoted amounts to a defence of absolute time. The point of the analogy with privative dimensions is that it is possible for such dimensions to contain a body, and hence that privative dimensions are relative to potential body-containment. On the analogy, privative time is relative to potential motion. And in any case the *Quodlibet* passage is explicitly about the temporal extension of periods of *rest*, not the duration of permanent items (see *Quod.* 11, n. 9 (Wadding edn., xii. 266; Alluntis and Wolter, 262–3 n. 11. 23), quoted in the previous note).

reductionistic account he opts for is one which has recently been labelled 'modal reductionism', according to which time is reducible to actual or possible motion.

So far, however, I have given an account only of *static* time in Scotus: time considered as a (static) ordered linear continuum bounded by instants of fixed location. It is generally thought that Scotus's basic account of time fixes on *flowing* time, time constituted by the flow of events from future to past. In the next chapter, I will try to show that Scotus does not have a coherent account of flowing time. Given Scotus's clear assertion of the reality of static time, as outlined in this chapter, Scotus has little difficulty giving an account of the reality of perduring items. Perdurance seems to entail the reality of static time, since perduring items do not have their properties all at once. They therefore require the existence of an extended temporal continuum—static time—for their existence. I will return to this in the next chapter. In principle, Scotus's account of motion and static time entails that perduring or successive items will count as H-unities, in some sense containing potentially infinitely divisible parts. But Scotus's commitment to the claim that motion consists in the generation and corruption of things, coupled with his account of the infinite (temporal) divisibility of motion, seems to entail his commitment to the position that at least perduring items are composed of an infinite number of (temporal) slices (and hence that they will not count as H-unities).

13

The Reality of Time

Ever since McTaggart first proposed the idea, it has been customary to distinguish between A-series (or flowing) time and B-series (or static) time.[1] We talk about the A-series using token-reflexives, words which include a reference to their utterer. The relevant set of token-reflexive words for talk about the A-series includes 'past', 'present', 'future', 'now', and indeed all tensed verbs. To use such words successfully, their utterer must have a temporal location. We talk about B-series time tenselessly, fixing temporal location by means of temporal indices which are related to each other changelessly. We can conveniently use terms and phrases such as 'earlier', 'simultaneous', 'later', 'on 8 December 1996', for this purpose. Richard Sorabji has argued that the distinction between flowing and static time is first found in the Neoplatonist Iamblichus.[2] Norman Kretzmann, however, claims to find the distinction in Aristotle.[3] I do not think that we can trace the distinction explicitly to Aristotle, for reasons which will become clear below. Neither do I think we can agree with a further claim made by Kretzmann on behalf of Aristotle, that A-series terminology is *inessential* to time: that what time is essentially can be captured simply by B-series terminology. On Kretzmann's reading of Aristotle, Aristotle holds that the passage of time is merely imaginary.

Kretzmann's second claim seems to be countered by a passage in *Physics* 4. 11 where, at least on a prima facie reading, Aristotle makes explicit reference to a flowing now:

---

[1] J. M. E. McTaggart, 'The Unreality of Time', *Mind*, NS 17 (1908), 457–74.

[2] Richard Sorabji, *Time, Creation and the Continuum: Theories in Antiquity and the Early Middle Ages* (London: Duckworth, 1983), 37–45.

[3] Norman Kretzmann, 'Aristotle on the Instant of Change', *Proceedings of the Aristotelian Society*, suppl. vol. 50 (1976), 91–114.

Just as motion is a perpetual succession, so also is the time. But every simultaneous time is the same, for the now is the same in substrate—though its being is different—and the now determines time in so far as time involves before and after.

The now in one sense is the same, in another it is not the same. In so far as it is in succession, it is different (which is just what its being now was supposed to mean), but its substrate is an identity: for motion, as was said, goes with magnitude, and time, as we maintain, with motion. Similarly, then, there corresponds to the point the body which is carried along, and by which we are aware of the motion and of the before and after involved in it. This is an identical substrate (whether a point or a stone or something else of the kind), but it is different in definition. . . . And the body which is carried along is different, in so far as it is at one time here and at another there. But the now corresponds to the body that is carried along, as time corresponds to the motion. For it is by means of the body that we become aware of the before and after in motion, and if we regard these as countable we get the now. Hence in these also the now as substrate remains the same (for it is what is before and after in movement), but what is predicated of it is different; for it is in so far as the before and after is numerable that we get the now. This is what is most knowable: for, similarly, motion is known because of that which is moved, locomotion because of that which is carried. For what is carried is a this; the movement is not. Thus the now is in one sense always the same; in another it is not the same: for this is true also of what is carried.[4]

(I will return to Scotus's discussion of this passage below.) Less controversially, Sorabji draws our attention to Aristotle's standard claim that *tensed* language is essential to all statements.[5] Sorabji argues further, with reference to Kretzmann's first point, that Aristotle was insensitive to the distinction between flowing and static time. Aristotle tends to run together 'in his conception of the now the static idea of an instant and the flowing idea of presentness'.[6]

That an account of flowing time caused Aristotle difficulties is evidenced by the three paradoxes about time proposed in *Physics* 4. 10. The third of these, which I give here, is a crucially important source for Scotus's discussion of the same issues:

The now, which seems to bound the past and future—does it always remain one and the same or is always other and other? It is hard to say.

(1) If it is always different and different, and if none of the parts in time which are other and other are simultaneous (unless the one contains and the

---

[4] Arist. *Ph.* 4. 11 (219^{b}9–33).
[5] Arist. *Cat.* 5 (4^{a}23–8); see Sorabji, *Time, Creation and the Continuum*, 51.
[6] Sorabji, *Time, Creation and the Continuum*, 48.

other is contained, as the shorter time is by the longer), and if the now which is not, but formerly was, must have ceased to be at some time, the nows too cannot be simultaneous with one another, but the prior now must always have ceased to be. But the prior now cannot have ceased to be in itself (since it then existed); yet it cannot have ceased to be in another now. For we may lay it down that one now cannot be next to another, any more than point to point. If then it did not cease to be in the next now but in another, it would exist simultaneously with the innumerable nows between the two—which is impossible.

Yes, but (2) neither is it possible for the now to remain always the same. No determinate divisible thing has a single termination, whether it is continuously extended in one or in more than one dimension: but the now is a termination, and it is possible to cut off a determinate time. Further, if coincidence in time (i.e. being neither prior nor posterior) means to be 'in one and the same now', then, if both what is before and what is after are in this same now, things which happened ten thousand years ago would be simultaneous with what has happened today, and nothing would be before or after anything else.[7]

The three paradoxes seem to be directed against the possibility of a flowing now. The third, quoted here, might also preclude both a flowing now and a static instant.[8] (As we saw in the last chapter, Scotus understands the paradox to apply to the static instant, and, given his claim that such things as static instants exist, tries to show how the paradox might be solved. I discussed his claim above, pp. 228–30.)

I do not now want to enter into a discussion of Aristotle on time. But it is well to be aware of at least the minimal account just given, since Scotus's account is based closely on the two passages quoted above. Scotus takes the passage quoted first, from *Physics* 4. 11, as providing the relevant tools for a solution to the third paradox, quoted second above. But, as we shall see, Scotus denies that the first passage entails accepting the existence of a flowing now (and hence accepting the reality of the A-series). Scotus stresses the B-theoretic elements of Aristotle's account. But there is a deep tension in Scotus's account, since, just like Aristotle, he effectively accepts that A-series language is essential to a correct understanding of time. In the next section, I try to describe Scotus's thoughts on A-series time, showing that he is dogged by a consistent failure to give an account of a flowing now.

---

[7] Arist. *Ph.* 4. 10 (218[a]10–30). We encountered part of this paradox in Ch. 12.

[8] On this, see Sorabji, *Time, Creation and the Continuum*, 47. Michael Inwood argues that the paradox of the ceasing instant is most naturally read in terms of static instants: see 'Aristotle on the Reality of Time', in Lindsay Judson (ed.), *Aristotle's Physics: A Collection of Essays* (Oxford: Clarendon Press, 1991), 151–78, p. 163. His reading thus bears some relation to Scotus's—as indeed (as we saw in Ch. 12) does his solution.

2. SCOTUS ON A-SERIES TIME

Scotus does not make an explicit distinction between A-series and B-series time. But this does not mean that it is not helpful to look at his writing on the reality of time with the distinction in mind. If we keep the A- and B-series distinction clearly in mind, we shall be able to see the extent to which Scotus may have been able to give a coherent account of one or other of these series—or even of both. What emerges, I think, is that Scotus has a clear account of B-series time. I gave an account of what Scotus has to say about the topology of B-series time in the previous chapter, and there is no need to rehearse the material again here. His attitude to the A-series is more problematic. I shall first present evidence that Scotus uncritically regards A-series terminology as essential to time. Secondly, I shall consider an early attempt to give an account of the A-series in terms of a flowing now. Thirdly, I shall assess Scotus's later rejection of a flowing now, when discussing five related Aristotelian texts:

(i)   The now is the same according to substance, but different according to existence.[9]

(ii) The now corresponds to the body that is carried along.[10]

(iii) The now cannot be without time, or vice versa, since movement cannot be without the moving body.[11]

(iv) No determinate divisible thing has a single termination . . . but the now is a termination, and it is possible to cut off a determinate time.[12]

(v)   If both what is before and what is after are in this same now, things which happened ten thousand years ago would be simultaneous with what has happened to-day.[13]

(i), (ii), and (iii) come from the first Aristotelian passage cited above (from *Physics* 4. 11); (iv) and (v) from the third time paradox in *Physics* 4. 10, also cited above. As we shall see, Scotus's interpretation of these two passages is central to his later understanding

---

[9] Arist. *Ph.* 4. 11 (219^{b}10–15), cited in Scotus, *Ord.* 2. 2. 1. 2, n. 96 (Vatican edn., vii. 199). As we just saw, Aristotle's precise claim is that the now is the same in substrate, but different in definition.

[10] Arist. *Ph.* 4. 11 (219^{b}22–5), cited in Scotus, *Ord.* 2. 2. 1. 2, n. 97 (Vatican edn., vii. 199).

[11] Arist. *Ph.* 4. 11 (219^{b}33–220^{a}4), cited in Scotus, *Ord.* 2. 2. 1. 2, n. 98 (Vatican edn., vii. 200).

[12] Arist. *Ph.* 4.10 (218^{a}21–5), cited in *Ord.* 2. 2. 1. 2, n. 101 (Vatican edn., vii. 201).

[13] Arist. *Ph.* 4.10 (218^{a}25–30), cited in Scotus, *Ord.* 2. 2. 1. 2, n. 100 (Vatican edn., vii. 201).

of A-series time. In this later understanding, Scotus rejects the possibility of a flowing now; and his failure to replace it with any other account
of the structure of the A-series makes the A-series appear unreal.

Despite this, Scotus clearly regards talk of A-series time as essential
to our understanding of time, and he clearly holds that such talk
corresponds to some real properties of time. He is happy, in a number
of different contexts, to claim that many statements are essentially
tensed. For example, he follows Aristotle in holding that some statements can change their truth-values over time.[14] Equally, when discussing God's timelessness, he suggests that tensed propositions, when
applied to God, should be parsed in terms of tenseless ones:

'God begot [his Son]' consignifies the now of eternity, such that the sense is
'God has the act of generation in the now of eternity in so far as that now
coexisted with the past'; and 'God begets' means 'has the act of generation in
the now of eternity in so far as it coexists with the present'. Thus, since the now
[of eternity] truly coexists with any difference of time, we can truly predicate of
God the differences of all times.[15]

When we use tensed propositions in referring to God, then, we are
drawing attention to the fact that the proposition 'God exists' (tenseless) is always true. But of course, there is a *contrast* implied between
God and creatures. Tensed propositions can be used of creatures,
though not of God. Perhaps most significantly of all, Scotus consistently talks of time as *flowing*.[16]

Of course, none of this amounts to any sort of A-*theory*: that is, to
any sort of account which could provide a theoretical understanding of
A-series time. It is sometimes suggested that Scotus has such an
understanding. Famously, in *Lectura* 1. 39 Scotus criticizes Aquinas's
account of God's timelessness on the grounds that it entails a B-theory
of time—that is, that the A-series does not exist. I have discussed
Scotus's two arguments elsewhere.[17] Basically, he argues that Aquinas's

---

[14] Scotus, *In Periherm.* 3 (Wadding edn., i. 189ᵇ); see Arist. *Cat.* 5 (4ᵇ5–8). In Scotus,
Ord. 4. 6. 10. n. 10 (Wadding edn., viii. 357), Scotus makes the basis for this clear: 'An act
passing into the past, after it passes, simply is not.'

[15] Scotus, *Ord.* 1. 9. un., n. 17 (Vatican edn., iv. 336–7). We shall see more evidence for
this in section 4 of this chapter.

[16] Perhaps the best example is in Scotus, *Quod.* 11, n. 9 (Wadding edn., xii. 266;
Alluntis and Wolter, 263 n. 11. 23), cited Ch. 12. See also *idem, Ord.* 2. 2. 2. 8, n. 510
(Vatican edn., vii. 384) which I discuss below.

[17] See my 'Duns Scotus on Eternity and Timelessness', *Faith and Philosophy*, 14 (1997),
3–25. For standard discussions of the implications of Scotus's account here, see William
Lane Craig, *The Problem of Divine Foreknowledge of Future Contingents from Aristotle to*

account of God's timelessness, according to which 'All temporal things are present to God',[18] is false. Scotus criticizes this view for entailing that all things are actual, and hence temporally present. His reason is that he accepts

(A) Only temporally present things are actual,[19]

a claim which itself is true only if A-series terminology reflects an essential feature of time.

Unfortunately, the *Ordinatio* account is incomplete at this point, and the scribe notes that Scotus left a blank space to fill in the discussion later—presumably when he had worked out what he wanted to say on the matter.[20] To make up for this deficiency, the scribe copied another version of the relevant discussion, a version which the Vatican editors regard as at best only dubiously authentic— possibly reconstructed by a disciple of Scotus's from lost notebooks, but certainly not representing Scotus's last thoughts on the matter.[21] The account in *Lectura* 1. 39 is unique in Scotus's oeuvre. Elsewhere— including elsewhere in the *Lectura*—Scotus adopts an account of God's timelessness which is remarkably similar to the one he rejects in *Lectura* 1. 39, and which certainly entails a B-theory of time, according to which none of time is ontologically privileged. Crucially, Scotus standardly rejects (A), and accepts in its place

(A') It is timelessly the case that all things, past present and future, are actual,[22]

a claim which requires the existence of the B-series for its truth, and is *probably* inconsistent with the existence of the A-series. Given that both the *Lectura* and the *Ordinatio* discussions offer support for the claim that Scotus's conception of divine timelessness commits him to a

---

Suarez, Brill's Studies in Intellectual History, 7 (Leiden: Brill, 1988), 130; Marilyn McCord Adams, *William Ockham*, Publications in Medieval Studies, 26 (2 vols., Notre Dame, Ind.: University of Notre Dame Press, 1987), ii. 1124.

[18] Aquinas, *ST* 1. 14. 13 (ed. Petrus Caramello (3 vols., Turin and Rome: Marietti, 1952–6), i. 86[b]).   [19] Scotus, *Lect.* 1. 39. 1–5, n. 27 (Vatican edn., xvii. 487).

[20] See Vatican edn., vi. 308.

[21] See ibid. 26*–30*. The text (*Ord.* 1. 39. 1–5) is printed in an appendix in Vatican edn., vi. 401–44.

[22] I have argued for this at length, with extensive textual support from the *Lectura* and the *Ordinatio*, in 'Duns Scotus on Eternity and Timelessness'. Representative texts include *Ord.* 1. 13. un., n. 83 (Vatican edn., v. 110) and *Lect.* 1. 13. un., n. 30 (Vatican edn., xvii. 174–5); *Ord.* 1. 30. 1–2, nn. 41–2 (Vatican edn., vi. 187–8) and *Lect.* 1. 30. 1–2, nn. 48–51 (Vatican edn., xvii. 412–13).

B-theory of time, I infer that the account in *Lectura* 1. 39, which seems to entail that Scotus rejects a B-theory of time (according to which the A-series does not exist), is atypical of Scotus's general approach to time, at least as time is discussed in the context of Scotus's account of divine timelessness.

In book 5 of the *Metaphysics* questions, Scotus seems to imply that we can give some theoretical content to our talk of time's flow by appealing to the possibility of a flowing now or present, constructing time as it flows along:

Let there be imagined a point in motion, and that through its motion it makes a line. The point is simple, because it is immutable according to its essence. But in so far as a line flows from it, it is mutable. It is the same for the now. Considered according to its essence, since it is simple, it is immutable and at rest; but in so far as it causes time through its flux, it is mutable and variable according to its being.[23]

(Scotus claims to derive this account from Averroës.[24]) This passage is exceptional in Scotus. In his *Sentence* commentaries, Scotus consistently rejects the possibility of a flowing now, on the Aristotelian grounds that an indivisible cannot move. (I discuss this rejection in a moment.) So I think we should conclude that in all probability book 5 of the *Metaphysics* questions should be dated either *before* all the *Sentence* commentaries or *after* them. Allan Wolter has recently noted that book 7 of the *Metaphysics* commentary pre-dates the *Reportatio*.[25] Supposing, as is likely, that Scotus worked on the *Metaphysics* questions more or less sequentially, we should date book 5 before the *Reportatio*; and therefore before all the *Sentence* commentaries. This would make book 5 of the *Metaphysics* date from before 1300. Given this, the general picture is that Scotus early on accepted the existence of an A-series constituted by a flowing now (possibly following the lead of Averroës), and later came to reject it.[26] Most notable of all,

---

[23] Scotus, *In Metaph.* 5.10, n. 4 (Wadding edn., iv. 632^b).

[24] At ibid., Scotus refers to Averroës, *In Ph.* 4. 104 (*Aristotelis Opera cum Averrrois Commentaria* (11 vols., Venice, 1550), iv. 84vb); perhaps he has in mind the following passage: 'The instant makes time, just as that which moves [*translatum*] makes motion [*translationem*], and a point [makes] measure, as the geometers say.'

[25] See Allan B. Wolter, 'Reflections about Scotus's Early Works', in Ludger Honnefelder, Rega Wood, and Mechthild Dreyer (eds.), *John Duns Scotus: Metaphysics and Ethics*, Studien und Texte zur Geistesgeschichte des Mittelalters, 53 (Leiden, New York, and Cologne: Brill, 1996), 37–57, p. 52.

[26] In *Ord.* 2. 2. 2. 8, n. 510 (Vatican edn., vii. 384–5), Scotus states: 'No part of time

the *Metaphysics* passage just quoted makes clear reference to the Aristotelian claim

> (i) The now is the same according to substance, but different according to existence,

noted above. And, as we shall see, Scotus is anxious in the *Sentence* commentaries to reject just the interpretation of (i) which he accepted in the *Metaphysics* questions.

When Scotus attends more closely to talk of past, present, and future, his account tends—despite the language which he uses—to collapse into a B-theory of time, according to which the A-series is in some sense unreal. The account does this by rejecting the possibility of a flowing now. To see this, it is necessary to look quite closely at the relevant Aristotelian texts (i)–(v) cited above. The catalyst for Scotus's discussion is (i), which he takes to constitute Aristotle's solution to his third paradox about time. *Prima facie,* (i) looks to be a defence of a flowing now—as, indeed, Scotus reads it in the early *Metaphysics* questions, just discussed. Scotus is convinced in the *Sentence* commentaries both that Aristotle does not have a conception of a flowing now, and that we do not need such a conception. So Scotus tries to offer a different interpretation of (i). He does so on the basis of two of the Aristotelian texts pin-pointed above:

> (ii) The now corresponds to the body that is carried along

and

> (iii) The now cannot be without time, or vice versa, since movement cannot be without the moving body.

Aquinas is Scotus's opponent here. Aquinas takes both of these claims to mean that there is a flowing now inhering in a mobile substance.[27] The basic point of this interpretation is that there is a flowing now. The interpretation also assigns a *subject* to this now: presumably, the outermost (mobile) heavenly sphere. This would mean that a flowing now would be a feature of the forward motion of the outermost heavenly sphere.

---

can pass from future to past except through the present,' a claim which perhaps suggests, but certainly does not entail, the existence of a flowing now. Perhaps Scotus's abandonment of his early A-theory was reluctant.

[27] Aquinas, *In Ph.* 4. 18, n. 585 (ed. P. M. Maggiòlo (Turin and Rome: Marietti, 1965), 287[b]).

Scotus tries to show that it is radically mistaken to understand either of Aristotle's two claims about the now as claims about a flowing now. Scotus supports his interpretation of Aristotle by appealing to

> (iv) No determinate divisible thing has a single termination . . . but the now is a termination, and it is possible to cut off a determinate time

and

> (v) If both what is before and what is after are in this same now, things which happened ten thousand years ago would be simultaneous with what has happened today.

Scotus supposes that these two problems are fatal for a flowing now, and notes that Aristotle nowhere proposes a solution to them.[28]

Given this basic understanding, Scotus attempts an exegesis of (ii) and (iii). According to Scotus, (ii) is not to be understood as if there is just one now, corresponding to a substance (i.e. a mobile substance). Rather, what Aristotle is referring to in (ii) is the starting and stopping at the beginning and end of a whole motion token; to these there correspond two different *instants*. It is by means of our knowledge of the relative positions of these two changes (i.e. starting and stopping) that we become aware of the different temporal positions of the two instants.[29] On this reading of (ii), it amounts to (iv). Scotus's treatment of (iii) also carefully rejects any reading which might allow a flowing now. He construes (iii) to mean that there are different temporal instants corresponding to the beginnings and ends of changes.[30]

Of course, it is one thing to argue that Aristotle has no account of a flowing now, and quite another to argue that no such account is possible. Scotus, however, offers two independent arguments against the possibility of a flowing now. Oddly, as we shall see in the next section, the first and most forceful of the objections is based on an Aristotelian presupposition which Scotus elsewhere rejects. But he does not appeal to his rejection of the relevant Aristotelian claim here to show how a flowing now might be possible. I label the two arguments '(F.1)' and '(F.2)'.

---

[28] Scotus, *Lect.* 2. 2. 1. 2, n. 86 (Vatican edn., xviii. 127); *idem, Ord.* 2. 2. 1. 2, *textus interpolatus* (Vatican edn., vii. 201, ll. 12–13).

[29] Scotus, *Ord.* 2. 2. 1. 2, n. 97 (Vatican edn., vii. 199–200); *Lect.* 2. 2. 1. 2, n. 88 (Vatican edn., xviii. 127); *Lect.* 2. 2. 1. 3, n. 115 (Vatican edn., xviii. 137).

[30] Scotus, *Ord.* 2. 2. 1. 2, n. 98 (Vatican edn., vii. 200); *Lect.* 2. 2. 1. 2, n. 89 (Vatican edn., xviii. 128).

(F.1) Accepting the Aristotelian claim

(B) Every moving item will necessarily traverse a distance smaller than or equal to itself before traversing a distance greater than itself,[31]

Scotus infers

(1) It is not possible that an indivisible moves continuously,[32]

presumably on the grounds stated by Aristotle in the relevant passage: namely, that it is not possible that an indivisible traverses a distance smaller than itself, and that

(C) Every moving item whose first movement is equal to itself moves discontinuously

(i.e. in leaps).

(F.2) Accepting the further claim

(D) Necessarily, every quantitative indivisible is either (a) the limit of a continuum or (b) part of a whole composed of indivisibles,

Scotus infers

(2) A flowing now is either (a) the limit of a continuum or (b) part of a whole composed of indivisibles.

But it is not the case that a flowing now could be the limit of a continuum. A flowing now retains identity over time; hence, the same now would mark both the beginning and the end of any continuum, which is impossible. Neither could a flowing now be part of a whole composed of indivisibles, since time is not composed of indivisibles.[33] So

(2′) It is not the case that a flowing now is either (a) the limit of a continuum or (b) part of a whole composed of indivisibles.

Given that, necessarily, any putative flowing now is a quantitative indivisible, (D) and (2′) entail that there is no such thing as a flowing now.[34]

Scotus suggests—and refutes—a way for his opponent to defend the claim that a flowing now could be the limit of a continuum (and hence

---

[31] Arist. *Ph.* 6. 10 (241^{a}6–14), cited in Scotus, *Ord.* 2. 2. 1. 2, n. 99 (Vatican edn., vii. 200–1).   [32] Scotus, *Ord.* 2. 2. 1. 2, n. 99 (Vatican edn., vii. 200–1).

[33] Scotus cites Arist. *Ph.* 6. 9 (239^{b}8–9).

[34] Scotus, *Ord.* 2. 2. 1. 2, n. 101 (Vatican edn., vii. 201–2); *idem, Lect.* 2. 2. 1. 2, n. 84 (Vatican edn., xviii. 127); 2. 2. 1. 3, n. 116 (Vatican edn., xviii. 137–8).

satisfy the first criterion in (2)). Could it not be the case that one flowing 'now' retains substantial identity 'over time', but that it gains and loses the successive accidental properties of being different limits? On this model, for any flowing now *n* and any continuum *c*, *n* could first have the property of being the beginning of *c*, and later have the property of being the end of *c*. The idea, I think, is that it is an essential feature of the now that it is the limit of a continuum, but that the *identity* of the continuum which it limits is constantly changing as the now flows along, dividing time up into ever-changing segments of past and future.

Scotus knows three different replies—which I label '(F1)'–'(F3)'—to his opponent's position.

(F1) It is an essential property of a quantitative indivisible that it is either (a) the limit of a continuum or (b) part of a whole composed of indivisibles. But on the position defended by Scotus's opponent, these will be non-essential features of a flowing now. So a flowing now is not a quantitative indivisible—which is absurd.[35]

(F2) On Scotus's opponent's position, a flowing now has the attribute of being the limit of a continuum as an accidental property. But accidental properties in Scotus's ontology are things. Let '*a*' refer to this thing (viz. the accidental property of being the limit of a continuum). To which category does *a* belong? If it is a quantity, then it would be superfluous to posit a flowing now as the subject of *a*. If *a* is not a quantity, then something that is not a quantity will be the limit of an extended continuum—which is absurd.[36]

(F3) If a flowing now has successive accidental properties, then a flowing now undergoes change. But the claim that a flowing now can change seems to entail that there is some even more basic temporal sequence to measure the change of the temporal now.[37]

All of these replies would require more work to make them cogent. The third in particular reveals fairly clearly Scotus's failure to appreciate the distinction between flowing and static time. His opponent could easily respond that he could index the various positions of the flowing now in terms of positions on the B-series. And it would, I

[35] Scotus, *Ord.* 2. 2. 1. 2, n. 102 (Vatican edn., vii. 202); *idem, Lect.* 2. 2. 1. 3, n. 118 (Vatican edn., xviii. 138).
[36] Scotus, *Ord.* 2. 2. 1. 2, n. 103 (Vatican edn., vii. 202–3); *idem, Lect.* 2. 2. 1. 3, n. 119 (Vatican edn., xviii. 138).
[37] Scotus, *Ord.* 2. 2. 1. 2, n. 104 (Vatican edn., vii. 203); *idem, Lect.* 2. 2. 1. 3, n. 120 (Vatican edn., xviii. 138–9).

think, be difficult for Scotus to find a response to this. On (F1), Scotus's opponent is committed to the claim that being the limit of a continuum is an accidental feature of a flowing now. But this is not right. The opponent agrees with Scotus that it is an essential property of a now that it is the limit of a continuum. But he argues that there is no *one* continuum *c* such that it is essential to *n* to be a limit of *c*. (F1) commits just the same fallacy in scope that we have encountered frequently.

Having given a series of arguments against the possibility of a flowing now, Scotus gives his own account of Aristotle's

> (i) The now is the same according to substance, but different according to existence.

Because Scotus rejects the concept of a flowing now, he clearly cannot interpret the claim to refer to a flowing now that retains substantial identity 'over time'. In fact, he interprets the claim to refer to different instants on the static series—even though his language sometimes suggests reference to the flowing series. Scotus offers the following reading of Aristotle's 'intended' meaning. Any one (static) instant has substantial (i.e. numerical) identity. But the instant has two different roles to play. The first is to end the past; the second is to begin the future. Thus, the instant is distinguished according to its existence: it exists in two different ways, or (in my way of putting the issue) has two different roles to play.[38] What Scotus means by this is that the instant is, as it were, midway between two extremes—the past and the future—and, as Aristotle notes, something that is midway between two extremes *has* something of both extremes. Thus, an instant has something of the past and something of the future. And this is what is meant, according to Scotus, when Aristotle claims that a now is distinguished according to its existence.[39]

This appears to be a discussion about A-series time. Scotus talks about 'past' and 'future', solid A-series terms. But I think we will be led astray if we perceive it in this way. First, Scotus does not cast the parallel discussion in the *Lectura* in terms of a discussion of past and future. Further, the *Ordinatio* discussion is clearly not a discussion of a flowing now. The claim is that any instant is self-identical; and the

[38] Scotus, *Ord.* 2. 2. 1. 2, n. 106 (Vatican edn., vii. 203); *idem, Lect.* 2. 2. 1. 2, n. 91 (Vatican edn., xviii. 128–9).
[39] Scotus, *Ord.* 2. 2. 1. 2, n. 107 (Vatican edn., vii. 203–4).

instants that Scotus is talking about do not flow or move. In fact, he later clarifies what he means by discussing the same issues in language that is unequivocally about static time. Thus, he claims that instants join different *parts* of time (not 'past' and 'future', but different segments of static time), and expressly claims that there is substantial (i.e. numerical) distinction between all time atoms:

If any one mobile precisely has identity according to substance (i.e. to itself) and distinction according to existence (i.e. according to an order to different parts of motion), it is the same with regard to an instant in relation to the parts of time. For there is not such great identity of an instant in the whole of time as there is of one instant. Therefore an instant in the whole of time is different according to substance.[40]

In fact, it is difficult to make sense of Scotus's claim both that now joins the past and the future and that 'now' refers to a set of static instants, not to a flowing indivisible. I do not see how Scotus can claim that the present divides the past from the future, since, on his own admission, the present will *not* be a time atom (a flowing time atom). The only way for a temporal instant to have a discernible position is for it to be located on the static series (e.g. at the beginning of a change). On this showing, A-series time—at least if spelt out in terms of a flowing now—is unreal.

3. THE PROBLEM OF THE PRESENT: A POSSIBLE SCOTIST SOLUTION

In the previous section, I argued that Scotus rejects any talk of a flowing now, and hence the reality of the A-series. His strongest reason for this, I suggested, is his acceptance of the Aristotelian claim that an indivisible cannot move. Oddly, however, Scotus does not generally accept Aristotle's claim that it is impossible for an indivisible to move. Aristotle's main reason for his claim is that

(B) Every moving item will necessarily traverse a distance smaller than or equal to itself before traversing a distance greater than itself.[41]

---

[40] Ibid. n. 108 (Vatican edn., vii. 204); Scotus, *Lect.* 2. 2. 1. 2, n. 92 (Vatican edn., xviii. 129).

[41] Arist. *Ph.* 6. 10 (241ᵃ6–14), cited in Scotus, *Ord.* 2. 2. 1. 2, n. 99 (Vatican edn., vii. 200–1); also ibid. 2. 2. 2. 5, n. 303 (Vatican edn., vii. 285).

As we saw above, this claim, coupled with

> (C) Every moving item whose first movement is equal to itself moves discontinuously

entails that an indivisible cannot move continuously. The idea is that

> (C*) Every continuously moving item necessarily traverses a distance smaller than itself before traversing a distance equal to itself.

But why should this be so? Scotus has an argument to show that (C*) is false. (I label it '(F.1′)', since, although Scotus does not use the argument against (F.1), he could—and in my view should—have done so.)

(F.1′) As Scotus understands it elsewhere, when discussing angelic motion, what (C*) aims to guarantee is just that

> (E) There is no smallest distance which a continuously moving item must first traverse.

Clearly, in the case of an extended item, satisfying (C*) is necessary (though not sufficient) for satisfying (E). But this is not so in the case of an unextended item. In the case of an indivisible, (E) can be satisfied without (C*) being satisfied. Invoking (C*) to prove that an indivisible cannot move continuously is just question-begging.[42] But, given this argument for the possibility of an indivisible's moving, by far the strongest of Scotus's arguments against a flowing now evaporates.

On the other hand, this proposed solution is not without its difficulties. Scotus expressly notes, in his 'official' rejection of A-series time, that we cannot talk of a flowing now inhering in a subject. But, given a relativistic account of time, I take it that we would want to be able to assign a subject to our flowing now. Perhaps we could speculate that, given Scotus's account of privative time, where time can be both relative to (potential) motion and have no subject, an inability to assign a subject for the flowing now might not be a problem for him (though it might constitute a fairly strong rejection

---

[42] Scotus, *Ord.* 2. 2. 2. 5, nn. 424–5 (Vatican edn., vii. 342–4). Scotus notes when expounding (B) that however close we get to the beginning of any given motion, we can always find a point closer to the beginning. So I take it that he expounds (B) in terms of (E). Given (E), Scotus notes that, paradoxically, in the case of the motion of an indivisible, any motion segment which we identify in the motion of an indivisible will actually be *larger* than the indivisible. Hence (B) actually turns out to be false in the case of a moving indivisible.

of Aristotle's basic claim that time is an *accident*, or it might constitute a very strong rejection of Aristotle's claim that properties
always have subjects).[43]

4. ENDURING THROUGH TIME: A SCOTIST APORIA

Scotus clearly thinks that perduring items, including quiescent forms,
are essentially temporal, having temporal parts. But he also argues that
only perduring items are essentially temporal. Enduring things—such
as substances—are at best *accidentally* temporal. They are essentially
eviternal:

> It should properly be conceded that generable and corruptible substances are
> essentially measured by the *aevum*; though they are accidentally (i.e. in virtue
> of some natural quality consequent upon them) measured by time.[44]

Eviternity is the 'durational' property of changeless things. To claim
that a substance is 'measured by' the *aevum* is equivalent to claiming
that the substance is an eviternal. Puzzlingly, as I hinted in the previous chapter, Scotus argues that, topologically, the *aevum* is just one
instant. So Scotus probably thinks that enduring things have no essential temporal extension at all. (Again, I take it that this is strong
evidence against the view that Scotus has any sort of account of
absolute time of the kind we later find in Newton.) Scotus takes this
line against Bonaventure. According to Bonaventure, eviternals have
some kind of non-spatial extension (let us label this 'broadly temporal
extension', since topologically it is taken to involve more than one
instant):

> We should posit before and after in the *aevum*, just as we should posit some
> [kind of] succession—though a different succession from [that which we
> posit] in time. In time, there is succession with variation, and 'before' and
> 'after' with ageing [*inveteratio*] and renewal [*renovatio*]. In the *aevum* there is

---

[43] Given the rejection of (C) and (C*) implied here, I think that Scotus should simply
reject the (F.2) claim

> (D) Necessarily, every quantitative indivisible is either (a) the limit of a continuum
> or (b) part of a whole composed of indivisibles,

which entails the damaging conclusion that there is no such thing as a flowing now.
[44] Scotus, *Ord.* 2. 2. 1. 4, n. 180 (Vatican edn., vii. 235); see also n. 172 (Vatican edn., vii.
232).

truly the 'before' and 'after' which mean the extension of duration, but which do not mean variation or renewal [*innovatio*].[45]

The idea seems to be that an eviternal will have broadly temporal extension without undergoing any other change. Bonaventure here has a conception related to Newton's absolute time. Because Scotus holds that nothing can have the topological properties of time unless there are real or potential natural processes, he rejects Bonaventure's position.[46] He replaces Bonaventure's account of the *aevum* with one entailing the claim that the *aevum* has the topological properties of an instant. He refers to the *aevum* as a 'now',[47] and, equivalently, repeatedly claims that there is no 'before' or 'after' in the existence of eviternals.[48] Likewise, he is clear that the *aevum* has no parts.[49]

What happens when we predicate tensed verbs of an eviternal?

For [an angel] to be, to have been, and to be about to be, is not other (for the angel); although these [tenses] denote different relations to time.[50] . . . And if it is said that the past cannot not have been: . . . here, there is no past in itself.[51]

Presumably, in the case of at least material substances (Socrates, for example), coexisting with time is equivalent to being accidentally temporal: having real accidental relations to temporal things. But Scotus clearly does not think that coexisting with time is in every case equivalent to being accidentally temporal. His paradigm case of a substance coexisting with time is God; and he is quite clear that God is not accidentally temporal.[52] Raphael the Archangel seems to be more like God than like Socrates in this respect:

That [e.g. an angel] in which there neither can be flux, nor in anything naturally consequent upon it . . . invariably remains the same while it remains,

[45] Bonaventure, *In Sent.* 2. 2. 1. 1. 3 (10 vols., Quaracchi: Collegium Sancti Bonaventurae, 1882–1902), ii. 62[b])

[46] Scotus, *Ord.* 2. 2. 1. 1, nn. 58–62 (Vatican edn., vii. 182–3).

[47] Ibid. nn. 71, 81 (Vatican edn., vii. 188, 192).

[48] See e.g. ibid. nn. 66, 80 (Vatican edn., vii. 186, 192).

[49] Ibid. 2. 2. 1. 2, n. 122 (Vatican edn., vii. 210); 2. 2. 1. 3, n. 132 (Vatican edn., vii. 213–14). In making this claim, Scotus again marks his disagreement with Bonaventure. Bonaventure expressly claims that an eviternal has durational parts: '[An angel] has some sort of composition: but composition in duration entails before and after': *In Sent.* 2. 2. 1. 1. 3 (ii. 62[a]).   [50] Scotus, *Ord.* 2. 2. 1. 1, n. 66 (Vatican edn., vii. 186).

[51] Ibid. n. 68 (Vatican edn., vii. 187); see nn. 73, 76–8 (Vatican edn., vii. 189–91).

[52] Ibid. 1. 30. 1–2, nn. 30–1 (Vatican edn., vi. 181–2); see also discussion of this and related passages in my 'Duns Scotus on Eternity and Timelessness'.

Scotus clearly believes that the coexistence of permanent *material* substances with time can be cashed out in terms of their being accidentally temporal—a view which seems to make some sense. The accidents of a substance are (essentially) related to time in virtue of their being essentially changeable;[54] and a substance is accidentally related to time in virtue of the relations it has to its essentially temporal accidents. This, I take it, is more or less equivalent to the claim that a substance endures, gaining and losing relations to different times. Furthermore, I take it that Scotus is committed to the view that substances endure through time (gaining and losing relations to different times) in virtue of their relations to *perduring* things.[55]

Scotus's account of the topology of eviternity seems puzzling. But I think that we can make some sense of his account on the following fairly conjectural reading. It seems clear that talk of perduring items entails that we can talk of B-series time. Perduring items have temporal parts; and we can only make sense of the existence of temporal parts if we allow some sense to the claim that the whole of time 'exists'—a claim that has to be made by anyone accepting the reality of the B-series, and that cannot be made by anyone denying reality to the B-series. Consistent with this, Scotus sees that his account of perduring items—motion and suchlike—entails the existence of the B-series. Enduring items, however, fail to have temporal parts. They have all their parts at once. *We* would perhaps want to claim that the existence of enduring items entails the existence of A-series time, according to which the present is ontologically privileged. The argument would be that it is only on a theory allowing for the reality of the A-series that we could speak of something having its parts *at an instant*—that is, at the *present* instant. Scotus's account of the *aevum* capitalizes on the (correct) insight that talk of enduring items entails talk of things having their parts at an instant. But Scotus, as I have indicated, does not have an explicit account of a flowing present

[53] Scotus, *Ord.* 2. 2. 1. 4, nn. 171–2 (Vatican edn., vii. 231–2).

ERRATUM

The quotation, which begins at the bottom of page 254, should continue:

and thus is in no way measured by time (neither as a whole in itself, nor in virtue of any part, nor even accidentally).[53]

instant. So instead, he postulates the existence of an instant that both will not admit of reduction to the B-series (i.e. that is not the limit of a continuum) and is static. The conclusion cannot be right: but the basic insight—that talk of enduring entails talk of a substance having all of its parts at an instant—seems to be correct.

Despite its limitations, Scotus's nuanced account of time represents an advance on Aristotle's in several ways. First, and most importantly, Scotus's account of angelic motion provides him with the tools—which unfortunately he does not use—to give an account of a flowing now. Secondly, Scotus's account of H-unity allows him to give a clear account of the unity of time. Thirdly, Scotus's use of the medieval distinction between permanence and succession allows him to get closer than Aristotle to a distinction between A- and B-series time. Scotus sees that talk of (static) temporal extension—the B-series—can only be appropriate in the case of successives. Fourthly, Scotus sees the desirability of modal reductionism over any more straightforward reductionism. This move allows him to sever Aristotle's straightforward identification of time from the actual rotation of the outermost heavenly sphere, while at the same time avoiding anything like Newton's absolute time.

But there are limitations to Scotus's account too. In particular, like Aristotle, he tends to reduce time to the B-series. Where Scotus should appeal to the A-series, to explain the temporality of permanent items, he instead has recourse to the obscure medieval concepts of the *aevum* and eviternity.

APPENDIX
The Metaphysics of Generation and Corruption

In Chapter 2, I showed that Scotus's major arguments in favour of the existence of prime matter all show that

(1) Matter exists

is entailed by

(A) Generation exists,

and likewise by

(A*) Corruption exists.

So, clearly, if generation and corruption exist, then, according to Scotus, matter exists. And it is actually the case that both generation and corruption exist. But could God have made a world in which substances produce other substances by some means other than generation? If not, then I take it that the existence of matter will be a logically necessary feature of any world containing substances capable of producing other substances.

Scotus argues that no created substance could ever produce another substance other than by generating it, or destroy another substance other than by corrupting it. So Scotus holds that the existence of matter is a logically necessary feature of any world containing substances capable of producing other substances. Generation and corruption are instances of *change*. Scotus often cites a definition of change derived broadly from an Aristotelian claim: 'A change is that in virtue of which something can exist now in a different way from before.'[1] According to Scotus, this definition has two distinct elements. The first is that substantial mutation involves the existence of one substance *after* another. I shall refer to this as the *succession* of one substance after another, and the stipulation that such succession is required I shall call the 'succession condition'. The second is that substantial mutation involves a substrate. The idea is that *something* must exist in successively different

---

[1] 'Mutatio est qua aliquid potest aliter se habere nunc quam prius': Scotus, *Ord.* 4. 11. 1, n. 5 (Wadding edn., viii. 588); 4. 12. 4, n. 1 (Wadding edn., viii. 760); see also 2. 2. 1. 4, n. 181 (Vatican edn., vii. 236). The definition is based on: 'A thing rests when it is now in the same state as it was earlier': Arist. *Ph.* 5. 8 (239^{a}15–16).

ways. I shall refer to the stipulation that a substrate is required as the 'substrate condition'.[2]

Generation and corruption satisfy both of these conditions. Using these two conditions, we can contrast generation and corruption with two other related processes: creation and transubstantiation. Creation satisfies neither the succession condition nor the substrate condition. Since it fails to satisfy the succession condition, Scotus argues that creation does not count as an instance of mutation or change at all.[3] Transubstantiation is the change of a whole into a whole without any substrate. (It cannot involve a substrate since, according to Church definitions, no matter remains in common between the bread and Christ's body.) Thus, transubstantiation satisfies the succession condition, but not the substrate condition.[4] Scotus is not clear whether or not transubstantiation can correctly be labelled a mutation, since it does not satisfy the substrate condition; but the issue is semantic, and does not fundamentally affect Scotus's ontological commitments.[5] (It is worth keeping in mind that satisfying the substrate condition entails satisfying the succession condition, since the substrate must be something *pre-existent*.)

As we saw in Chapter 2, Scotus identifies the substrate of a substantial change with matter. So the issue here—whether or not the existence of matter is necessary in a world which contains created substances capable of producing other substances—concerns the necessity of the substrate condition being satisfied in creaturely activity. Both creation and transubstantiation take place without a substrate. But of these two processes, creation is easier than transubstantiation. Scotus reasons that the presence of some preexistent substance (which entails satisfying the succession condition) requires the agent to expend more effort in producing some new substance than would be required if there were no pre-existent substance.[6] Thus, any agent

[2] Scotus, *Ord.* 4. 11. 1, n. 10 (Wadding edn., viii. 590).

[3] For a Scotist definition of 'creation', see Ch. 3.

[4] Scotus, *Ord.* 4. 11. 1, n. 10 (Wadding edn., viii. 590).

[5] Ibid. n. 5 (Wadding edn., viii. 588). Scotus sometimes speaks as though changes which do not satisfy the substrate condition can still be classified as generation and corruption: see ibid. 4. 12. 5, n. 5 (Wadding edn., viii. 774); also Tamar M. Rudavsky, 'The Doctrine of Individuation in Duns Scotus', *Franziskanische Studien*, 59 (1977), 320–77, and 62 (1980), 62–83, p. 336. What is significant here, of course, is that Scotus is giving a non-Aristotelian interpretation of the words translated 'generation' and 'corruption'. The account gives us no warrant for suggesting that Scotus would have thought that, given Aristotle's definitions of 'generation' and 'corruption', we could dispense with a substrate. He is simply suggesting that substances could be produced in a different way from generation, and destroyed in a different way from corruption, without this entailing that the produced substance is created or that the destroyed substance is annihilated. Rather, the substances would be produced and destroyed by transubstantiation.

[6] Scotus, *Lect.* 2. 12. un., n. 15 (Vatican edn., xix. 73–4). Scotus justifies his position by arguing that the presence of some other substance is what prevents a natural agent from

capable of transubstantiating other things will be capable of creating them, but not vice versa.

So the question I want to look at here is: Could God have made a world that contains created substances capable of *creating* other substances? Scotus thinks that the correct answer is negative, though, as I shall try to show, his arguments for this negative conclusion leave something to be desired. Scotus's opponent is William of Ware. William argues that

(2) A created agent cannot create

has to be accepted on faith alone.[7] Scotus, however, believes that arguments can be found for (2). He argues for (2) by means of the following claims:

(3) It is not possible for a material form to be that in virtue of which anything is created;[8]

(4) A created substance cannot create the form of a material substance;[9]

and

(5) An immaterial substance cannot create another substance.[10]

Scotus argues that accepting (3), (4), and (5) entails accepting (2). According to Scotus, (3) entails that a material substance cannot create, since to do so, it would have to create in virtue of a material form; (4) entails that a created immaterial substance cannot create an accident; and (5) states that a created immaterial substance cannot create another substance. And this covers all the

---

producing its effect all the time. Hence, *ceteris paribus*, it must make it harder for an agent to produce its effect: ibid. n. 16 (Vatican edn., xix. 74). See also Scotus, *In Metaph.* 7. 5, n. 2 (Wadding edn., iv. 680[b]), where Scotus argues for

(1) Matter exists

by reasoning that someone denying both (1) and that creatures can create substances (and at the same time wishing to avoid occasionalism) would be committed to the absurd claim that creatures could produce substances by the harder process of transubstantiation rather than by the easier process of creation.

[7] Scotus, *Ord.* 4. 1. 1, n. 29 (Wadding edn., viii. 50[a]). The opinion is William's, though not the argument which Scotus gives for it. For William's argument, see *In Sent.* 2. 1. 6 [qu. 107] (MS F, fo. 95[r]); for the argument offered by Scotus on William's behalf, see Scotus, *Ord.* 4. 1. 1, n. 27 (Wadding edn., viii. 49; MS A, fo. 186[ra]).

[8] Scotus, *Ord.* 4. 1. 1, n. 28 (Wadding edn., viii. 50[a]). Scotus also argues for the further thesis

(3*) A material substance cannot produce matter,

a principle which is in fact entailed by (3). Briefly, Scotus holds that a substantial form is that in virtue of which a substance produces its effect. But matter is prior to form; and something prior cannot be produced in virtue of something posterior to it: ibid. n. 29 (Wadding edn., viii. 50[a]–51[a]). [9] Ibid. n. 28 (Wadding edn., viii. 49[a]–50[a]).
[10] Ibid. (Wadding edn., viii. 49[a]).

possibilities. So we can infer that (2) is true.[11] Thus, Scotus believes that any world which contains finite agents capable of producing substances will have to contain matter. Hence, (1) will be true of any such world.

Why accept (3), (4), and (5)? In favour of (3), Scotus reasons that the uncontroversial

(B) Material forms naturally inhere in prime matter

coupled with a general principle (which Scotus does not spell out, but which he explicitly defends elsewhere)

(6) A naturally inherent item requires a passive substrate for its activity,

entails

(7) A material form requires a passive substrate (prime matter) for its activity,

which entails (3).[12]

Scotus argues for (6) by appealing to the general principle that no agent can produce an effect more perfect than itself. This principle would be violated if (6) were false. If (6) were false, a material form could create an immaterial substance. But according to Scotus, independence from matter is a perfection-increasing property, such that an immaterial substance is necessarily more perfect than a material one. So if (6) were false, some agents could produce effects more perfect than themselves. So (6) is true.[13]

In favour of

(4) A created substance cannot create the form of a material substance,

Scotus argues that the possibility of form's existing without matter, coupled with the contradictory of (4)

(4') A created substance can create the form of a material substance,

entails

(8) A created substance can conserve a material form without any matter.

---

[11] Ibid. n. 29 (Wadding edn., viii. 50ᵃ); MS A, fo. 186ʳᵇ, reads: 'Ex his concluditur propositum sic. Nullus angelus potest substantiam creare, ex prima, nec accidens aliquod, ex secunda, quia accidens a creatura creari non potest: igitur angelus nihil potest creare. Nec substantia materialis potest aliquid creare, quia non potest agere nisi per formam suam (accidentalem vel substantialem, non curo). Nam materia, etsi aliquod ens sit, tamen ita infimum est, quod non est principium alicuius actionis productivae. Forma autem materialis non potest esse principium creandi aliquid, nec aliquod accidens potest esse principium creandi, ex tertia conclusione. Igitur substantia materialis non potest creare. Igitur nec substantia materialis nec immaterialis potest creare, nec aliquod accidens potest esse principium creandi, ex tertia, ut dictum est.'

[12] Scotus, *Ord.* 4. 1. 1, n. 28 (Wadding edn., viii. 50ᵃ).

[13] Ibid. n. 18 (Wadding edn., viii. 31ᵃ).

But (8) is false in the actual world, so (4′) is too; in which case (4) is true.[14] The argument is not wholly satisfactory. Scotus does not provide any reason for supposing that (4) is about what is *logically* (as opposed to naturally) possible. So the argument does not help us determine the necessary or contingent status of (A), and hence (1).

Scotus defends

(5) An immaterial substance cannot create another substance

against Avicenna, who denied it.[15] Scotus's argument against Avicenna is fairly complicated. Central is the following thesis, which, according to Scotus, Avicenna accepts:

(C) For every immaterial substance x, x can produce another substance y only if x has a cognitive act concerning y.

On (C), an immaterial substance has to *think* about the item it produces.[16] Given (C), Scotus reasons that

(D) A cognitive act is an immanent accident of an immaterial substance

and

(9) It is not possible that an immanent accident is a necessary condition for the production of a substance

entail

(5) An immaterial substance cannot create another substance.[17]

Scotus spends some time justifying (D).[18] But it looks obvious to me that (D) is true, and I will not discuss it further here. Scotus does not bother with a

---

[14] Ibid. n. 28 (Wadding edn., viii. 49ᵃ–50ᵃ). I discuss Scotus's defence of the possibility of form existing without matter in Ch. 3 above.

[15] Avicenna argues that the first cause cannot produce directly more than one simple entity. He reasons that the production of two entities—or even one complex entity—would mean that the first cause would cause in virtue of two or more different modes, and that the first cause would thus contain multiplicity and division: Avicenna, *Metaph.* 9. 4 (ed. S. van Riet, Avicenna Latinus (3 vols., Louvain: Peeters; Leiden: Brill, 1977–83), ii. 479). Avicenna instead argues that lower intelligences are created by higher intelligences (ibid. (ii. 483)).

[16] Scotus is wrong to think that Avicenna actually accepts (C). Avicenna affirms instead

(C*) For every immaterial substance x, if x has a cognitive act concerning y, then x produces y.

On (C*), x's cognitive act is *sufficient* for the production of y. (C*) is an odd principle. But implicit in Avicenna's argument is that understanding is a sufficient condition for multiplicity; and hence, as Avicenna sees it, for production *ad extra*: see *Metaph.* 9. 4 (ii. 481–2). [17] Scotus, *Ord.* 4. 1. 1, nn. 18 and 28 (Wadding edn., viii. 31ᵃ and 49ᵃ). [18] Ibid. n. 23 (Wadding edn., viii. 38ᵃ–39ᵃ).

justification for (C), since he thinks that it is accepted by his opponent here, Avicenna.[19] But (C) looks highly questionable. There seems to be no reason why an immaterial created substance (such as an angel) could not produce another substance by some process which does not require conscious thought. And this would be an instance of creation.

(9) is justified at length.[20] The relevant sort of immanent accident is a causal power in virtue of which a substance can produce an effect. Scotus's example is the heat of fire with respect to the heating of a stick.[21] Accepting

(6) A naturally inherent item requires a passive substrate for its activity,

along with

(E) An accident naturally inheres in a substance,

Scotus infers

(9) It is not possible that an immanent accident is a necessary condition for the production of a substance.[22]

The inference to (9) looks reasonable enough. But the whole argument, which attempts to prove (5), seems to me to fail since I do not see that (C) is true.

So Scotus's attempts to show, by means of (3), (4), and (5), that (2) is true cannot be counted a success. He fails to show that (4) is logically necessary, and he fails to show that (5) is true at all. In fact, as I pointed out above, Scotus does believe (2) to be true. The *real* reason for this—if I may so speak—is that he affirms

(F) Creation requires infinite power.

For example,

A created agent requires a patient for two reasons: viz. on its own account, since a patient causes along with the created agent, since it has limited power in acting and therefore requires some other cause, viz. a material cause concurrent in the production; and on account of the effect.[23]

Scotus thus holds that (F) entails (2). He even argues that (F) is 'perhaps the explanation' for (2).[24] But he expressly denies that (F) is any use in proving (2), since he holds that (F) is 'not much more evident than the conclusion [viz.

---

[19] As I have just noted, it seems to me that Scotus is in fact wrong to ascribe this view to Avicenna.   [20] Scotus, *Ord.* 4. 1. 1, nn. 18–21 (Wadding edn., viii. 31ᵃ–34ᵃ).

[21] Ibid. n. 18 (Wadding edn., viii. 31ᵃ).

[22] Ibid. For a further argument, see ibid. nn. 18–19 (Wadding edn., viii. 31ᵃ–32ᵃ).

[23] Ibid. 4. 12. 4, n. 23 (Wadding edn., viii. 768); see also ibid. 4. 1. 1, n. 27 (Wadding edn., viii. 49).

[24] Ibid. 4. 1. 1, n. 27 (Wadding edn., viii. 49); MS A, fo. 186ʳᵃ, reads: 'Ratio ista . . . dic<i>t forte propter quid consequentis': Wadding omits 'forte'.

(2)]'.[25] Likewise, Scotus does not appeal to (F) in his discussions of the proof of God's infinite power, for much the same reason.[26]

Scotus notes—and rejects—the attempt of Bonaventure to prove (F) by means of

(G) Only an infinite power can traverse an infinite distance

and

(10) There is an infinite distance between nothing and something.

Bonaventure justifies (10) by

(H) There is an infinite distance between contradictories.[27]

Scotus argues, however, that (H) is false. The salient feature of contradictories is that, however small (or large) the 'distance' between them, they are incompossible. For example, in (10), 'something' can be instantiated by a very small-scale object. Scotus, like all the schoolmen, holds that any created item is finite, and thus in principle quantifiable in some way or another. And his point concerning (H) is that, where 0 is the value that can be assigned to 'nothing', and where some positive value can be assigned to created objects which satisfy the conditions for being 'something', there is necessarily a *finite* distance between nothing and something, just as there is a necessarily finite distance between 0 and any natural number.[28] Since (H) is false, it cannot be used to buttress an inference to (F).

All this amounts to the conclusion that Scotus holds that (A) obtains in every possible world which contains finite agents which can produce substances. But the only reason he can offer for this is (F). He believes that (F) is true, but he rejects the available argument in favour of it, and does not replace this argument with any other. I thus conclude that Scotus is forced to accept William's theory, according to which the truth of (2) is a matter of faith. Nevertheless, since Scotus holds that (A) obtains in every possible world which contains created agents which can produce substances, we can conclude that he holds that matter exists in every possible world which contains such agents—even if this conclusion is not one which he successfully demonstrates.

---

[25] Scotus, *Ord.* 4. 1. 1, n. 27 (Wadding edn., viii. 49).

[26] See Scotus, *Quod.* 7 (Wadding edn., xii. 168–91; Alluntis and Wolter, 159–97); *idem*, *De Primo Princ.* 4. 73 (p. 132/3).

[27] See Bonaventure, *In Sent.* 1. 43. 1 (10 vols., Quaracchi: Collegium Sanctae Bonaventurae, 1882–1902), i. 765ª); Scotus, *Ord.* 4. 1. 1, n. 6 (Wadding edn., viii. 9ª).

[28] Scotus, *Ord.* 4. 1. 1, nn. 11–12 (Wadding edn., viii. 20ª–22ª); see also *idem*, *De Primo Princ.* 4. 73 (p. 132/3).

BIBLIOGRAPHY

MANUSCRIPTS

Assisi, Biblioteca Communale, MS 137 [= A] [John Duns Scotus, *Ordinatio*].
Cambridge, Gonville and Caius College, MS 448/409, fos. 172–543 [=G] [Walter Burley, *Super Octo Libros Physicorum*]
Erfurt, Staatsbibliothek, MS Amplon. F. 135 [William Heytesbury, *Regulae Solvendi Sophismata*].
Florence, Biblioteca Laurenziana, MS Lat. Plut. 33 Dext. 1 [= F] [William of Ware, *In Sententias*].
Oxford, Merton College, MS 59 [= M] [John Duns Scotus, *Reportatio*, 1 A].
Oxford, Merton College, MS 87 [John Duns Scotus, *Additiones Magnae*].
Oxford, Merton College MS 138, fos. 138^v–338 [Thomas Sutton, *Quaestiones Ordinariae*].
Rome, Vatican Library, MS Vat. Lat. 868, fos. 1^r–129^r [Richard of Middleton, *Quaetiones Disputatae*].

PRINTED PRIMARY SOURCES

Abelard, Peter, *Ouvrages inédits d'Abélard*, ed. V. Cousin (Paris: Imprimerie Royale, 1836).
Albert of Saxony, *Quaestiones . . . in Octo Libros Physicorum* (Paris, 1518).
Albert the Great, *Opera Omnia*, ed. S. C. A. Borgnet (38 vols, Paris: Vivès, 1890–9).
Aquinas, Thomas, *Quaestiones Quodlibetales*, ed. R. M. Spiazzi (Turin and Rome: Marietti, 1949).
—— *In Aristotelis Libros De Caelo et Mundo, De Generatione et Corruptione, Meteorologicum Expositio*, ed. Raymundus M. Spiazzi (Rome and Turin: Marietti, 1952).
—— *Summa Theologiae*, ed. Petrus Caramello (3 vols., Turin and Rome: Marietti, 1952–6).
—— *In Octo Libros Physicorum Aristotelis Expositio*, ed. P. M. Maggiòlo (Turin and Rome: Marietti, 1965).

Aristotle, *Opera*, ed. Immanuel Bekker (5 vols., Berlin: Georgius Reimer, 1831); English translation: *The Complete Works of Aristotle: The Revised Oxford Translation*, ed. Jonathan Barnes, Bollingen Series, 71 (Princeton: Princeton University Press, 1984).

Augustine, *Confessions*, ed. James J. O'Donnell (3 vols., Oxford: Clarendon Press, 1992).

Averroës, *Aristotelis Opera cum Averrois Commentaria* (11 vols., Venice, 1550).

Avicenna, *Opera* [*Liber Primus Naturalium, tractatus* 2 and 3] (2 vols., Venice, 1508).

—— *Liber de Philosophia Prima sive Scientia Divina* [*Metaphysica*], ed. S. van Riet, Avicenna Latinus (3 vols., Louvain: Peeters; Leiden: Brill, 1977–83).

—— *Liber Primus Naturalium: Tractatus Primus de Causis et Principiis Naturalium*, ed. S. van Riet, Avicenna Latinus (Louvain: Peeters; Leiden: Brill, 1992).

—— *al-Shifāʾ al-Tabīʿiyyāt: al-Samāʿ al-Tabīʿī* [*Liber Primus Naturalium*], ed. by S. Zāyid (Cairo, [1985]).

Bacon, Roger, *Opus Maius*, ed. John Henry Bridges (3 vols. London, Edinburgh, and Oxford: Williams and Norgate, 1900).

—— *Questiones super Libros Octos Physicorum Aristotelis*, ed. Ferdinand M. Delorme and Robert Steele, Opera hactenus inedita a Rogeri Baconi, 13 (Oxford: Clarendon Press, 1935).

Boethius, *In Isagogen Porphyrii Commenta, Editio Secunda*, ed. Samuel Brandt, Corpus Scriptorum Ecclesiasticorum Latinorum, 48 (Vienna: Tempsky; Leipzig: Freytag, 1906).

—— *The Theological Tractates: The Consolation of Philosophy* [*De Trinitate*], ed. H. F. Stewart, E. K. Rand, and S. J. Tester, Loeb Classical Library (Cambridge, Mass.: Harvard University Press; London: Heinemann, 1978).

Bonaventure, *Opera Omnia* (10 vols., Quaracchi: Collegium Sancti Bonaventurae, 1882–1902).

Buridan, John, *Quaestiones super Octo Physicorum Libros Aristotelis* (Paris, 1509).

Burley, Walter, *De Intensione et Remissione Formarum* (Venice, 1496).

—— *In Physica Aristotelis Expositio et Questiones* (Venice, 1501).

—— 'De Primo et Ultimo Instanti des Walter Burley', ed. Herman and Charlotte Shapiro, *Archiv für Geschichte der Philosophie*, 47 (1965), 157–73.

Cartularium Universitatis Parisiensis, ed. H. Denifle and E. Chatelain (4 vols., Paris: Delalain, 1889–97).

Duns Scotus, John, *Opera Omnia*, ed. Luke Wadding (12 vols., Lyons: Durand, 1639).

—— *Opera Omnia*, ed. C. Balić *et al.* (Vatican City: Vatican Polyglot Press, 1950–)

—— *Ordinatio* [book 2, distinction 3, part 1, questions 1–6], trans. and ed. Paul Vincent Spade in *Five Texts on the Mediaeval Problem of Universals:*

Porphyry, Boethius, Abelard, Duns Scotus, Ockham (Indianapolis and Cambridge: Hackett, 1994), 57–113.

—— *Ordinatio* [book 2, distinction 12, from MS A], ed. Prospero Stella in *L'Ilemorfismo di G. Duns Scoto*, Pubblicazione del Pontifico Ateneo Salesiano. II. Testi e studi sul pensiero medioevale, 2 (Turin: Società Editrice Internazionale, 1955), 309–12.

—— *God and Creatures: The Quodlibetal Questions*, ed. Felix Alluntis and Allan B. Wolter (Princeton and London: Princeton University Press, 1975).

—— *A Treatise on God as First Principle* [*De Primo Principio*], ed. Allan B. Wolter, 2nd edn. (Chicago: Franciscan Herald Press, [1982]).

Ghazālī, *Algazel's Metaphysics: A Medieval Translation*, ed. J. T. Muckle, St Michael's Medieval Series (Toronto: St Michael's College, 1933).

Giles of Rome, *In Libros de Physica auditu Aristotelis* (Venice, 1502).

—— *Quodlibeta* (Venice, 1504)

—— *Theoremata de Corpore Christi* (Rome, 1554).

Godfrey of Fontaines, *Les Quatre Premiers Quodlibets de Godefroid de Fontaines*, ed. M. de Wulf and A. Pelzer, Les Philosophes Belges. Textes et Études, 2 (Louvain: Institut Supérieur de Philosophie de l'Université, 1904).

—— *Les Quodlibet cinq, six et sept de Godefroid de Fontaines*, ed. M. de Wulf and J. Hoffmans, Les Philosophes Belges: Textes et Études, 3 (Louvain: Institut Supérieur de Philosophie de l'Université, 1914).

—— *Les Quodlibets treize et quatorze de Godefroid de Fontaines*, ed. J. Hoffmans, Les Philosophes Belges: Textes et Études, 5/3–4 (Louvain: Institut Supérieur de Philosophie, 1935).

Grosseteste, Robert, *Die philosophischen Werke des Robert Grosseteste, Bischof von Lincoln* [*De Luce seu Inchoatione Formarum*], ed. Clemens Baeumker, Beiträge zur Geschichte der Philosophie des Mittelalters, Texte und Untersuchungen, 9 (Münster: Aschendorff, 1912).

—— *Commentarius in VIII Libros Physicorum Aristotelis*, ed. Richard Dales (Boulder, Colo.: University of Colorado Press, 1963).

Henry of Ghent, *Quodlibeta* [*Quodlibets* 3–5, 8, 11, 14–15] (2 vols., Venice, 1613).

—— *Opera Omnia* [*Quodlibets* 1–2, 6–7, 9–10, 12–13], ed. R. Macken *et al.*, Ancient and Medieval Philosophy, De Wulf–Mansion Centre, Series 2 (Leuven: Leuven University Press; Leiden: Brill, 1979–).

Hugh of St Victor, *De Sacramentis Christianae Fidei*, ed. J.-P. Migne, Patrologia Latina, 176 (Paris: J.-P. Migne, 1854). Trans. Roy J. Deferrari as *On the Sacraments of the Christian Faith* (Cambridge, Mass.: The Medieval Academy of America, 1951).

Marston, Roger, *Quodlibeta* [quodlibet 2, question 22], ed. Roberto Zavalloni in *Richard de Mediavilla et la controverse sur la pluralité des formes*, Philosophes médiévaux, 2 (Louvain: L'Lnstitut Supérieur de Philosophie, 1951), 180–99.

Olivi, Peter John, *Quaestiones in Secundum Librum Sententiarum*, ed. Bernardus

Jansen, Biblioteca Franciscana Medii Aevi, 4–6 (3 vols., Quaracchi: Collegium S. Bonaventurae, 1922–6).

Peter of Spain, *Parva Logicalia* (Venice, 1494).

—— *Syncategoreumata*, ed. by L. M. de Rijk, trans. Joke Spruyt, Studien und Texte zur Geistesgeschichte des Mittelalters, 30 (Leiden, New York, and Cologne: Brill, 1992).

Porphyry, *Porphyrii Isagoge et in Aristotelis Categorias Commentaria*, ed. Adolfus Busse, Commentaria in Aristotelem Graeca, iv/1 (Berlin: Georgius Reimer, 1887); trans. and ed. Paul Vincent Spade in *Five Texts on the Mediaeval Problem of Universals: Porphyry, Boethius, Abelard, Duns Scotus, Ockham* (Indianapolis and Cambridge: Hackett, 1994), 1–19.

Richard of Middleton, *De Gradu Formarum*, ed. Roberto Zavalloni in *Richard de Mediavilla et la controverse sur la pluralité des formes*, Philosophes médiévaux, 2 (Louvain: L'Institut Supérieur de Philosophie, 1951), 35–169.

Siger of Brabant, *Questions sur la physique d'Aristôte*, ed. Philippe Delahaye (Louvain: L'Institut Supérieur de Philosophie, 1941).

Simplicius, *Commentaire sur les Catégories d'Aristote: Traduction de Guillaume de Moerbeke*, ed. A. Pattin, W. Stuyven, and C. Steel, Corpus Latinum Commentariorum in Aristotelem Graecorum, 5 (2 vols., Louvain: Publications Universitaires; Paris: Béatrice-Nauwelaerts, 1971 [vol. 1]; Leiden: Brill, 1975 [vol. 2]).

William of Auxerre, *Summa Aurea*, ed. Jean Ribailler, Spicilegium Bonaventurianum, 16–19 (4 vols., Paris: CNRS; Grottaferrata: Collegium S. Bonaventurae ad Claras Aquas, 1980–6).

William of Ockham, *Opera Theologica*, ed. Iuvenalis Lalor *et al.* (10 vols., St Bonaventure, NY: St Bonaventure University Press, 1967–86).

—— *Quodlibetal Questions*, trans. Alfred J. Freddoso and Francis E. Kelley, Yale Library of Medieval Philosophy (2 vols., New Haven and London: Yale University Press, 1991).

Wodeham, Adam, *Tractatus de Indivisibilibus: A Critical Edition with Introduction, Translation, and Textual Notes*, ed. Rega Wood, Synthese Historical Library, 31 (Dordrecht, Boston, and London: Kluwer, 1988).

SECONDARY SOURCES

Adams, Marilyn McCord, 'Universals in the Early Fourteenth Century', in Kretzmann et al. (eds.), *Cambridge History of Later Medieval Philosophy*, 411–29.

—— *William Ockham*, Publications in Medieval Studies, 26 (2 vols., Notre Dame, Ind.: University of Notre Dame Press, 1987).

—— 'Aristotle and the Sacrament of the Altar', in 'Aristotle and his Medieval

Interpreters', Richard Bosley and Martin Tweedale (eds.), *Canadian Journal of Philosophy*, suppl. vol. 17 (1991), 195–249.

Balić, C., *Les Commentaires de Jean Duns Scot sur les quatre livres des Sentences*, Bibliothèque de la Revue d'Histoire Ecclésiastique, 1 (Louvain: Bureaux de la Revue d'Histoire Ecclésiastique, 1927).

—— 'The Life and Works of John Duns Scotus', in Ryan and Bonansea (eds.), *John Duns Scotus, 1265–1965*, 1–27.

Baudoux, Bernardus, 'De forma corporeitatis Scotistica', *Antonianum*, 13 (1935), 429–74.

Bettoni, E., *Saint Bonaventure*, trans. Angelus Gambatese (Notre Dame, Ind.: University of Notre Dame Press, 1964).

Boler, John F., 'The Ontological Commitment of Scotus's Account of Potency in his *Questions on the Metaphysics*, Book IX', in Honnefelder *et al.* (eds.), *John Duns Scotus*, 145–60.

Bostock, David, 'Aristotle on Continuity in *Physics* VI', in Judson (ed.), *Aristotle's* Physics, 179–212.

Boulnois, Olivier, 'La Présence chez Duns Scot', in Sileo (ed.), *Via Scoti*, i. 95–119.

Broadie, Alexander, *The Shadow of Scotus: Philosophy and Faith in Pre-Reformation Scotland* (Edinburgh: T. and T. Clark, 1995).

Buescher, Gabriel, *The Eucharistic Teaching of William Ockham*, Franciscan Institute Publications, Theology Series, 1 (St Bonaventure, NY: The Franciscan Institute, 1950).

Burr, D., 'Scotus and Transubstantiation', *Mediaeval Studies*, 34 (1972), 336–60.

Butler, Joseph, *The Analogy of Religion* (Oxford: Clarendon Press, 1874).

Charles, David, 'Matter and Form: Unity, Persistence, and Identity', in T. Scaltsas, D. Charles, and M. L. Gill (eds.), *Unity, Identity, and Explanation in Aristotle's Metaphysics* (Oxford: Clarendon Press, 1994), 75–105.

Charlton, William, 'Aristotle's Potential Infinites', in Judson (ed.), *Aristotle's* Physics, 129–49.

Clagett, Marshall, 'Some General Aspects of Medieval Physics', *Isis*, 39 (1948), 29–44.

—— *The Science of Mechanics in the Middle Ages*, Publications in Medieval Science, 4 (Madison: University of Wisconsin Press; London: Oxford University Press, 1961).

Clavelin, Maurice, *The Natural Philosophy of Galileo: Essay on the Origins and Foundations of Classical Mechanics*, trans. A. J. Pomerans (Cambridge, Mass., and London: MIT Press, 1974).

Cohen, S. M., 'Essentialism in Aristotle', *Review of Metaphysics*, 31 (1977–8), 387–405.

Courtenay, William J., 'Scotus at Paris', in Sileo (ed.), *Via Scoti*, i. 149–64.

Craig, William Lane, *The Problem of Divine Foreknowledge of Future Contingents from Aristotle to Suarez*, Brill's Studies in Intellectual History, 7 (Leiden: Brill, 1988).

Crombie, A. C., *Augustine to Galileo: The History of Science AD. 400–1650* (London: Falcon Educational Books, 1952).

—— *Robert Grosseteste and the Origins of Experimental Science 1100–1700* (Oxford: Clarendon Press, 1953).

Cross, Richard, 'The Doctrine of the Hypostatic Union in the Thought of Duns Scotus' (unpublished doctoral thesis, Oxford University, 1991).

—— 'Duns Scotus's Anti-Reductionistic Account of Material Substance', *Vivarium*, 33 (1995), 137–70.

—— 'Aquinas on Nature, Hypostasis, and the Metaphysics of the Incarnation', *Thomist*, 60 (1996), 171–202.

—— 'Duns Scotus on Eternity and Timelessness', *Faith and Philosophy*, 14 (1997), 3–25

—— 'Aquinas and the Mind–Body Problem', in John Haldane (ed.), *Thomistic Papers* (forthcoming).

—— 'Identity, Origin, and Persistence in Duns Scotus's Physics', *History of Philosophy Quarterly* (forthcoming).

Daniels, A., 'Zu den Beziehungen zwischen Wilhelm von Ware und Johannes Duns Scotus', *Franziskanische Studien*, 4 (1917), 221–38.

Decorte, Jos, '"Modus or "Res": Scotus' Criticism of Henry of Ghent's Conception of the Reality of a Real Relation', in Sileo (ed.), *Via Scoti*, i. 407–29.

Dedekind, Richard, *Essays on the Theory of Numbers* (Chicago: Open Court, 1901).

Dhanani, Alnoor, *The Physical Theory of Kalām: Atoms, Space, and Void in Basrian Muʿtazilī Cosmology*, Islamic Philosophy, Theology and Science: Texts and Studies, 14 (Leiden, New York, and Cologne: Brill, 1994).

Dolnikowski, Edith Wilks, *Thomas Bradwardine: A View of Time and a Vision of Eternity in Fourteenth-Century Thought*, Studies in the History of Christian Thought, 65 (Leiden, New York, and Cologne: Brill, 1995).

Duhem, Pierre, *Le Système du monde: histoire des doctrines cosmologiques de Platon à Copernique* (10 vols., Paris: Hermann, n.d.–1959); extracts trans. and ed. Roger Ariew as *Medieval Cosmology: Theories of Infinity, Place, Time, Void, and the Plurality of Worlds* (Chicago and London: University of Chicago Press, 1985).

Dumont, Stephen D., 'The Question on Individuation in Scotus' "Quaestiones super Metaphysicam"', in Sileo (ed.), *Via Scoti*, i. 193–227.

Eagleton, Terry, *The Illusions of Postmodernism* (Oxford and Cambridge, Mass.: Blackwell, 1996).

Effler, R., *John Duns Scotus and the Principle 'Omne quod movetur ab alio movetur'*, Franciscan Institute Publications, Philosophy Series, 15 (St Bonaventure, NY: The Franciscan Institute, 1962).

Emden, A. B., *A Biographical Register of the University of Oxford to A.D. 1500* (3 vols., Oxford: Clarendon Press, 1957–9).

Emerton, Norma, *The Scientific Reinterpretation of Form* (Ithaca, NY: Cornell University Press, 1984).

Frank, William A., 'Duns Scotus on Autonomous Freedom and Divine Co-Causality', *Medieval Philosophy and Theology*, 2 (1992), 142–64.

Freddoso, Alfred J., 'Human Nature, Potency, and the Incarnation', *Faith and Philosophy*, 3 (1986), 27–53.

Frede, Michael, *Essays in Ancient Philosophy* (Oxford: Clarendon Press, 1987).

Gál, Gedeon, 'Gulielmi de Ware, O. F. M. Doctrina Philosophica per Summa Capitula Proposita', *Franciscan Studies*, 14 (1954), 155–80, 265–92.

Geach, Peter, 'Form and Existence', in Anthony Kenny (ed.), *Aquinas: A Collection of Critical Essays*, Modern Studies in Philosophy (London and Melbourne: Macmillan, 1969), 29–53.

Gill, Mary Louise, and Lennox, James G. (eds.), *Self-Motion from Aristotle to Newton* (Princeton: Princeton University Press, 1994).

Gilson, Etienne, *The Christian Philosophy of St Bonaventure*, trans. Illtyd Trethowan and F. J. Sheed (London: Sheed and Ward, 1938).

—— *Jean Duns Scot: Introduction ses positions fondamentales*, Études de philosophie médiévale, 42 (Paris: Vrin, 1952).

—— *The Christian Philosophy of Saint Augustine*, trans. L. E. M. Lynch (London: Gollancz, 1961).

Goddu, André, *The Physics of William of Ockham*, Studien und Texte zur Geistesgeschichte des Mittelalters, 16 (Leiden and Cologne: Brill, 1984).

Gracia, Jorge J. E. (ed.), *Individuation in Scholasticism: The Later Middle Ages and the Counter-Reformation 1150–1650*, SUNY Series in Philosophy (Albany, NY: State University of New York Press, 1994).

—— 'Individuality and the Individuating Entity in Scotus's *Ordinatio*: An Ontological Characterization', in Honnefelder *et al.* (eds.), *John Duns Scotus*, 229–49.

Graham, Daniel W., *Aristotle's Two Systems* (Oxford: Clarendon Press, 1987).

Grajewski, Maurice J., *The Formal Distinction of Duns Scotus: A Study in Metaphysics*, The Catholic University of America Philosophical Series, 90 (Washington: Catholic University of America Press, 1944).

Grant, Edward, 'Place and Space in Medieval Physical Thought', in Machamer and Turnbull (eds,), *Motion and Time*, 137–67.

—— 'The Condemnation of 1277, God's Absolute Power, and Physical Thought in the Middle Ages', *Viator*, 10 (1979), 211–44.

—— *Much Ado About Nothing: Theories of Space and Vacuum from the Middle Ages to the Scientific Revolution* (Cambridge: Cambridge University Press, 1981).

—— 'The Medieval Doctrine of Place: Some Fundamental Problems and

Solutions', in Maierù and Paravicini Bagliani (eds.), *Studi sul xiv secolo*, 57–79.

—— 'The Effect of the Condemnation of 1277', in Kretzmann *et al.* (eds.), *Cambridge History of Later Medieval Philosophy*, 537–40.

—— *Planets, Stars, and Orbs: The Medieval Cosmos, 1200–1687* (Cambridge, New York, and Melbourne: Cambridge University Press, 1994).

Harris, C. R. S., *Duns Scotus* (2 vols., Oxford: Clarendon Press, 1927).

Henninger, Mark G., *Relations: Medieval Theories 1250–1325* (Oxford: Clarendon Press, 1989).

Henry, Desmond Paul, *That Most Subtle Question (Quaestio Subtilissima): The Metaphysical Bearing of Medieval and Contemporary Linguistic Disciplines* (Manchester and Dover, NH: Manchester University Press, 1984).

Hissette, R., *Enquête sur les 219 articles condamnés à Paris le 7 Mars 1277*, Philosophes médiévaux, 22 (Louvain: Publications Universitaires de Louvain; Paris: Vander Oyez, 1977).

Hocedez, Edgar, *Richard de Middleton: sa vie, ses oeuvres, sa doctrine*, Spicilegium Sacrum Lovaniense. Études et documents, 7 (Louvain: 'Spicilegium Sacrum Lovaniense' Bureaux; Paris: Honoré Champion, 1925).

Hödl, Ludwig, 'Untersuchungen zum scholastischen Begriff des Schöpferischen in der Theologie des Wilhelm von Ware OM', in Burkhard Mojsisch and Olaf Pluta (eds.), *Historia Philosophiae Medii Aevi: Studien zur Geschichte der Philosophie des Mittelalters* (2 vols., Amsterdam: Grüner, 1992), i. 387–408.

Hoeres, W., 'Wesen und Dasein bei Heinrich von Gent und Duns Scotus', *Franziskanische Studien*, 47 (1965), 121–86.

Honnefelder, Ludger, *Ens Inquantum Ens: Der Begriff der Seienden als Solchen als Gegenstand der Metaphysik nach der Lehre des Johannes Duns Scotus*, Beiträge zur Geschichte der Philosophie und Theologie des Mittelalters, N. F., 16 (Münster: Aschendorff, 1979).

—— Wood, Rega, and Dreyer, Mechthild (eds.), *John Duns Scotus: Metaphysics and Ethics*, Studien und Texte zur Geistesgeschichte des Mittelalters, 53 (Leiden, New York, and Cologne: Brill, 1996).

Hughes, Christopher, *On a Complex Theory of a Simple God: An Investigation in Aquinas' Philosophical Theology*, Cornell Studies in the Philosophy of Religion (Ithaca, NY, and London: Cornell University Press, 1989).

—— 'Matter and Individuation in Aquinas', *History of Philosophy Quarterly*, 13 (1996), 1–13.

Inwood, Michael, 'Aristotle on the Reality of Time', in Judson (ed.), *Aristotle's Physics*, 151–78.

Jammer, Max, *Concepts of Mass in Classical and Modern Physics*, Harper Torchbacks Science Library (New York, Evanston, Ill., and London: Harper and Row, 1964).

—— *Concepts of Space: The History of Theories of Space in Physics*, 2nd edn. (Cambridge, Mass.: Harvard University Press, 1969).

Judson, Lindsay (ed.), *Aristotle's* Physics: *A Collection of Essays* (Oxford: Clarendon Press, 1991).

Kenny, Anthony, 'The Use of Logical Analysis in Theology', in *Reason and Religion: Essays in Philosophical Theology* (Oxford: Blackwell, 1987), 3–20.

King, Peter, 'Duns Scotus on the Reality of Self-Change', in Gill and Lennox (eds.), *Self-Motion from Aristotle to Newton*, 229–90.

Klima, Gyula, 'On Being and Essence in St Thomas Aquinas's Metaphysics and Philosophy of Science', in Knuuttila *et al.* (eds.), *Knowledge and the Sciences in Medieval Philosophy*, ii. 210–22.

—— 'The Semantic Principles Underlying St Thomas Aquinas's Metaphysics of Being', *Medieval Philosophy and Theology*, 5 (1996), 87–141.

Knuuttila, Simo, *Modalities in Medieval Philosophy*, Topics in Medieval Philosophy (London and New York: Routledge, 1993).

—— Työrinoja, Reijo, and Ebbesen, Sten (eds.), *Knowledge and the Sciences in Medieval Philosophy: Proceedings on the Eighth International Conference on Medieval Philosophy*, Publications of the Luther–Agricola Society, 19B (3 vols., Helsinki: Yliopistopaino, 1990).

Kretzmann, Norman, 'Aristotle on the Instant of Change', *Proceedings of the Aristotelian Society*, suppl. vol., 50 (1976), 91–114.

—— 'Incipit/Desinit', in Machamer and Turnbull (eds.), *Motion and Time*, 101–36.

—— 'Continuity, Contrariety, Contradiction, and Change', in Kretzmann (ed.), *Infinity and Continuity*, 270–96.

—— 'Continua, Indivisibles, and Change in Wyclif's Logic of Scripture', in Anthony Kenny (ed.), *Wyclif in his Times* (Oxford: Clarendon Press, 1986), 31–65.

—— (ed.), *Infinity and Continuity in Ancient and Medieval Thought* (Ithaca, NY, and London: Cornell University Press, 1982).

—— Kenny, Anthony, and Pinborg, Jan (eds.), *The Cambridge History of Later Medieval Philosophy* (Cambridge: Cambridge University Press, 1982).

Lang, Helen S., 'Bodies and Angels: The Occupants of Space for Aristotle and Duns Scotus', *Viator*, 14 (1983), 245–66.

—— *Aristotle's* Physics *and its Medieval Varieties* (Albany, NY: State University of New York Press, 1992).

Lechner, Joseph, 'Die mehrfachen Fassungen des Sentenzkommentars des Wilhelm von Ware, O.F.M.', *Franziskanische Studien*, 31 (1949), 99–127.

Lerner, Ralph, and Mahdi, Muhsin (eds.), *Medieval Political Philosophy: A Sourcebook* (New York: The Free Press of Glencoe, 1963).

Lewis, David, *On the Plurality of Worlds* (Oxford: Blackwell, 1986).

Lobato, Abelardo, 'El cuerpo human en Duns Escoto y Tomás de Aquino', in Sileo (ed.), *Via Scoti*, ii. 951–66.

MacDonald, Scott, 'The *Esse/Essentia* Argument in Aquinas's *De ente et essentia*', *Journal of the History of Philosophy*, 22 (1984), 157–72.

McEvoy, James, *The Philosophy of Robert Grosseteste* (Oxford: Clarendon Press, 1982).

Machamer, P. K., and Turnbull, R. G. (eds.), *Motion and Time, Space and Matter: Interrelations in the History and Philosophy of Science* (Columbus, Oh.: Ohio State University Press, 1976).

McMullin, Ernan (ed.), *The Concept of Matter* (Notre Dame, Ind.: University of Notre Dame Press, 1963).

McTaggart, J. M. E., 'The Unreality of Time', *Mind*, NS 17 (1908), 457–74.

Maier, Anneliese, *Die Vorläufer Galileis im 14. Jahrhundert* (Studien zur Naturphilosophie der Sptscholastik, [1]), Raccolta di Studi e Testi, 22 (Rome: Storia e Letteratura, 1949).

—— *An der Grenze von Scholastik und Naturwissenschaft: Die Struktur der materiellen Substanz. Das Problem der Gravitation. Die Mathematik der Formlatituden* (Studien zur Naturphilosophie der Spätscholastik, 3), 2nd edn., Raccolta di Studi e Testi, 41 (Rome: Storia e Letteratura, 1952).

—— *Metaphysische Hintergründe der spätscholastischen Naturphilosophie* (Studien zur Naturphilosophie der Spätscholastik, 4), Raccolta di Studi e Testi, 52 (Rome: Storia e Letteratura, 1955).

—— *Zwischen Philosophie und Mechanik* (Studien zur Natur philosophie der Spätscholastik, 5), Raccolta di Studi e Testi, 69 (Rome: Storia e Letteratura, 1958).

—— *Zwei Grundprobleme der scholastischen Naturphilosophie: Das Problem der intensiven Grösse. Die Impetustheorie* (Studien zur Naturphilosophie der Spätscholastik, 2), 3rd edn., Raccolta di Studi e Testi, 37 (Rome: Storia e Letteratura, 1968).

—— *On the Threshold of Exact Science: Selected Writings of Anneliese Maier on Late Medieval Natural Philosophy*, ed. Steven D. Sargent, The Middle Ages (Philadelphia: University of Pennsylvania Press, 1982).

Maierù, A., and Paravicini Bagliani, A. (eds.), *Studi sul xiv secolo in memoria di Anneliese Maier*, Raccolta di Studi e Testi, 151 (Rome: Storia e Letteratura, 1981).

Marenbon, John (ed.), *Aristotle in Britain during the Middle Ages*, Société Internationale pour l'Étude de la Philosophie Médiévale: Rencontres de Philosophie Médiévale, 5 (Brepols, 1996).

Marmo, Costantino, 'Ontology and Semantics in the Logic of Duns Scotus', in Umberto Eco and Costantino Marmo (eds.), *On the Medieval Theory of Signs* (Amsterdam and Philadelphia: John Benjamins, 1989), 143–93.

Martin, C., 'Walter Burley', in R. W. Southern (ed.), *Oxford Studies Presented to Daniel Callus*, Oxford Historical Society, NS 16 (Oxford: Clarendon Press, 1964), 194–230.

Martin, Christopher, *The Philosophy of Thomas Aquinas: Introductory Readings* (London and New York: Routledge, 1988).

Massobrio, Simona, 'Aristotelian Matter as Understood by Thomas Aquinas and John Duns Scotus' (unpublished doctoral dissertation, McGill University, 1991).

Mendell, Henry, 'Topoi on Topos: The Development of Aristotle's Concept of Place', *Phronesis*, 32 (1987), 206–31.

Mendoza, Celina A. Létora, 'Escoto y el hilemorfismo aristotélico: Cuestiones metodológicas', in Sileo (ed.), *Via Scoti*, ii. 765–81.

Merricks, Trenton, 'On the Incompatibility of Enduring and Perduring Entities', *Mind*, 104 (1995), 523–31.

Miller, Fred D., 'Aristotle against the Atomists', in Kretzmann (ed.), *Infinity and Continuity*, 87–111.

Miralbell, Ignacio, 'La distinción entre metafísica, matemática y física según Duns Escoto', in Sileo (ed.), *Via Scoti*, i. 348–58.

Moody, Ernest A., and Clagett, Marshall, *The Medieval Science of Weights (Scientia de Ponderibus): Treatises Ascribed to Euclid, Archimedes, Thabit ibn Qurra, Jordanus de Nemore and Blasius of Parma* (Madison: University of Wisconsin Press, 1952).

Moore, A. W., *The Infinite*, The Problems of Philosophy: Their Past and their Present (London: Routledge, 1990).

Murdoch, John E., 'Henry of Harclay and the Infinite', in Maierù and Paravicini Bagliani (eds.), *Studi sul xiv secolo*, 219–61.

—— 'Infinity and Continuity', in Kretzmann *et al.* (eds.), Cambridge History of Later Medieval Philosophy, 564–91.

—— and E. Synan, 'Two Questions on the Continuum: Walter Chatton (?), O.F.M and Adam Wodeham, O.F.M.', *Franciscan Studies*, 26 (1966), 212–88.

Newton, Isaac, *Opera [Principia Mathematica Philosophiae Naturalis]*, ed. S. Horsley (5 vols., London: John Nichols, 1779).

—— *Mathematical Principles of Natural Philosophy*, trans. Andrew Motte, ed. Florian Cajori (2 vols., Berkeley, Los Angeles, and London: University of California Press, 1971).

Newton-Smith, W. H., *The Structure of Time*, International Library of Philosophy (London, Boston, and Henley: Routledge and Kegan Paul, 1980).

Noone, Timothy B., 'Scotus' Critique of the Thomistic Theory of Individuation and the Dating of the 'Quaestiones in Libros Metaphysicorum', vii q. 13', in Sileo, (ed.),*Via Scoti*, i. 391–406.

O'Brien, A. J., 'Duns Scotus' Teaching on the Distinction between Essence and Existence', *New Scholasticism*, 38 (1964), 61–77.

O'Leary, Conrad John, *The Substantial Composition of Man According to Saint Bonaventure* (Washington: Catholic University of America Press, 1931).

Olejnik, Roman M., 'Attualità delle leggi logiche in Giovanni Duns Scoto', in Sileo (ed.), *Via Scoti*, ii. 1073–90.

O'Meara, W., 'Actual Existence and the Individual According to Duns Scotus', *Monist*, 49 (1965), 659–69.

Owens, Joseph, 'Thomas Aquinas', in Gracia (ed.), *Individuation in Scholasticism*, 173–94.

Park, Woosuk, 'The Problem of Individuation for Scotus: A Principle of Indivisibility or a Principle of Distinction?', *Franciscan Studies*, 48 (1988), 105–23.

—— 'Understanding the Problem of Individuation: Gracia vs. Scotus', in Honnefelder, *et al.* (eds.), *John Duns Scotus*, 273–89.

Paulus, Jean, *Henri de Gand: Essai sur les tendances de sa métaphysique*, Études de philosophie médiévale, 25 (Paris: Vrin, 1938).

Plantinga, Alvin, *The Nature of Necessity*, Clarendon Library of Logic and Philosophy (Oxford: Clarendon Press, 1974).

Quinn, John Francis, *The Historical Constitution of St Bonaventure's Philosophy* (Toronto: Pontifical Institute of Medieval Studies, 1973).

Quinton, Anthony, 'Spaces and Times', *Philosophy*, 37 (1962), 130–47.

Roensch, Frederick J., *Early Thomistic School* (Dubuque, Ia.: Priory Press, 1964).

Rudavsky, Tamar M., 'The Doctrine of Individuation in Duns Scotus', *Franziskanische Studien*, 59 (1977), 320–77, and 62 (1980), 62–83.

Ryan, John K., and Bonansea, Bernardine M. (eds.), *John Duns Scotus, 1265–1965*, Studies in Philosophy and the History of Philosophy, 3 (Washington: Catholic University of America Press, 1965).

Santogrossi, Ansgar, 'Duns Scotus on the Potency Opposed to Act in *Questions on the Metaphysics*', *American Catholic Philosophical Quarterly*, 67 (1993), 55–76.

Sharp, D. E., *Franciscan Philosophy at Oxford in the Thirteenth Century*, British Society of Franciscan Studies, 16 (Oxford: Oxford University Press; London: Humphrey Milford, 1930).

Shoemaker, Sydney, 'Time without Change', *Journal of Philosophy*, 66 (1969), 363–81.

Sileo, Leonardo (ed.), *Via Scoti: Methodologica ad mentem Joannis Duns Scoti. Atti del Congresso Scotistico Internazionale, Roma 9–11 Marzo 1993* (2 vols., Rome: Antonianum, 1995).

Sorabji, Richard, *Time, Creation and the Continuum: Theories in Antiquity and the Early Middle Ages* (London: Duckworth, 1983).

—— *Matter, Space and Motion: Theories in Antiquity and their Sequel* (London: Duckworth, 1988).

Stella, Prospero, *L'Ilemorfismo di G. Duns Scoto*, Pubblicazione del Pontificio Ateneo Salesiano. II. Testi e studià sul pensiero medioevale, 2 (Turin: Società Editrice Internazionale, 1955).

Stump, Eleonore, 'Theology and Physics in *De Sacramento Altaris*: Ockham's Theory of Indivisibles', in Kretzmann (ed.), *Infinity and Continuity*, 207–30.

Swinburne, Richard, _Space and Time_, 2nd edn. (London and Basingstoke: Macmillan, 1981).

—— 'God and Time', in Eleonore Stump (ed.), _Reasoned Faith: Essays in Philosophical Theology in Honor of Norman Kretzmann_ (Ithaca, NY, and London: Cornell University Press, 1993), 203–22.

Sylla, Edith, 'Medieval Concepts of the Latitude of Forms: The Oxford Calculators', _Archives d'histoire doctrinale et littéraire du moyen-âge_, 40 (1973), 223–83.

Sylwanowicz, Michael, _Contingent Causality and the Foundations of Duns Scotus' Metaphysics_, Studien und Texte zur Geistesgeschichte des Mittelalters, 51 (Leiden, New York, and Cologne: Brill, 1996).

Theron, Stephen, 'Esse', _New Scholasticism_, 53 (1979), 206–20.

Thijssen, J. M. M. H., 'Roger Bacon (1214–1292/1297): A Neglected Source in the Medieval Continuum Debate', _Archives internationales d'histoire des sciences_, 34 (1984), 25–34.

Trifogli, Cecilia, 'The Place of the Last Sphere in Late-Ancient and Medieval Commentaries', in Knuuttila _et al._ (eds.), _Knowledge and the Sciences in Medieval Philosophy_, ii. 342–50.

Wald, Berthold, '_Accidens est Formaliter Ens_: Duns Scotus on Inherence in his _Quaestiones Subtilissimae_ on Aristotle's _Metaphysics_', in Marenbon (ed.), _Aristotle in Britain during the Middle Ages_, 177–93.

Weisheipl, James A., 'Aristotle's Physics and the Science of Motion', in Kretzmann _et al._ (eds.), _Cambridge History of Later Medieval Philosophy_, 521–36.

White, Michael J., _The Continuous and the Discrete: Ancient Physical Theories from a Contemporary Perspective_ (Oxford: Clarendon Press, 1992).

Wieland, Georg, _Untersuchungen zum Seinsbegriff im Metaphysikkommentar Alberts des Großen_, Beiträge zur Geschichte der Philosophie und Theologie des Mittelalters, N. F., 7 (Münster: Aschendorff, 1971).

Williamson, Timothy, _Vagueness_, The Problems of Philosophy: Their Past and Their Present (London and New York: Routledge, 1994).

Wilson, Curtis, _William Heytesbury: Medieval Logic and the Rise of Mathematical Physics_, Publications in Medieval Science, 3 (Madison: University of Wisconsin Press, 1956).

Wippel, John F., 'Aquinas's Route to the Real Distinction: A Note on _De Ente et Essentia_, c. 4', _Thomist_, 43 (1979), 279–95, reprinted with additional matter as 'Essence and Existence in the _De Ente_, ch. 4', in _Metaphysical Themes in Thomas Aquinas_, 107–32.

—— _The Metaphysical Thought of Godfrey of Fontaines_ (Washington: Catholic University of America Press, 1981).

—— _Metaphysical Themes in Thomas Aquinas_, Studies in Philosophy and the History of Philosophy, 10 (Washington: Catholic University of America Press, 1984).

—— 'Essence and Existence in Other Writings', in *Metaphysical Themes in Thomas Aquinas*, 133–61.

Wolter, Allan B., *The Transcendentals and their Function in the Metaphysics of Duns Scotus*, Franciscan Institute Publications, Philosophy Series, 3 (St Bonaventure, NY: The Franciscan Institute, 1946).

—— 'The Formal Distinction', in Ryan and Bonansea (eds.), *John Duns Scotus, 1265–1965*, 45–60; repr. in Wolter, *Philosophical Theology of John Duns Scotus*, 27–41.

—— *The Philosophical Theology of John Duns Scotus*, ed. Marilyn McCord Adams (Ithaca, NY, and London: Cornell University Press, 1990).

—— 'Reflections on the Life and Works of Scotus', *American Catholic Philosophical Quarterly*, 67 (1993), 1–36.

—— 'John Duns Scotus', in Gracia (ed.), *Individuation in Scholasticism*, 271–98.

—— 'Duns Scotus at Oxford', in Sileo (ed.), *Via Scoti*, i. 183–91.

—— 'Reflections about Scotus's Early Works', in Honnefelder *et al.* (eds.), *John Duns Scotus*, 37–57.

Wood, Rega, 'Walter Burley's *Physics* Commentaries', *Franciscan Studies*, 33 (1984), 275–327.

—— 'Individual Forms: Richard Rufus and John Duns Scotus', in Honnefelder *et al.* (eds.), *John Duns Scotus*, 251–72.

Zavalloni, Roberto, *Richard de Mediavilla et la controverse sur la pluralité des formes*, Philosophes médiévaux, 2 (Louvain: L'Institut Supérieur de Philosophie, 1951).

Zupko, Jack, 'Nominalism Meets Indivisibilism', *Medieval Philosophy and Theology*, 3 (1993), 158–85.

INDEX LOCORUM

GENERAL INDEX